OLD CANADIAN CEMETERIES

Places of Memory

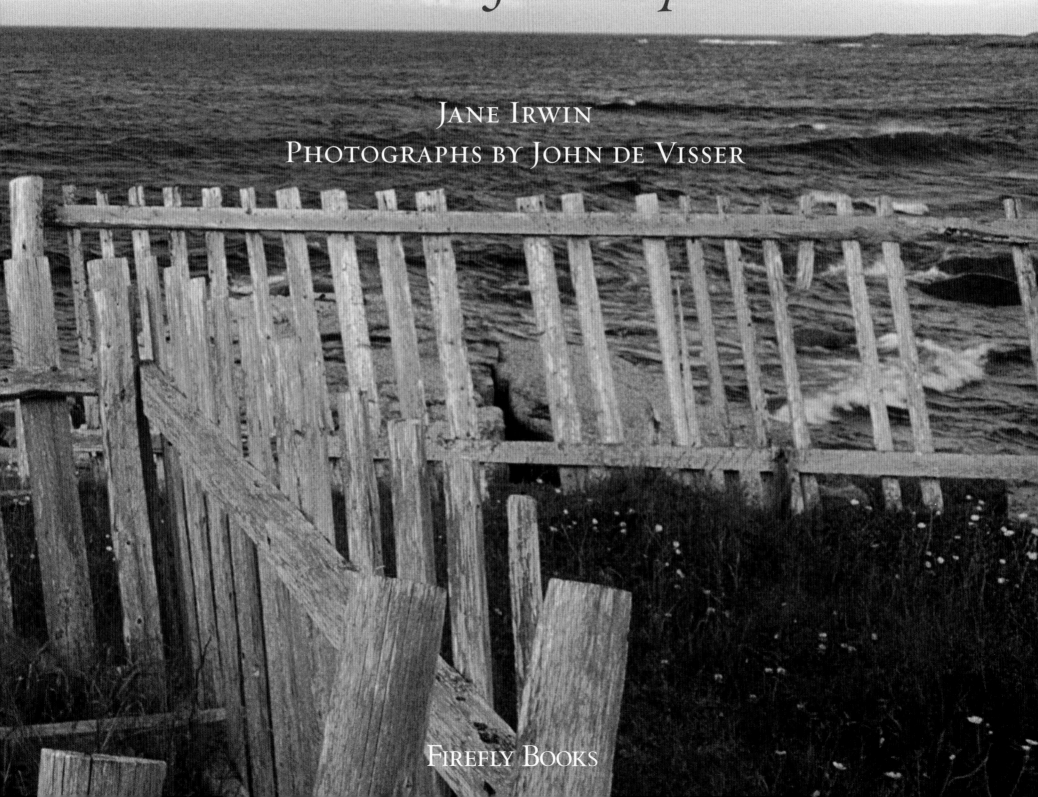

OLD CANADIAN CEMETERIES

Places of Memory

Jane Irwin

PHOTOGRAPHS BY JOHN DE VISSER

Firefly Books

A FIREFLY BOOK

Published by Firefly Books Ltd. 2007

First printing

Publisher Cataloging-in-Publication Data (U.S.)

Irwin, Jane, 1941-
    Old Canadian cemeteries : places of memory / Jane Irwin ; photographs by John de Visser.
[ ] p. : col. photos. ;   cm.
Includes bibliographical references and index.
Summary: A look at historical cemeteries from across Canada. Topics include burial traditions from various religions, war memorials, graveyard symbols and their meanings, and historic graveyard conservation.
ISBN-13: 978-1-55407-146-3
ISBN-10: 1-55407-146-1
1. Cemeteries — Canada — History. I. de Visser, John, 1930- II. Title.
971 dc22   F1010.I7956   2007

Library and Archives Canada Cataloguing in Publication

Irwin, Jane, 1941-
    Old Canadian cemeteries : places of memory / Jane Irwin ;
photographs by John de Visser.
Includes bibliographical references and index.
ISBN-13: 978-1-55407-146-3
ISBN-10: 1-55407-146-1
    1. Cemeteries--Canada--History. 2. Cemeteries--Canada--Pictorial works. I. De Visser, John, 1930- II. Title.
FC215.I79 2007   971   C2007-900791-0

Published in the United States by
Firefly Books (U.S.) Inc.
P.O. Box 1338, Ellicott Station
Buffalo, New York 14205

Published in Canada by
Firefly Books Ltd.
66 Leek Crescent
Richmond Hill, Ontario L4B 1H1

Design concept: Kathe Gray/Electric Pear
Cover and design: Bob Wilcox
Page Production: Tinge Design Studio
Copy Editor and Proofreader: Jane McWhinney

Printed in China

The publisher gratefully acknowledges the financial support for our publishing program by the Government of Canada through the Book Publishing Industry Development Program.

PHOTO CREDITS.

T = Top, M = Middle, B = Bottom, R = Right,
L = Left, C = Centre

Front Cover: John de Visser
Back Cover: John de Visser

John de Visser: 2-3, 5, 6-7, 8-9, 10, 13, 18-19, 20, 22, 25, 27, 42-43, 44, 46, 53, 58, 61BC, 65, 67, 78, 79 B, 84, 85, 86, 87, 88, 89, 91, 92, 94, 96, 98-99, 100, 103, 107 T, 109, 111, 113, 115, 116, 117, 118, 119, 120, 121 BL, 122, 124-125, 126, 129, 131, 133, 136, 140, 142, 147, 150, 151, 157, 158, 166-167, 168, 169, 170, 171, 172-173, 174, 175, 176, 177, 178-179, 180, 181, 182, 183, 184, 185, 186, 187, 188-189, 190, 195, 197, 199, 200 R, 201 L, 204, 206, 210, 211, 212, 215, 218-219, 220, 224, 225, 228, 230, 234 L, 238, 240, 241, 244, 245, 249, 252, 256, 260, 261B, 262, 265, 266, 268-269, 270, 272, 273 T, 275 BL&C, 276 L, 279, 284-285, 286, 296

Jane Irwin: 15, 31, 49, 51, 54, 55, 57, 61 TL ML BL TC MC, 63, 68, 69, 70, 72, 73, 76, 79 TR&L, 105, 107 B, 121 BC, 127, 132, 134, 135, 139, 141, 146, 148, 149, 153, 154, 155, 159, 160, 162, 163, 164, 165, 193, 196, 200 L, 201 R, 203, 223, 226, 227, 229, 231, 232, 233, 234 R&T, 235, 236, 237, 239, 242, 243, 246, 248, 251, 253, 255, 257, 258, 259, 261 T, 273 BC&BL, 274, 275 T, 276, 277, 278, 281, 283, 289

FRONT COVER: *Old Military Cemetery at Fort Anne, Annapolis Royal, Nova Scotia*

BACK COVER TOP: *Old Burying Ground, Halifax, Nova Scotia*

BACK COVER BOTTOM: *Cataraqui, Kingston, Ontario*

PAGE 2—3: *United Church Cemetery, Cape Freel, Newfoundland*
Known as Cabo de Frey Luis when it was a Portuguese village, Cape Freel predates all other European settlements in Newfoundland except L'Anse aux Meadows. The village was abandoned under Premier Smallwood's resettlement program.

PAGE 5: *Cemetery at Chantry, Leeds County, Ontario*

PAGE 6—7: *Brigus, Newfoundland*
One of Newfoundland's oldest settlements.

PAGE 8—9: *Union Cemetery, Cobourg, Ontario*

PAGE 10: *Old Burying Ground, Halifax, Nova Scotia*

For Richard, all-weather companion,
patient supplier of tech support
and tireless reader.

— *Jane Irwin*

For Carole, Joanne and John.

— *John de Visser*

Acknowledgements

Over the years, my on-the-road journeys preparing for this book have brought me many delights and debts. I am grateful for the kindness and generosity of friends and fellow cemetery enthusiasts, as well as historians and those with professional interests.

Among those who have shared my graveyard visits in all kinds of weather and countless miles on roads and off the roads to out-of-the-way spots, or who have offered hints about special places to visit and much appreciated hospitality at the end of the day, I wish to thank Barbara and Robert Bishop, Steve Blacksmith, Barbara Bonner, Carol Bristow-Savile, Lois Corey, Gar Darroch, Ivy and Merlin Ernst, Heather Gilmour and Charlie Hogg, Judy and David Goodings, Jim Green, John Grenville, Maureen Harris, Lawrence Hill, Judy Horsley, Jean Johnston, Corey Keeble, Bev Kovacs, Ann Langille, Marion Leonard, Holly Levine, David Lillico, Norma Lundberg, Robin McKee, Jennifer McKendry, Marie Minaker, Amy Morassut, Clay Prescott, Donna Reid, Douglas Richardson, Peter Richardson, Mary Schofield, Rosemary Silvera, Marjorie Simmons, Anne Simpson, Bronwyn Smith, Shannon Smith, Karen Stauss and David Smith, Elizabeth Strathdee, Janis Topp, Dorothy Turcotte, Sharon and Paul Van Nest, Margaret and George Wallace, Elizabeth and Paul Watkinson, Anne West, Pamela Williams, Anne and Bob Wingfield and Sylvia Wray.

Some years ago, members of the Burlington Historical Society – Peggy and Les Armstrong, Marianne Hubbs and Harold Sears – made it possible for me to prepare a "Virtual Tour of Burlington's Heritage Cemeteries" as part of a Heritage of Ontario Cemeteries workshop sponsored by the Ontario Historical Society. That day I was fortunate indeed to meet two featured speakers, stalwart supporters and defenders of Ontario cemeteries: Marjorie Stuart, genealogist and Cemetery News editor of the *OHS Bulletin*, and Rob Leverty, OHS Programme Coordinator. I thank them for their help and encouragement.

Others who have worked for decades to preserve Canadian cemeteries and their historical records have also been extraordinarily generous in sharing their expertise. I am very grateful to those who read parts of my draft manuscript and offered valuable comments and suggestions: John Adams, Pleasance Crawford, David Kho, Helen Meredith, Randall Reid, Sally Ross, Peter Schell and George Wright. Deborah Trask, the authority on Nova Scotia burial grounds and gravestones, stands out as one whose comprehensive scholarship has not diminished her "amateur" enthusiasm and love of graveyard visits and her generosity to newcomers in the field.

Other debts are recorded in the Bibliography and Notes. I want particularly to acknowledge one internet source, the *Dictionary of Canadian Biography Online* (*DCBO*), "a major research and publishing project launched by the University of Toronto and the Université Laval in 1959, [providing] a much easier access to the published biographies and the information that interests you," at www.biographi.ca. As leaders of cemetery tours well know, the "reading" of monuments is much enhanced by biographical information supplementing what is inscribed in stone. My insight into commemorated lives owes much to easily accessible *DCBO* entries.

SACRED

To the Memory of

Margaret

Infant Daughter of

RICHARD & CATHARINE

SCOTT

who Departed this Life

the 2nd. January 1818

Aged 1 year and Six Months

Our pleasant Child is gone before
And but a little while
For life with us will soon be o'er
Then wherefore weep or wail.

SACRED

to the Memory of

ARCHIBALD SCOTT.

Who departed this life

on the 26th march 1827.

in the 82nd Year

of his Age.

Also

CHRISTIANA NEILSON

wife of JAMES SCOTT

RECTED

In Memory of

EDWARD BOND

SACRED

To the memory of

WILLIAM SCOTT,

who died Jan. 19. 1822

aged 42 years.

Also his Wife

EUPHA

who died 1826

aged years

CONTENTS

Discovering Historic Canadian Graveyards

Canada abounds in historic burial places. You may be driving along a two-lane country road and catch a sudden glimpse of a stone obelisk, glinting rays of sunlight from the middle of a field of tall grass and wildflowers. A low brick wall, a wide gate, or a quaint metal arch naming an old burying place invites you to stop for a brief investigation. More surprisingly, from a busy highway you may get a brief glance at a small group of gravestones beneath old trees, a quiet place despite its situation beside the unremittting roar of traffic. Once you begin noticing their presence, old cemeteries seem to turn up everywhere.

My own enthusiasm for historic graveyards grew from a general interest in local history. The area where I live was once a small village on the north shore of Lake Ontario. When I walk out my front door, I have merely to turn the corner to find myself beside St. Luke's Anglican Church, founded in 1832. The way to the lake naturally takes me through the churchyard, where old gravestones stand beneath tall locust trees, firs and maples. The trees were planted long ago and have shared the lifetimes of many churchgoers now resting peacefully beneath them. When my transplanted family put down its roots in this neighbourhood, I began to recognize that the names carved into the gravestones were the names of those who had founded the village, constructed its houses and established its businesses. The houses they built are now the homes of newcomers like myself. It was satisfying to know that my predecessors were, in a sense, still present here.

Canada is sometimes said to be a country lacking sufficient awareness of its history. The rueful admission by Stephen Leacock is often quoted: "I never realized that there was history, close at hand, beside my very own home. I did not realize that the old grave that stood among the brambles at the foot of our farm was *history*." Indeed, Canadians must acknowledge that too many of our nation's historic landmarks have been unrecognized, removed or forgotten. Their loss makes the monuments that remain ever more valuable.

FACING PAGE: *Milton Cemetery, Pittsburgh Township, Ontario*

PAGE 15: *Stoney Beach Cemetery, Annapolis County, Nova Scotia*
View over the Annapolis Basin from the Stoney Beach Cemetery, believed to have originally been an Acadian cemetery. Its earliest monument is dated 1780.

It is the future that gives meaning to history. Memorials seem to be about the past, but in reality they always stand for the future. Remembrance is essentially about the life to come. "Eternal life" may mean various things to various people, but common to all its meanings is the concept of something that survives the passing of time. Burial places are places of memory. Set apart from the mundane pressures of our everyday lives, they have an inherent power to provide a brief respite from temporary concerns and a chance to see our own life in a longer perspective. A graveyard sets our present in the once and future continuum of other people's lives.

We walk by history daily, but not always our own ancestral history. If I were to travel northward and eastward from my home, I'd find 20 pioneer graveyards before reaching the urban borders of modern Burlington. Not one of them would contain the monuments or remains of my own ancestors. Even the graves of my mother and father are so far from where I now live that I seldom visit them. As for my more distant relatives, I recall one expedition made in the 1960s, to seek out genealogical information in an overgrown pioneer rural graveyard. From treacherous small holes in the ground issued little snakes. I was too disconnected from my rural heritage to identify them as harmless garter snakes, and both my young children and I were genuinely spooked that day. Had I only known then what I know now, surely I'd have photographed the gravestones. Instead I merely noted names and dates, as if those bare facts were all that mattered.

In the past 40 years much has been lost from the inscribed records of pioneer gravestones. When I compare 1970s photographs of early gravestones to the same stones today, how I regret that I was not one of the pioneers who saw the need to make a pictorial record of what since has been worn away by time and environment. I was not in any way ahead of my time, and it is small consolation that not many people were. Even the acclaimed American author and photographer Eudora Welty, who took "a lot of cemetery pictures" in Mississippi in the 1930s and 1940s, did not see them published until some years after the publication of her other photographs. Her book *Country Churchyards* finally appeared in 2000, when she was in her nineties.

I took a lot of cemetery pictures in my life ... My family were not "Old Jackson," so I had no kin buried at Greenwood Cemetery, but I grew up near it. It was the view from the sleeping porch on our house on North Congress Street. We could look right down on it. I used to go over there and play...

How surprising it is that the author who lived for more than 75 years in the house her father built, and whose stories created for her readers a virtual experience of Old Mississippi, felt herself to be a stranger, a newcomer. But how typical she was, too, as a cemetery enthusiast. Without having any kin or family buried there, she was susceptible to a feeling of kinship with all kinds of families. In a graveyard, what might usually be a gossipy interest in other people's lives is tempered by our sense that death has made superfluous any passing judgement by the living.

Welty also comments that "Mississippi had no art except in cemeteries." Many people have, like her, come to appreciate cemeteries as *plein-air* art galleries. Older graveyards are filled with wonderful examples of sculpture, and handcrafted lettering too, of a quality that is rarely produced today. As with all artistic appreciation, the pleasure to the eye is matched by the appeal to the mind. The visual symbols on gravestones are part of ancient iconographical traditions, and their interpretation often requires exploring several layers of meaning.

Cemetery visitors should be given an early warning: fascination with graveyards tends to grow with each exposure to them. Searching out favourite themes, even such seemingly innocuous ones as willows, urns and obelisks, may develop into a kind of addiction. Soon a mania develops for collecting these representations (by camera, of course). One begins to perceive certain patterns of repetition-with-variation, and to find individual traits identifying the hand of a regional school or even a particular sculptor. Connoisseurship of gravestone art is a career open to all talents. Those who are already hooked are generous in sharing their knowledge and their discoveries. Once having reached this stage, one might as well join the Association of Gravestone Studies and exchange stories with other AGS members about how, without quite intending to, we got into this field. But anyone can enjoy visiting old graveyards. Although a smattering of art and history and natural history is helpful, no scholarly expertise is required.

Old cemeteries are also places of great natural beauty and diversity. Many are sites for meetings with remarkable trees, some planted a century or more ago. Smaller plants in our earliest pioneer burying grounds may be easily overlooked, or even regularly mowed down, but they are equally remarkable survivors too, and rare specimens of our natural heritage. Many old roses and varieties now known as "heritage flowers" were planted at the graveside in pioneer family burying grounds and are seldom found elsewhere. Naturalist groups such as the Nature Conservancy of Canada have raised public awareness about extremely rare survivals, in a few "abandoned" rural cemeteries, of native plant life from even before the time of European settlement. The Russ Creek Cemetery in the Township of Alnwick-Haldimand, Ontario, is one

such remnant of the dry tallgrass prairie that once covered extensive tracts over the Rice Lake Plains and the Oak Ridges Moraine but is now considered one of the most endangered ecosytems in Canada. For Ontario Nature (the Federation of Ontario Naturalists), that old cemetery, less than a hectare in size, is "a priceless jewel of Ontario's natural and cultural heritage." Historical gravestones are also treasured by specialists in fibre arts – hand-weavers, spinners and dyers – as sustenance for rare lichens. It is not uncommon for naturalists who set off on a quest for a rare sighting of the prairie buttercup, say, to find themselves becoming enthusiastic about old cemeteries. They are places to experience uniqueness and variety in the natural world.

The great Rural Cemeteries established, from the 1840s, in cities across Canada were created to illustrate "the beauties of nature combined with art." Often chosen for their scenic or even sublime vistas of mountains, rivers, lakes and oceans, the sites of these cemeteries were artfully transformed by landscape architects. They are comparable to the celebrated public parks created about the same time by Frederick Law Olmsted and others. Central to their vision was the planting of trees, both native and exotic. More than a century later, these cemeteries are among the finest aboretums in Canada. Long since surrounded by the restless activity of growing cities, they have become havens of treasured greenspace. Not at all far from the madding crowd of urban occupations, they provide habitats for birdlife and peaceful retreats for visitors. They were expressly designed to be admired, visited and appreciated. Picturesque and full of diversity, they invite extended browsing. Whether alone, in company or on a guided tour, enjoy them, treasure them.

STORIES IN OLD STONES

Those who love to explore old graveyards find in the monuments there an immediate and unique link with the past. Many people make pilgrimages to gravesites of famous men and women and feel an oddly intimate connection with them. Every day in Père Lachaise Cemetery in Paris, throngs come to honour the memory of Oscar Wilde and Jim Morrison. In Canada the gravesites of Glenn Gould, Emily Carr and Sir John A. Macdonald are much visited. But monuments with names unknown to us also exert a strong attraction and arouse our curiosity. Who were these people? We want to know their stories. We may begin looking into local histories and archives to fill in some blanks and sketch out a biography. Graveyard tours, where guides and costumed re-enactors bring selected stories to life, are immensely popular across the nation.

Many old stones, however, do not yield the information needed to piece together the stories of those whose lives were filled with "unhistoric acts" (in the finely ironic words of George Eliot's *Middlemarch*), those who lived "a hidden life, and rest in unvisited tombs." It is the creative artist who brings these "unhistoric" people to life. In "The View from Castle Rock," Alice Munro creates a distinctly Canadian viewpoint for her story of a family who emigrated from Ettrick, Scotland, in June 1818. Her story ends with a sudden shift from their lives midway through their voyage, to a 21st century perspective.

Those travellers lie buried — all but one of them — in the graveyard of Boston Church, in Esquesing, in Halton County, almost within sight, and well within sound, of Highway 401 north of Milton, which at that spot may be the busiest road in Canada ... Old James is here ... Nearby, close to the graves of her father and her brother Andrew and her sister-in-law Agnes, is the grave of Little Mary, married after all and buried beside Robert Murray, her husband ... She and Robert did not have any chil-

dren together, but after Mary's early death he married another woman and by her he had four sons who lie here, dead at the ages of two, and three, and four, and thirteen. The second wife is there too. Her stone says Mother. *Mary's says* Wife.

This summary is not much different from the Finale of *Middlemarch*, where readers learn what happens to the characters after the story leaves them in the middle of their lives. The following sentences seem to reverse Isabel's lifespan, from death in old age to difficult birth:

On the stone commemorating Andrew and Agnes ... there appears also the name of their daughter Isabel, who, like her mother Agnes died an old woman ... Born at Sea. And here, also, is the name of Andrew and Agnes's firstborn child, Isabel's elder brother. His dates as well.

The final paragraph delivers the reader an unexpected blow:

Young James was dead within a month of his family's landing at Quebec. His name is here but surely he cannot be. They had not taken up their land when he died, they had not even seen this place. He may have been buried somewhere along the way from Montreal to York or in that hectic new town itself. Perhaps in a raw temporary burying ground now paved over, perhaps without a stone in a churchyard where other bodies would some day be laid on top of his. Dead of some mishap in the busy streets of York, or of a fever, or dysentery – of any of the ailments, the accidents, that were the common destroyers of little children in his time.

The strength of Alice Munro's writing comes from the stark contrast between what any visitor to an old graveyard may plainly see – for instance, the names of Robert Murray's wives, the ages of his four sons – and our intimate acquaintance with the family during their crossing to Canada.

The end of the story devastates us in two ways. Having come to know the active little boy, to feel Mary's anguish when she fears young James is lost, readers feel a pang to learn of his death. And then, like any ordinary graveyard visitor 200 years later, we have no way of knowing how he died, where he died, nor where he was buried. All we know is that neither was he "swallowed [live] in the ocean," nor was his dead corpse "thrown overboard sewed up in a piece of canvas with a large lump of coal at its feet," like "the child [with] the name of Ormiston." Young James survived the crossing to come to a land that, for him, would be little more than the haunting image seen from Castle Rock in Edinburgh by his father and grandfather – the view of "a land as light as mist, sucked into the sky."

This poignant story reminds us that it was all too common in the 19th century for little children to die, and for adults to meet death before they had children to survive them. At the same time, in Canada's earliest pioneer graveyards we also see markers commemorating the ancestors of very large families. A man and wife who started their family before 1820 and remained hale and well, may now have hundreds of descendants dispersed all over the nation or even the world. The clan may have pursued genealogical research, published an extensive family tree, organized family reunions and supported the maintenance of their ancestral grave plot. But the burial places of other early pioneers, those who never became ancestors, are not "unhistoric." Having no surviving families to rally in their defence, their graves are vulnerable to modern redevelopment pressures.

For graveyard visitors who are not single-mindedly tracing the roots and branches of their own family trees, it is obvious that all these pioneers held shares in the early history of Canada. The honouring of their memory is a matter of national public interest.

CHANGING

BURIAL TRADITIONS

CHANGING BURIAL TRADITIONS

A New World

❦ Canadian cultural landscapes have been shaped and reshaped by waves of immigration. Arriving in a world that is new to them, each group of settlers brings cultural traditions from the world they have had to leave behind. Emigration to new dwelling places emphasizes the great divide between those who are still living and moving, and those who have gone to their long home. In such transitional contexts, burial customs are most tenaciously preserved. For the first generations, traditional burial practices are essential links to their ancestors in the old country. So the places of early Canadian settlement are also places where grave markers continue to signify cultural identities.

The earliest known graves of European settlers are those of two miners who were part of Martin Frobisher's settlement of Qallunaat Island in 1578 (*qallunaat* is the Inuktitut word for "white people"). "Two upright boulders in a field of gravel may be makeshift headstones marking miners' graves ... The sense of an historical landscape, of a place where the past is very close, pervades the atmosphere. On a quiet walk around the island one is conscious of the same unchanged vistas seen by Frobisher and his men, the same rocks and patches of gravel underfoot, the same constant, bitter wind."

The oldest known gravestones with European inscriptions date from the 16th or 17th century. Newfoundland is England's oldest colony, but Basque fishermen were among the first Europeans to frequent the island. Captain George Drake, visiting Placentia Bay in 1592, counted 60 Basque fishing ships in the area. The Basque "Plaisance" was authorized as a French settlement by Louis XIV in 1660. Two years later a chapel was built, perhaps on the site of a Basque churchyard. A church built on the same site by the Recollet friars in 1689 and taken over by the Church of England following the Treaty of Utrecht was surrounded by the original burying ground. The medieval tradition of burying the dead in consecrated ground close to the house of worship had been carried over to the new-found land.

FACING PAGE: *'Namgis First Nation Burial Ground, Alert Bay, British Columbia*

PAGE 18–19: *Union Cemetery, Cobourg, Ontario*

It is said that the English and Irish settlers who came to Placentia after 1713 removed many of the old gravestones and put them to new uses, such as doorsteps. In more recent times, five remaining fragmentary stones were removed to St. Luke's Anglican Church and are now preserved at the Castle Hill Historic Site. The oldest, bearing the date 1676, reads (in translation): "Here lies, having died on May 1, 1676, John de Sale Cesana, son of the House of the Sweetest Odour."

Another stone was studied in 1902, when it was in much better condition. What remained of the epitaph was the first, but hardly the last, memorial in Canada to record details of a military career.

CY.GIS.JOVANNES.
DE.SVIGARAICHIPI.
DIT.CROISIC.CAPIT
AINE.DE.FREGATE
.DV.ROY.
1694

ENVIEUX.POUR
L'HONNEVR.DE.MON
PRINCE.JALLOIS.NE
SVIVANT.SA.CARRIERE
ATTAQVER.LES.ENNE
MIS.EN.LEVR.MESME
[...]
+ DM

"Here lies John de Suigaraichipi called Croisic, Captain of the King's Frigate. 1694. Craving the honour of my Prince I went following his career to attack enemies in their own [...] **+ DM**." Le Croisic in Brittany was a port town for privateers, who were commissioned by Louis XIV to attack the commercial shipping of the enemy Dutch, Spanish and English. John de Suigaraichipi may have met his death while sailing in Newfoundland waters to protect the annual fishing convoy.

Mounds and Cairns

The earliest known sacred burial grounds are roughly contemporaneous in both the Old and New Worlds. "New World" is perhaps a Eurocentric term. The American continents, after all, are no more *arriviste* than those on the other side of the tectonic divide known as the Mid-Atlantic Ridge. In fact, Wayland's Smithy in Oxfordshire (built some 5,500 years ago), Cuween Hill in Orkney (5,000 years old) and Cairnpapple Hill in West Lothian (in use 4,300 to 3,500 years ago) are more recent than the oldest known aboriginal cairn in Canada.

Along the road to the village of L'Anse Amour in southern Labrador, a rock cairn about nine meters wide and less than one meter high had escaped notice until 1973, when road maintenance crews partially uncovered it. Archaeologists who excavated it a year later, expecting to find the burial place of a person of importance, found only a small stone chamber with no traces of a burial, apart from a few stains of red ochre. Beneath the chamber, however, they discovered a child's well-preserved skeleton and a collection of artifacts placed there 7,500 years ago. The child had been buried lying face down with an ivory walrus tusk placed in front of his face and a rock resting on his back. Ceremonial paint objects and two upright stones with charcoal and fish remains suggest that a ritual ceremony was associated with his burial. Buried with him were stone and bone spearheads, an ivory toggling harpoon head and hand toggle, a bone pendant and a bird-bone flute, or whistle. Both the harpoon and the burial mound are among the oldest in the world.

Aboriginal burials were usually communal. Was this child a person of importance? His isolated single grave may suggest that he had a special status. The meaning of aboriginal burial sites cannot be wholly understood, however, by speculating about individual identities or relics. In the absence of traditional knowledge, our interpretation is limited. The cairn has been restored to its original form. Seventy-five centuries ago it probably looked much as it does today. This

FACING PAGE: *Placentia, Newfoundland* Fragment of the gravestone for "Jouannes de Suigaraichipi dit Croisic," who died in 1694.

is by far the most ancient burial place in Canada to have become a restoration project. Until some 30 years ago, however, it suffered from neither environmental degradation nor deferred maintenance. Undisturbed and entirely forgotten, no restoration was necessary. It had merely passed from human memory.

Thousands of mounds were built throughout North America between 3,000 and 500 years ago. The Mound Builders on the prairies sought to honour their dead, to ensure for them a happy and peaceful afterlife in the spirit world, and to leave a lasting monument to be revisited. Mound burial was the final step in a long and complex ritual of mourning. A few days after a death, the body was tightly wrapped in buffalo hides and placed upon a scaffold with gifts of tools and food. Mourning, distribution of possessions and a feast accompanied these ceremonies. About a year later, the band ended its mourning by constructing a mound. Sod was stripped from a circular area to make a depression, and a wooden post was erected in the centre. Bones were gathered from scaffolds, rubbed with ochre, rebundled, placed on the ground around the central post and surrounded by grave offerings of goods required in the next life – decorated pottery vessels, birchbark containers, tubular stone pipes and bone tools. A low tipi-like structure was built, and many tons of earth were hauled in to cover the burial chamber.

The Moose Bay Mound in Crooked Lake Provincial Park, near Fort Qu'Appelle, Saskatchewan, is a grassy conical dome 15 meters in diameter and 1.5 meters high, located on a steep hill high above the lower Qu'Appelle River. Archaeological excavation in 1968 uncovered the bundled skeleton of a young woman near the surface. Included with her burial were stone scrapers, bone awls, pipes and a pottery vessel covered by two birchbark containers. A small hole in the bottom of the vessel is thought to represent the traditional killing of goods meant to serve the dead. Next to the central post at the base of the mound were multiple burials with grave offerings – a birchbark container, a curved bone knife, pottery shards and fragments of a turtle shell gorget.

Mounds were also built in what is now Ontario. The Rainy River was a gathering place for indigenous people from all over North America, and the centre of a continental trading network. Copper from Lake Superior was exchanged for stone for tool-making from the north and west, and marine shells from oceans far to the east and south. From about 3,000 to 2,300 years ago, people now known as the Laurel Culture buried their most honoured dead with grave offerings in earthen mounds, which grew over time, some to more than 12 meters high. The 17 or more Manitou Mounds form the largest ancient structure in Canada. Medicine bags, pipes, food, clay pots and tools, so useful in life, were provided for the afterlife of the spirit. *Manitou* is the Anishinaabe (Ojibway) word for "spirit." The Anishinaabeg of the Rainy River First Nation are the modern guardians of this rich spiritual heritage at *Kay-Nah-Chi-Wah-Nung*, "Place of the Long Rapids."

On a high point of land comanding a view over the magnificent marsh and wildlife-filled waters of Rice Lake are nine burial mounds. The zigzag or serpentine form of the largest (the only one of its kind in Canada) is thought to have been formed from a series of smaller mounds, later joined together. Mounds were made between 2,400 and 1,300 years ago by Woodland communities as they established more permanent settlements. The later Iroquoian people developed other burial traditions, such as the use of ossuaries. Their continuing use of the Rice Lake sacred burial place was exceptional.

The oldest community in New Brunswick is a fishing village where the Miramichi and Red Bank rivers join at the Oxbow. The history of the Miramichi Mi'kmaqs can be traced back over some 2,500 years. In 1909 artifacts taken from a sacred burial place in the Red Bank area were sold by a local man to the British Museum. The collection includes pipes, copper beads, gorgets, a boatstone, various implements and pottery shards. The mound from which they were taken was the ancient burial site for two people whose remains had been wrapped in birchbark. Until the 1970s, when Red Bank Elder Joseph Augustine determined to follow up traditional lore, the location of the mound remained apparently unknown. On a high terrace above the Miramichi River, he discovered what is now known as the Augustine Mound. Archaeologists found lavish grave offerings, including copper salts from thousands of copper beads, which had helped preserve organic materials such as braided thongs, textile fragments, cedar bark matting, twilled and pleated basketry, hafted beaver teeth and a wood spear shaft fragment.

For the Mi'kmaqs, Augustine's discovery of the Mound has a meaning quite different from that of non-aboriginal researchers. A cultural landscape is valued by aboriginal people because of their complex relationship with it through the seasonal round of life. A place is seen not as property to be owned, but as a resource for supporting life – for harvesting, social gatherings and sacred ceremonies.

The day-to-day activities of drawing a living from the land depend on an intimate link between human and animal movements. For them, land includes water and sky, the home of fish and fowl as well as earthbound creatures. All living things – animals, plants, people – must breathe, and breath has been associated with soul or spirit since Paleolithic times. The Latin word *anima* expresses all three meanings – breath, soul and spirit. Animals, spirits and people are interrelated in significant aboriginal landscapes, places of particular spiritual and emotional power. The people's relationship to the land is embodied in traditional knowledge, transmitted orally from generation to generation in stories associating spirit beings with kinship to place. Material remains of this association may be evident, but they may also be minimal or even (apparently) absent.

Serpent Mound, overlooking Rice Lake, Ontario

First Nations and Christian Missions

❧ Before the arrival of Christian missionaries, the First Peoples of the northwest coast had many local varieties of mortuary practices – cairns, tree burial, grave houses, cremation and mortuary poles. The Europeans' first reactions to these traditions are represented in the published report of Alejandro Malaspina, the Spanish naval officer and explorer whose ships visited Yakutak Bay, Alaska, in 1792. His book includes a drawing of the large bear totem holding in its paws a box containing cremated ashes, which is described as follows:

We do not know whether the colossal monster ... is an idol or merely a frightful record of the destructive nature of death, but the fact that in its vicinity are various pyres on which bodies have been cremated inclines us to the first idea. In a casket which lay between its claws or hands was a bowl-shaped basket, a European hat, and otter skin and a piece of board ... In the upper chambers of the two sepulchral deposits were two baskets, one greater than the other, the contents covered with loose boards, containing a basket with some calcined bones, broken up very small so that it was scarcely possible to distinguish between parts of the cranium and the two first cervical vertebrae.

Shocked by the "pagan" practice of cremation, suspecting that totem sculptures were idols for heathen worship, and confident that unburied remains were a health hazard, missionaries linked their conversion of native people to Christianity with the suppression of what they perceived to be uncivilized practices. Consecrated burial grounds were established, while existing memorial and mortuary posts were destroyed, or were not renewed when they decayed.

Among many First Peoples, grave houses sheltered not only the remains of the dead but also their personal belongings, or grave goods provided for their spirits' journey to the spirit world. The goods were sometimes damaged to signify their transition to spiritual form. In 1926 the artists A.Y. Jackson and Edwin Holgate and the anthropologist Marius Barbeau made a trip to the west coast, seeking to document native traditions. Jackson recalled: "One day Holgate and I were making drawings of the Indian grave houses at Hazelton. They were made of wood and were of odd design. Inside were placed all kinds of objects the deceased might have use for in the spirit world, such as clothes, tools, and a broken sewing machine." He also noted in his autobiography that "American archeologists, ethnologists and others had cleaned up everything of value in the country." Totem poles were no longer being made, but the few remaining "kept alive the memory of days when the tribes were numerous and powerful. They were regarded as idols by many people who encourage the Indians to destroy them."

Like Emily Carr, these artists could appreciate (to a degree) what was being lost. In his journal, Holgate wrote that he felt they "were witnessing the rapid decline of a splendid race of creative and well-organized people." Jackson deplored the "absurd" restoration of totem poles in "a complete line of garish colours from Vancouver," promoted by the CNR and government officials: "The poles were made to look ridiculous. The Indians were suspicious of the project and the people in charge of it, and they had good reason to be." But even crass exploitation for tourism development did not spell the end of ancient traditions.

The Shingwauk Cemetery in Sault Ste. Marie, Ontario, is a tranquil wooded area beside the picturesque Bishop Fauquier Memorial Chapel, a one-of-a-kind structure built in 1883 of local red sandstone. Its design, by the evangelical Anglican missionary Edward Wilson, combines Gothic and Tudor elements under the influence of the British Arts and Crafts movement. The monuments include one for the first Bishop of Algoma, Frederick Dawson Fauquier, who in 1874 had supported the founding of residential schools, one for boys and one for girls, the Shingwauk and Wawanosh Indian Homes. Fauquier and his wife both died in Toronto in the winter of 1881 and their remains were brought to the Sault for burial the following spring.

FACING PAGE: *St. Anne's Church Cemetery, Chapel Island, Nova Scotia* Catholic Mission for the Eskasoni Mi'kmaq First Nation.

Edward Wilson ran the schools from 1874 to 1893, and his account of his experience there, *Missionary Work Among the Ojebway Indians*, was published by the Society for Promoting Christian Knowledge in 1886. Wilson himself had experienced a religious epiphany, and his mission was to encourage his nominally Christian boys to be converted through a vital, highly emotive religious experience, and then to train them as missionaries who would proselytize their own people. After the death in 1882 of a star pupil and model Christian, William Sahqucheway, whom he had adopted as a son, Wilson found it comforting that, as the gravestone epitaph states, the boy had been at the age of 19 "a young soldier of the cross who led 20 of his companions to love the Saviour."

In November 1877 John Rodd died at age 15, nine months after his conversion experience. Wilson's correspondence gives a vivid account of the religious discourses and rituals associated with his final days: "I had all the boys in to see him as he lay in a sort of stupor to bid him farewell – then about a dozen of the elder boys remained for singing & prayer. We sang 'Sweet bye & bye', 'Safe in the arms of Jesus', 'Over there', & 'There is a fountain.'" At the funeral the following day the pallbearers wore white sashes and other boys wore black crepe bands and bows: "I was glad we had the little cemetery done up – it looks nicely now with its grass, gravel walks & flower beds ... I shall place a neat slab at the head of his grave with his name, age, place of abode ... & the verse 'Them also which sleep in Jesus shall God bring with him.'"

The following May the school had a ceremony to install the tombstone, which still stands. Part of its epitaph records that it was "Erected by the Sunday School of St. Peter's Church, Toronto." Chief Buhkwujjenene delivered an address. He was a brother of Chief Shingwauk, whose idea had originally been to build an industrial school.

For these men, their newly adopted Christian faith was assimilated to the Anishinaabe belief system, in which religious power came from other-than-human persons, often referred to as "our grandfathers." Traditional spiritual aid helped the Anishinaabeg to achieve the Good Life here on earth, rather than the eternal afterlife promised by Christianity. It was also very clear that, since the initial encounter between them in the 16th century, the Christians had had a better life than native peoples. As one scholar has put it: "Conversion to Christianity was essentially a phenomenon of the moon of wintertime, when ancestral spirits had ceased to perform their expected functions satisfactorily and angel choirs promised to fill a spiritual vacuum." In addition, access to literacy and other economic powers was seen as a part of the package of conversion. But the old beliefs (or "superstitions," as Christians usually termed them) were not given up.

The Anishinaabeg did not greatly fear death, but neither was it welcomed, and "they traditionally went to considerable trouble to prevent the spirits of those who had just died from giving in to their loneliness and taking others with them to the land of the dead." For instance, they blocked up windows of their homes to prevent lingering spirits from entering in search of their loved ones. They believed that the dead could receive gifts from the living, such as food or tobacco placed in the fire, and friends and relatives often left food, tea and tobacco at grave shelters, so that passersby could visit with the dead in their last homes. It was an exchange of hospitality that was thought to make the dead man "glad that [the living] should stop and visit him." The families of the children who died in the residential schools may have wished them to be close by, where the living could communicate with them, but their families' requests for the return of the bodies were resisted.

As for Edward Wilson, another turning point was to be marked by the Northwest Rebellion in 1885. He attended the conclusion of Riel's trial, visited Poundmaker (Pitikwahanapiwiyin) in prison, and began to rethink the destruction of native autonomy and the promotion of assimilation. After an extended journey in 1888, he was particularly impressed by the Cherokee of Oklahoma, who had adopted aspects of European culture but retained their own government, schools, judicial system and collective ownership of land. Using the pseudonym "Fair Play," he published articles advocating self-government for natives in Canada.

Christian Burial and Cemetery Reform

The practice of burial in churches and churchyards had its origins in the early history of Christianity. All communities in Rome, including the Christians, followed Hellenistic custom and complied with the laws of the Roman Empire, purchasing burial land along the main roads outside the city walls. In the subterranean layer of tufa (a stone that is easy to work, yet stable), galleries were cut with *loculi* or niches for the dead and altars were erected for funeral rites, again following Roman custom. Later, churches were built over the relics of the first Christian martyrs and confessors of the faith, and fragments of bone were placed as venerated relics within the altar. The burial place beneath the basilica of San Sebastiano on the Via Appia in Rome was called *Coemetrium ad Catacumbas*. It was the holiest of Christian places of pilgrimage, the final resting place of the relics of the Apostles and Saints Peter and Paul, along with Saint Sebastian and some 174,000 other martyrs or faithful witnesses from the era when the sect was persecuted. Its name was the origin of the terms "catacomb" and "cemetery." The source and original meaning of the Latin *catacumbus* is still obscure. The Latin *coemetrium,* derived from the Greek word for "dormitory," was adopted by the Christians to express their faith that a cemetery is a temporary place where many lie slumbering for a while, awaiting the Second Coming and the day of Resurrection.

As Christian congregations increased in number, more churches were built, and they exerted a gravitational pull on burial practices. The dead of the parish were buried beneath church floors, or beside churches in ground enclosed by walls and consecrated by a bishop. Church crypts became filled with the remains of the great and the good, while the less privileged churchyard places were periodically cleared of bones, which were stored in charnel houses, leaving room for more burials.

By the 17th century, with the great expansion of population in cities and towns, old churchyards became overused. There was also a reaction in England against the practice of transferring remains to ossuaries and charnel houses. The results were further overcrowding of English churchyards and consequent concerns about hygiene and public health. Finally, there was a reaction by Dissenters, whose religious convictions separated them from the established Church. Wishing neither to pay burial fees to the Church nor to be buried in ground consecrated by an Anglican bishop, Dissenters acted on the radical idea of establishing a cemetery, rather than a churchyard. Bunhill Fields, near Moorgate in the old London Wall, opened in 1665. By the time it closed in 1860, that particular Nonconformist idea (so radical 200 years earlier) had found general acceptance. Most of the great English cemeteries opened in the 19th century were outside the liturgical and economic control of the Church of England.

Dissenters continued to found small cemeteries where funerals could be conducted by ministers of Nonconformist congregations. In 1819 they opened the first large private cemetery for multi-denominational use in Norwich, and followed almost immediately with cemeteries in Manchester, Liverpool and other major cities during the 1820s. These enterprises were funded by the incorporation of joint-stock companies, which rapidly became extremely successful ventures, returning substantial annual dividends to their shareholders. Private enterprise, following the example of philanthropic non-profit corporations, was motivated to use the joint-stock model to set up a great number of cemeteries throughout Britain, wherever population growth created sufficient demand and suitable land was available for purchase at the right price. St. James's Cemetery in Liverpool, for example, sited to spectacular effect in an abandoned sandstone quarry, was opened in 1829. Its shareholders received a handsome annual dividend of 8 per cent.

These market conditions prompted a certain spirit of competitiveness among cemeteries. In Greater London, the

"Magnificent Seven" private cemeteries were opened within a decade: Kensal Green (1833), Norwood (1837), Highgate (1839), Nunhead, Abney Park and Brompton (all in 1840), and Tower Hamlets (1841). Excellence in architectural and landscape design was well recognized as essential to a private cemetery's success. The purchase of family burial plots became a form of real estate investment, in which sufficient wealth could secure a desirable location at a good address. In these circumstances, cemetery design in Victorian Britain was quite transformed from the traditional church and churchyard pattern, not only entirely different from the crowded city site, but also far from the modest country churchyard which had been idealized by the "Graveyard Poets" of the previous century.

A century earlier, Thomas Gray's "Elegy Written in a Country Church-Yard" (1751) had very memorably paid tribute to "some mute inglorious Milton," an unknown genius whose potential had not even achieved the success of the poet known as "Anon." In this secluded spot, the anonymous "rude Forefathers of the hamlet sleep" in their lowly bed "far from the madding crowd's ignoble strife." Having passed through "the cool sequester'd vale of life," they now rested "to fortune and to fame unknown." Gray's "Elegy" was often quoted by urban Victorians: "The paths of glory lead but to the grave." But in the fashionable new Victorian cemeteries, its message was seldom heeded. "Nor you, ye Proud, impute to These the fault / If Mem'ry o'er their Tomb no Trophies raise" was a moral admonition quite generally ignored.

Those grandly ambitious 19th century descendants of their almost-forgotten forefathers were not to be dissuaded from spending their newly acquired fortunes on the production of storied urns or animated busts as proud memorials for their families and even – perhaps especially – for themselves. They aspired to lasting fame. Not for them the neglected spot for the interment of "th'unhonour'd Dead." They were only one or two generations away from rural life, and knew all too well the harsh realities of farm labour. No matter how celebrated by Gray's smooth poetic diction –

"Their furrow oft the stubborn glebe has broke ... How bow'd the woods beneath their sturdy stoke!" – tree-felling, ploughing and harvesting by hand-sickle held no attraction for them. No doubt they felt some sentimental attachment to the rustic graveyards where their forefathers lay, but they themselves had no intention of returning to rural life, and the new Rural Cemeteries were to be completely different from the kind of place where "the ploughman homeward plods his weary way."

Two major influences on Victorian cemetery design came from outside Britain – Calcutta and Paris. The historian of cemeteries and commemorative structures James Stevens Curl has pointed out that some of the earliest modern cemeteries were laid out in the 17th century by Europeans in India, as the hygienic necessities of the "sick season" were combined with the delight experienced by European colonial settlers when they viewed supreme examples of Islamic tombs in the sub-continent. These astonishingly beautiful tombs and mausoleums were derived from Persian prototypes. Free-standing in their settings of formal gardens, gates and water features, they are undeniably magnificent. Since Roman times, Europeans had not been accustomed to seeing grand tombs outside of churches. Moghul mausoleums standing in formal enclosed gardens were potent examples for them as they began to establish their own modern cemeteries. Impressive tombs were built for them by local craftsmen, using brick covered with stucco in imitation of stone.

One of the best-known European cemeteries in India was established in 1767. South Park Street Cemetery, in what was then the out-skirts of Calcutta, was renowned for its large numbers of tombs, arranged along streets in the pattern of a modern necropolis or "city of the dead." Rudyard Kipling observed that "the tombs are small houses. It is as though we walked down the streets of a town, so tall are they and so closely do they stand."

Many mausoleums at South Park Street took Imperial forms, including frequent design references to the Roman Empire. Domed gazebos, kiosks and temples were derived

FACING PAGE: *Père Lachaise Cemetery, Paris, France*
A streetscape of mausoleums and trees.

from Classical plans and patterns, and were crowned by obelisks, urns, pyramids and truncated columns inspired by the French Neoclassicist architectural style. This influence on cemetery architectural form returned to France in 1804, when Emperor Napoleon decreed the purchase of land on Mont-Louis east of Paris for the site of a new cemetery, now the renowned Père Lachaise Cemetery. Like South Park Street, Père Lachaise has an urban flavour, with paved streets lined with house-tombs. The mausoleums, with their prominent doors, resemble detached villas. The urban aspect of Père Lachaise, with its surveyed arrangement of divisions and sub-divisions and the numbering of each plot, is enhanced by its landscaping and a great variety of plantings. The formality of roads along Classical symmetrical axes is also complemented by winding paths in the Romantic English landscape tradition. The effect was to create a second modern version of the Champs Elysées, or Elysian Fields, evoking the Classical Greek abode of the happy and grateful dead.

Since 1804, the appeal of Père Lachaise Cemetery as an attraction for casual visitors and tourists has not waned, but has been enhanced by the patina of time and the corresponding increase of historical content. When it was first opened, the initial sense that it was too new was mitigated by its well-publicized acquisition of the remains of famous authors, transferred from older burial grounds: Molière, La Fontaine and – most brilliantly – the 12th century lovers Abélard and Héloïse. Père Lachaise quickly became an extraordinarily successful investment story. It is said that the previous owner of the grounds, James Baron, who was buried there in 1822, paid more to acquire his own small plot than he gained for the entire 17 hectare site. Père Lachaise now has 44 hectares and is considered the largest park in Paris. It has more than 5,000 trees and more than 70,000 plots for its permanent residents, and every year is visited by two million visitors from all over the world. Perhaps the greatest aspect of its success, however, was its potent influence on the design and marketing of new 19th century cemeteries in Europe, America, Britain and British colonies around the world.

The Rural Cemetery Ideal

Private cemeteries in Britain were quick to emulate the design aspects and marketing tactics of Père Lachaise. Cemetery companies promoted architecture competitions to achieve excellence in the designs of their entrance gateways, keepers' lodges and chapels. Talented landscape architects were also in demand. Although no English lovers quite equivalent to Abélard and Héloïse were available for reburial, Kensal Green, the first of Greater London's "Magnificent Seven" cemeteries, gained fashionable status when it was chosen for the interment of Princess Sophia and the Duke of Sussex, royal offspring of George III. Within six years, the Kensal Green Company was a flourishing concern, and its shares had doubled in value.

Despite the great success of these private cemeteries, the continuing problem of severely overcrowded urban graveyards, where corpses were often buried only a couple of feet below the surface, was far too great to leave to private enterprise alone to solve. In the Victorian era of public sanitation reform, old churchyards were understandably seen as a prime menace to public health. The first cholera epidemic (1831–32), which killed 52,000 people in Britain, heightened public awareness of the urgency of the issue, but it was the second cholera epidemic of 1848–49 that stirred the dilatory government into action. The *Burial Act* of 1857 established a national system of public cemeteries.

During the decades of public debate about cemetery reform that preceded the passing of this Act, there was a shift away from the ideal urban necropolis pattern of South Park Street and Père Lachaise, toward a particularly British rural ideal. Among the influences on this shift were the publications of John Claudius Loudon. He edited many gardening magazines, was a prolific writer in all of them and in 1843 produced a final book, *On the Laying Out, Planting, and Managing of Cemeteries, and on the Improvement of Churchyards.* Loudon, like his precursor John Strang, advocated what they called the "garden cemetery" as "the most convincing token of a nation's progress in civilization and the arts." They were confident that the garden cemetery would mark the defeat of "preternatural fear and superstition" and would be beneficial in improving public morals, manners and taste, in cultivating the intellect, and in extending virtuous and generous feelings. Lofty ambitions, indeed.

Loudon's numerous publications reveal his interest, as a practising landscape gardener, in practical recommendations. Cemetery locations ought to be distant from human dwellings and situated "in an elevated and airy place" with a southern aspect, so that the surface soil would be dried by the sun. They should be secured by boundary walls of "an architectural character." Entrance lodges at the gate should house the superintendent and also an office containing the layout map book and register of burial locations. Evergreen trees should be planted – cedars, yews, pines, firs and cypresses – not because of any symbolic *semper vivens* (everliving) value, but for quite practical reasons – to avoid the maintenance problems of falling leaves and to allow light and air to reach to the ground surface. Similarly, weeping willows were in Loudon's view a sentimental mistake, with implications of poor drainage.

Despite the "garden cemetery" name, he advocated planting "no flowers at all" because their cultivation required disturbing the soil. The general impression is of an extensive list of gardening do's and don'ts, gained from his long experience, and combined with a utilitarian and hygienic approach. For Loudon, even the cemetery chapels, to be located in conspicuous positions as focal points, have a practical function. He describes the installation in the chapels of new systems to rotate or lower coffins.

Loudon's writings offer much guidance on how to design modern cemeteries, but little understanding of how they will "extend virtuous and generous feelings." His advice does not explain the radical shift of taste in a matter so intimately connected with religious beliefs and emotional attachments. Taste is not ultimately about beauty as an impersonal quality of things in themselves, but results from the association of feelings blended with recollection. A revolution in taste is therefore connected essentially to a shift in emotional association. Also, the 19th century was characterized by a tremendous increase in the number of varieties of religious experience, comprising not only the established Church of England, but also Dissenters of all kinds, as well as Jews, Catholics, agnostics and atheists. The new cemeteries had to be inclusive of a great many various beliefs about death and mourning.

The essence of the new taste was comprehensively grasped and expressed by Charles Dickens. Capturing the popular imagination as no other novelist had ever done, he has been credited with embodying the central consciousness of the Victorian age. A campaigner for numerous reforms, Dickens voiced his concerns about church and churchyard burial in many of his works. His account of the London churchyard named by him "Saint Ghastly Grim" was published in his magazine *All the Year Round*, which sold an impressive 300,000 copies every week. His novels were even more effective in influencing his vast range of readers. *Bleak House* was published serially between 1851 and 1853, during the public debate preceding the *Burial Act*. The novel mingles many themes, all of them addressed in two ways by his narrative's double-sided perspective. First, Dickens made his readers conscious of what was generally ignored by polite society. In burial practices, for instance, Lady Dedlock's world includes not only the "ancient, solemn, little church" in Chesney Wold, "which smelt as earthly as the grave," and where "there is a general smell and taste of the ancient Dedlocks in their graves," but also the London "hemmed-in churchyard, pestiferous and obscene" where the unknown pauper with the pen-name Nemo ("No One") is buried.

Lady Dedlock herself will be laid in the modern family mausoleum in the park of the Dedlock estate. Dickens has taken pains to describe this park for us at a significant moment, just before her entrance into his story. The chapter is related in the second side of his narrative, from the perspective of Esther Summerson. Her primary experience of acute unhappiness as a young child of unknown parentage has given Esther an intensely perceptive sensitivity. Her lush descriptions are characteristically filled with sentiment. Her voicing of this description is most poignantly set in the chapter where she will briefly glimpse the family connection that she has always longed for. In this emotionally loaded context, Dickens draws a picture that erases the foul image of corruption and replaces it with an idealized view that epitomizes the look and the spirit desired by advocates of the Rural Cemetery Movement.

As Esther arrives for the first time in Chesney Wold, she rapturously describes a picturesque old house in a fine richly wooded park:

O, the solemn woods over which the light and shadow travelled swiftly, as if Heavenly wings were sweeping on benignant errands through the summer air; the smooth green slopes, the glittering water, the gardens where the flowers were so symmetrically arranged in clusters of the richest colours, how beautiful they looked! The house, with gable and chimney, and tower and turret, and dark doorway, and broad terrace-walk, twining among the balustrades of which, and lying heaped upon the vases, there was one great flush of roses, seemed scarcely real in all its light solidity, and in the serene and peaceful hush that rested all around it. To Ada and to me, that, above all, appeared the pervading influence. On everything, house, garden, terrace, green slopes, water, old oaks, fern, moss, woods again, and far away across the openings in the prospect, to the distance lying wide before us with a purple bloom upon it, there seemed to be such undisturbed repose.

Dickens has here depicted both the desired look of the landscape and the desired psychological effect of the Rural Cemetery. The picturesque house becomes the gatehouse or superintendent's lodge in the Rural Cemetery design. The formal viewing terrace, balustrades, water features, floral beds, mature trees, broken and open prospect views and finally the purple bloom of almost infinite vistas at the horizon – all are quintessential elements in the design of Rural Cemetery landscapes. And all of these features are fused to create the pervading atmosphere of solemn repose and union with the natural world.

There is even a hint that the natural and spiritual worlds may unite, so that the alternating light and shadow of swiftly passing clouds may be seen as visions of "Heavenly wings … sweeping on benignant errands." Dickens' decision to capitalize the "H" in Heavenly makes a kind of subliminal reference to angelic messengers, but the reference is not intrusive. He does not insist on a religious message. The presence of the church in the landscape view is, in fact, not even mentioned here. This park is a non-denominational place of slumber in "the serene and peaceful hush that rested all around it." The reader is very subtly made to view Chesney Wold park as a cemetery, long before coming to know that in this park there is a mausoleum. Only the dark doorway to the house gives that hint.

At the end of the novel, the reader is given a last look at the park, where the elderly Sir Leicester "holds his shrunken estate" in the Dedlocks' ancestral house, the greater part of which is shut up, a "showhouse" no longer. Dickens shows the light of the drawing room dwindling until it shall soon be no more "and the damp door of the mausoleum which shuts so tight, and looks so obdurate, will have opened and relieved him." A bleak house, indeed. But the final chapter reminds readers that Esther's two houses, which actually bear the "Bleak House" name, are filled with "happy years" and "much dear remembrance." The balance of these viewpoints was the ideal of the Rural Cemetery Movement.

Mount Auburn Cemetery

Rural Cemeteries throughout America, including Canada, were inspired by the example of Mount Auburn Cemetery, founded in Cambridge (near Boston) in 1831. Still an active cemetery as well as a National Historic Landmark, it is exemplary in the quality of its landscape maintenance, its magnificent horticultural collection and array of interpretive materials, special events and guided walking tours prepared to welcome tourists from all over the world. It was the first large-scale designed landscape in America open to visits by city dwellers wanting to experience nature, and in the 19th century it influenced not only other rural cemeteries but also the first public parks and the first designed suburbs. A guidebook for visitors was produced: *Dearborn's Guide through Mount Auburn with Seventy-six Engravings, for the Benefit of Strangers, desirous of seeing the clusters of monuments with the least trouble; with the established rules for the preservation of the Cemetery, purchase of Lots, and other concerns, with an Engraved Plan of the Cemetery.* By 1856 it had reached its tenth edition.

Mount Auburn's site was distinguished by its irregular and varied topography. It included a network of ponds and wetlands and a mature forest of native pines, oaks and beeches, which created a place of special rural beauty. Harvard University students had nicknamed it "Sweet Auburn," in reference to Oliver Goldsmith's poem "The Deserted Village" (1770), and so its highest hill was named Mount Auburn. The landscape of the cemetery was designed to mingle together monuments, tree plantings and winding roads, so that interrupted viewpoints produced multiple vistas that succeeded each other like tableaux.

The picturesque beauty of the rugged site was complemented by the layout of roads and paths, and ample space was provided for burials in a tranquil natural setting. Monuments were scattered widely throughout the rather dense native forest growth, in contrast to the flat, barren, unplanted burying grounds of the city. The philosophical basis for the Rural Cemetery Movement (not always explicitly acknowledged) was that death was not to be regarded as merely synonymous with destruction and decay, but as part of the complete biological cycle. The natural landscape was subtly, almost subliminally, a reminder that the return to the earth of mortal remains was essential to provide the elements for the continuance of life.

Equally important to the philosophy of the Rural Cemetery Movement was the perpetuation of historical continuities of family roots and social networks. Mount Auburn's founders intended it to be a place for the living as well as the dead, where nature would provide comfort and inspiration, and family values and the enduring regeneration of the family would be celebrated. Reserving the family burial plot and establishing the appropriate monument would become an essential part of estate planning:

Lots of ground, containing each three hundred square feet, are set off, as family burial places, at suitable distances on the sides of the avenues and paths ... It is confidently expected that many of the proprietors will, without delay, proceed to erect upon their lots such monuments and appropriate structures as will give to the place a part of the solemnity and beauty which it is destined ultimately to acquire.

These family monuments, as much as the horticultural plans and road layouts, were to change the landscape of cemeteries.

Cemetery Reform in Canada

In Canada the 2,000-year history of Christian faith and practice is condensed into just a few centuries of European settlement. In New France, Catholics were buried in consecrated ground near convents, hospitals or churches, while non-Catholics (whose settlement in New France was not officially sanctioned) were buried in paupers' or strangers' fields. In Catholic teaching, a permanent monument is not of prime importance. The wooden crosses on Acadian graves in Nova Scotia, and on graves of aboriginal peoples converted by Catholic missionaries on the prairies, have naturally decayed with time. In Quebec, as in some European countries, burial plots may even today be leased for a certain term, rather than purchased outright. Lists of surnames connected with plots whose lease is about to expire are published locally. If the lease is not renewed, the remains are reburied a few feet deeper, and the plot is made available for a new interment. The inscription on a gravestone may even be sandblasted off for the stone's reuse.

In its first European incarnation, Montreal was Ville-Marie, a town dedicated to the Blessed Virgin Mary, or "our Lady," the mother of Jesus. The church of Notre-Dame put its first parish under her protection. The first Catholic graveyard, founded in 1642 not far from the St. Lawrence River, was built over as Ville-Marie became Montreal. In 1992 it was incorporated as a crypt in the Montreal Museum of Archaeology and History, Pointe-à-Callière. Museum visitors can now descend underground and see, in the vestiges of the city's ancient cemetery, the oldest extant structure associated with its birthplace. Other 17th century burying grounds, in Quebec City and elsewhere, lie hidden far below busy urban streets and commercial developments of later centuries. In some places – Port Royal (now Annapolis Royal) and Fort Frontenac (now Kingston) – evidence of their location is to be found only on old maps.

Following the Seven Years' War, the new settlers were mostly Protestants, members of either the established Church of England or many nonconforming or dissenting sects. For a time, Anglican churches perpetuated the English practice of burying important church officials and congregation members in crypts below the church floor. St. Paul's, Halifax (1750) has 20 graves beneath its floor and is said to have more memorial tablets on its walls than any other church building in North America. The Anglican Church did not always exclude adherents of other faiths from burial in its churchyards. Nevertheless, many immigrants had come to the New World precisely because they could not in conscience conform to the established church in their old country. They strove to build their own chapels and set aside land for their own burial grounds.

When Halifax was founded in 1749, an acre of land was set aside for burial grounds outside the wooden palisade which then encircled the town. Governor Cornwallis, during the 1749–50 typhus epidemic, ordered the immediate removal of the dead to the extra-mural, non-denominational burial grounds. In this respect he was a pioneer of the early cemetery reform movement since the Halifax burying ground predates Calcutta's South Park Street Cemetery by 18 years. Like many 18th century military officers, Cornwallis was a member of the order of Freemasons, who were early proponents of cemetery reform. And like other colonial administrators, he perhaps felt less constrained by opposition from the establishment, whose power was centred across the ocean.

By the 1830s the Old Burying Ground in Halifax had more than doubled in size. It was no longer on the outskirts of town and had become a noisome neighbour to Government House. The satirical writer Thomas Chandler Haliburton, speaking through his Sam Slick *persona*, described it as "a nasty dirty horrid lookin' buryin' ground ... filled with large grave rats as big as kittens, and the springs of black water there, go thro the chinks of the rocks and flow into all the wells, and fairly pyson the folks – it's a dismal place, I tell you."

Halifax was, in its beginnings, cousin to another British colony, Boston. Both colonial parishes were part of the Diocese of London. The structural timbers of St. Paul's had been cut in Boston and shipped to Halifax. Like Christ Church in Boston, it emulated London churches designed by James Gibbs and Christopher Wren. The two cities retained numerous commercial and cultural connections in the 1830s, and many Halifax residents, including Haliburton, knew about Boston's recently opened Mount Auburn Cemetery. Halifax's response to the need for cemetery reform was Camp Hill Cemetery, established by legislation in 1833 in what was then the suburban area beyond the fort. Although its setting and landscape layout are less picturesque than those of later cemeteries, it is probably the earliest Rural Cemetery in Canada.

The pressures of overpopulation affected several fast-growing towns in the British colonies. In 1832 the town of York was little more than a large village with just over 9,000 residents, almost all of whom lived within a 10-minute walk of the shore of Lake Ontario; but by 1844 the population had doubled, and the town was incorporated as the City of Toronto. The burial ground adjacent to the Cathedral of St. James (1797), at King and Church streets in downtown Toronto, was becoming too crowded. The Church purchased a large plot of land on the hill overlooking the ravine of the Don River – far outside the city boundaries, miles away from the city's homes and shops, and surrounded only by family farms. The picturesque layout of St. James' Cemetery was designed in 1842 by the eminent Toronto architect and engineer John Howard, after he had borrowed a copy of *Dearborn's Guide through Mount Auburn*. Although established by the Anglican Church, the cemetery was open to all religious affiliations. Interred there, for example, are several children and descendants of Egerton Ryerson, the outstanding Methodist opponent of the Anglican domination of political and educational institutions in Upper Canada. Ryerson himself, however, is buried in the non-denominational Mount Pleasant Cemetery.

In 1848 the United Empire Loyalist Burial Ground in Saint John, New Brunswick, (founded in 1783) was closed, and Fernhill Cemetery was opened in a pastoral setting, with winding roads and islets in the Rural Cemetery style. The same year marked the opening of Mount Hermon Cemetery in the suburban area of Quebec City and Burlington Heights Cemetery on the outskirts of Hamilton, Ontario.

Yarmouth, Nova Scotia, had in 1842 established a public graveyard, to be "open and free for the interment of all classes and denominations of the inhabitants of, or persons coming to, or being within the township of Yarmouth, and according to the rite and ceremonies as the friends of the deceased shall think proper." No church would receive "any charge or fee to be paid therefore," but a fee "not exceeding two shillings for each interment" would be paid to the Trustees and be "applied to and for the use of such cemetery." But as the port came into its own as a major shipping centre, the Yarmouth Free Discussion Club raised the question one evening in 1859: "Is it sound policy, or compatible with reason, to continue burying the dead in the centre of the town?" It was resolved, and passed unanimously: "That the public graveyard is situated where in time it is likely to be surrounded by a dense population, and as the existence of a burying ground in such a locality may be considered a grave obstacle as regards health and convenience; that therefore from motives of expediency and humanity the practice of burying the dead in the aforesaid graveyard ought at once to be discontinued."

The Yarmouth Mountain Cemetery Company was founded in the same year and incorporated in 1860 as a non-profit company dedicated to the burial of persons of all denominations, on an eleven-acre section on high ground "in back of town." Yarmouth Mountain Cemetery was designed by H.W.S. Cleveland, the visionary landscape architect whose "organic" design aesthetic (based chiefly on the writings of Ralph Waldo Emerson) was first expressed in 1855 at Sleepy Hollow Cemetery in Concord, Massachusetts. He was later to work on Brooklyn's Prospect Park with his better-known colleagues Frederick Law

Olmsted and Calvert Vaux. The plan was developed by an English landscape gardener, and "the magnificent trees, many of which date to the original laying out of the ground," continue to set "the cemetery apart from its surroundings." As the cemetery grounds explanded to 40 acres, the characteristically Rural plan of winding roads and irregular islets was extended to preserve the character of its landscape design. In 1861 the earlier graveyard in the centre of town was closed and converted into a public park, with a fountain, walks and benches. Tombstones were removed, but a few still remain, "as a reminder that it was once a cemetery."

On the Pacific Coast, Fort Victoria was founded by the Hudson's Bay Company in 1843. Six years later, the pallisaded fort become the capital of the Colony of Vancouver Island, and Victoria grew rapidly to become incorporated as a city in 1862. To make way for development of the new city, its first small graveyard was closed in 1855, and most of the remains buried there were relocated to the new grounds in what is now known as Pioneer Square, next to Christ Church Cathedral. During the next 18 years, the Old Burying Ground was the site of some 1,000 burials. Most of the few grave markers that remain were crafted by local artisans from sandstone brought from Haddington Island, on the northeast side of Vancouver Island. As in Yarmouth, the stones have been relocated and no longer mark particular graves.

The cities of Victoria, Yarmouth, Quebec City, Saint John, Halifax and Charlottetown are exceptional in having preserved remnants of their oldest burial grounds. In other cities, the graveyards of 17th or 18th century founding settlers have been covered over by layers of more recent history, obliterated and almost entirely forgotten. Some families moved older ancestral monuments to new family plots acquired in the cemeteries founded in the 19th century. Families of substantial means might also choose to build private mausoleums in the new cemeteries. Among other reasons, they may have felt that, whereas earlier burial grounds had been developed for other uses, a large structure would discourage future applications for redevelopment.

Cremation

The 19th century cremation movement was a modern revival of an ancient practice. The burning of dead bodies had been practised at many times and by many civilizations. The ashes and bone fragments were collected and stored in urns, buried, thrown to the winds, or immersed in rivers or the sea. In Europe, burial of the whole body was established at the beginning of the Roman Empire when the Egyptian cults of Isis and Osiris were embraced. Educated Victorians were aware that cremation had been practised in Classical Antiquity and also among Northern Europeans, including pre-Christian people in the British Isles. The British in India were familiar with Hindu practices, and some advocated cremation themselves. For others, cremation, like the "towers of silence" of the Parsees, seemed unpleasantly foreign and lacking in respect for the dead. Decades passed before its advocates began to find tolerance, let alone acceptance.

John Claudius Loudon, when publishing his recommendations for improved "garden cemeteries" in 1843, had already foreseen that population growth in the great metropolitan centres would result in a "great mass of the dead." Loudon predicted that the "practice of burning" would replace what he called the suffering of bodies "decomposed in the soil": "Every large town will have a funeral pile, constructed on scientific principles, instead of a cemetery; and the ashes may be preserved in urns, or applied to the roots of a favourite plant." Ever the man for practical gardening advice, Loudon failed to anticipate that his hard-headed utilitarian views would win few converts to the cause. The cremation movement had already found support among those whose concerns were hygienic and economic, and whose character was rationalist, scientific, secular, or even anti-clerical. But others were offended by pro-cremation publications that treated the disposal of the dead as strictly a matter of scientific sanitary reform. They were not at all ready to contemplate the direct application of their loved one's bonemeal to the roots of a favourite rosebush.

Again, a shift in sensibility brought a gradually increasing general acceptance of cremation. The large rural cemeteries began to be surrounded by expanding urban development, and their new neighbours began to view cemeteries with a distaste similar to that felt toward crowded churchyards a century earlier. Cemetery boards with limited space removed water features and wooded areas to make room for more and more interments and memorials, so that the park-like atmosphere of the landscapes began to diminish. Popular taste was influenced by the Aesthetic Movement, which reacted against the ornate, over-embellished style of the previous era. Also influential was the Arts and Crafts Movement, with its revulsion toward ugly industrialization. The decline of modest hand-carved head stones and the blight of oversized machine-made products offended the Arts and Crafts ethos. Finally, there were just too many gravestones. People living in the recently enlarged metropolitan centres did not want to be reminded that death had undone so many.

These negative reactions to the cemetery reforms accomplished just 50 years earlier met a positive response in William Robinson's *God's Acre Beautiful or The Cemeteries of the Future*, first published in 1880. A gardener, a garden writer and a publisher of gardening magazines, Robinson was an advocate of the wild or "natural" garden in the Arts and Crafts style. He argued in favour of both cremation and the ideals of the Rural Cemetery Movement. Urn-burial would provide the solution for the aesthetic problems of overcrowded cemeteries as well as the practical and hygienic problems. The book's frontispiece, depicting "two Classical temples facing each other in a landscaped park entirely uncluttered with any memorials or tombstones," evokes the ancient Arcadian ideal.

Robinson's book is illustrated with examples of Classical urns from the collections of the British Museum and the Vatican Museum. The Arts and Crafts aesthetic is combined with Classicism in Robinson's statement that the "simplest urn ever made for the ashes of a Roman soldier" was more beautiful than "the costly funeral trappings used in the most imposing burial pageant of modern times." The practice of cremation would transform cemeteries into places of "sylvan charms ... greater than ... usually obtained in public gardens."

Near country seats urn-burial would lead to the family burial place within the grounds — a quiet inclosed glade in some sunny spot with hardy native or naturalised flowers only — so as to prevent any frequent attention on the part of workmen. Such a spot, with its carpet of turf, and walls of musical-leafed trees, wholly free from the long-lasting and many-staged horror of decomposition, which makes the ordinary churchyard so far from inviting to many persons, would form a fitting place of meditation for the living, as well as repose for the ashes of the dead.

This word picture suggests an aversion to the ordinary church as well as its churchyard and progresses some way into the future far beyond Dickens' picture of the family country estate in *Bleak House*.

Robinson's personal vision was not merely independent of Christian beliefs. His Stoic resignation was indebted to Classical pagan beliefs. Even the colonnades of the temples in his book's frontispiece seem to hint at the philosophy of Stoicism, which was named for its origins in Athens at the colonnade (*stoa* in Classical Greek) where Zeno met with his students. The project of beautifying "God's Acre" — a traditional folk-name for a burial place — took Robinson far from the traditions and beliefs common in his time.

Cremation is now widely accepted in Canada. At the turn of the past century, however, the ambivalence about cremation contributed a certain *frisson* to Robert Service's immortal verses "The Cremation of Sam McGee" (1907). A decade-long debate about legalizing cremation was resolved too belatedly for John H.R. Molson, who left a bequest toward the cost of the "workings of a crematory furnace" in Mount Royal Cemetery in 1897, but whose body had to be taken by train to Forest Hills Crematorium in Boston.

The construction of the crematorium in 1901 was funded by Sir William Macdonald, a successful tobacco manufacturer and a philanthropist who was very generous in his support for the advancement of science, funding the

Macdonald Physics, Engineering, and Chemistry buildings at McGill University, the Macdonald Institute of Home Economics in Guelph and many other educational projects. His gifts and bequests to McGill alone exceeded $13 million, a sum unparalleled in Canada and other countries. An unpretentious "self-made" man, who initially declined the honours of a knighthood, he disliked his company's product: "I am not proud of my business, and that feeling, perhaps, has been the reason for my donations." His advocacy of cremation was based on scientific principles — it was technologically advanced, clean, and efficient. Macdonald's body was cremated without religious observances at his request. His longtime aversion to religion had been exacerbated by the lengthy struggle over legislation permitting the operation of the crematorium, which had been strongly opposed by the Catholic Church. The dean of the Faculty of Theology at Laval University had attacked cremation as "a pagan invention which fits badly with the spirit and traditions of a Christian country like ours." Only when provincial legislation was revised to restrict it to Protestants was the opposition of the Catholic Church withdrawn.

Green Burial

❧ William Robinson's 1880 vision of the future has found its culmination in some 21st century cemeteries whose designs feature native plantings, natural ecosystem preservation and sustainable development plans. Permanent name plaques are optional. Ashes may be freely scattered over certain areas of the grounds. These landscapes may not differ much in appearance from other natural places that might be chosen for the private scattering of ashes, but their shared purpose and common experience make them communities of commemoration.

Green or natural burial grounds, also known as woodland cemeteries, memorial nature preserves or eco-cemeteries, are not uncommon in parts of Britain and Europe and have begun to be established in North America. In place of monuments, native trees are planted as living memorials in a wildlife conservation area, to be protected in perpetuity from the pressures of modern development. Ashes, which would have an impact on the ecological balance of soil and air, are not scattered there. Instead, remains are buried in simple shrouds or environmentally friendly cardboard or wicker coffins.

Embalming is avoided. It became a generally acceptable practice in the United States only after the shocking assassination of the president in 1865, when an estimated one million citizens viewed Lincoln's embalmed body as it lay in state in 13 cities along the funeral train's route from Washington to Springfield, Illinois. The arsenic then used was replaced by formaldehyde in the 20th century.

Advocates of natural burials believe that interfering with the return of our bodies to the biosphere denies our spiritual and material relationship with it. Just as embalming and cremation practices were linked with then-advanced scientific concepts, green burial is linked with recent advances in popular understanding of the cellular basis of human life. Most of the living cells in our bodies are not human and will survive our deaths. A recent article in *The New York Times* included the news that "of the trillions and trillions of cells in a typical human body — at least 10 times as many cells in a single individual as there are stars in the Milky Way — only about 1 in 10 is human. The other 90 percent are microbial." A distinguished professor of Molecular Biology expresses it so that even non-scientists can understand: "Microbes colonize our body surfaces from the moment of our birth. They are with us throughout our lives, and at the moment of our death they consume us." In our lives we depend on these microbes, and it seems ungrateful to immolate them when we no longer need them.

The trend away from investment in individual monuments and burial sites is not entirely new, but in some ways a return to a much older tradition of communal burials and unconcern about permanently marked graves. William Wordsworth's poem "The Brothers" is a reminder that some 200 years ago there were many churchyards with "neither epitaph nor monument / Tombstone nor name – only the turf we tread / And a few natural graves." At about the same time Wordsworth also published an "Essay on Epitaphs," in which he noted:

There is not anything more worthy of remark in the manners of the inhabitants of these mountains, than the tranquillity, I might say indifference, with which they think and talk upon the subject of death. Some of the country churchyards ... do not contain a single tombstone, and most of them have a very small number.

"The Brothers" is a dialogue that takes place in a country churchyard between the Vicar and a Stranger who has returned *incognito* to his home after 20 years abroad as a mariner in foreign parts of the Empire, including a period of "slavery among the Moors / Upon the Barbary coast." "Your Churchyard," he observes to the Vicar, seems to say "that you are heedless of the past."

> *An orphan could not find his mother's grave:*
> *Here's neither head nor foot-stone, plate of brass,*
> *Cross-bones nor skull ...*
> *Nor emblem of our hopes: the dead man's home*
> *Is but a fellow to that pasture-field.*

That pasture-field is an implicit allusion to a scriptural symbol for the brevity of mortal life: "As for man, his days are as grass; as a flower of the field, so he flourisheth. For the wind passeth over it, and it is gone; and the place thereof shall know it no more" (Psalm 103: 15–16).

Taking him for a tourist, the Vicar acknowledges that "The stone-cutters, 'tis true, might beg their bread / If every English churchyard were like ours," but explains: "We have no need of names and epitaphs, / We talk about the dead by our fire-sides." To this the supposed Stranger responds: "no doubt / You, Sir, could help me to the history / Of half these graves?" The underlying irony of the poem is that while the Vicar enacts, at some length, his powers of almost total recall as he memorializes the orphan brothers – the one who left and the stay-at-home – he fails to recognize the brother, who has returned with "a determined purpose to resume / The life he had lived there." The Stranger had expected to "possess a kind of second life" on his return. Instead, he departs again in sorrow, still unknown to the man who has treated him to a second-hand narrative of his life. The living brother is, somehow, even more anonymous than the brother who died 12 years earlier and lies in an unmarked grave. Wordsworth prompts his readers, as usual, to think again about the variable nature of memory and commemoration. His poem includes a vignette of the mariner brother becalmed in the tropics "for days and weeks," filling "hours of tiresome indolence" with vivid memories of his "Paternal home." Twenty seasons can be a very long time, although memories do bring a distant past back to a kind of second life.

The poem speaks for both sides of the experience that has been all too familiar to generations of immigrants to the New World, and which was to influence commemorative traditions in Canadian burial grounds. Its timeless message is relevant today, when families continue to be dispersed to all parts of the world, and those who move away cannot regularly visit their family graves. In such circumstances, when an orphan no longer seeks to find his mother's grave, it may well be unmarked. The contemporary movement toward "natural graves" with neither epitaph nor monument stems in part from our patterns of diaspora and absence from home. Like earlier cemetery reforms, it is also not unrelated to the many problems of maintaining historic burial places. Preserving these places of memory for the future will be the task of those who are not, narrowly speaking, kin to individuals buried there. That human kindness will have deeper roots.

ANCESTRAL TIES

ANCESTRAL TIES

Historic Burying Grounds

❧ Many of Canada's historic burying grounds have been lost to us because they were never consecrated or registered as cemeteries. In rural areas where travel was difficult and churches were not yet established, deaths in pioneer families meant that a corner of the family lot was set aside for burials. Two descriptions of pioneer family graveyards, by Catherine Parr Traill and the Reverend James Jones, reveal glimpses of them when they were new.

Jones, a travelling missionary for the Church of England, Diocese of Quebec, wrote a letter in 1852 about a family graveyard in an isolated part of his parish in the Eastern Townships. He had to turn aside from his regular round to bury an infant child "in a corner of the farm belonging to the family ... the same place I had sometime before interred the mortal remains of the Grandmother of the infant." He admired the "strikingly picturesque spot":

Sheltered upon one side by a craggy rock surmounted by a few stunted bushes, the lofty eminence upon which this unwonted burial took place ... commanded on all other sides a most extensive view of the surrounding country ... large tracts of the un-reclaimed forest dotted here and there by distant settlements. Two or three mountains at various distances bounded the prospect ...

The sun shone brightly forth, the clear blue sky overhead broken by intervals of fleecy clouds, and the balmy air of coming spring imparted an inexpressible feeling of elevated enjoyment and could not fail to raise the reflective mind in contemplation to that bright and glorious world beyond the grave and which by the Redeemer's death and resurrection is opened out to each believer.

Jones' description combines missionary zeal with an enthusiasm for the picturesque school of landscape painting, without quite expressing what this corner of the family farm might have meant to the family most concerned. The scene reminded the priest of his reading in the Bible about "primitive times" and "Macpelah (I think that I have that right) the burying place of the Patriarchs and their wives."

FACING PAGE: *Union Cemetery, Port Hope, Ontario*

PAGE 42–43: *St Joseph's Catholic Church Cemetery, Deschambault, Quebec*

IN MEMORY OF
JOHN DENISON, ESQUIRE,
SON OF GEORGE DENISON, ESQ.,
OF ROTHERHAM, YORKSHIRE ENGLAND,
BY HIS WIFE, MARY PARKINSON,
BORN AT HEADON, YORKSHIRE, 20 NOV. 1755.
DIED AT TORONTO, 28 OCT. 1824
AND ALSO OF HIS WIFE,
SOPHIA TAYLOR,
DAUGHTER OF ARTHUR TAYLOR, ESQ.,
OF HARWICH, ESSEX, ENGLAND
BY HIS WIFE HANNAH HARWOOD,
BORN AT DOVERCOURT, HARWICH, ESSEX, 13 OCT. 1765,
MARRIED 19 DEC. 1782
AND DIED AT QUEBEC, 26 NOV. 1852.
HAVING DETERMINED TO LEAVE ENGLAND AND GO TO
OUR CANADA UPON THE SOLICITATION OF FRIENDS
THEN GOING TO OUR NEW COLONY, THEY SAILED
FROM HULL ON 11 JULY, 1792 WITH THEIR SONS,
GEORGE TAYLOR, THOMAS JOHN, AND CHARLES.
SETTLED AT KINGSTON IN OCT. OF THAT YEAR
AND RESIDED THERE UNTIL OCT. 1796
WHEN THEY MOVED TO YORK, (NOW TORONTO)
BEING THEN JUST SURVEYED FROM THE WILDERNESS,
TO BE CAPITAL OF UPPER CANADA,
JOHN DENISON SET APART THIS BURIAL GROUND
ABOUT THE YEAR 1800 AND FULLY ESTABLISHED IT
AS A CEMETERY UNDER THE NAME OF
"ST. JOHN'S CEMETERY ON THE HUMBER"
WITH RIGHT OF BURIAL TO ALL THOSE
ONLY OF HIS BLOOD WITH THEIR WIVES AND HUSBANDS
RESPECTIVELY.
THIS TABLET WAS ERECTED IN THEIR MEMORY
BY THEIR GRANDCHILDREN.
SUBSEQUENTLY REPLACED IN JUNE 1992
TO COMMEMORATE THE 200TH ANNIVERSARY OF
JOHN DENISON'S ARRIVAL IN CANADA.

*St. John's Cemetery on the Humber,
Toronto, Ontario*
Monument for the patriarch John
Denison.

In the book of Genesis are several references to the cave of Machpelah, purchased by the patriarch Abraham after his wife's death: "I am a stranger and a sojourner with you: give me a possession of a buryingplace with you, that I may bury my dead." Machpelah became the ultimate family burial place for Abraham, Isaac and Jacob, whose descendants were to become "a multitude" (Genesis 23: 1–20, 25: 9–10; 47: 29–30). According to Biblical accounts, the long-lived patriarchs of the Middle East might in three generations live for hundreds of years – "the days of Isaac were an hundred and fourscore years" when he "gave up the ghost, and died, and was gathered unto his people, being old and full of days" (Genesis 36: 28, 29). In the Eastern Townships, by contrast, grandmother and infant grandchild might be buried within a brief span of time. It was far from certain that a family taking up a land grant from the Crown in this wilderness would clear it and make of it a successful homestead, much less establish a settlement where a multitude would come to live in the future.

Catherine Parr Traill's view of pioneer life was more down-to-earth and charged with empathy. Her book, *The Backwoods of Canada* (1836), includes her poem "The Scottish Emigrant's Song," in which the emigrant mother sings a lament about the "bairns' wee graves" in the "auld kirk yard" that she'll never see again. Traill also observed the unfenced burying-grounds of Upper Canada, quoting from a letter written to her own mother in England:

... my attention was attracted by the appearance of open burying-grounds by the roadside. Pretty green mounds, surrounded by groups of walnut and other handsome timber trees, contained the graves of a family, or maybe some favoured friends slept quietly below the turf beside them. If the ground was not consecrated, it was hallowed by the tears and prayers of parents and children. These household graves became the more interesting to me on learning that when a farm is disposed of to a stranger, the right of burying their dead is generally stipulated for by the former possessor.

Traill's record bears witness to emotional truths about emigration, which resulted in painful family separations.

Having to leave behind a family burial place intensified the pain of bereavement. The generality of the stipulation she mentions is questionable, however. When former landowners moved far away from the district, few had the resources to return to claim a family burial right. They were not in the position of the Patriarch Jacob, who stipulated with his son Joseph that he would be buried not in Egypt, where he died, but in Machpelah. After almost 4,000 years, Machpelah is still venerated as a holy spot, the burial place of the patriarchs and matriarchs of three faiths. Canadian pioneer burial grounds might be unrecognized and forgotten after less than a century.

In the spring of 1792, two men sailed from London, on board different ships. Both Richard Hatt and John Denison were bound for the new Province of Upper Canada, where both found great success, and both now lie in family graveyards. When Hatt died in 1819, he was one of the wealthiest men in the province and one of its most successful businessmen. He owned 10,000 acres of land, extensive livestock, numerous mills and shops, several houses and a distillery. He had also been a judge, Member of Parliament, school trustee and newspaper proprietor. Since the local church, St. John's Anglican, was not built until seven years after his death, he was buried on the Cooley farm, the property of his wife's family. His father-in-law, Preserved Cooley, was an American Loyalist who had applied for his land grant in 1794. Local historians have found a record that in 1801 Cooley came in to the village to purchase two handkerchiefs and a baby's shroud. The infant was perhaps the first burial on the Cooley family farm.

Meanwhile, after four years in Kingston, John Denison and his wife, Sophia, settled in Castle Frank, the log house built by Governor Simcoe in York, and after 1798 established a farm on the Humber River.

While still residing at York, he lost an infant daughter, Elizabeth Denison, but there being at that time no public burying ground, no churchyard, no church and no clergyman, he was obliged to bury his child in his garden. Later when he settled himself on the Humber he had this child removed to a lovely spot overlooking the valley of the river.

He was buried near her in 1824. Following the intent of his will, his son made an Indenture for a Deed of Trust to "the Right Reverend John [Strachan], by divine providence Lord Bishop of Toronto":

... being the eldest brother of the said Charles Denison, and the eldest son of the said John Denison, and the male heir of them respectively, and now seised in his demesne as of fee tail, as such heir male as aforesaid, is desirous to set apart and preserve for ever, that portion of the said land and premises herein mentioned, including the ground wherein the said John Denison and Sophia his wife, and their descendants and family, are now interred, for consecration as a burial ground, to be called "ST. JOHN'S CEMETERY ON THE HUMBER," for the use and burial of those of the blood of the late John Denison, and the wives and husbands respectively, of such blood for ever ...

This was the first of several occasions when the family had to hire "a clear headed lawyer" to negotiate with the Church and other authorities. Title to the land was divested in 1928 to a newly founded non-profit family corporation. Descendants, now scattered around the globe, have continuously maintained the family cemetery through bequests and subscription fees. A visitor today will see many monuments bearing the family crest and its motto, *Perseverando*, and evidence of the family's proud tradition of military service. A cenotaph commemorates members of the family killed during the First and Second world wars. A Chronicle of St. John's Cemetery on the Humber includes an appendix listing those buried there in 1969. Half of the 200 surnames then were Denison, and six descendants of Captain John were named John Denison. The cemetery is still open for burials of those of his blood.

The Hatt-Cooley farm stayed in private ownership. The burial ground was never officially registered as a cemetery and began to sink into obscurity. Richard Hatt's gravestone was "discovered" in 1947 and removed, leaving his grave unmarked. As part of the Centennial celebrations in 1967, Hatt was recognized as the founder of the town of Dundas (now part of Hamilton), and his gravestone was installed in the Grove Cemetery. The almost-forgotten Hatt-Cooley pioneer graveyard was rediscovered in 2004, following an application for the development of a housing subdivision. Archaeologists surveying the site as part of the plan-approval process expected to find perhaps a half-dozen graves, but found more than 100. The seventh-generation Richard Hatt has said that "finally find[ing his] great, great, great grandfather's grave" was an "eerie" experience. The future of this unregistered burial ground remains uncertain.

Acadian Churchyards

❧ The name "Acadie" is thought to derive from the district of Arcadia in Greece, which in classical times represented the ideal region of pastoral contentment, the setting for the simple joys of the shepherds' life, tending flocks and making music. Acadian life in 17th and 18th century New France, however, was not quite so leisured. In 1604 Pierre Du Gua, Sieur de Mons, was granted a monopoly of the fur trade in the land known as Acadie (now Nova Scotia and New Brunswick). In return, he was to promote its colonization and also the conversion of its native Mi'kmaq people to the Christian, that is, Catholic, faith.

By the time of their deportation in 1755, the Acadians in the British colony of Nova Scotia numbered approximately 10,000. According to a list made by the British Lt. Col. John Winslow, the "French Inhabitants belonging to Grand-Pré" alone included 483 men, 337 wives, 527 sons and 576 daughters. Winslow also made an inventory of their livestock – 1,269 oxen, 1,557 cows, 2,181 young cattle, 8,690 sheep, 4,197 hogs and 493 horses, which stayed behind. Despite numerous alternations between French and English rule, the Acadians had greatly improved their lands during their tenure. To emphasize their loss and discourage their hope of return, British troops (many from colonial New England) set fire to the thatched roofs of the Acadians' half-timbered buildings. Virtually all visible traces of their barns, houses, churches and burial grounds have disappeared. As one historian of the Acadians has observed, "to fully appreciate Acadian cemeteries, one has to value and respect invisible heritage."

Mather B. DesBrisay's *History of the County of Lunenburg* (1870) includes a description of one disappearing Acadian graveyard:

There is a burying ground near a sand beach at Petite Riviere, which is filled with graves. In one corner of it, twenty or thirty were once visible, but they are now covered to the depth of over five feet, with sand blown from the beach. The head stones, many of which are of immense size, and rounded at the top, are without inscriptions. A circular stone wall, over four feet in height, was built to enclose the place of sepulture; but much of it has fallen down, and is hidden by sand. In the same vicinity are the graves of ship-wrecked Americans, and others, including the crew of a vessel wrecked at Indian island, and the captain of a Norwegian barque. There, far from home, "They keep / The long, mysterious exodus of death," awaiting reunion with those they loved on earth, in that eternal city, "Where every severed wreath is bound."

In the Parish of Sainte-Famille in the Pigiguit (Falmouth) area, a burying ground was founded in 1722, abruptly closed in 1755 when the Acadians were deported, and rediscovered only in 1996, when the land was being redeveloped for new housing. It is thought to contain 300 graves. Modern archaeological techniques confirmed the accuracy of oral tradition, and a memorial was placed in time for the 400th anniversary of French settlement in North America. In a sense, the Sainte-Famille memorial represents all those Acadians whose burial places are invisible and unknown. They were not Unknown Warriors, however. Their fault was a futile wish to maintain neutrality in a war-torn land.

Acadian exiles were permitted to return after 1764, but the place they had named *le paradis terrestre*, the earthly paradise, in the Annapolis Valley was ultimately a paradise

Sainte-Marie Cemetery, Pointe-de-l'Église, Nova Scotia
The grave of Joseph Dugas.

lost to them. Their home and native land had been granted to Protestant Planters, settlers from the New England colonies. The returning Acadians of the diaspora were dispersed again to small communities on the margins of their former homeland. Because Catholics in Nova Scotia were denied land titles until 1783 and were not emancipated until the 1820s, for many years they had no resident priests or churches. Mass was said in private homes or small chapels. The Catholic tradition of a community of the living and the dead keeps active cemeteries alongside, or very near to, parish churches. When larger churches were later built in more convenient locations, the earlier chapels and burial grounds were abandoned and gradually disappeared from the landscape.

Wooden crosses were common, perhaps reflecting the long European custom of the temporary use and reuse of burial sites. Grave markers were also made from locally available stone. Some stones were imported, but the usual preference was for grave markers crafted in the community. If Acadian mourners had money to spare, they spent it on masses and prayers for the soul rather than grand monuments. In the early days, at least one parish, Chéticamp in Cape Breton, observed the ancient custom of *la criée des âmes* (the auction of souls). Mourners would donate produce such as a sack of potatoes, a pig, or a ewe to be auctioned off on the steps of the church. The money raised by the auction would pay the priest for masses and prayers of intercession. The memoirs of Anselme Boudreau (1890–1991) record another Chéticamp custom, *l'encan des morts* (the auctioning of the dead person's clothes) in front of the church before Mass on the Sunday after a death. Again, the proceeds were to pay for celebrating masses for the soul of the dead, with any surplus given to the family. These customs of a community with a restricted economy reflect their Catholic faith. The departed souls no longer needed food and clothing. Neither did they need permanent markers for their earthly remains. Boudreau recalls wooden crosses bearing the name of the dead, the date and the age. Only the most prosperous

could afford to erect a tombstone.

In Chéticamp, where sandstone is readily available along the shore, there is a local tradition of whitewashing the stones and highlighting their inscriptions with black paint. The old St. Pierre burial ground in Chéticamp has the oldest known Acadian gravestone, the painted sandstone marker for Jean LeLièvre, which is inscribed simply "1817 / J LL." The stone also bears an incised outline of a cross with a triangular support base. The painted sandstone tablet for Pierre Aucoin in Chéticamp has a simple incised cross above "IHS," the Greek monogram for Jesus. "P.O.Q" abbreviates a phonetic variant of his name (O'Quin for Aucoin). Abbreviations "M 1863. A. 67" (M for *mort* and A for *âgé*) indicate the year of his death and his age.

The Sainte-Marie graveyard in the village of Pointe-de-l'Église (Church Point) is located across the road from the Église Ste-Marie, the largest wooden church in North America, built in 1903–05 by Acadian volunteers from the parish. Several handcrafted gravestones, modest in size and made of rough-hewn rock, are notable for the quality of their inscriptions. The lettering is well cut, but not uniform. The stone for Joseph Dugas, who died in 1858 at the age of 92, states that he was the first Acadian born in Clare, a township granted to returning Acadians in 1768.

ICI REPOSE LE CORPS
DE JOSEPH DUGAS
DÉCÉDÉ LE 29 OCTOBRE
1858 AGÉ DE 92 ANS
IL ÉTAIT LE PREMIER ACA
DIEN NÉ A CLARE
REQUIESCAT
[IN PACE]

Another rock has the incised outline of a tablet with tympanum and a delicately cut cross with arms ending in trefoils or fleurs-de-lys. The very shallow lettering in the space around the cross is scarcely legible, but commemorates

ASSEM LE BLANC
DCDE 1843
AGEE 75 ANS.

"ASSEM" is a phonetic spelling reflecting a variant pronunciation of Anselme, and "DCDE" is a variant of a commonly used homonym (DCD) of *"décédé,"* "died." If the readings of the death date and age are correct, Anselme le Blanc was born a few years before the return from Boston in 1772 of the family of Pierre le Blanc. According to the *Dictionary of Canadian Biography*, the le Blanc descendants and those of François Doucet constitute the majority of the population of the Church Point area today.

A third stone is a smoothly finished tablet with a large and a small cross and a tympanum filled with inscribed letters. Points separate the words, and line breaks occur wherever the lettering meets the edge of the stone:

LE.CORPS.DE.CHA
RLOTTE.DEVEAULT.EPO
USE.DE.MARC.SONIER.DECE
DEE.LE/NEUF.AOUT.MIL.HUIT
CENT.CINQUANTE.CINQ
AGEE.DE.QUARANTE.ET.UN.AN

("The body of Charlotte Deveault, wife of Marc Sonier, died the 9th August 1855, aged 41 years.") In keeping with earlier French custom, her maiden name is recorded, and then her status as *épouse* (wife) of Marc Sonier.

The doctrine of veneration of the Cross is markedly Catholic, as is the Crucifix, portraying Christ on the Cross. Acadian graveyards, like other Catholic burial places, include a large Calvary Cross, and many markers depict the Crucifix. The Latin inscription *Requiescat in pace* or simply R. I. P. and the phrase *Priez pour l'âme de ...* (Pray for the soul of ...) are signs of a Catholic belief in the efficacy of prayers of intercession for departed souls in Purgatory. These symbols stand as public witnesses of Catholicism in a colony where Protestant forces had triumphed over the dispossessed settlers.

Sainte-Marie Cemetery, Pointe-de-l'Église, Nova Scotia
Charlotte Deveault's headstone.

Foreign Protestants

The settlement of some 2,500 Foreign Protestants in Nova Scotia, in the years between 1749 and 1752, included French Huguenots, Calvinists from Switzerland and Lutherans or Mennonites who had been recruited from southern and central Germany. Their Protestant faith motivated these immigrants to seek refuge in a new world, but also ensured that they would not form alliances with the Acadians, who had yet to be deported. In 1750 the ship *Ann*, sailing from Rotterdam, entered the harbour of the newly founded city of Halifax carrying 300 immigrants, many of them suffering from typhus or "ship fever." Thirty or more of them soon died and were hastily buried in a communal grave on land in the north suburbs of Halifax, outside the palisade. The surviving newcomers laboured to work off the cost of their passage while awaiting the allocation of town lots, garden lots and farm lots in the hinterlands of Lunenburg County.

In 1753 about 20 families chose to remain in the Halifax area, and three years later they established the earliest Lutheran church in Canada. Now called the Little Dutch Church (a mis-translation of *die Deutsche Kirche*, the German church), it was a former cottage that was moved to the burial ground and placed above the *fosse commune*. The rebuilt church, with its added steeple, its bell taken from a former convent of New France in Louisbourg, and its weathercock made from the discarded blade of a shovel, is a complex symbol of renewal. The shovel and the bell are both symbols of burial of the dead. The church was meant to be not only a house of worship, but also a monument to victims of the typhus epidemic. Some of them died without even having their names recorded, and all of them without having translated their identities into new lives in this world. The church stands where it does to identify death as a rite of passage out of this world and into another.

The churchyard continued to be used as a burial ground until 1843. Meanwhile, in 1760 the church was made a chapel of St. Paul's Anglican Church. It was consecrated to St. George, a good choice, given that the saint's namesake, the German-speaking George II, was Defender of the Faith of the Church of England. Only in 1786 was a suitable German-speaking pastor found. The Reverend Bernard Houseal was a Loyalist who had been a Lutheran pastor in New York and had gone to London to be ordained an Anglican priest before taking up his mission in Halifax. He ministered to the German community until his death in 1799 and was buried according to the old world tradition, beneath the church floor. The congregation had expanded and included many non-Germans; English was increasingly spoken there. In 1800 construction began on the magnificent Round Church of St. George's. Under such circumstances, it is not surprising that the gravestones at the Little Dutch Church are not unlike those in the Old Burying Ground associated with St. Paul's. For example, the stone "Sacred / To the Memory of / THOMAS BAUER / who departed / this life / 3rd Novr 1827" is from the same workshop as the stone "Sacred / To the Memory of / RACHEL SMITH / who departed this life / Octr 25th 1827" in the Old Burying Ground. Both stones have identical flourishes around "Sacred." By 1827, the descendants of the Foreign Protestants who had remained in Halifax were no longer on foreign ground. The persistence of Germanic traditions is seen more clearly in the graveyards of Lunenburg County.

Lunenburg was the second British colonial settlement in Nova Scotia. Its name honoured the Hanoverian King George II, who had been born into the title of Duke of Brunswick-Luneburg. The Germanic name of Lunenburg was appropriate, since most of its settlers were German-speaking. The Hanoverian monarchs had themselves been considered by some of their subjects to be foreign Protestants. It was because they were not Catholics that they had come from foreign parts to reign over Britain. Before the defeat of Charles Stuart at the Battle of

FACING PAGE: *Little Dutch Church Burial Ground, Halifax, Nova Scotia*

Culloden in 1746, the Hanovers' title to the monarchy had continued to be threatened by the Jacobite cause. Unlike George II, who was *ex officio* the head of the Church of England, and whose military success was celebrated in 1745 in the new anthem, *God Save the King*, most of the Germans who came to Lunenburg were Lutherans, Anabaptists or Mennonites.

The Mennonites are named after Menno Simons, a priest who withdrew from the Roman Catholic Church in 1536 and became the leader in the Netherlands and Germany of a pacifist wing of the Anabaptists. After the Thirty Years' War (1618–48), a terribly destructive series of campaigns and battles fought by various European powers over various religious, dynastic, territorial and com-

mercial rivalries, some surviving Mennonites sought refuge in the Bavarian Palatinate. The ravaging of the Palatinate by the French troops of Louis XIV during the War of the Grand Alliance caused many Protestant Germans to emigrate at the end of the 17th century. Many of the so-called Pennsylvania Dutch settlers of the American colonies were refugees from the Palatinate. They included Anabaptists and Mennonites who accepted the Quaker William Penn's offer of religious protection in America and settled in Germantown in Pennsylvania. Both they and the Quakers shared pacifist convictions, and their conscientious refusal to participate in wars made them notably unpopular in regions frequently contested by military campaigns. The American Revolutionary War forced many of them to move once again to British North America. By 1800 Mennonites from the United States began settling the German Company Tract in Ontario, now the Waterloo Region.

Mennonites had a particular horror of what they called the "hardness of heart" required for practising war and other sinful actions. The "Heart of Peace" image often seen in their folk art has several layers of meaning, but foremost is its representation of the penitent and believing heart of God's elect. Having for centuries suffered many tribulations, they had a particularly strong faith in the promise of the Spirit of the New Testament: "Be thou faithful unto death, and I will give thee a crown of life" (Mark 16: 14; Revelation 2: 13). In Hillcrest Cemetery in Lunenburg, the repentant and faithful heart is incised on the slate gravestone for Cathrina Maragreta Läs[s]le, who was buried in 1808. The inscription is in German. Within the outlined heart are the words "*gott ist*" and beside the heart, "*die ruhe.*" *Ruhe* connotes the calm repose attainable only after a life of struggle and oppression. The message is that God is peace, and God is rest.

Some gravestones in Lunenburg County begin with the words, "*Hier ruhet in Gott*" (Here rests in God) followed by the name of the person who has found this peaceful rest. The lettering of one very early stone in Mahone Bay's Bayview Cemetery is comparatively primitive. The letters are carved in Roman capitals, and the N is sometimes reversed. The words are separated by vertical dots and are broken wherever the stonecutter ran out of space.

HIR:RVET:IN

GOTT:ANA:CA

THARIENA:GE

STORBEN:27

OCTOBER:1780

ANA:ZWICKRIN

(Here rests in God Ana Cathariena, died 27 October 1780, Ana Zwicker.")

For many foreign Protestants, their most treasured possession was the Bible, brought with them from the old country. In it they could read in their own mother tongue both the scriptural basis for their faith and their personal record of their family history. Johann Michael Schmitt, a settler in La Have near Lunenburg, brought the family Bible from Leimen, a small town near Heidelberg. An incident he noted in the Bible illustrates the strength of connections with family left behind in Germany: "1759: The 12th of April, my wife's sister, Anna Catharina STRUMPF, the wife of the head pheasant-keeper at Sandhausen, appeared in person to my wife Maria Barbara Elisabetha SCHMITT here in Leehöff. At the time I did not know what it signified; but later we learned that she died on the same day in Mannheim." The "visit" by the dying sister had a poignant spritual and religious significance .

In another family Bible, Johan Philip Heyson, senior, recorded the most pertinent turning-points of his family's life. In translation it reads: "1737 – I ... was born on October 20 in ... the Palatinate. The town was called Hering; ... 1751 – moved to this country. 1759 – married Magdalene Zwicker on March 4, 1760 – on March 19 were my two sons brought into the world, and on March 21 brought to holy baptism." The details of this record parallel those inscribed on a slate gravestone in Mahone Bay:

ABOVE: *Bayview Cemetery, Mahone Bay, Nova Scotia*
Grave marker with a heart and an abbreviated inscription, "I:P:H x JNRY25 / 1797," for 6-day-old Johan Philip Heyson, Jr.

BELOW: *Bayview Cemetery, Mahone Bay, Nova Scotia*
Slate stone for Johan Georg Eisenhauer, with a three-petalled dancing tulip with trefoil leaves.

Hier ruhet in Gott
Maria Magdalena Zwickerin
Gebohren in Chur Pfalz in
Zeibham bey Landau im
Jahr 1709 & gestorben den
11 Oktober 1787. Sie ist im
Ehestand gewesen 52 Jahre
6 monath und hat darinnen
erlebat 49 kinder & Enckelkin[der]
& Uhrenkel von welchen 9 im
Herrn entschlafen, 40 her nach
[inscription illegible]

("Here rests in God Maria Magdalena Zwicker born in the Palatinate in Zeibham near Landau in the year 1709 and died on 11 October 1787. She was married for 52 years 6 months and lived to see 49 children and grandchildren and great grandchildren, of whom 9 have died in the Lord, and 40 will later follow her.")

This stone is unadorned by imagery, but it is a significant example of *Frakturschrift*, a decorative calligraphy developed from 15th century Gothic type, named *Fraktur* for its angular, fractured appearance. The distinctive style was dominant in northern Germany, while the more classically inspired Roman lettering was preferred in the rest of Europe. Protestant German emigrants were familiar with Gothic "black-letter" type in their Bibles and on hand-lettered deeds and documents, where great attention was paid to artistic calligraphy. In the new world, they continued to mark rites of passage in which legal significance was yoked with spiritual significance.

The slate stone for Johan Georg Eisenhauer has a three-petalled dancing tulip with trefoil leaves, the central leaflets being heart-shaped, and a full summary of his life in mixed Roman and *Fraktur* lettering:

Hier Ruhet Johan Ge
org Eisenhauer. Ist ge
bohren zu WILHELMS

FELD *in Teutschl,* ANNO
1733 22d Jan. Kömt nach NO
VA SCOTIA *1751. Heyr. 1759*
Lebt in der Ehe 46 J. Zeuget
13 Kinder. Stirbt 1805 d. 10 Jun

The gravestone for George Jung in Hillcrest Cemetery in Lunenburg shows a transition from original *Fraktur*. Its inscription is brief, in English, and elegantly cut in large Roman lettering.

Here Lieth
the Body of
GEORGE IUNG
Born Febry 19th 1770
Died Janry 7th 1794
[...] 23 Year

The tympanum is decorated with a *Fraktur* emblem, the blooming heart. In Protestant German poetry the heart blooming with the lily and the rose is a frequent image, representing faith in Christ as the bringer of the promise of life after death.

Another English-language gravestone in Lunenburg has hearts and flowers with strong curved lines. Fergus Byers was born in Scotland in 1798, and his name is not German. His death by drowning in 1822, and the deaths "Also [of his] children Fergus and Catherine / Aged 6 Weeks," had "Left a Widow to LAMENT their loss." It is possible that his widow had no Lutheran or Mennonite background, and made a sentimental choice of the hearts-and-flowers motif without understanding that it was meant to express joy. The traditional *Fraktur* bloom is the dancing three-petalled lily-tulip or Rose of Sharon. The source for the image is a Biblical text: "The wilderness and the solitary place shall be glad for them; and the desert shall rejoice, and blossom as the rose. It shall blossom abundantly and rejoice even with joy and singing: ... they shall see the glory of the Lord" (Isaiah 35: 1, 2).

Congregationalist Planters

Between 1759 and the eve of the American Revolution, some 8,000 Planters emigrated to Nova Scotia from the New England colonies, where their forebears had lived since the 1630s, when the Great Migration had brought some 20,000 Pilgrims from England. The Planters were descendants of the English Puritans (a disparaging name given them because they regarded the Elizabethan reformation of the Church as incomplete and called for its further purification). In England and Scotland, Puritanism was fragmented into Congregationalism and other dissenting churches by disputes over doctrine or polity. The Congregationalists who came to New England in order to build a New Zion also sought full reformation of their churches. The task of being in this world, but not of it, was a difficult one. Many Puritans fell from grace, and the religious motivation of others was moderated by time and circumstance. Nonetheless, their piety persisted, especially in rural New England.

Puritan gravestones may at first appear grim and strange to cemetery visitors who are familiar only with the conventions of Victorian grave art. The earlier stones in particular are cut in a rough, almost primitive, way that is nevertheless very expressive. Neither the provincial character of these carvings nor their status as a branch of folk art should detract from the full appreciation of their artistic qualities. Twentieth-century modernism has introduced us to a new way of seeing primitive images. Allan Ludwig, who photographed hundreds of New England gravestones, recalled his conversion experience in the 1960s: "I stumbled into what was then considered the chaos of low culture when I got lost on the way to an outdoor pig roast and found myself looking at the Thomas Cushman stone of 1727 in Lebanon, Connecticut. I remarked at the time that it looked like the kind of stylization that would have appealed to Paul Klee."

FAR LEFT: *Old Barrington Meeting House Burial Ground, Barrington, Nova Scotia*
Slate marker imported from New England for Thomas Doane, who died in 1873.

LEFT: *Old Burying Ground, Halifax, Nova Scotia*
Winged skull motif with crossbones on the monument for Mrs. Jane Giffin, who died in 1775.

Ludwig's study brought a higher level of attention to this so-called low culture. As his title *Graven Images* implies, the visual symbolism on these gravestones raises a number of questions, since Puritanism was associated with an avoidance of imagery and even with iconclasm. For casual cemetery visitors, it is enough to recognize that the imagery is meant to overcome the dreadful aspect of death. For Puritans the commonplace fact of death was not the end of the story.

Winged skull images are not, as sometimes assumed, mere death heads, unadorned examples of *mementi mori*. Rather, they are winged victories, signifying the living soul's triumph over death. Wings are very ancient symbols of power and swiftness. The wings are not a decorative frill, but utterly transform the meaning of the skull into an emblem of startling change: "It is sown a natural body; it is raised a spiritual body." The grim features of these winged skulls — their hollow eye sockets and prominent teeth — should not deter us from recognizing them as expressions of aspiration, hope and faith in the resurrection of the mortal body. They are images of transformation. The stylized

leaves flourishing in the borders of many of these stones reinforce the message of continually renewed life.

The Planters' emigration did not separate them from their past. In Nova Scotia they were not far from the more established British colonies, and the new settlers retained links with their friends and former neighbours. When gravestones were needed, they were ordered from stonecutters in Boston. Imported slate markers for three of Edmund Doane's relatives stand in the burial ground next to the Barrington Meeting House, built in the traditional New England Congregationalist style.

Here lies the Body of
Mrs LETTICE DOANE
Wife of Mr THOMAS
DOANE. She died In
Chield Berth & was
Buried with her Chield
In her armes July
the 26th 1766
Aged 30 Years

Old Burying Ground, Halifax, Nova Scotia
Winged skull on a gravestone for Robert and Susanah Wiston's 3-year old daughter, who died in 1778.

Chebogue, in Yarmouth Township, which had been an Acadian settlement from 1714 to 1758, was resettled by New England Planters in 1761, when the families of Captain Moses Perry, Sealed Landers and Ebenezer Ellis arrived aboard the shallop *Pompey Dick*. Captain James Kelley from Massachusetts and Captain Amos Hilton landed later, each bringing a shallop and their family. The Town Point Cemetery is the burial place of these pioneers and their descendants.

The slate marker for Captain Hilton's wife, Mary (1742 –1774), is signed by the maker, "Abraham Codner Next the Drawbridge, Boston." The winged skull emblems for Captain Moses Perry and his wife, Elenor, have a strong family resemblance, although she died in 1772 and he in 1801. As Deborah Trask noted in her study of gravestone carving in Nova Scotia, *Life How Short, Eternity How Long*, the emblem was old-fashioned in New England by the time of the American Revolution, but continued to be standard in parts of Nova Scotia. "The people of Liverpool and Chebogue, even though they were sending to the Boston area for their stones anyway and could have had the latest design, chose instead to purchase what had been to them a traditional gravestone design when they lived in that area." The appeal of the traditional emblem to them illustrates their wish to conserve family and ancestral ties to their homeland.

The memorial for Margaret Kelley, who died in 1804, combines the winged skull motif with a lengthy verse epitaph that introduces softer sentiments usually associated with the sensibilities of a man of feeling, not a Puritan. The grieving widower died three years later.

Here lie the remains of
Mrs. MARGARET KELLEY
Wife of James Kelley Esq.
who departed this Life Janry 6th 1804
aged 60 Years, 11 Months & 14 Days
Lo! where this silent marble weeps
A friend, a wife, a mother sleeps,
A heart, within whose sacred cell
The peaceful virtues lov'd to dwell
Affection warm, and faith sincere
And soft humanity was there.
In agony, in death, resign'd,
She felt the wound she left behind.
Her darling issue here below
Sits mourning on a father's woe,
Whom what awaits while he strays
Along the lonely vale of days?
A pang to secret sorrow dear,
A sigh, an unavailing tear,
Till time shall ev'ry grief remove
With life, with mem'ry and with love.

The mid-Victorian stone of Miss Maria K. Scott, who died in 1858, has a more fitting match between the epitaph and the emblem of a dove bearing the olive branch of peace:

Sister thy loved form is lying
Peaceful in the grave's still gloom,
And the mourning winds are sighing
Sadly o'er thy lonely tomb.

The New Light and Soul Effigies

Many of the Planters who settled in Horton Township in 1760–61 were experienced landowners who appreciated the fertile soil of the Minas Basin, which had been so richly prepared by the recently dispossessed Acadians. The De Wolf families in Wolfville were descended from De Wolfs who had emigrated from the Netherlands to New Amsterdam. When the British captured the colony and renamed it New York, some of the family returned to Europe, but Balthasar De Wolf retired to inland Connecticut. These De Wolfs were educated people. Nathan De Wolf, for instance, was an M.A. from Yale College (as it then was), a lawyer and property owner in Connecticut.

Other Planters, who had never farmed in New England but had been attracted to the new settlement by free land grants, were to discover the economic hardships of frontier agrarian life. The Allines, whose forebears had arrived on the *Mayflower*, were such a family. The outbreak of the American War of Independence, and their poverty, prevented their second son, Henry Alline (1748–1784), from returning to New England to be educated for the ministry. But the self-educated Henry was "moved upon by the spirit of God" to lead a second Great Awakening that recalled the Puritan Great Awakenings of the 1730s and 1740s. An enthusiastic evangelist, self-taught theologian and writer of many hymns, he established several somewhat ephemeral churches before his early death from consumption, shortly after the end of the war between Britain and the United States, while expanding his mission in New Hampshire.

Despite the fact that his New Light churches either collapsed or were absorbed into the Baptist movement, Henry Alline is now recognized as the leader of the major popular movement of his era. He insisted that "new birth" was the sole qualification for the ministry and encouraged audience participation in his services. "A woman in Windsor, in a typical response, became 'so overjoyed, that she could not contain, but cried out in divine raptures, with shouts of praise to God, and exhorting souls to come and share with her.'" Alline often preached from the text "Awake thou that sleepest, and arise from the dead, and Christ shall give thee light" (Ephesians 5: 14). For enthusiastic followers of the New Light, the central image of the conversion experience and the escape from "the unfruitful works of darkness" and the things done in secret, which "it is a shame even to speak of" (Ephesians 5: 11, 12), was resurrection of the dead.

The mental turmoil that preceded such enthusiastic conversions may be suggested by a brief outline of the life of Alline's successor as a leader of the New Light movement. The Huguenot parents of John Payzant (1749–1834) fled to Jersey, where he was born, to escape religious persecution in France, and then came to the Lunenburg area in 1753 as Foreign Protestants. Three years later, his father was killed by Indians, who took John and one of his brothers for adoption, while his mother was sent to Quebec. The family was reunited there in 1757, and John was educated at the Jesuit College until Quebec was taken by the British in 1859. The family then returned to Nova Scotia, where the widow was granted land adjoining that of the Alline family. John then resumed his education with a fellow Huguenot and learned Latin, Greek and some Hebrew, to add to his French and English and the Indian language he had learned during his captivity. John Payzant's religious calling as an adult was based on an intensely personal spiritual rebirth. A period of religious anxiety followed his marriage to Henry Alline's sister, leading him to his experience of finding his peace in the Lord in 1775, just one week after Alline's conversion experience.

St. Ignatius Loyola, the founder of the Society of Jesus, famously emphasized the importance of early Jesuit education: "Give me the child until he is seven and I will show you the man." Already seven when he was kidnapped and taken to a Jesuit mission, John Payzant was exposed to more than one doctrine in his childhood and youth. He may not have

TOP LEFT: *Old Horton Burying Ground, Wolfville, Nova Scotia*

MIDDLE LEFT: *Liverpool Common Burying Ground, Liverpool, Nova Scotia*

BOTTOM LEFT: *Old Burying Ground, Halifax, Nova Scotia*
Two soul effigies on one stone for brothers James Nicholson Cook and Robert Cameron Cook, who died on December 15 and 16, 1806, "Aged 3 Years & 6 Months" and "1 Year & 3 Months." "These Babes who Prattled on the Knee / Are Gone to Realms Above."

TOP, MIDDLE AND BOTTOM RIGHT: *Old Burying Ground, Halifax, Nova Scotia*

been thoroughly indoctrinated by his Jesuit schooling, but his disrupted childhood experience certainly formed the character of the man. As a New Light Congregational minister, he sought continuously to make peace between Congregationalists and Baptists and between paedobaptists and antipaedobaptists, and to reconcile sectarian differences fomented by the Great Awakening.

The imagery seen on so many gravestones in areas where the New Light Awakening was most active, including Horton Township, Liverpool and Chebogue, witnesses to the intensity of the conversion experience and the faith in life after death. After the 17th century the winged skull symbol began to be replaced by a new representation of the resurrected spiritual body. The Soul Effigy is quite distinct from the traditional effigy, the likeness or portrait of someone, associated before the Reformation with monuments inside churches. Those elaborate effigies were part of much more exclusive funerary art in the Middle Ages, when altar-tombs of aristocrats or wealthy merchants bore full-size sculpted figures lying recumbent beneath a canopy, with their heads on a stone pillow and their eyelids either wide open or closed as if in sleep. The rich and powerful represented in these effigies endowed chantries, where prayers would be said for the repose of their souls. Intercession, or the defending of these well-endowed souls against the prolonged horrors of Purgatory, became part of the economy of the medieval church. During the reign of Henry VIII, these payments were prohibited in England, the "vain opinion" of Purgatory was denounced, and chantry funds were confiscated by the Crown. The immediate impact was the closing of hundreds of hospitals, schools and alms-houses throughout England. Perhaps a longer-range impact of this reform in opinion may be seen on 18th century gravestones.

A Soul Effigy is not an individual portrait of the natural man or woman, but rather an image of his or her perfected spirit. Puritans and adherents of other Protestant sects, who rejected the doctrine of pain and purification after death, saw no need for intercessory prayer for the repose of the soul. Their monuments do not bear the inscription "RIP"

("Rest in Peace" or the Latin "Requiescat in Pace"). Instead, they drew from the letter of St. Paul to the Corinthians a dynamic vision of instantaneous transformation "in a moment, in the twinkling of an eye." Many of them were convinced that, since the souls of the elect were to be raised incorruptible, there was no need for them to await a Last Judgement Day in some distant future. Rather, on passing from this life, they could immediately and vigorously enter eternal life. Soul Effigies are symbols of transformed vitality, making an impression of instantaneous radiance – with no allusion to an intermediate process of corruption, which is implicit in the earlier image of the winged skull.

Some of the earliest Soul Effigies carved in Nova Scotia were made by James Hay, the Scottish stonecutter and carver to whose Halifax workshop the Bulkeley monument is attributed. Their rounded facial features are similar to those of Adam and Eve on the Bulkeley tomb in the Old Burying Ground, Halifax. The wings sculpted by Hay, buoying up the spirit from beneath, show distinctive feather patterns. Long wing plumes are joined in two layers and are attached to a short-feathered bib below the chin. The pattern of these breast feathers is often echoed in the petals of sunflowers on each side. Some of Hay's Soul Effigies wear what seem to be old-fashioned wigs with tight side curls, while others have a short and more Romantic hairstyle that waves upwards.

Stone carvers developed their own characteristic representations of Soul Effigies, and their individual works can be easily recognized. Those cut by Abraham Seaman, working in Horton and Cornwallis between 1812 and 1821, have finely incised details that make them appear to be wearing glasses. The identity of Seaman's contemporary, the "Annapolis Carver," is not known, but his works are readily identifiable. On his stones high-curved tympanums restrict the wing-spreads, so that they do not appear to be doing the work of elevation, but trail downward, almost like a short cloak, as if under the influence of a strong energy field. Carved in shallow relief, the faces have semi-circular pates, behind which curly locks of hair roll down to meet feathery ruffles that join the wings beneath definite chins. Despite his tag, the

"Annapolis Carver" is thought to have worked out of Saint John, New Brunswick, where the Old Loyalist Burying Ground has a large number of stones that look like his work.

Soul Effigies in Horton Township have been attributed to the Horton Carver and the Second Horton Carver. Both men worked in sandstone. The first was a master of simplicity. The wings flowing under the chin and the features of each circular face – eyebrows, mouth, eyes-and-nose in one continuous line – show what can be done with a strict economy of incised lines. The works by the second carver gain three-dimensional relief, with ribbing detail in the wings and sometimes a sprouting of curly hair in the recessed halo area. The first Horton Carver gives his rising souls radiant crowns of glory with pointed rays. They resemble the sun's rays in three unusual stones by an unknown carver in the Chebogue Town Point Cemetery, which also are drawn with finely incised lines. These suns may be a solar symbol of resurrection. They set only to rise again. Their eyes on the horizon and their effortful expressions give them a strange animation, but they are not typical Soul Effigies.

The most idiosyncratic carver of gravestones in Nova Scotia – if not all of Canada – is the man who prominently identified himself as "J.W. Sculptor" but whose name is yet unknown. His markers are full of texts addressed to "READER." They exhort others to find salvation before it is too late.

READER!

How ought you on earth to live
While God prolongs the kind reprieve
And props the house of clay!
Your sole concern, your single care
To watch, and tremble, and prepare
Against the fatal day!

———

Hark!
Life is uncertain,
Tyrant death approaches
The Judge is at the door.
Prepare to meet your GOD.

ABOVE: *Town Point Cemetery, Chebogue, Nova Scotia*
Rays of a rising sun inscribed on the tympanum of a gravestone for "Ephraim / son of Mr. Seth / & Mrs. Susanna / Tinkham / died Aprl. 17 / aged 4 years / & 2 mos."

BELOW: *Liverpool Common Burying Ground, Liverpool, Nova Scotia*
Elizabeth Riggs, "(Rev. J. PAYZANT'S only daughter)" and Henry Alline's niece, "died in childbed with her infant son" in 1815. Her gravestone bears an unusual image of New Light resurrection.

United Empire Loyalists

Ancestral and family ties of long duration are at the heart of the United Empire Loyalist Association of Canada (UELAC), which was incorporated in 1914 and has the mandate "to enrich the lives of Canadians through knowledge of the past, in particular the history of the United Empire Loyalists and their contribution to the development of Canada." Some 40,000 to 50,000 colonists of British North America came to what is now Canada as refugees following the American Revolutionary War. It is estimated that today, as a result of this immense influx of immigrants from the older American colonies, about 3 million Canadians – one in 10 – have Loyalist ancestors.

The Loyalists' contribution to the development of Canada was most immediately political, resulting in the separation of New Brunswick from the colony of Nova Scotia in 1784, and the 1791 division of Quebec into two Canadas: Lower, with the original seigneurial system of landholding, and Upper, with the British tradition of freehold land tenure. Upper Canada, so called because the older part of Quebec was downstream, later became the Province of Ontario, whose coat of arms still bears the Latin motto *Ut incepit sic permanet fidelis* ("Loyal she began, loyal she remains"). This loyalty to the Crown, or opposition to republicanism, was the Loyalists' one shared characteristic. Otherwise they had little in common. In economic status, racial origin and religious affiliation, they were as varied as their fellow colonists who had supported the successful Patriot rebels. Their burial grounds reflect this variety.

The first landings in Nova Scotia of United Empire Loyalists evacuated from New York City were at Port Roseway (now Shelburne) on May 4 and Saint John on May 18, 1783. The Loyalist Burial Ground, in use from 1784 to 1848, may be the least altered part of the original Saint John

settlement. Even so, many grave markers have apparently been lost; some 500 grave markers remained intact in 1883, but by 1955 only half that number were to be seen. Of the 3,300 recorded burials there, some 3 per cent were described as "Colored." Among the Loyalists there were 3,500 African-Americans – slaves, indentured servants or free Blacks loyal to the Crown. Birchtown in Shelburne County, with 1,500 Black Loyalists, was the largest free Black community outside Africa at that time. Their numbers fell when 1,200 emigrated to Sierre Leone in 1792, but the community endured. The Black Burial Ground in Birchtown now has a plaque from the Historic Sites and Monuments Board of Canada, but there are no land title records for it, most of the old church records were destroyed in a fire, and no grave markers remain. Its location was identified by people remembering that as children they were told not to play on the site because it was sacred ground.

In Upper Canada, the 2nd Battalion of the King's Royal Regiment of New York landed at Cataraqui on July 30, 1783, to rebuild Fort Frontenac and prepare for the arrival of the Loyalists in Kingston. The Mohawks landed at Tyendinaga, the first Loyalists reached the Bay of Quinte on May 22, 1784, and three weeks later, Peter Van Alstine's band of Loyalists landed in Adolphustown. Pioneer burying grounds in these Loyalist settlements were connected with new churches, both Anglican and Methodist. In the 1790s John Ferris gave one acre of land as a burial place for Methodist Loyalists in the village of Waterloo (renamed Cataraqui in 1868) near Kingston. In form and content, Nicholas Herchmer's headstone is typical of early Methodist monuments. A simple tablet with round tympanum and square shoulders, it records the age and death date, but not the year of birth.

Here lies
the Body of
NICH. HERCHMER
who departed this

Life on the 15 OCT
1809
AGED 38 YEARS ...

Refugees from the Revolutionary War crossing the border at the Niagara River began the history of European settlement in the Niagara Peninsula and to the west, sometimes even before the Crown acquired tracts in several "Indian Treaties" with indigenous peoples from 1781 to 1792. Settlers not infrequently squatted on unsurveyed land before formal grants of land titles were available. The St. Andrew's Anglican churchyard in Grimsby contains monuments for generations of the founding Loyalists, including the Nelles and Pettit families. The designs of their gravestones show similarities, but also distinctive family traditions. The "de Nelles" ancestors had been Huguenot refugees from France and later from the Palatinate, and as Loyalists to the British cause had left behind their established home in the Mohawk Valley of New York State. The "Petit" ancestors had also lived in France, but had moved to England with the conquest of 1066 and had come to the American colonies in the 17th century. The Pettits arrived in Grimsby in the second group of Loyalists, coming from Pennsylvania and New Jersey.

Three large white marble gravestones for members of the Nelles family stand side by side. All three are plain rectangular tablets with a simple rectangular panel at the top, each filled with the same design carved in shallow relief – two willows flanking a flaming urn on a plinth. Stylized palm fronds fill the spaces around the biographical oval medallions below, and near the bases are labels with finely inscribed Biblical texts. One label reads: "Eye hath not seen, nor ear heard, neither / have entered into the heart of man, the things / which God hath prepared for them that love Him. / I Cor. 2.9." This stone for Catharine, who died in 1829, was ordered from a factory in Buffalo, New York. Those for her husband, who died 10 years later, and for Henry Nelles, who died in 1842, were made locally by B. Hicks in Beamsville. Although all the design elements are Neoclassical, their total effect is thoroughly Victorian, and somewhat provincial – even the stone made in Buffalo, whose willows have comparatively slender trunks and display their roots.

The slate memorial for Ashman Pettit uses the willow and urn motif to very different effect. It has the profile of an earlier style, with small shoulders on either side of a tympanum, which is topped by a circular rosette whose geometrical form is far more archaic than the Classical period. The information given about Pettit's age is also from an earlier tradition. Both he and Henry Nelles died in 1842 – Nelles "in the 45th year of his age," and Pettit more explicitly "Aged 53 Years 5 Months & 28 Days." The elegant economy of the incised lines links the design of the Ashman Pettit stone to those of the 18th century.

Pioneer Loyalist graves manifest a complex diversity of family histories and beliefs. Loyalists' descendants share that diversity but, as represented by the United Empire Loyalist Association of Canada, they also share one characteristic strongly connected with American descendants of the Patriots: their dedication to honouring the graves of their ancestors. UELAC branches in various communities restore and rededicate tombstones commemorating Loyalists and post permanent signs to identify Loyalist cemeteries.

Protestant Burying Ground, Quebec City

In urban burying grounds, family stories are often inscribed on gravestones in much greater detail than in rural pioneer family graveyards. On the family farm, spelling out relationships on each small individual grave marker might have seemed unnecessary, but in the more anonymous situation of towns newly settled by immigrants from many different places, the grave inscription became a kind of public notice.

In Quebec City, the Protestant Burying Ground was founded in 1771 by the new English and Irish community in the Saint-Jean-Baptiste quarter of Haute-Ville (Upper Town).

Previously, the Church in New France had expected the faithful to be baptized and buried according to the sacraments, by their parish priests. Protestants, prohibited by royal edict from settling in the French colony, had not been permitted burial in consecrated ground. They were buried in separate paupers' and strangers' fields, which were never intended to be more than temporary and were soon built over. The Protestant Burying Ground, closed in 1860, is today preserved for use as a town park.

St. Matthew's Church, which began as a chapel in the for-

Protestant Burying Ground, Quebec City, Quebec

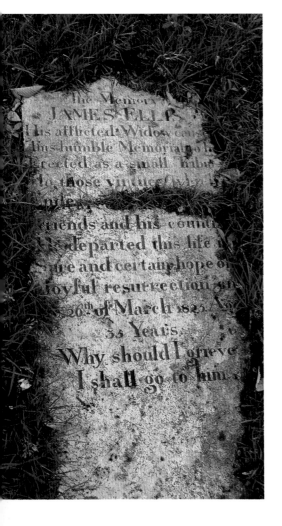

mer gravedigger's house, was rebuilt in a neo-Gothic style and consecrated in 1897. Since 1980 it has been recognized by the province as an historic monument and has served as a branch of the public library, the Bibliothèque Saint-Jean-Baptiste. The library patrons no doubt add to the numbers of people who stroll through the former burying ground and stop to read the gravestone inscriptions. Besides the many biographies available on the library shelves, a good number of brief lives can be read out-of-doors. The epitaphs of the early stones give striking glimpses of family stories, often told from a woman's point of view.

> The Memory
> *JAMES ELLIS*
> *His afflicted Widow caused*
> *This humble Memorial to be*
> *Erected as a small Tribute*
> *To those Virtues which*
> *Endeared [... him to?]*
> *Friends and his country*
> *He departed this life in*
> *Sure and certain hope of a*
> *Joyful resurrection on*
> *26th of March 1825 Aged*
> *35 Years.*
> *Why should I grieve*
> *I shall go to him*

One memorial stone summarizes an-all-too-common family story. It was erected by the widow of Alexander Munn (1766–1812), one of at least five contemporary shipbuilding Munns who established themselves in Lower Canada and Scotland, where he was born. His Quebec shipyard between 1798 and 1812 produced "at a conservative estimate ... 17 vessels having an aggregate of 4,470 tons," 10 of which were registered in his own name – and in those years his wife bore 11 children. Left a widow with a large estate, she commissioned a memorial "in affectionate memory" of her husband and their six children who predeceased him. The stone also commemorates one son who survived to adulthood but died in Bombay three years before his mother. The horizontal slab grave covering is by necessity very large, to accommodate entries for all the children who died not long after their lives were launched.

ERECTED
BY
AGNES GALLOWAY
IN AFFECTIONATE MEMORY
OF HER HUSBAND
ALEXANDER MUNN
OF QUEBEC, SHIPBUILDER
WHO DIED 19TH MAY 1812
AGED 43 YEARS, 7 MONTHS, & 25 DAYS
AND OF THEIR CHILDREN
JOHN WHO DIED 1ST OF APRIL 1803
AGED 7 MONTHS AND [?] DAYS
AGNES WHO DIED 24TH APRIL 1804
AGED 3 YEARS AND 5 MONTHS
ALEXANDER WHO DIED 20TH JULY 1805 AGED 18
MONTHS AND 15 DAYS
ALEXANDER WHO DIED 21ST SEPT 1807 AGED 7
MONTHS AND 15 DAYS
MARIA WHO DIED 20TH MAY 1809
AGED 10 MONTHS
JOHN WHO DIED 10TH OCT 1811
AGED 9 DAYS
ALSO OF
JAMES WHO DEPARTED THIS LIFE
AT BOMBAY JULY 1842
AGED 31 YEARS AND [?] MONTHS
AGNES GALLOWAY
AGED 67 YEARS, WIFE OF THE LATE
ALEXR MUNN ESQR SHIPBUILDER
QUEBEC, DIED ON THE 12TH DEC 1845

Anglican Churchyards

Two of the most beautiful Anglican churchyards in the Niagara region – St. Andrew's in Grimsby, and St. Mark's in Niagara-on-the-Lake – had Loyalist beginnings and show traces of the American invasion and occupation in 1813. These churchyards approximate the historical depth of Thomas Gray's "Elegy Written in a Country Church-Yard." Almost the whole chronology of a parish may be found in them. The same family names recur on the oldest and more recent gravestones.

St. Andrew's began in 1794, when Robert Nelles gave land at Forty Mile Creek for building "a Church and burying ground for the use of the Episcopal congregation ... and also to be free for all other Christian Denominations, except it be in Church hours when it is previously engaged by said Episcopal congregation." When a larger frame church was completed in 1804, the churchyard became the second burying ground and was surveyed for burial plots, many of which were bought by families. By April of the following year, another subscription was taken up to fund the building of a fence:

The Burying Ground contiguous to the church in Grimsby where the remains of so many of our dead are depositted, being unenclosed, and therefore in an indecent condition, the subscribers will pay the sums affixed to their respective names in money or such specific articles as are affixed to their names, by the first day of January next.

"Viewers of fences" were elected to make sure that rails were no more than five inches apart, and the fences were to be "bull high and hog low," a necessary specification when the road to market ran right in front of the churchyard. In 1824 the present historic stone church was built, consecrated and named St. Andrew's. That name, somewhat unusual for a Church of England rather than a Scottish kirk, hon-

oured the memory of Andrew Pettit, who until the appointment of a clergyman in 1817 had conducted services as an unremunerated volunteer. In 1843 the churchyard was officially registered, confirmed and consecrated as a burial ground by the bishop of Toronto, John Strachan.

The fence has been replaced several times. In 1916 the lych-gate was built, a copy of one made in 1886 for a parish church in Hythe, England. *Lic* was the Old English word for body (alive or dead) and so became embedded in archaic words like lich-way, the path along which the corpse was

St. Andrew's Anglican Church Cemetery, Grimsby, Ontario
Lych-gate.

carried for burial, and lich-stone, the resting place for the coffin near the lich-gate (or lych-gate, the more apparently archaic spelling that was adopted in the 19th century). The Arts and Crafts movement, active in England from the 1870s, was associated with a revival of medieval traditions such as stained-glass windows and lych-gates, which were meant not for use but as decorative entrances for church-yards. The Woolverton family in Grimsby made bequests to St. Andrew's for two memorials in 1915 and 1916: an Easter window, made by Robert McCausland of Toronto, and the lych-gate, made by Thaddeus Southward. The latter was funded by a bequest from Linus Woolverton, who in 1907 had chaired the first committee for "the beautifying of the old Churchyard" so that "the yard could be kept in a pre-sentable state with a lawn mower":

The neglect and unkempt condition of the greater portion, with high mounds, occasional hillocks and many hollows, with tangle of vines and weeds made the undertaking a serious problem ... This seemed at first too great an undertaking for the first year, but ... this formidable task was completed ... at an outlay of only $116.10 ... and a balance in hand for further work at $30.00.

Inside the gate are very beautifully lettered memorials, one for "Men of the Parish / who for the Empire went / out to battle and died" in the Great War 1914–1918" and a second for those who died in battle in 1939–1945. Both bear four-sided inscriptions. The first is in Latin – "IN LUCE SPES: / IN OBITU PAX: / POST TENEBRAS LUX: / POST OBITER SALUS" ("in light, hope: in death, peace: after the darkness, light: after death, life"). The second, with a sundial, is in English:

> *FROM THE RISING UP OF*
> *THE SUN UNTO THE GOING*
> *DOWN OF THE SAME THE*
> *LORD'S NAME BE PRAISED.*

During the War of 1812, when American forces invaded and then retreated through the settlement, battle came right into the Forty Mile Creek area. The gravestone for Isaac Walker, who died as a casualty of war in November 1812, bears an inscription expressing hope in life after death:

> *I sleep in dust,*
> *but soon shall rise,*
> *dwell with the Just*
> *beyond the skies.*

The St. Andrew's churchyard contains a rare group of table stones for members of the Crooks family. The table-stone tradition is common in parts of Scotland. William and Margaret Crooks came from Scotland to Upper Canada with five sons; another son was born here. The large flat stones covering each burial place are elevated on corner

St. Andrew's Anglican Church Cemetery, Grimsby, Ontario
Memorial for the men of the parish who died in battle during the Great War.

posts, preventing anyone from walking over the grave. The inscriptions follow Scottish tradition by giving biographical information without a poetic epitaph. Sometimes only a biblical reference is provided, with the expectation that viewers will recognize the passage, or will look it up in their own Bibles.

Sacred to the memory of William Crooks; who was born at Kilmarnock, Scotland, 6th August, A.D. 1776, and after a residence of 44 years in U. C. died at Niagara 31st December, 1836. Job. 9, 12.

———

Sacred to the memory of Mary Butler, relict of Wm. Crooks, who departed this life at St. Anns, Nelson, 30th Dec., 1851, aged 70. Watch for the morning. – Ps. 130, 6.

———

Beneath this stone lieth the
Remains of Margaret Crooks
Relict of William Crooks, late
of the Kingdom of Scotland,
who was born in Edinburgh,
the 23rd day of April AD 1753.
Died at Ancaster
in the Province of U.C.
the 2nd Day of October
1827
Aged 71 years, 5 months & 9 days
This testament of Filial Respect is
erected to her memory
by her Affectionate Children.

Although the Crooks' sons moved away from Grimsby – to go into fur-trading with John Jacob Astor, to establish the busy Crooks' Hollow in West Flamborough, and to set up another Crooks' Mills on Dundas Street in Nelson Township – many of the family returned for burial in St. Andrew's. In 1930, when the United States government finally paid reparation for the American seizure in 1812 of James Crooks' schooner, the *Lord Nelson*, there was no difficulty in finding 25 of his descendants to share the $15,546.63 payment.

Niagara-on-the-Lake has been fortunate in having citizens who were dedicated, early on, to the preservation of its history. Its Historical Society, formed in 1895, in 1906 built Memorial Hall, the first museum in Ontario, to commemorate the region's United Empire Loyalist founders. The society's first president, Janet Carnochan, gathered extensive and detailed documentation for many publications on the history of Niagara, including her pioneering *Graves and Inscriptions in the Niagara Peninsula* (*circa* 1920). Through most of its history, the town grew slowly. Newark (originally Butlersburg, later Niagara and Niagara-on-the-Lake) was briefly the seat of the first parliament of the new province of Upper Canada, from 1792 to 1796. After being burned by retreating American forces, who had occupied it from May to December 1813, much of the town had to be rebuilt. The colonial military presence is evident throughout Niagara-on-the-Lake. In the Servos family burial ground, for instance, is a monument for Elizabeth Johnson, who died in 1811, aged 104 years, She was the widow of Col. Johnson, who was killed at the British capture of Fort Niagara in 1759.

St. Mark's Anglican Church was built in 1804 on a site that had been an aboriginal burial place. When the church was under construction, one old stone marker was uncovered. The spelling is crude and the characters roughly incised, with the letter N reversed:

LEИERDBLAИCK / DESEaCED 5 / AUG.T 1782.

Since the burial place of "Lenerd Blanck" is unknown, the stone has been placed inside the church.

The churchyard, now full of peace, contains many graves of military men and their families, and bears marks of war. During the occupation by the Americans, the church was converted into a barracks. The invaders also dug up the cemetery to make trenches, mounds and a cave for storing their munitions. The resulting abrupt changes in ground level are still visible. Traditional lore holds that the Americans used tombstones to shore up the walls of their trenches, and that one grave marker in particular, a large

recumbent slab, was used as a butcher's block by soldiers billeted in the church. Cleaver marks can be seen on the face of the stone, although its inscription suggests that ill-feeling, not merely the need for a convenient horizontal surface, may have contributed to its ill use:

To the memory of Charles Morrison, a native of Scotland, who resided many years at Michilimackinac as a merchant and magistrate, and since the cession of that post to the United States, became a British subject by election. For loyalty to his Sovereign and integrity in his dealings he was ever remarkable. He died here on his way to Montreal on the 6th day of Sept., 1804, aged 65 years.

A tablet shaped as a double memorial for John and Margaret McFarland, with thistle emblems emphasizing their Scottish origins, has an epitaph outlining another aspect of the devastation of the American occupation.

SACRED
to the memory of
JOHN McFARLAND
A native of Paisley
SCOTLAND.
He was taken Prisoner
at the capture of Fort Geo-
rge and Escaped from
Green Bush near the close
of the war 1815 returning
to this place (Niagara) and
finding his property
burnt up and destroyed
by the Enemy, it Enervated
him so much that he Died
in a few months after.
IN THE 64 YEAR
of his age.

ABOVE: *St. Andrew's Anglican Church Cemetery, Grimsby, Ontario*
Table stones for members of the Crooks family.

RIGHT: *St. Andrew's Anglican Church Cemetery, Grimsby, Ontario*
Urn and willows design on the gravestone for Catharine Nelles.

The memorial tablet for Robert Wilson, a native of Sunderland County, Durham, England, who died in 1839, bears a strange device – a Neoclassical urn combined with a serpent – and the legend "Upon thy belly shalt thou go," a

reference to the story of the Fall, with a second legend, "I am the resurrection and the life," taken from the story of the raising of Lazarus from the dead (Genesis 3: 14 and John 1: 25.) These verses from scripture frame a secular verse addressed to his family:

> Farewell dear wife and children all
> Wherever you remain,
> The Lord of Hosts be your defence
> Till we do meet again.

This unusual image illustrates Christian faith in the promise of resurrection to redeem death, caused by original sin in Eden. The serpent is cursed – "upon thy belly shalt thou go, and dust shalt thou eat all the days of thy life" – and the first man, Adam, is told he must "return unto the ground, for out of it wast thou taken: for dust thou art, and unto dust shalt thou return" (Genesis 3: 14, 19). The latter verse is part of the Anglican burial service.

ABOVE & RIGHT: *St. Mark's Anglican Church Cemetery, Niagara-on-the-Lake, Ontario*

FAR RIGHT: *St. Mark's Anglican Church Cemetery, Niagara-on-the-Lake, Ontario* Double tablet for John and Margaret McFarland.

Methodist Burying Grounds

Methodism began as a movement within the Church of England in 1739, with the ministry of John Wesley. It was strongly evangelical, both in Britain and in its American colonies. Wesley preached deliverance from sin and guilt in *this life*, a Christian salvation known and enjoyed as present reality, in contrast to the Anglican concept of bliss in the life to come. A charismatic preacher, Wesley offered an inclusive message: "All needed to be saved, could be saved, could know they were saved, and could be saved to the uttermost," a message that inspired many Methodists to become missionaries. Lawrence Coughlan, the first Methodist missionary in what is now Canada, began preaching in Newfoundland in 1766 and made many converts there.

Many pioneer Methodists, however, experienced their conversion before the promise of a better life made them decide to emigrate from Britain, then in a period of economic depression. Wesley's outdoor revival-meetings had won thousands of converts in the East Riding of Yorkshire that was visited in 1769–70 by Michael Francklin, the Lieutenant-Governor of Nova Scotia. His purpose was to recruit settlers to purchase the homestead lands not taken up by New England Planters. The Yorkshiremen were mostly tenant farmers who emigrated, they said, "in order to seek a better livelihood" or "due to rents being raised by my landlord." From 1772 to 1775, shiploads full of staunch Wesleyan Methodists arrived – a thousand or more, at a time when the total population of Nova Scotia was just 17,000. Most of them settled in the Chignecto Isthmus. They met in private houses before building their first chapel in Pointe de Bute in 1788, the year their first ordained minister arrived from England. No longer having to rely on the Anglican clergy to administer burial rites, they founded their own burial place. The Old Methodist Burying Ground in Sackville, New Brunswick, is the oldest in Canada. The epitaph on one gravestone there tells a tale imbued with Methodist ideas and concludes with pointed advice: "Reader be thou also ready."

William Fawcett (1770–1832)
He was a plain industrious hospitable and
deeply pious man whose uniformly
Christian conduct gained him the respect
of all who became acquainted with him.
While reading one of Mr. Wesley's sermons,
his immortal soul was instantly
precipitated into the eternal world of his
final rest by some monster of iniquity that
will be discovered at the last day who
intentionally shot him through the kitchen
window the evening of June 10, 1832 in the
63rd year of his age. Reader be thou also ready.

Fawcett's son Rufus was suspected, but not convicted, of being the "monster of iniquity" and soon after left the country for the United States.

Early gravestones bear witness to a strenuous Methodism and a strong faith in salvation. The epitaph for Jacob Powley records his peaceful death, which was believed to be a sign of blessing.

Here Lays
The Body Of
Jacob Powley
Who Gave Much
Satisfaction Until
The Last Period When He
Sat In His Chair Facing The
Door On The 21st day of June

2 o'clock Afternoon Year 1814
He Lay Down His Head With
Out A Struggle Or a Groan
To Sleep In Silence Being
Aged 69 yrs 8 M 7 Dys

The influence of Wesley's inclusiveness – his message that *all* could be saved – is evident in the history of the Methodism in Canada. The British Methodist Episcopal Church developed from the African Methodist Episcopal Church in the American slave-owning colonies. A later wave of settlers from the United States included Methodist Episcopals, members of an independent church founded in 1784. They were noted for their saddlebag preachers, whose zeal and adaptability to frontier conditions made them highly effective missionaries. When the War of 1812 exposed them to the suspicion of being pro-American, many Methodist Episcopals severed their American ties and joined the Wesleyans. Both Census records and the large number of Methodist sects make it evident that distinctions between different forms of Methodism were matters of importance to individual members. In 1874, perhaps inspired by the forces leading to the Confederation of Canada, the separate churches merged to found the Methodist Church of Canada, and the smaller church buildings and their burying grounds were made redundant.

In Ontario it is not uncommon for pioneer graveyards to be the only visible remnants of vanished churches. Perhaps the best known, or at least the most frequently glimpsed, is Richview Cemetery at the intersection of highways 427 and 401. The drivers and passengers of more than 300,000 vehicles pass by it every day. The pioneer settlers near Richview hamlet (now part of Etobicoke in Metropolitan Toronto) included a number of Primitive Methodists. The Primitives in Britain were expelled in 1808 for refusing to stop holding camp meetings and preaching in the open air, in the manner of the original, or "primitive," Methodists. Their opponents nicknamed them "Ranters" and complained that their practice of singing hymns loudly while parading in the streets made people's heads ache.

In 1819 Joseph Stonehouse came to Canada from Yorkshire with one of his sons and settled on a farm in Etobicoke Township. In 1839 a small part of the Stonehouse farm was deeded for a Primitive Methodist chapel and burying ground. Fourteen years later, Robert Stonehouse broke away and deeded land from his farm just across the road for a Wesleyan Methodist chapel. In the same year William Knaggs, another Methodist – perhaps with a wish for unification – deeded land from his farm at the crossroads of Richview hamlet for a "chapel and lot without belonging to any particular church or denomination, to be respectively devoted exclusively to religious purposes in the discretion of certain trustees." This became the Union Chapel at the time of the Methodist Union, and was replaced as the congregation expanded by the larger Richview Methodist (later United) Church.

Today not even the heartiest hymn-singing Primitives could hold an open-air meeting amid the noise of encircling traffic. Land was expropriated in 1959 for the interchange and the vast expansion of Highway 27 (now 427). The congregation was relocated and the church demolished, but descendants of those buried in the cemetery refused to let it be closed, and the roadways were rerouted around it. The descendants of Richview's founders are tenacious in keeping faith with their ancestors. They have restored most of the headstones through funding from the Ontario Heritage Foundation, the Etobicoke Historical Society and the Heritage Etobicoke Foundation, as well as many private donors, and have had the cemetery designated under the *Ontario Heritage Act*. The cemetery was officially rededicated with a memorial service in the summer of 2005.

The New Connexion had been formed in 1792, after a quarrel with the Methodist Church about the representation of lay members in Church administration. Bethel Chapel, on a country sideroad near the village of Kilbride (now part of Burlington, Ontario) was built in 1853 by members of the New Connexion Wesleyan Methodists. It closed in 1874, but the descendants of the families who formed its original congregation have preserved its beautiful wooden structure and maintained its burial ground. They gather annually in the second week of September for a service of remembrance and thanksgiving for their pioneer ancestors.

The social position of Methodists in Canada began to change in the mid 19th century. According to one historian. "Earlier the Church of Scotland and the Church of England had formed social elites inaccessible to Methodists, the latter being poor and frequently despised. Zealous in evangelism and ardent in their pursuit of godliness, however, their sobriety, industry and thrift fuelled their social ascendancy. Some Methodists became wealthy: the Gooderhams from grain and railways, the Masseys from farm implements, and the Flavelles from meat-packing."

Egerton Ryerson's role in reforming the provincial educational system and the establishment of Victoria College empowered Methodists to challenge the Anglican monopoly on education and political power. The Methodist challenge was also evident in the cemetery reform movement, especially in the founding of the Necropolis and the Mount Pleasant Cemetery in Toronto. The 1925 union of the Methodist Church with the Congregationalists and most Presbyterian churches formed the United Church of Canada, now Canada's largest Protestant denomination.

This epitaph for Laura Miles records a sign of blessing:

Sacred to the memory of
LAURA
Late Companion of
STEPHEN MILES, and third
daughter of the late ELI-
JAH SPAFFORD. — Her happy
Soul took its flight on the 31st
of July, 1821, (her birthday) age-
d 27 years.
A few minutes before she
breathed her last, she was
heard to whisper the blessed
name of
JESUS! JESUS!

Quaker Cemeteries

"Quaker" is the name commonly given to the religious society, founded in the mid 17th century, that calls itself the Society of Friends. British Quakers settled in the Province of Pennsylvania, granted in 1681 to William Penn by Charles II, just 21 years after he had been the recipient of the Quaker Declaration of Pacifism:

We utterly deny all outward wars and strife, and ... with outward weapons, for any end, or under any pretense whatever ... The Spirit of Christ by which we are guided is not changeable ... and we ... testify to the world, that the Spirit of Christ, which leads us into all truth, will never move us to fight and war against any man with outward weapons, neither for the kingdom of Christ, nor for the kingdoms of this world.

Quakers in the American colonies did not fight on either side during the Revolutionary War, and so were not forced to flee as Loyalists, but nevertheless some of them felt uncomfortable in the new republic. Lieutenant-Governor John Graves Simcoe invited them to settle in East Gwillimbury, north of York. Arriving in 1800, they paid for their land rather than receiving it as a United Empire Loyalist grant from the Crown. Like other pioneer settlers, each family had two years to clear and fence 10 acres, build a log house no smaller than 16 by 20 feet, with a shingled roof, and clear 35 feet of their half of the public road in front of their property – Yonge Street. When some Quakers established a new market to save traders from having to travel to the York market, the place eventually gained the name Newmarket.

In 1807 one member donated two acres for a burial ground, and in 1810 a simple frame meeting house was built next to it. The Society of Friends still meets there. The Quaker principles of plain and truthful language and indifference to the vanities of outward observances are evident in their burial grounds. Quakers believe that all ground is "God's ground" and that special consecration of burial places is unnecessary. Not recognizing any privileges of rank or established status among the living, they guard against any special distinctions between rich or poor being made in their places of burial. When they first settled on Yonge Street, they did not permit grave markers at all, as these were seen as creating distinctions between members on the basis of worldly wealth. The earliest graves followed the Quaker custom of ordering burials according to the date of death, with no regard to family relationships. When they were later permitted to use markers, they chose fieldstones, wood, or modest stone tablets – simple, small and unadorned by images.

Most stones in the burial ground beside their first Meeting House have a standard format. The person's name is followed by a plain-spoken statement of facts. "*DIED*" or "*DECEASED*" is centred and often the most emphasized word, followed by the date of death and the duration of life. The date is usually in the plain Quaker form, where the month is simply numbered in order to avoid using names that honour pagan Roman deities like Janus, or Mars, or the deified emperors Julius and Augustus. A typical Quaker inscription reads, in its entirety, "Joel Hughes / died / 15th of 7th mo. 1872 / AE 80 yrs. 5 mo. / 1 day."

In 1818 a dissident Quaker group calling themselves the Children of Peace broke away from the Yonge Street Meeting. In the hamlet then known as Hope (later the Village of Sharon, now the town of East Gwillimbury) they built their beautiful Temple of Peace. Their burial ground is a short distance to the south. The earliest graves here follow the Quaker custom of ordering burials according to the date of death, but in time this custom was modified to a more conventional preference for family plots. The Children of Peace prized the aesthetic appeal of good architecture and music, and many of their gravestones incorporate sculpted symbols. The dove, emblem of peace, is a favourite. Air pol-

Children of Peace Cemetery, East Gwillimbury, Ontario

lutants from automotive emissions have worn away the carving on the soft white marble stone; two figures reclining above a dove on one grave marker are becoming almost unreadable. Bearing an olive branch, the dove symbolized the peaceable kingdom and the Quaker testimony against military power and warfare.

Quakers were not entirely apolitical, however, and not every member of the Society of Friends avoided "outward wars and strife, and fightings with outward weapons." They were early opponents of slavery, active in the abolitionist movement and the underground railroad for escaped slaves. In the Sharon burial ground is a weathered white marble monument for James Lundy, who died in 1864 while fighting in the American Civil War. He is one of thousands of British North Americans (that is, Canadians) who died for the Union cause in that war. The inscription indicating his regimental affiliation is no longer legible, but the carved relief emblematic scene on his grave marker shows a militant eagle perched against a backdrop of furled flags and above a palm branch of victory.

FAR LEFT: *Children of Peace Cemetery, East Gwillimbury, Ontario*
The dove was a favourite emblem of the Children of Peace.

LEFT: *Cataraqui Cemetery, Kingston, Ontario*
A Friends burial ground established in 1802 near Kingston was absorbed by Cataraqui Cemetery in 1907. Quaker and non-Quaker graves now coexist there. The marker for Quaker "MARY FERRIS / died 16th of / 4th month 1893 / Aged 82" is a typically plain statement of the facts.

BELOW: *Children of Peace Cemetery, East Gwillimbury, Ontario*

African-American Cemeteries

When slavery was legal, men and women of African descent were brought to the colonies that are now part of Canada as slaves owned by their masters. In 1791, the year that Governor Simcoe arrived in Canada, William Wilberforce first presented a bill to abolish the slave trade to the Bristish House of Commons. That bill was defeated, but Simcoe exerted his political influence to make Upper Canada the first British territory to legislate against slavery. The *Anti-Slavery Act* of 1793 did not free any slaves, but it prohibited the importing of new slaves in Upper Canada and declared that all children born into slavery would be freed when they reached the age of 25.

The result was a great immigration of African-American settlers. Philip Sovereign deeded a corner of his farm property in 1830 as a burial ground for people of "all orders, sects, nations and parties," including those who had escaped from slavery.

In Niagara-on-the-Lake, the site of a former Baptist church with a racially mixed congregation, built in 1829, is marked by an Ontario Heritage Foundation plaque. Only a few gravestones are left standing. Janet Carnochan's *Graves and Inscriptions in the Niagara Peninsula* included a record of the "Baptist (Colored) Church":

At one time several hundred escaped slaves found shelter under the British flag, and here are buried many of these dusky Africans ... Here too is buried a hero whose name should not be forgotten, though it is unrecorded in marble or granite. Herbert Holmes, a teacher and exhorter, who organized a band of colored men of several hundreds to surround the jail and prevent the return of Mosely, an escaped slave from Kentucky, who was by law ordered to be given up. The civil and military authorities were called out, soldiers, constables, sheriff, and the Riot Act read. The prisoner escaped, but Holmes and Green were shot and lie buried here, having given their lives to save their brother from slavery. Were not they heroes indeed, and should not their names be commemorated?

Before 1865, when slavery in the United States finally came to an end, an estimated 30,000 to 40,000 fugitives settled in Upper Canada, and there were 20 African-American settlements in what is now Ontario. Where, then, are the graves of these settlers? And the burial places of their children and grandchildren? A rough estimate for pioneer graveyards is that typically one in 10 graves retains its marker or can be identified from records. The disappearances that have affected so many pioneer burial places have been much more comprehensive in African-American graveyards, many of which have almost completely vanished.

An extreme example of such a disappearance is New York City's African Burial Ground. From the late 17th century to 1796, an estimated 10,000 to 20,000 people were buried on a five-acre site in lower Manhattan, but when it was accidentally uncovered in 1991 during excavations for the foundations of a new Federal Government Building, its past had been completely forgotten. The fact that so many slaves had lived in New Amsterdam and New York had been erased from public memory. In 2006 the Burial Ground was designated a National Monument, and preparations are being made to nominate it as a UNESCO World Heritage Site. Of the 400 remains that archaeologists have found in the site, about 45 per cent were children under the age of 12. Nevertheless, the thousands of adults buried there undoubtedly include ancestors of a great many 21st century Canadians, as well as Americans. Genealogical research, which has played a significant role in increasing public recognition of historical cemeteries, has been less effective in preserving African-American burial places, since only those who have already traced their African descent tend to support such research. For others, the revelation of an African ancestor would be even more surprising than the discovery of an African Burial Ground, and for some, finding this hidden ancestry would be unwelcome news. In some cases, as has been alleged of the Old Durham Road Pioneer Cemetery near the village of Priceville, Ontario, denial of racially mixed ancestry has played a role in suppressing evidence about a former cemetery's location.

Lack of familiarity with traditional African burial practices may also contribute to a failure to recognize their value. One instance is recorded in South Carolina, where an anthropologist sent to check out the Charles Towne Landing area returned, reporting that there appeared to be nothing other than some late period garbage scattered throughout the area. The location was written off as being of no interest. William Faulkner was one white man who knew better than such common misunderstandings of Black experience. His story "Pantaloon in Black" begins with a burial:

... the grave, save for its rawness, resembled any other marked off without order about the barren plot by shards of pottery and broken bottles and old brick and other objects insignificant to sight but actually of a profound meaning and fatal to touch, which no white man could have read.

The broken objects placed on grave sites served to break spiritual links, so that the souls or spirits would not "walk" and tantalize the living, tempting loved ones to join them. Other grave goods were personal items or things last used by the deceased. No one would ever remove grave goods, for the discontented spirit would follow them. Graves were also sometimes covered with shells, or marked with a large rock for a headstone and a smaller one at the foot. Unfortunately, these objects have occasionally been removed in well-intentioned clean-ups of cemeteries. Traditional conservation of the African-American burial places is "let it be." It was not uncommon for them to become overgrown after burials were no longer taking place. This was not a sign of neglect, but resulted from a wish not to disturb the dead.

The Toronto Necropolis includes conventional monuments for men who found not only liberty but also success in business and life in the city. William Peyton Hubbard, the city's first African-American councillor, nicknamed the "Cicero of Council" by his colleagues, was elected 15 times between 1894 and 1913. A large obelisk commemorates Thornton Blackburn and his wife, Lucie, former slaves from Kentucky whose dramatic escape to Upper Canada from Detroit caused a race riot in 1833 and an international incident when Lieutenant-Governor Sir John Colborne refused to extradite them to the United States. Blackburn very successfully established the first taxi company in Upper Canada, with a four-passenger one-horse cab, painted red and yellow and called "The City."

A sarcophagus bearing only the inscription "ABBOTT" marks the grave of a man born in 1837 to parents who had moved to Toronto a year or two earlier, following the ransacking of their store in Alabama. Educated at William King's school in Buxton and then at the Toronto Academy, Oberlin College, and the Toronto School of Medicine, Anderson Ruffin Abbott became in 1861 the first Canadian-born doctor of African descent licensed to practise by the Medical Board of Upper Canada. During the American Civil War, he served as a surgeon in the Union Army. Returning to Canada, he was admitted to the College of Physicians and Surgeons of Ontario. In later life he published articles on topics including the importance of Black history. He was confident that "the color line [would] eventually fade out in Canada" – "It is just as natural for two races living together on the same soil to blend as it is for the waters of two river tributaries to mingle with each other."

Abbott's wife had blended ancestry, and his son married a white woman and became a heart surgeon in Chicago, where his race was apparently not questioned. In 1975 Catherine Slaney, a great-great-granddaughter of Anderson Ruffin Abbott, was surprised to discover her eminent Black ancestors. Her book about tracing her lost family history is called *Family Secrets: Crossing the Colour Line.*

New Germany

The village of Maryhill, Ontario, was so named in 1941. Its original name had been New Germany or, in the German-language newspapers, *Neu Deutschland*. The first generation of settlers was composed of Mennonites who came from Pennsylvania after the American Revolution and created a distinctive German society and culture in Waterloo Township. Their tolerance of other religions attracted later waves of Catholic German immigrants from Alsace Lorraine, Bavaria and Prussia. The Weiler family, for instance, came from Umzhurst, Baden, in two crossings in 1829 and 1831 – four brothers and their wives, a sister and her husband, and their father, Ignatius, a widower. Ignatius "carved a statue of Mary, the mother of Jesus, to invoke her intercessory protection for the treacherous Atlantic crossing." His statue is still kept in the church they helped to found, and the new name of their village celebrates their Marian devotion. Other branches of the Weiler family came later and lived in Maryhill before resettling in parts of Bruce County, where there are six churchyards with graves marked by wrought-iron crosses. Of the three Catholic burial sites in Waterloo Region, the one in Maryhill is notable for having many wrought-iron crosses of various designs, both simple and ornate. St. Boniface, a substantial stone church named after the eighth-century English missionary to Germany, was built on the hill, so that its spire (with a plain cross) is the first thing a visitor sees when driving along the irregular rural road leading to the village.

While the Mennonites from New England were farmers, Germans coming direct from Europe brought varied craft and trade skills. Those of the blacksmith are on display in the St. Boniface churchyard, which is enclosed by a high stone wall. Its elaborate wrought-iron entrance gate introduces the visitor to a dazzling array of intricately embellished hand-crafted grave crosses, displaying a balance of cultural tradition and individual creativity. The Latin crosses, the principal symbols of the Catholic faith, often bear a small cast-iron crucifix. The iron crosses represent a necessary frugality, made rich by skillful labour. Their material came from the village blacksmith's scrap heap. In fledgling agricultural communities blacksmiths were practical men whose metalworking skills were essential to the village economy. They shaped and welded iron to refit horseshoes and to repair wagon wheels and ploughshares. Wrought iron resists corrosion, seldom breaks and is reclaimable from old scrap iron. It is soft and malleable and can be worked by hand, but making the iron crosses took skill, patience, strength and effort. A simple unadorned cross probably took a day or two to make, while an ornate one could take weeks. Some elaborate designs required more than 30 pieces.

The heart motif found on Lunenburg gravestones is also seen in German Catholic settings. The spirals, coils, floral and leafy ornaments on the crosses transform the Cross of Salvation into a Tree of Life symbol, which has its source in pre-Christian times. The inventiveness and variety of designs, with decorative scrolls, filigree and curlicues are signals that these works of art were fashioned in a spirit of celebration and joy. The German words frequently used to refer to cemeteries were *Friedhof* (courtyard of peace) and *Gottesacker* (God's field, an acre God had under cultivation). The burial grounds of these deeply religious people were expressions of personal faith integrally connected with their active lives.

Ghost Town Graveyards

The Coal Branch, a rail line running through the Rocky Mountains in a long loop between Edmonton and Yellowhead Pass, was built in 1912 by the Canadian National Railway. The branch line serviced various mining operations that supplied high quality bituminous coal to fuel the railway's locomotives. The more than twenty collieries and towns on the Coal Branch drew thousands of miners, and in some cases their families, including a large number of immigrants from Italy, Britain and Central Europe. After more than thirty years of prosperity and a boom period during the Second World War, the mines and mining towns were closed in the 1950s, as diesels replaced coal-burning steam engines. The closures created many "Ghost Towns" – some quite deserted, and some now supporting small seasonal cottage communities.

During its peak years, the mining town of Lille had three operating mines producing close to one million tons of bituminous coal. Despite their early success, by 1913 the mines and the town were closed, and the workers and their families moved away. For another thirty years scores of homes were left standing at the Lille site, but more recently treasure hunters have picked apart its material remnants, including its magnificent brick coke ovens.

Some fifteen minutes away from Lille a faint path leads to the town's pioneer graveyard. It is believed that about a dozen former citizens and miners were buried there, but today only one tombstone still stands. No one has assumed responsibility for preserving the final remnants of this pioneer cemetery. A rusty pail from pioneer times hangs from a tree near a Lille grave. A memorial plaque is nailed to a tree.

The town of Mercoal is located just outside the eastern ranges of the Rockies near Jasper National Park. Mercoal's pioneer burial ground, hidden in a forested area outside of town, is cared for by the town's remaining cottage residents. A sign records the restorations of the burial ground by groups of students, junior forest wardens and air cadets, whose tasks were sponsored by the local branch of the Canadian Legion.

Fewer than twenty-five wooden crosses and other simple markers now remain, standing as sparse and reticent memorials to the many who were buried in what has become, once more, an isolated place. Beyond the neat wooden fence, the second-growth forest is replacing trees cut down by the logging and sawmill operations that were also part of the pioneer economy.

Mountain Park was the first community along the western line of the Coal Branch, and also the highest inhabited point in the British Commonwealth, at almost 1,900 meters above sea level. Its graveyard, with the Rocky Mountains as a backdrop, has the highest elevation of any in Canada. Some 150 marked graves remain, with modest wooden picket fences defining their boundaries against the wilderness. Although the town and its mining facilities are gone, former residents are active in preserving memories of their lives here. Some have expressed their wish to be remembered in the graveyard. It has been enlarged to include scattering grounds for cremated ashes, and small metal plaques include epitaphs such as "Resting in the Mountains He Loved" and "At Peace in the Mountains She Loved."

New Iceland

Iceland is situated on the Mid-Atlantic Ridge, a deep fissure in the earth's crust where the North American and Eurasian continental plates drift apart several millimeters every year, periodically causing molten lava to come to the surface in eruptions, slow or explosive, from its many volcanoes. In 1783 an eight-month-long eruption of Laki led to the death by famine of about one-quarter of the island's population, when their crops failed because of acid rain and their livestock perished after grazing on grass contaminated by fluorine gas emissions. Some 60 years later, Iceland's economy was devastated again by an epidemic that killed 200,000 sheep. Many Icelanders resolved to emigrate and to found a colony they could govern and administer by themselves, free from the burden of Danish tariffs and trade restrictions. Between 1870 and 1914, over a quarter of Iceland's population emigrated to North America.

In Iceland, Christmas Eve is a family day that includes visits to cemeteries to lay flowers and candles on family graves. In a world built on lava, burial does not involve digging in the ground. Instead, the casket is set on the ground and covered by a cairn of stones, covered by strips of sod that grow and hold the stones in place. Walking in an Icelandic graveyard, one is knee-deep among the graves. The landscape of their new world was quite different.

Immigration agents encouraged Icelandic settlement in the remote interior of Nova Scotia, offering cheap land where large stands of virgin forests had to be cleared. The Icelander pioneers, coming from a country that had few trees, found this no light task. They named the place Markland – "treeland" – the name given to an unknown location by the Norse explorer Leif Ericson, during his visit to North America almost 900 years earlier. The Markland Settlement lasted from 1875 to 1882, just long enough for the settlers to earn the Crown grants for their poor land. They then sold it for whatever price they could get and moved West. Some went to the Dakota Territories (later the state of North Dakota), and others to the colony of New Iceland (*Nýja Island*), which had been established in 1875 on the west shore of Lake Winnipeg, then part of the vast wilderness of the Northwest Territories.

The colony at Willow Point was called Gimli, a name that comes from Norse mythology and means "Home of the Gods" or, some say, "paradise." As one of their descendants has commented, "the Icelanders have always had a wry sense of humour." But Gimli also illustrates the Icelanders' trait of positive thinking, which is a powerful characteristic of the Markland settlers' written accounts.

Icelandic Cemetery, Grund, Manitoba

An intense interest in genealogy is part of Icelanders' heritage. Their extensive written records, including medieval sagas, make it possible for most to trace their ancestry back to the colonization of Iceland in the ninth and 10th centuries. Written records and printed memoirs of their experience in their 19th century pioneer settlements in America are now treasured by their descendants. Sigurur Jóhannesson's letter in December 1877 to the "esteemed editor" of the newspaper in his old home town, written from *Hljéskógar*, his new home in Markland, had "little to report, apart from good news":

The weather has been fine and pleasant. Actually, this past summer and fall were rather rainy, but there were dry periods now and again so that the hay crop and harvest were good ... Here in Nova Scotia we had a better than average harvest this past summer, except for potatoes. Those ... rotted to some extent ... It is now two years since there has been a death among our group and, in the two and one-half years we have been living in this colony, only one individual has died. There are now about 100 of us here.

A cheerful outlook was also expressed in the memoir published in 1916 by Gudbrandur Erlendsson, who describes his departure from his Markland homestead, *Grænavatn*:

This place, where I had lived for six years, was truly beautiful. In this place, I had known great poverty, but in spite of that, my wife and children had been happy there. How often, on my return from work, I had heard her lovely voice raised in song in which she was joined by my children. How wonderful it was that all my children had inherited her beautiful singing voice. We had never been visited by disease, not even so much as a cold. Would we always be that lucky? The future held the answer.

The settlers' cheerful resiliency was tested again in New Iceland, where clearing the land was arduous and agricultural development was hampered by poorly drained, rocky soils. A smallpox epidemic in 1877 afflicted one-third of the settlers and was even more devastating to their aboriginal neighbours. In 1879 a mass exodus for the Dakota Territory left behind only 50 of the original 200 families. The traditional Icelandic celebration of "burning the old year" must have been especially significant on the subsequent New Year's Eve. But the remaining settlers persevered, and Gimli began to grow again. At the end of the century, the opening up of the area to homesteaders brought a surge of settlers from Ukraine, Poland, Hungary and Germany. The arrival of the railroad in 1906 made the area accessible to summer cottagers, who came from Winnipeg to enjoy the recreational activities of the lake and the beaches.

Markland remained quite uninhabited. By the end of the 20th century, only one unmarked grave and the foundations of 25 houses remained. In the summer of 2000, members of the Icelandic Memorial Society of Nova Scotia dedicated a memorial cairn there. They also reprinted Erlendsson's memoir in two books, Icelandic and English. His *Markland: Remembrance of the Years 1875–1881* has become a strand braided into the long written record of Icelandic history.

Cemetery on Lake Winnipeg, Hecla, Manitoba

Ukrainian Cemeteries

Between 1892 and 1914, some 170,000 immigrants from the provinces of Galicia and Bukovina in the Austro-Hungarian empire settled on prairie farm homesteads in Manitoba, Saskatchewan and Alberta. The national awakening among the peasantry in the Austro-Hungarian and Russian empires was reflected in their choosing to identify themselves in the New World as Ukrainians, rather than Austrians, Galicians or Bukovinians. They built their pioneer communities on the prairies with others who had arrived at different times, and from different villages, districts and provinces, even different empires. They also practised different religions (the Ukrainian Greek Catholic Church and the Ukrainian Orthodox Eastern Church) and built separate churches with separate burial grounds.

As the earlier pioneers in the eastern provinces had done, before churches could be built they buried their dead on private homesteads or burial grounds. Their first graves were marked by wooden crosses or posts, which soon vanished. Prairie residents may drive down their local road today without even recognizing that "the fenced-off rectangle overgrown with brush in an adjacent pasture holds a long-forgotten grave."

Especially poignant is the place at Patterson Lake, Manitoba, where 40 children and two adults were buried on Crown land in 1899, having died of scarlet fever and exposure while *en route* to their homesteads near Shoal Lake. Their survivors marked the graves with wooden crosses and again took up their way. The first owner of the land, not a Ukrainian, pastured his cows among their graves, and the markers disappeared. In 1915 a Ukrainian schoolteacher bought the property and ploughed it up before discovering what the site was and fencing it off. The families returned to build a large mound topped with a wooden cross.

Elsewhere on the Canadian prairies, Ukrainians combined Christian monuments with pre-Christian earthen burial mounds. In Alberta they built a symbolic *mohyla,* or mound, like those of the ancient Scythians, still evident in the landscape of the Ukrainian steppe. Their grave markers were made of wood, wrought iron, stone or cement cast in moulds. The crosses in Ukrainian graveyards have footrests, which make allusion to the death of Christ on the Cross, without depicting the crucified Saviour. The ends of the cross are trefoils, the three leaves representing the Trinity and also the vitality of new growth. The Orthodox cross has a slanted footrest, while the cross of the Byzantine Rite, or Greek Catholic church, has a horizontal footrest.

Few of the earliest grave markers told personal life stories. Often, just the person's name and year of death were inscribed or painted. Only a minority of grave markers recorded European birthplaces, whose names were continually altered anyway, through tides of historical and

RIGHT: *Ukrainian grave marker near Andrew, Alberta*

FACING PAGE: *St. Michael's Ukrainian Orthodox Cemetery, near Gardenton, Manitoba*
The oldest Ukrainian Orthodox church in Canada, established in 1899.

political change. Occasionally there is an inset photograph. More recent gravestones are personalized by laser technology. Ukrainian stones tend to show images of their workplaces, and particularly aerial views of their farmsteads, including details like "the television antenna on the house, the van in the driveway, and the dogs barking at the gate." Since Ukrainians tended to stay on the homestead through several generations, these images show the result of their family's long cultivation of the land.

Gravestone engravings also show farmers driving their combines and traditional images of wheat sheaves and stooks. These are symbols of both the earthly harvest and the Second Coming of Christ, according to the vision of St.

John: "And I looked, and behold a white cloud, and upon the cloud one sat like unto the Son of man, having on his head a golden crown, and in his hand a sickle. And another angel came out of the temple, crying in a loud voice to him that sat on the cloud, Thrust in thy sickle, and reap: for the time is come for thee to reap; for the harvest of earth is ripe" (Revelation 14: 14–15). For the faithful Christian, the sickle is not only the sign of the grim reaper, death, but also a promise of a final resurrection.

Traditional graveside rituals, practised according to the liturgical calendars of both the Orthodox and Catholic churches, made connections between the old and new land. In Ukrainian tradition, the relationship between the living

Ukrainian church and cemetery, Vita, Manitoba

and the dead is linked to ancient customs connected with the planting and harvest of wheat. Like generations of peasants before them, Ukrainian settlers in western Canada saved from the harvest a particular sheaf of wheat whose kernels were believed to contain the souls of the dead. On Christmas Eve they brought the sheaf into the house, and on New Year's Eve burnt it in their fields, returning the souls to the soil. Since they had brought the first handful of seed grain with them from Ukraine, the souls of their ancestors who had planted and gathered the seed for generations became incorporated into their new Canadian farms, just as generations of kernels from each year's crop were planted anew in the following year.

In both Orthodox and Catholic churches, the time between Easter and Pentecost is celebrated by *provody*, when families gather in the cemetery and tidy the family plots. The priest blesses the grave sites and baskets of food. Then people break bread together, sharing their braided loaves and fruit or Easter eggs, and symbolically sharing with those whose time is past but who are still present to the living. The name of the festival derives from the word meaning "to accompany," and signifies that all who rest in the faith are together in the company of those awaiting the final resurrection.

St. Julian Ukrainian Orthodox Catholic Cemetery, near Batoche, Saskatchewan

Chinese Cemeteries

The experience of the Chinese who emigrated to Canada in the 19th century from the Kwangtung Province of South China was typical of immigrant experience in some ways, but in others most distinctive. Proper burial is exceptionally important in traditional Chinese society, where death represents a person's transformation to a new status as ancestor. The subsequent fortunes of the ancestor's family are believed to be shaped by the observation of prescribed burial rites, and above all by the *feng shui*, or harmonious balance, of the grave site. The care and respect shown for the dead in a well-chosen site imply a reverence for life, a devotion to the successful outcomes of lifetime enterprises and a commitment to the collective good fortune of the family lineage. Conversely, an unbalanced site is believed to have unfavourable implications both for the repose of the dead and for their living descendants. In pre-revolutionary China, auspicious sites were in short supply, and quite commonly an ensuing family misfortune led to reburial, called the "lucky burial" after a period of five to 12 years.

Most Chinese who entered Canada before 1923 were men who came as sojourning workers, sending their earnings to their families back home, but isolated from the deep family ties and support that traditionally characterized their society. Their shared belief was that they would find peaceful repose after death only if they were buried near their home villages. Many managed to return to China in their old age, but for those who died in Canada, arrangements were made for reburial in China after interment for some seven to 10 years in Canadian graves. The men joined clan or county organizations that took responsibility for reburial arrangements. The practice of exhuming and returning bones to China, added to the transitory nature of the earliest Chinese settlements in Canada, often resulted in the abandonment of their burial sites after the

Chinese dispersed to work elsewhere.

In Victoria, which contained the largest urban population of Chinese in Canada during the 19th century, the earliest Chinese interments were in a corner of the pioneer burial ground on Quadra Street. Then, in 1873 a section of Ross Bay Cemetery was reserved for "Aboriginals and Mongolians" who were not members of Christian churches. Ross Bay was a low-lying area, subject to flooding and erosion at seasonal high-tides, and graves were sometimes washed away in winter gales. The Chinese Consolidated Benevolent Association was established in 1885 to coordinate and fund reburial arrangements, and also to acquire a suitable site for permanent burials where traditional funeral rites could be observed.

The site at a promontory beside Gonzales Bay in the municipality of Oak Bay, a few miles east of Ross Bay in Victoria, was chosen after another location was thwarted by opposition from neighbours. The Harling Point Cemetery, which opened in 1903, incorporates the history of shifts in Chinese settlement during the 20th century. In 1923 Chinese immigration to Canada was prohibited by federal legislation (not repealed until 1947). The subsequent postwar growth of the Chinese-Canadian population included second- and third-generation families with changing circumstances and cultural values, so that Canada rather than China was seen as the home country. Shipments to China of exhumed remains came to a stop with the outbreak of the Sino-Japanese War in 1937, and their repatriation continued to be blocked after the war. By 1950 the cemetery was filled to capacity, with more than 1,000 burials. It was briefly reopened in 1961 so that 13 mass graves, arranged according to the original home villages, could be prepared for the remains of 849 Chinese sojourners, pioneers in the history of the Chinese-Canadian community, whose bones had since 1937 been

Chinese Cemetery, Harling Point, Oak Bay, British Columbia

stored in the cemetery's bonehouse, awaiting the end of international hostilities.

After 1961 Harling Point became a contested site subject to conflicting views about its use, including attempted closure and expropriation by the municipality, proposed residential development and creation of a public park. The Chinese Cemetery was declared a National Historic Site in 1996, and its recent restoration includes plaques interpreting many botanical and geological features of the point. In the spring the turf includes a wide variety of flowering plants found only in a gentle Mediterranean climate, and the shoreline reveals the meeting of two pieces of the earth's crust. The exposed rocks bear long deep grooves from glaciers of the Ice Age, and several large erratic rocks are left by the withdrawal of those glaciers. One erratic, known as "Harpoon Rock," is the place of a transformation legend in the creation myths of the Songhees Nation.

Visitors who may be unfamiliar with the principles of *feng shui* may learn from an interpretive plaque that the

Chinese words mean "wind and water," the two forces of nature that are literally the shapers of Chinese landscape. They are the agents of the magnificent work of nature. By force of erosion, wind and water carved out the lofty mountains and hills that form the greater portion of the land in China. In the Harling Point site, the earth's surface has a natural configuration that is smooth in form and outline, not rugged or steep. The ground slopes gently, backed by a "Pillow Mountain" (Gonzales Hill). A course of "Living Water," a symbol of wealth and affluence is open to view in the bay and strait. The site is flanked on the west by the lower ground of the crouching "White Tiger" and on the left by the higher elevation of the "Azure Dragon." These cosmic energies of Yin (female) and Yang (male) converge and interact vigorously on the auspicious secluded ground, producing *sheng ch'i*, or life breath. The powerful ancestors buried here are oriented to face south, the realm of life and vigour. Like high-ranking officials on an elevated platform, they command a "Grand Hall" – the Juan de Fuca Strait – and the distant "Worshipping Mountain Range," the Olympic Mountains in Washington State. Perhaps most foreign to visitors new to *feng shui* is the notion that the snow-capped mountains are not merely a scenic view but also represent a circle of worshipful descendants.

There is no longer a wooden pagoda shelter, as seen in Chinese areas of community cemeteries elsewhere. The most striking features are the altar and incinerator towers. The most common singular feature of overseas Chinese cemeteries is the "burner," a tall brick or masonry structure serving as a safe place for the ritualized burning of spiritual tributes. Paper facsimiles of money, clothing, possessions and houses are burnt to pass them to the spirit realm, where they serve the spirits of the dead in the afterlife. At Ching Ming (grave-sweeping day), descendants visit to maintain the grave sites, light incense and burn imitation paper money at the altar, and leave food offerings such as candies and oranges.

Japanese O-Bon

Buddhists have many ceremonies devoted to honouring earlier generations. During the spring or fall equinox festival, Japanese Buddhists memorialize the dead, visiting the cemeteries of their loved ones, cleaning their graves and offering them food. Buddhist rites are also common on anniversaries of a family member's death-day.

The most important annual festival is the *Bon Matsuri* or O-Bon, the Festival of the Dead. The festival has its origin in a story of a Buddhist monk or disciple who had a disturbing vision of his dead mother in the Realm of Hungry Ghosts, where he saw her indulging her own selfishness. When he petitioned to find out how to release her, the Buddha advised him to perform some charitable act in her memory. After doing so, the monk saw more truly: not only the release of his mother from the Realm of Hungry Ghosts, but also her unselfishness during her lifetime and the many sacrifices she had made for him. From his dance of joy and gratitude comes *Bon Odori* or Bon Dance, a time in which ancestors are remembered and appreciated.

In July or August, Buddhists invite the spirits of their dead ancestors to return to the world of the living. This three-day festival is also a family reunion, in which many of the living return to their original family homes. On the first day of O-Bon, after thoroughly cleaning their houses, people go to family gravesites – the columbaria containing the ashes of their ancestors – to invite the spirits of their dead to visit them. They light small fires or hang lanterns in front of their houses to guide the spirits, or they may lead the way home with a shining lantern. For the next two days, they act as though the spirits are among them, conversing with them and offering them food. On the second day, the Japanese set up the *tamadana*, or spirits' altars, at their homes: ancestral cenotaphs are placed on a woven mat, along with vegetarian dishes and cucumbers formed to symbolize horses for the spirits to ride on. On the third day, hundreds of people congregate for the *Bon Odori*, a slow and mesmerizing dance

that moves in circles or multiple lines. Then they offer the spirits a farewell meal, and the fires and lanterns are relit to help the ancestors find their way back to the spirit world. During the evening, people may place small paper lanterns on the river or sea to lead the spirits back to shore (*Toro-Nagashi*).

The first known Japanese immigrants to Canada settled in Victoria in 1877. Others began arriving in British Columbia in the 1890s, and migration to the prairies began in the early 1900s. Their immigration and citizenship were restricted: they were not permitted to vote, and their work opportunities were effectively limited to fishing, logging, farming and mining. During the Second World War the hostilities with Japan led to invoking the *War Measures Act*, whereby Japanese Canadians who had been living on the west coast – 22,000 men, women and children – were treated as enemy aliens. More than 2,000 were sent to work small sugar beet farms near Lethbridge, Alberta. Others were sent to mass internment camps such as Slocan City, a ghost town in the Kootenays that had boomed during the silver rush of the 1890s. When the wartime laws were finally revoked in 1949, many did not return to live where their properties had been sold, their temples and community halls dismantled and their graveyards desecrated.

Those who had worked since 1903 at the Knight Sugar Factory in southern Alberta continued to observe the most important festival of their Buddhist tradition, and in 1929 they established the Raymond Buddhist Church. During the 1960s the town councillors of Raymond, having noted their fellow citizens' observance of O-Bon, asked the Japanese community if it would be suitable to extend this festival to all citizens, and established Cemetery Day as a civic holiday. Like the Nikka Yuko garden of friendship in nearby Lethbridge (a city where Japanese Canadians had been prohibited from living during the war), this extension of O-Bon to include the entire town manifests something at the heart of Japanese Buddhism – a response coming from hardship, motivated by compassion and understanding. It also seems a fitting illustration of a changing community, one with a high rate of intermarriage. Generations to come will inherit mingled traditions of East and West.

On August 10, 1991, the surviving former Japanese Canadian residents of Chemainus, the town they had known as Chimunesu, returned to celebrate O-Bon there for the first time since August 1941. One of the men who returned had been only six months old when his family was removed. He had never been able to visit the grave of his infant brother, left behind in the Japanese Canadians' burial ground. After 50 years of absence, the 50 years of their living presence in Chemainus, previous to their relocation, had been obliterated. Even their graveyard had been cleared with a backhoe earth mover. Only a few grave markers remained, leaning against the fence in an overgrown corner. The wooden markers disintegrated into fragments. Stone markers had been removed for use elsewhere; a few of these have since been quietly returned. Modern stone plaques now record the names of those known to be buried there.

On Vancouver Island, annual O-Bon Tours have become a manifestation of traditional Buddhist respect for ancestors. Most families of Japanese descent did not return to the Island after the war, and there are now few descendants to pay their respects to those buried there. The O-Bon Tours compensate for that lack. A three-day chartered bus tour visits the cemetery sites of Nanaimo, Cumberland, Port Alberni, Ucluelet, Chemainus, Duncan and Victoria before returning to the ferry for Vancouver and the mainland. This invitation to join the holiday tour emphasizes the enjoyment of socializing and visiting many places (not least the great beauty of Clayoquot Sound) while observing the Buddhist tradition of tending the graves, and points out that much history can be learned from tombstones. As the decades pass, it is natural to expect that tour participants will be learning about, rather than recalling, Japanese communities on Vancouver Island in the late 19th and early 20th centuries. Formerly described as "forgotten," those historic communities are now said to be "relegated to memory."

Chemainus, British Columbia
Japanese Canadian Memorial monument.

Jewish Cemeteries

The patterns of Jewish settlement in Canada reflect the Jews' long history of exile and the necessity of journeying in strange lands. In New France the immigration of both Jews and Huguenots (French Protestants) was prohibited by a royal edict, and Jews did not officially settle in what is now Canada until 1749 in Halifax. In 1759, the year of the Battle of the Plains of Abraham, the children of Abraham first officially resided in Quebec City. The following year a dozen merchants established themselves as permanent settlers along the St. Lawrence Valley, in Montreal, Quebec and Trois-Rivières. Known today as the Pioneer Jews, they were well-educated businessmen who maintained close religious, social and commercial links to New York and London.

By Jewish tradition, the presence of 10 men is required for a *minyan*, or congregation, for communal prayer and reading the Torah with the benedictions. Smaller numbers may study the Torah, but without the blessings that come with a community sharing in the faith. The first Jewish congregation in Canada, Shearith Israel (Remnant of Israel), built its first synagogue in Montreal in 1777, a year after its first cemetery (near present-day Dominion Square) was consecrated. It has since disappeared, but some of its early grave markers were relocated to the Jewish cemetery on Mount Royal, which includes both the Shearith Israel and the English, German and Polish congregation of the Shaar Hashomayim.

The diaspora of the Jews into lands far from Israel, their spiritual home, began with the Roman destruction of the Temple in Jerusalem in 70 AD. Some still wish to return to the Holy Land to die, or at least to have a bag of its soil placed in their graves in foreign lands.

From their long experience as strangers in strange lands, Jews learned to be prepared to provide a respectful burial place for all members of their community. Bodies were prepared, according to the traditional rituals of purification, by the community's *Chevra Kadisha* (burial society). Membership in this society is held as a high honour. Respect for the dead is expressed in traditional Jewish burial practices and extends to their place of burial. An essential part of that respect is protection of the grave. Although fences or walls surround many non-Jewish cemeteries, locked gates are more characteristic of Jewish sites. Even when their gates are open, casual visiting is not encouraged. A Jewish cemetery is not a place intended for idle contemplation. Friends and family come to the graveside for one purpose, to pay their respects and mark their visit by leaving a small pebble on the gravestone. Groups of pebbles are tokens of numerous remembrances. The modest scale of these tokens echoes the understated arrangement characteristic of Jewish cemeteries. Burial plots are usually of a uniform size, organized closely together in linear rows with fairly narrow paths between the rows. In such a place, it would be vanity to deny the truth that death is the universal leveller. The material circumstances contingent to life become irrelevant here. There are no preferred or reserved sites. Graves are generally arranged according to the date of death, although double plots for married couples may be reserved in all but the most Orthodox cemeteries.

The oldest Jewish cemetery in Canada is now the Beth Israel (House of Israel) Cemetery, established in the 1850s just outside the boundary of Quebec City, in the parish of Sainte-Foy. It was designated a National Historic Site in 1992. The Jewish population in Quebec City today is small, and the rows of graves fill only part of the space within the cemetery's fenced boundaries. This arrangement of the graves suggests that the founders of Beth Israel were aware of the decision made in 1829 by the congregation of the Shearith Israel Cemetery in New York:

that each person should be Buried in the Row as it shall please God in his own good time to call unto Himself for whatever distinction exists in Life, there is none in Death; and to give to the opulent a preference over the pious and religious poor, might tend to cause to them feelings which in no manner could be compensated, and which we should on all occasions avoid.

We pray the Board to take this into their serious Consideration and direct that each person shall be interred regularly in the Row, without any Space being left but next to the last Grave.

In the 19th century, Ashkenazim (Jews from Germany and Central Europe) immigrated to Canada. The oldest Jewish cemetery in Toronto was established in 1849 to the east of the city on Pape Avenue. Seventeen men founded the Toronto Hebrew Congregation (Sons of Israel) in 1856. Later renamed Holy Blossom, it outgrew its first synagogue in the 1890s and in 1937 moved again to Bathurst and Eglinton, then the outer northwest edge of the city. Its relocation meant that the land purchased for the Pape Avenue Cemetery was never filled. The cemetery site, reduced from two acres to half an acre, is enclosed by a high fence. The beautiful wrought-iron gate is locked and "No Trespassing"

signs are posted to discourage vandalism. The Jones Avenue cemetery, not far to the northeast, was consecrated in 1896 on a steeply sloped site that is terraced to hold the rows of graves. On the street side, the graves and *Chevra Kadisha* buildings are protected by a buttressed and whitewashed high wall.

On the west coast, the Fraser River gold rush in 1858 attracted an influx of immigrants including Jewish merchants, traders and provisioners, as well as miners. The number of Jews in the territory rose rapidly in five years from 50 to 242. They had come from Germany, England and Eastern Europe, many by way of California. The construction in 1863 of their Congregation Emanu-el Temple, the oldest surviving synagogue in Canada, followed the first task of building their community. During the early years, while Sabbath services were held in a private home, they established the Victoria Hebrew Benevolent Society, whose first act was to send $185 to aid the Jews of Morocco. In May 1859, the society placed a notice in the *British Colonist*: "THE ISRAELITES of this city are respectfully invited to attend the meeting at Mr. Simpson's Store on Yates street, above Broad st., at 3 o'clock P.M., on Sunday, 22nd inst., for the purpose of procuring a suitable place for a Burying ground."

Roselawn Cemetery, Toronto, Ontario

Soon after its consecration, it received its first burial when Morris Price was shot dead in his store in the gold rush town of Cayoosh. The post of the entrance gate bears the Hebrew phrase "*Bays Ha Chayim*" (House of the Living). Nearby is a memorial to the martyrs of the Holocaust in Europe. The rows of graves fill only part of the cemetery space, reflecting the smaller population following the waning of the Gold Rush. The rest of the enclosed space is a tranquil landscape of trees and lawn with outcroppings of Victoria's bedrock.

In 1892 the Montreal United Hebrew Cemeteries purchased land on Avenue de la Savane, then outside the city limits. Enclosed within its walls are many sections for various burial societies and synagogues. Its name, the Baron de Hirsch Affiliated Cemeteries, honours the memory of the great German financier and philanthropist. Baron Maurice de Hirsch amassed an immense fortune from investments in sugar, copper and the construction of a railway through the Balkans, linking Europe and Constantinople. After his only son died, he dedicated his wealth to the education and welfare of impoverished Ashkenazim. Worsening conditions in Russia made their mass emigration a necessity. Hirsch chose not to support the Zionist project of establishing a Jewish state in Palestine. Intstead, he was convinced that emigration to nations with no history of antisemitism, where Jews might be treated as equal citizens, would lead to a rebirth of Jewry. To facilitate the mass emigration of Jews from Russia to agricultural colonies in North and South America, this "Moses of the New World" funded the Jewish Colonization Association in 1891. His vision was to transform Eastern European Jewish refugees into independent farmers and craftsmen. Hirsch himself had begun by investing an inheritance from his grandfather, who was the first Jew in Bavaria permitted to own agricultural land, and wanted to give Jewish colonists the opportunity to own land in the Americas and to provide an inheritance for their descendants. The land was not a gift, however. Colonists were required to pay for it, and for loans received during their transfer through to their first harvests, with interest.

In the event, most of the colonists' children and grandchildren left the rural settlements for better opportunities in urban centres. Krugerdorf, Ontario, was a farming community supported by the Baron de Hirsch Institute and the Jewish Colonization Association. The subsequent development of northern Ontario's mining industries brought more immigrants to the region and attracted many of the settlers to new towns, including Kirkland Lake, where the community prospered for many years. In the 1930s there were 125 Jewish families, but as the region's economy declined following the Second World War, most of them moved away. For the rededication service a few years ago of the Krugerdorf Hebrew Cemetery, founded near Engelhart in 1909, a *minyan* could be formed only by gathering former residents of the area.

Between 1886 and 1906, six Jewish farming communities were established in the District of Assiniboia, Northwest Territories (now Saskatchewan). Today, the village of Hirsch, near Estevan, is a small remnant of a Baron de Hirsch agricultural colony (1892–1942).

The Hirsch Community Jewish Cemetery contains more than 100 graves, of which 50 have markers. Many individual stories remain untold in this place, for some grave markers observe the not-uncommon Jewish tradition of recording only a name and the date of death. Some were inscribed only in Hebrew, with only the first name of the person interred, the first name of his father and the year of death according to the Hebrew calendar. Many other graves from the drought years of the 1930s had temporary markers that have since disappeared. The original cemetery records have also been lost. In 1976 almost 200 descendants, neighbours and friends of the former community came from distant cities – Montreal, Toronto, Sault Ste. Marie, Winnipeg, Vancouver, San Francisco and Los Angeles. They witnessed the cemetery's reconsecration and designation as an historic site and afterwards attended a reception hosted by the last Jewish couple remaining in Estevan. A commemorative plaque honours "Jewish immigrants who mostly came from Czarist Russia, Romania, Austria and Poland ... motivated by a keen desire to escape religious persecution and racial discrimination, with the rights to own and farm their land and freely adhere to their orthodox faith."

Exploring Canada's

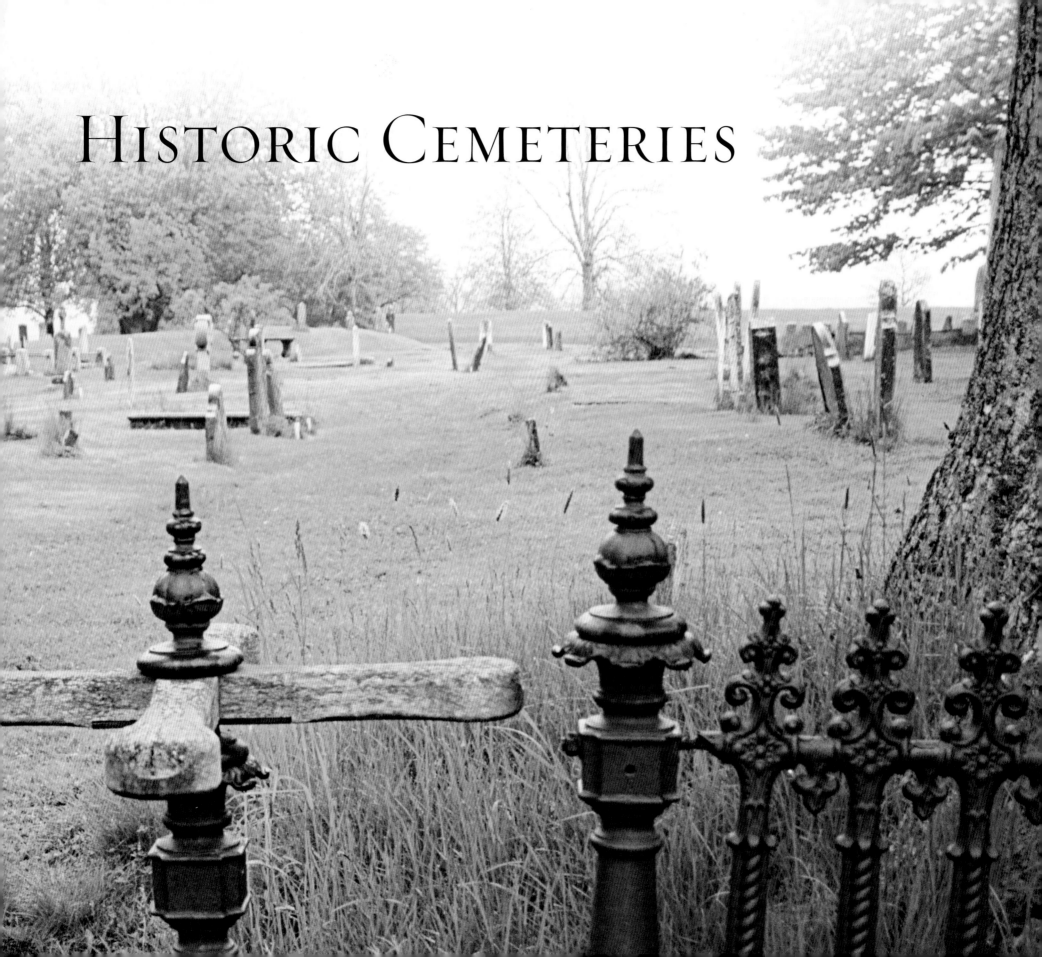

HISTORIC CEMETERIES

Exploring Canada's Historic Cemeteries

National Landmarks

Each of the dozen cemeteries presented here has its own distinct character, but all merit national historic landmark status. Five have been designated National Historic Sites of Canada: The Old Burying Ground in Halifax, Mount Royal and Notre-Dame-des-Neiges in Montreal, Beechwood in Ottawa and Mount Pleasant in Toronto. The others, and many more across the country, deserve such commemoration. Perhaps Canada will follow precedents set by the American National Register of Historic Places, which includes more than 900 cemeteries and burial grounds, and England's national Register of Parks and Gardens, where the number of cemeteries of national importance grew from only 14 in 1988 to 110 in 2003.

All eight cities associated with the cemeteries introduced in the following pages have been centres of national importance. Casual tourists or avid historians will seek out the last resting places of national political leaders and statesmen (Sir Wilfrid Laurier in Notre-Dame in Ottawa, Sir John A. Macdonald in Cataraqui in Kingston, Tommy Douglas in Beechwood, William Lyon Mackenzie King in Mount Pleasant). Other burial sites also have their pilgrims: celebrities in the arts and hockey (Émile Nelligan, Jean-Paul Riopelle and Maurice Richard in Notre-Dame-des-Neiges, William Notman, Howie Morenz and Toe Blake in Mount Royal, Yousuf Karsh in Notre-Dame, Archibald Lampman and Punch Broadbent in Beechwood, Foster Hewitt in Mount Pleasant, Emily Carr in Ross Bay), famous corporate family names (Eaton, Birks, Massey, Molson), great Canadian explorers and inventors, and more – many more.

Anyone setting out to explore these cemeteries may visit their offices or websites to obtain maps showing locations of the more famous grave sites, and information about guided tours. The number of fascinating places to explore in them cannot be exaggerated. Even with maps in hand, visitors will detour from suggested routes, being drawn by glimpses of monuments and vistas "just over there." None of these cemeteries can be adequately explored in one day. The ever-varying beauties of their nature as parks and gardens are revealed only in repeated visits during the changing seasons – "October with the rain of ruined leaves," deep winter's drifts of pristine snow, and the blossoms and greening of the reviving year.

FACING PAGE: *Notre Dame Cemetery, Ottawa, Ontario*
Trees planted to create an *allée*.

PAGE 98–99: *Old Military Cemetery at Fort Anne, Annapolis Royal, Nova Scotia*

The Old Burying Ground, Halifax

Halifax, from its founding in 1749, was a cosmopolitan town whose residents had lived in many other parts of the world. The Old Burying Ground contains some 1,200 grave markers, believed to represent approximately one-tenth of the actual graves. Most of them display the town's historic importance as a seaport and military garrison. Many were erected by colleagues and associates or by the Masonic fraternity, not by bereaved parents or spouses. One relatively unadorned tablet supplies a brief eulogy to a young naval volunteer who died at sea, followed by a roll-call of his fellows who also died on board.

SACRED
TO
the Memory of
MR WM B DECOURCY
*VOLr 1st Class who died on
the 2nd July 1842 at sea
of yellow fever aged 17 years.
This Stone is Erected
as a tribute of Respect and in
testimony of his worth and high
qualities by the Officers
of Her Majesty's Ship Volage.*
— ALSO OF—
*Wm Howlett R.M.
Saml Marvin, A.B.
Wm Baillie, Boy.
Robt Webb, Boy.
Saml Brummage, C. Mate.
Saml Gribbon, Ordy.
John Barnes, Capt Sted.*

*Robt Stimpson, R.M.
Benj Bennett, Ordy.
Wm Stone, Ordy.
All of the same Ship.
The Lord gave and the Lord hath taken away.
Blessed be the name of the Lord.*

Substantial altar tombs, low tablestones and recumbent slabs commemorate majors, lieutenant colonels and other officers. The large horizontal slabs of stone protect the grave and also provide a surface for lengthy inscriptions. One of the most notable tombs is that of British Major General Sir Robert Ross. He led the army whose burning of Washington – in retaliation for the Americans' burning of York (now Toronto) – was the cause of the repainting of the presidential mansion, thereafter named the White House. Ross was mortally wounded in the subsequent attack on Baltimore. His epitaph proclaims "the defeat and Rout" of the Americans, but the battle was also observed from a different point of view – Francis Scott Key saw that "the flag was still there" and was inspired to write "The Star-Spangled Banner." The major general's epitaph celebrates a record of distinction in his military career.

HERE
*On the 29th of September 1814
Was committed to the Earth*
THE BODY
OF
MAJOR GENERAL ROBERT ROSS
WHO
After having distinguished himself in all ranks as an officer

FACING PAGE: Tablestones, recumbent slabs and headstones in the dappled shade of the Old Burying Ground. St. Matthew's United Church stands in the background.

IN
EGYPT, ITALY, PORTUGAL,
SPAIN, FRANCE & AMERICA
WAS KILLED
At the commencement of an Action
Which terminated in the defeat and Rout
OF
THE TROOPS OF THE UNITED STATES
NEAR BALTIMORE
On the 12th of September
1814

A single monument in this colonial outpost was not sufficiently worthy of Major General Ross:

At ROSSTREVOR
The seat of his Family in Ireland
A MONUMENT
More Worthy of his Memory has been erected
BY
The Noblemen and Gentlemen of his Country
And
The officers of a gallant army
WHICH
Under his Conduct
Attacked and dispersed the Americans
AT BLADENSBURG
And the same day victoriously entered
The Capitol of the United States

He was important enough to be memorialized in St. Paul's Cathedral, London, also:

IN
ST. PAUL'S CATHEDRAL
A MONUMENT
Has also been Erected to His Memory
By
His Country

St. Paul's in Halifax became a cathedral in 1787 with the arrival of Charles Inglis as the first Anglican bishop of Nova Scotia, and the first bishop in the British colonies. (Before the American Revolution, the Anglican churches of Boston, Halifax and Lunenburg had been part of the London diocese in England.) St. Paul's in Halifax kept up the English practice of memorials in the church, and is said to have more memorial tablets on its walls than any other church building in North America. The wording of the tablet for Bishop Inglis, who died in 1816, celebrates his accomplishments in life. In some respects it bears comparison to the Major General's monument.

Sacred to The Memory of
THE RIGHT REV. AND HONBLE. CHARLES INGLIS, D.D.
(Third Son of The Rev. Archibald Inglis, of Glen and Kilcar, in Ireland)
Bishop of Nova Scotia and Its Dependencies;
Whose Sound Learning and Fervent Piety
Directed by Zeal According To Knowledge
And Supported by Fortitude, Unshaken
Amidst Peculiar Trials
Eminently Qualified Him For The Arduous Labours Of
The First Bishop
Appointed To A British Colony.
This Stone Is Raised By Filial Duty and Affection
In Grateful Remembrance of Every Private Virtue
That Could Endear a Father and a Friend.

Of The Ability, Fidelity and Success, with Which
He was Enabled By The Divine Blessing, To
Discharge All His Public Duties
The General Prosperity Of The Church In His Diocese
The Increase of His Clergy, And of The
Provision For Their Support,
The Establishment of a Chartered College
And The Erection of more Than Twenty new
Churches are The Best Monument.
Obiit annu salutis MDCCCXVI, ætatis lxxxi.

THIS PAGE: One of the most impressive monuments in the Old Burying Ground, Halifax is also the most mysterious, since no identifying inscription survives. It is a large elevated sarcophagus, looking much like an antique from somewhere in the Roman Empire – perhaps Arles or Turkey or Tunisia. It is rather plain, with the bearded heads of river gods as acroteria at the corners of its roof, elegant urns, or amphorae, carved in shallow relief on the lower support, and garlands in deeper relief on its sides. Where on earth did it come from, and how did it come to rest in Halifax?

In keeping with Anglican tradition, the bishop's grave lies beneath the floor of the church. Anyone curious to learn more about his "Zeal," "Fervent Piety," "Sound Learning," Unshaken Fortitude and "Arduous Labours," or seeking to supplement the monumental summary commissioned by his grateful son (who was left a wealthy heir), will find that there have been two opinions about him. One corresponds to his epitaph. According to the *Dictionary of Canadian Biography*, his "character and career have been distorted by hagiography":

Much of the historical praise is based on his distinction as the first colonial bishop of the Church of England, a landmark, admittedly, but hardly an adequate ground on which to assess his reputation. The other enthusiasms of Inglis's posthumous partisans have been more fundamentally misleading ...

In picturing him as an energetic, hard-working administrator, Inglis's champions have missed the underlying personal objective of his episcopate: a tranquil, comfortable retirement to compensate for his steadfast loyalty. By the same token they have misinterpreted his approach to official duties. Far from displaying the energy and zeal with which he has been credited, he studied to be quiet, to maintain a discreet presence, and to confine himself as much as possible to the less controversial concerns of his denomination.

Faint praise indeed, when set against a reputation fostered, at least in part, by words engraved in stone.

The Old Burying Ground is rightly viewed as an outdoor sculpture gallery, since it includes a large number of grave markers of outstanding artistic merit. Among its greatest treasures is the tomb erected in memory of Mary, the first wife of Richard Bulkeley, and their son Freke. Richard Bulkeley, a wealthy and educated man of cultivated tastes, was a British army officer who, from the time he arrived in 1749 as aide-de-camp to Governor Cornwallis until his death in 1800, held numerous senior government positions. He commissioned the monument from the Halifax workshop of James Hay. In 1776, the year after Mary Bulkeley's

death, Hay had placed an advertisement in the *Nova Scotia Gazette and Weekly Chronicle*:

James Hay, Stone Cutter and Carver
lately from Scotland:
Begs leave to acquaint the Public, that he cutts and
carves all Kinds of Stone Work; such as Tomb and
Head Stones, Chimney and Hearth Stones in the neatest maner

— Any Gentlemen in Town or Country favouring him
with their Commands will be duly acknowledged
and punctually attended to by Gentlemen Your
Most Obedient Servant,
JAMES HAY.

A native of Scotland, Hay would have been acquainted with the tableau of Adam and Eve as a not uncommon theme in Scottish grave art. In all North America, there are only three known gravestones representing what might be called the primal scene at the centre of Christian teaching about the death and resurrection of the body. One of the other stones was also found in Halifax, across the road from the Old Burying Ground, set flat into an asphalted parking surface. Much of the stone's sculptural detail was obliterated before it was removed to the safekeeping of the Nova Scotia Museum. Fortunately, the relief sculptures of the Bulkeley monument are still remarkably well preserved.

Its two end panels perfectly illustrate the oppositions set up in the argument of the Apostle Paul's First Epistle to the Corinthians: "For as in Adam all die, even so in Christ shall all be made alive" (see I Corinthians: 15). "The first man [Adam] is of the earth, earthy," according to Paul; "the second man [Christ] is the Lord from Heaven." Even in the natural world, he observes, "There are also celestial bodies, and bodies terrestrial." Paul's reference to the Fall (in the book of Genesis) is illustrated on the head panel of the Bulkeley tomb. Adam and Eve, the first man and woman, are tempted by the "subtil" serpent twining around the tree trunk and then eat the fruit, after specifically recalling that

FACING PAGE: Two end panels of the Bulkeley Monument: the Temptation of Adam and Eve by the Serpent in the Garden of Eden, and the Resurrection.

it is forbidden: "God hath said, Ye shall not eat of it, neither shall ye touch it, lest ye die" (Genesis 3: 1, 3). The fatal consequence, as recalled in the Anglican service for the burial of the dead, is that the first man and all his descendants must earn their bread in toil and sorrow: "till thou return unto the ground; for out of it wast thou taken; for dust thou art, and unto dust shalt thou return."

In his letter to the Corinthians, Paul develops his argument in the form of a dialogue. He imagines someone posing the question, "How are the dead raised up?" In reply, he strenuously works a metaphor familiar to all those who have earned their bread by sowing "bare grain" – "that which thou sowest is not quickened, except it die ... So also is the resurrection of the dead. It is sown in corruption; it is raised in incorruption ... it is sown in weakness; it is raised in power: It is sown a natural body; it is raised a spiritual body."

The opposite panel of the Bulkeley tomb illustrates Paul's dramatic image of victory over death and resurrection of the body: "Behold, I shew you a mystery; We shall not all sleep, but we shall be changed, In a moment, in the twinkling of an eye, at the last trump; for the trumpet shall sound, and the dead shall be raised incorruptible, and we shall be changed." We see the trumpet being sounded by a winged messenger, an angel; the natural body, sown in corruption in the grave and reduced to a supine skeleton; and the spiritual body being raised, its face showing no trace of sorrow, and its head crowned by a celestial glory.

In the 18th century, Paul's verbal image of "the manner of the resurrection" was known to Christians as part of the Anglican service for the burial of the dead. The familiar text was given a new and gloriously memorable musical form in 1741, in the libretto for Handel's *Messiah*. Any viewer of the Bulkeley monument who knows part three of that oratorio (following the "Halleluiah Chorus") can hardly help recalling Handel's airs and recitatives while contemplating these remarkable sculptures. Richard Bulkeley indeed may well have known Handel's music. He was an amateur organist who, through 50 years as a civil servant, also found time to promote music in the Charitable Irish Society and in the

church of which he was a founding member, namely St. Paul's. He even volunteered for a period as the church organist and choir master. *Messiah* had premiered in 1742 at a charity concert in Bulkeley's native Dublin, just seven years before he came to Halifax.

The resurrection trumpet sounds again on a monument for the Lawson children, on which the sculpted relief is splendid in its heraldic symmetry. The feet, arms, drapery and wings of the angelic messengers are designed to fit perfectly into the lunette of the tympanum, while centring our view upon the crown of glory awaiting a resurrected spiritual body. Above their heads, the flourish of trumpets is echoed visually by palm fronds, traditional symbols of victory since at least the time of the Roman Empire. (The Greek goddess Nike and her Roman derivation, Victoria, both carry palms of victory.) In this celebration of victory over death, the angels are not merely making a wake-up call, but welcoming new arrivals to celestial life.

The verse epitaph mixes the religious imagery of mansions reserved (or allotted) in heaven with the martial imagery of guards on patrol, watching a garrison: "Angels Watch around their Tombs / Pleased they Patrole nor Sleep nor Faint," until the Reveille call of the Resurrection "Relieves their Guards and bids them Rise."

The Lawson family was not a military one. The children's father was a merchant and politician, a member of the House of Assembly from 1806 to 1836. Their grandfather, Daniel Shatford, was a schoolmaster who had advertised on 5 January 1754 in the *Halifax Gazette* the opening of his school:

On the Parade, opposite the Church, on Monday the seventh, a school will be opened where will be taught, Writing, Arithmatick, Merchant's Accompts after the true Italian Method, Geometry, Trigonometry plain and spherical, Navigation and other branches of the Mathematicks; also the Latin tongue. By Daniel Shatford.

In 1769 John Lawson married Sarah Shatford, who bore him 14 children. It is likely that the schoolmaster composed

the verse epitaph for six of his grandchildren, which appears on their gravestone beneath a stark record of their names and their short lifespans, far too short to experience what learning might be offered in almost any school of life.

Here lies Interr'd the Bodies of the Children
of JOHN & SARAH LAWSON

	Aged		
	Year	M⁰	Dˢ

Aged

	Year	M⁰	Dˢ
JOHN SHATFORD LAWSON			
Ob 8 Sep 1772	1		8
JOHN LAWSON JUN			
Ob 8 Dec 1776	1		7
SARAH LOVE LAWSON			
Ob 27 Sep 1778	1		5
THOMAS RICHARD LAWSON			
Ob 30 March 1779			14
ROBERT LAWSON			
Ob 3 Feb^Y 1783			8
ELIZABETH SARAH LAWSON			
Ob 12th Jan^Y 1784	3		3

The Lord gave and the Lord hath taken away, and
Blessed be the name of the Lord.
What once had Virtue Grace and Wit
Lies mouldring now beneath our Feet.
Poor mansions for such lovely Guests
Yet here they sweetly take their Rest.
Cold is their Beds and dark their Rooms
Yet Angels Watch around their Tombs
Pleased they Patrole nor Sleep nor Faint
They only Watch their fellow Saints
Till the lottd mansions of the Skies
Relieves their Guards and bids them Rise.

FACING PAGE: Angels sounding the Reveille call of the Resurrection.

Here lies interr'd the Bodies of the Children
of JOHN & SARAH LAWSON

Aged
Year M^o D^s
JOHN SHATFORD LAWSON Ob^t 8th Sep^t 1772. 1. 8
JOHN LAWSON Junr Ob^t 8th Decr 1776. 1 7
SARAH LOVE LAWSON Ob^t 27th Sep^t 1778. 1 5
THOMAS RICHARD LAWSON Ob^t 30th March 1779. 14
ROBERT LAWSON Ob^t 3^d Feby 1783. 8
ELIZABETH SARAH LAWSON Ob^t 12th Jany 1784. 3 3

Mount Hermon and St. Patrick's Cemeteries, Sillery, Quebec

Mount Hermon Cemetery in Sillery near Quebec City, founded in 1848, was one of the first in Canada fully to adopt the design principles of the American Rural Cemetery Movement. Its name is shared with many Mount Hermon cemeteries throughout the United States. Their namesake, the highest mountain in the Holy Land, has from ancient times been a sacred place. The Hebrew name means "separate," "belonging to a sanctuary." On its slopes are remains of temples from many eras, and archaeologists have found 4,000-year-old funerary monuments there. The Psalmist links Hermon with the promise of everlasting life: "Behold, how good and how pleasant it is for brethren to dwell together in unity! ... As the dew of Hermon, and as the dew that descendeth upon the mountains of Zion: for there the Lord commanded the blessing, even life for evermore" (Psalms 133: 1, 3).

The symbolic appeal of the original Mount Hermon may be enhanced by the fact that melted snow from its dome-shaped summit is the source of the Jordan River, whose waters descend rapidly through its foothills, then run deeper than the level of the Mediterranean and empty into the Dead Sea. Passing through the Jordan's deep and chilly waters has long been a proverbial metaphor for dying, but the river is also linked with John the Baptist and a birth into new life. The motif is common in African-American spiritual songs – the Jordan's water "chills the body but not the soul." In John Bunyan's *Pilgrim's Progress*, Christian and Hopeful pass with difficulty through the deep waters and then mount the mighty hill with ease, scarcely noticing that "they had left their mortal garments behind them in the River." Mount Hermon's somewhat tenuous and indefinite scriptural associations may have contributed to its popularity as a name

for rural cemeteries, which, unlike churchyards, were not identified with any particular religious faith.

Sillery's Mount Hermon was designed by Major David Bates Douglass, an American military engineer who had won distinction in the Battle of Lundy's Lane in 1814. His more relevant experience included the landscape layout of Green-Wood Cemetery in Brooklyn, then a village near New York. His plan for Mount Hermon shows the typical layout of varied topography designed to offer sequences of picturesque views. A winding road leads down between mature trees to where the horizon opens up to the river view. At the entrance, placed so that it partly conceals the cemetery grounds, is a picturesque gate-lodge. Its style is American Carpenter Gothic, with prominent decorative elements picked out in paint trim in strong contrast with its wood siding. The bargeboards on steep gables and emphatic "labels" (flat hood mouldings above the windows) are likely those of the entrance lodge of the Cataraqui Cemetery, Kingston, built in 1853.

The Mount Hermon gate-lodge was designed by Edward Staveley, an English architect and surveyor who had practised in Baltimore before coming to Quebec. His architectural practice in Quebec and suburban Sillery thrived in a period of prosperity based on the expanding lumber and shipbuilding industry. Sillery's coves and bays on the St. Lawrence River were used for unloading, squaring off, warehousing and exporting timber. Not unlike Major Douglass' Green-Wood Cemetery in Brooklyn, which had a panoramic view of the harbour of New York City, Mount Hermon's riverside setting overlooked a busy scene of commerce. The rural quietude and serenity of these cemeteries were emphasized by their contrast to the power and flux of the mercantile world.

Mount Hermon's substantial monuments include celebrations of wordly success. For example, John Strang's elaborate monument supporting a sculpture of a female mourning figure was erected, not by his grieving widow, but by his business partners. This inscription fills one side of the pedestal:

TO
PERPETUATE THE REMEMBRANCE
OF HIS MANY AMIABLE QUALITIES
AND
TO TESTIFY THEIR DEEP REGRET
FOR THE LOSS OF A PARTNER
MOST DESERVEDLY ESTEEMED,
THIS PILLAR
CONSECRATED TO THE MEMORY OF
JOHN STRANG ESQUIRE
HAS BEEN ERECTED BY
HUGH ROBERTSON JOSEPH MASSON
AND CHARLES LANGEVIN
THE SURVIVING PARTNERS
OF THE COMMERCIAL FIRM OF
MASSON
STRANG LANGEVIN AND COMPANY
OF THIS CITY.

Strang had managed the Quebec company of the very successful import/export business built up in Montreal, Quebec and Glasgow by Joseph Masson, who had entered the business world as an apprentice clerk with a contract stipulating that he had to serve his employer for two years in return for board, lodging, light, heat and laundry, and £18 to be paid at the end of each year. Starting out in 1807 with no capital, by the 1840s Masson had increased his assets to about £200,000. Erecting a monument to Strang was not only a testimonial to a trusted partner, but also a business decision, a public tribute to the Masson commercial enterprises. As he wrote to his surviving partner, Hugh Robertson, in 1853, "You ought to have known that all my ambition and feelings [were] for the interest and honor of

my *Firms,* as I have all along determined to beat every house around me and bring *them down* which is all in the way of trade, and in which I have not failed yet." Masson's success was the product of unremitting effort and the grasping of every opportunity for commercial promotion, even in an idyllic cemetery.

Neighbours of Mount Hermon Cemetery were Spencer Wood (renamed Bois-de-Coulonge in 1947), which in 1852 became the residence of Lord Elgin, Governor General of the United Provinces of Canada, and other villas surrounded by landscaped parks, such as Villa Bagatelle and Staveley's Domaine Cataraqui. St. Patrick's Cemetery is located nearby, also on the shore of the St. Lawrence River. St. Patrick's Church was established in 1832 for Irish Catholics, who then formed about one-fifth of the population of Quebec City. In 1874 the Redemptorist Fathers, who were active with Irish and German immigrant communities in America, assumed the ministry of St. Patrick's, and land in Sillery was purchased for a new cemetery five years later. The name of its designer is unknown. Like Mount Hermon, St. Patrick's is modest in size, less than 50 acres. Both have views over the river, and both have their entrances on the south side of Chemin Saint-Louis, between Villa Bagatelle and Domaine Cataraqui.

The landscape layout of St. Patrick's, established 30 years after Mount Hermon, does not entirely follow the Rural pattern. Some roads curve, others are rectilinear, and in one section they form a cross. Its plan was influenced by Catholic doctrine, like that of Notre-Dame-des-Neiges on Mount Royal. But the Montreal cemetery, the largest in Canada, is located at a centre of power. St. Patrick's evokes an impression of a truly rural scene. Inside its entrance gates, a road leads through a woodland area before arriving at the graves. Trees planted alongside the road create an effect quite different from the rather stately procession of the *allées* in Notre-Dame-des-Neiges.

The approach in St. Patrick's is a quiet countryside lane, marking a zone of separation between the burials and the suburban streetscape beyond the cemetery's gates. After a

FACING PAGE, TOP: *Mount Hermon Cemetery, Sillery, Quebec* View of the St. Lawrence River.

FACING PAGE, BOTTOM: *St. Patrick's Cemetery, Sillery, Quebec*

fire destroyed much of the *faubourg* Saint Louis in 1876, the provincial parliament building was located on its present site, and the city's Grande Allée was transformed into a grand boulevard for official processions between Parliament and Spencer Wood. It was developed by Lord Dufferin, the Governor General, who worked with Charles Baillairgé, a Quebec-born architect, engineer and surveyor from the fourth generation of a distinguished family of artists and architects. (Baillairgé had also designed two very beautiful cemeteries, Saint-Charles, Quebec, in 1855 and Notre-Dame-de-Belmont, Sainte-Foi, in 1859.) Lord Dufferin also commissioned the Irish Protestant architect W. H. Lynn to design the new Porte Saint-Louis, which introduced the grandeur of the Chateau Style to Quebec City.

Inspired by the example of Edinburgh's New Town, Baillairgé made the Grande Allée, originally a mere country road leading to the Porte Saint Louis, into one of the city's main arteries. Now a busy thoroughfare, it claims to be the Champs Élysées of Quebec City. Like the famed Parisian avenue, it was originally lined with opulent residences, since replaced by an abundance of elegant restaurants, cafés, boutiques and offices. In both Paris and Quebec, the avenues obviously celebrate wordly success.

St. Patrick's Cemetery is more reminiscent of the classical ideal of the Elysian Fields, the happy or delightful abode assigned to the blessed after death. Its quiet burial places leave behind the parade of pomp and circumstance that busies the modern Grande Allée, the former country road. Outside the St. Patrick's entrance gates, even the part of the Chemin Saint Louis that has retained its old name has not kept its ancient character. The road inside is a reminder of bygone times. The celebration of worldly goals and aspirations is replaced by a different kind of return journey in this cemetery, named appropriately after the 5th-century saint whose earthly life was notable for so many journeys and return journeys.

Mount Royal and Notre-Dame-des-Neiges Cemeteries, Montreal

Ever since 1535, when Jacques Cartier named it "*un mont réal*," the Mountain has played a dominant role in the historical imagination of the residents of Montreal. The Sieur de Maisonneuve erected the first cross at its summit in 1643, thereby inaugurating its function as a place of monuments. For more than 150 years it has provided the site for two of the finest cemeteries in Canada, Mount Royal and Notre-Dame-des-Neiges. Both were designated National Historic Sites in 1998. Divided by a common fence, the cemeteries may be said to have formed two solitudes, one Catholic and predominantly francophone, the other non-denominational and predominantly anglophone. The two founding cultures of Montreal find expression in the origins and historical development of their literatures, their music, their art and their cemeteries. Mount Royal Cemetery is oriented toward American examples of the landscape management of wilderness. Notre-Dame-des-Neiges originally claimed Père Lachaise Cemetery in Paris as its exemplar and is a witness for a martyrology of nationhood.

The "highest point in the island of Montreal" was purchased in 1874 by Mount Royal Cemetery Board, with the expectation that in the future it would "in all probability, be one day deemed a fitting site on which to erect a memorial to the fame of some Canadian worthy, or as a record of some event in the history of our city or Dominion." It would be "a conspicuous beacon for many miles around." These words express the board's confidence that the most fitting location for a monument of ultimate historical greatness, not only in Montreal but for the entire Dominion of Canada, must be the peak of Mount Royal Cemetery. Indeed, at its lower elevations, one sees countless memorials for worthy men and women whose lives influenced events essential to the build-

ing or shaping of our nation. The people featured in guided historical walking tours in the cemetery include a good many knights, such as Sir Hugh Allan, Sir Mortimer Davis, Sir William Dawson, Sir Alexander Galt and Sir George Simpson, and also commoners of no common worth, such as Ernest (Chinese) Wilson, David Thompson, John Redpath, William Notman, Howie Morenz and the Molson family. But such tours name only a few of the great, the good, and the merely famous, interred there. Likewise, the Notre-Dame-des-Neiges Cemetery pamphlet *150 Ans d'histoire!* locates the burial places of 390 historical, famous and notorious personalities, including Sir George-Étienne Cartier, Clarence Gagnon, Gratien Gélinas, Sir Louis-Hippolyte La Fontaine, Thomas D'Arcy McGee, Lord Thomas George Shaughnessy and Maurice (the Rocket) Richard. Both founding cultures of Montreal have contributed extraordinary vitality to Canadian life. Even a non-resident must acknowledge that Montrealers have ample grounds to believe that their mountain must be the centre point for a great Canadian project of commemoration.

As for the famous peak, a picturesque path winding to the summit was created to provide a panoramic view of the entire surrounding country, a prospect that had no limits, or more precisely was "bounded only by the horizon." It was named Mount Murray in honour of the Cemetery Board's previous president. Following its controversial clear-cutting in 1979, the peak was renamed "Mountain View." The change of name of the peak was neither the first nor the last time that the memorial function of a natural or man-made feature had been lost or altered. In 1958 the Camillien Houde Parkway, following the former tramway line across the mountain, signalled the primacy of the automobile, as

FACING PAGE: *Mount Royal Cemetery, Montreal, Quebec*

PAGE 116: *Notre-Dame-des-Neiges Cemetery, Montreal, Quebec* Firefighters' monument.

PAGE 117: *Notre-Dame-des-Neiges Cemetery, Montreal, Quebec*

well as honouring the memory of the former mayor, who died that year. However, the parkway cannot yet be claimed as a more permanent memorial than Houde's tomb in Notre-Dame-des-Neiges Cemetery.

The mountain's division into two great cemeteries has added a certain element of rivalry to their development. Although they did not compete commercially, they strove jealously to guard the honour of their own Montrealers. Their endeavours may be seen in the two Firefighters' Monuments, each aspiring to be the grandest in its cemetery. The "Monument aux Pompiers catholiques" in Notre-Dame-des-Neiges was sculpted by Robert Reid, of Scottish origin, who had taken over his uncle's Montreal Sculpture and General Marble and Granite Works.

Both monuments are tall Corinthian columns that support a magnificent marble statue of a fireman in uniform. A long fire hose spirals down the column to the base, which is decorated with relief sculptures of hatchets and other fire-fighting tools arranged like trophies around the emblem of an inverted torch. Between these panels are memorial plaques naming firefighters who died from injuries received in the line of duty. In 1902 *La Presse* illustrated commemorative services on the same day at both locations. The duplication of these monuments reflected the simple truth that fire impartially ravaged the properties of Catholic and Protestant Montrealers, and that firefighters did not discriminate among the faiths of the victims.

The two cemeteries' sites for First World War soldiers who died of injuries in England are another sign of connection between the two great Montreal cemeteries. In 1921 the Imperial War Graves Commission, which had established a standard form for headstones and sites, purchased adjoining plots in both cemeteries and insisted on an open passage between the two. For years, the trustees had refused to open a gate in the "Catholic fence," but the opening was accomplished for this cause, and the remains of men previously buried in Last Post Fund plots in Mount Royal were relocated to the new official site. Sir Reginald Blomfield's Cross of Sacrifice, installed on the border in 1922, is

inscribed bilingually – on the Mount Royal side, "to the memory of those who died for King and country in the great war 1914–1918," and on the Notre-Dame-des-Neiges side, "à la mémoire des soldats morts pour la patrie dans la grande guerre 1914–1918," with no mention of any British monarch.

Preceding the founding of Mount Royal Cemetery there was a multiplicity of European burial places on the island of Montreal – 15 for the Parish of Notre-Dame-de-Montréal, nine for other Catholic parishes, 11 places reserved for Jesuits, Recollet friars and other religious members of convents, three for Indian converts at Sulpician missions, two military burial grounds, one Jewish, and five Protestant. As a major port, Montreal escaped neither the cholera epidemic of 1832 nor the devastation of typhus in 1847, and as population grew, the capacity of the old burial places was exceeded. In 1851 it was announced that burial within the city must cease, and two years later the final date of 1 May, 1854, was set.

For a brief time it had seemed that a combined rural cemetery might be established, with separate sections for various faiths. However, a joint meeting in 1846 between the trustees of the Protestant Burial Ground and representatives of the Jewish community and the Catholic parish church of Notre Dame did not result in an ecumenical joint venture. The founders of the chartered non-profit Montreal Cemetery Company in 1847 included 15 prominent members of the Protestant elite and one Jew. However, in 1854 the Congregation of Spanish and Portuguese Jews, Shearith Israel, purchased separate land adjacent to the entrance of Mount Royal Cemetery, and the German and Polish Jews, or Askenazim, belonging to the Congregation Shaer Hashomayim later bought land next to that.

By 1851 the new company had raised a sufficient number of subscriptions, had named Judge Samuel McCord as president, and sought to purchase a site. Their choice was part of an estate owned by McGill University professor Michael McCullough, on the north-east side of the mountain. The trustees described "Spring Grove" as:

a tract of land admirably adapted for their purpose; possessing sufficient depth of soil, rivulets and springs to make ponds and lakes, well wooded, and with an undulating surface and beautiful situation, – retired from the bustle and heat of the City, and yet near and convenient of access. A spot capable of being made one of the most beautiful and finest Cemeteries in America.

In fact the site was too heavily forested and too steeply sloped, with problematic spring run-offs in its watercourses and rather too rocky terrain. It presented picturesque capabilities, but also challenging requirements for taming its wilderness.

Wishing to emulate the finest American Rural Cemeteries, the trustees first wrote to Andrew Jackson Downing to ask his assistance in planning landscaping improvements, but got no response before he died tragically young in July 1852, during a steamboat fire and explosion on the Hudson River. The following year, Frederick Law Olmsted joined with Downing's partner, Calvert Vaux, to enter the design competition for Central Park in New York, to honour the memory of Olmsted's mentor, Downing, who had been among the first to propose the Central Park development. The partnership of Olmsted, Vaux and Company created hundreds of outstanding landscape architecture projects in America, including their design for Mount Royal Park, which opened to the public in 1876.

In his recent biography of Olmsted, Witold Rybczynski recalls that he "took the landscape of the Mountain for granted" when he was a student: "I thought that it was simply a nature preserve. Here was the most significant man-made object in Montreal – arguably the city's most important cultural artifact – and I thought of it as 'natural.' How wrong I was." Rybczynski alerts his readers to the artifice behind the Park's seemingly natural landscape. Comparable in their artificial construction of natural effects are the landscapes of the mountain's cemeteries, begun 20 years earlier and still works-in-progress today. It might be more comprehensively argued that the Mount Royal and Notre-Dame-des-Neiges cemeteries are, conjointly, the city's most important cultural artifact.

Not having a response from Downing, the Mount Royal Cemetery trustees consulted the superintendent of Philadelphia's Laurel Hill Cemetery (designed in 1836 by Downing's friend and colleague John Notman) and hired James Sidney in partnership with James Neff, of Philadelphia. The Sidney and Neff plan of 1852 shows roads curving naturally around topographic elevations in the usual Rural Cemetery style and with the usual rural names. Forest Drive circles sinuously around the perimeter, and irregular sections are shaped by avenues named after trees – Linden, Birch, Oak, Hawthorn, Hemlock, Chestnut, Myrtle and Larch. In the next 20 years several additional parcels of land were purchased. They were required for protecting and enhancing the site's picturesque character. It was considered "prudent," for instance, to acquire some "high ground covered with wood" which had "a fine appearance from the Cemetery," not because land was needed for more burial plots, but because "it was apprehended that it might be acquired by parties who might cut down the trees and erect unseemly buildings, thereby injuring the picturesque view from the Cemetery."

The ongoing work of physically transforming the topography of Mount Royal Cemetery was taken up by two families. Richard Sprigings was Gardener and Superintendent of the Grounds from 1852 until his death in 1890. His brothers William and Edward and two of his sons also worked there. His successor, Frank Roy, was the first of four generations of Roys to be employed in the cemetery. His son Ormiston, hired in his teens as a clerk in 1890, took up the superintendent's duties during his father's last illness and then succeeded him in 1898. He cemented the family connection by marrying Richard Sprigings' daughter Charlotte. Ormiston Roy wrote that New York's Central Park was for him a model landscape. Its open spaces, "a perfect imitation of country and nature ... would make an ideal cemetery." In fact, in preparing their design for Central Park, Olmsted and Vaux had been influenced by Laurel Hill Cemetery, which had also directly influenced Sydney and Neff's plan for Mount Royal. But Roy was ready to bring a more modern vision of American landscape architecture to Mount Royal.

In 1899 he attended a meeting of the Association of American Cemetery Superintendents and met Ossian Cole Simonds, the superintendent of Chicago's Graceland Cemetery and the progenitor of the "Prairie Style" of landscape gardening, based on ecological restoration, environmentally sustainable design and the use of native plants. Under the influence of Simonds, Roy recommended the replacement of the "cold, bare effects produced by too much stonework" with natural beauty in the form of trees, shrubs and hardy flowers. Grass would take the place of annual carpet beds and "monstrosities" like floral sundials. Imported tropical plants like palms and banana trees would be rejected as entirely out of place. Ground-level markers would replace raised stone copings, and large monuments would be discouraged. Roy's vision of a modern "Lawn Cemetery" was more completely accomplished in the satellite Hawthorn-Dale Cemetery, established in 1906 at Pointe-aux-Trembles. That even more remote suburban location provided sites for less expensive burials and was linked to the city centre by convenient public transit. Transit use had been foreseen by John Claudius Loudon in the 1840s. Roy also shared Loudon's preference for cremation, which was performed for the first time in Canada at Mount Royal Cemetery in 1902.

FACING PAGE AND LEFT: *Notre-Dame-des-Neiges Cemetery, Montreal, Quebec*

By 1935 Roy could report to the board that the Lawn Style cemetery was "the greatest American creation of Art-Out-of-Doors, and as original with the American people as their skyscrapers." In the Mount Royal Cemetery, he boasted:

We have demolished some very unsightly vaults and thousands of posts, bars, copings, iron fences and enclosures of all kinds inherited from the past; we have exerted a very large influence in getting smaller and more artistic monuments than in most places.

The tone of this report may make the superintendent sound all-powerful, but the cemetery landscape is actually the product of decades of compromise. Although many neglected stone and ironwork enclosures were demolished, characteristic stone copings and steps have survived in older sections. A photograph taken in 1898 (the year when Ormiston Roy inherited his father's position as superintendent) shows old-style cedar hedges surrounding individual lots. He had them cleared away and planted an abundance of flowering and fruit-bearing shrubs and trees – peonies, roses, Japanese crab apple, lilac, flowering almond, hydrangea, serviceberry, sumac and viburnum.

A photograph taken in the winter of 1891 shows the bare stone towers of the entrance gates in front of a dense thicket of immature trees. Roy planted the vines that have covered the gates. Like Olmsted, he considered stone structures to be cold, bare and best covered with living greenery. The thickets of young volunteer trees, all competing for light as in a natural new-growth forest, were transformed into small clearings on irregularly shaped "islets." Half the trees in the

cemetery's arboretum today are red oaks and sugar maples, most of them planted during or before Ormiston Roy's career. Among the other half are native and rare exotic specimens – ash, hemlock, white pine, birch, Kentucky coffee tree, ginkgo and dawn-redwood (metasequoia). The master list of trees in Mount Royal Cemetery names more than 500 species. Along with the hundreds of shrubs and perennials, they provide food and habitats for many small animals and some 150 species of birds. The clearing of Mount Royal's wilderness was designed to make it a place for a distinctly human purpose, the commemoration of the dead. But the life cycles of the natural world have been sustained as well.

Early in 1854 the Notre-Dame *fabrique* (parish corporation board) selected a very large piece of farmland, contiguous at the back property-line with Mount Royal Cemetery,

but located on a gently sloping plateau with a smaller more steeply inclined area behind it. Aside from a maple sugar bush, there were few trees. More than 80 per cent of the property had been cleared for farming in the early 18th century, and the land retained some of its agricultural character. Parts of the grounds continued to be cultivated until the 1920s, producing hay, barley, millet and clover for animal feed, and providing kitchen gardens for cemetery employees. It was only in the 1950s that the channelling of Raimbault Creek and the draining of the marshy pond entirely eliminated a small island where a miniature cottage had doubled as a goose house.

An extra layer of rural heritage was added in 1957, with the acquisition of a designated historical monument, an 18th century house that had been displaced by road con-

FACING PAGE: *Mount Royal Cemetery, Montreal, Quebec*

FAR LEFT: *Notre-Dame-des-Neiges Cemetery, Montreal, Quebec* Sir George-Étienne Cartier.

LEFT: *Notre-Dame-des-Neiges Cemetery, Montreal, Quebec*

struction. Between 1751 and 1781 Joseph-Henri Jarry had built his stone house in the vernacular style adapted by the earliest *habitants* from the traditional form originating in medieval Normandy. The "Maison de la Côte-des-Neiges," a typical example of rural architecture once common in the New France regime, and the rarest of survivors in the 20th century Montreal streetscape, thus became at a stroke the newest/oldest monument in a location steeped in memory.

Notre-Dame-des-Neiges was designed by a Montreal architectural firm. John Ostell's commissions included the Customs House, the McGill University Arts building, the Episcopal Palace, the Grand Seminary of St-Sulpice, the Court House and the Church of St-Jacques. The work of his nephew, Henri-Maurice Perrault, included the City Hall, the College of Montreal, and the Chapel of the Sacred Heart for Notre-Dame Basilica. Ostell and Perrault's professional experience as Montrealers working in a particular religious and national context gave them qualifications quite distinct from those of the imported American team of Sydney and Neff who designed Mount Royal Cemetery. Perrault was certainly aware of the Rural Cemetery Movement. He visited Mount Auburn and New York in 1854 and mentioned a preference for winding paths and irregular islets instead of the straight lines and checkerboard pattern of lots on the flat plateau. The landscape plan of Notre-Dame-des-Neiges, however, does not adhere faithfully to the American model. Indeed, the spiritual program of individuals communing privately with nature in a landscape devoid of religious symbolism and made to appear "natural" could not be entirely satisfactory to faithful Catholics.

The main entrances accent the differences between the two cemeteries. Mount Royal is approached from Outremont by a quiet road. Its stone gates in Rural Gothic style, made more picturesque by the growth of vines, were placed so as to screen any preliminary view of burial places. In contrast, the stone gates designed by Montreal architect Victor Bourgeau for the entrance at the well-travelled Chemin de la Côte des Neiges were far more imposing and

monumental. The central tympanum framed a sculpture of the Risen Christ and the flanking towers were crowned by sculpted angels of the Resurrection. After the demolition of the central gate in the 1920s, which left only the stone pavilions at each side, the Angels were installed on either side of the cross near the beginning of the road leading to the chapel. Both cemeteries could accommodate large public funeral processions, but the entrance settings have different emphases. Mount Royal makes available a discreet privacy. Notre-Dame-des-Neiges celebrates a more dramatic procession toward a shared, general (or, more accurately, universal) destination.

The straight lines of the processional routes in Notre-Dame-des-Neiges were bordered by regularly planted trees to create *allées* leading from the entrance to the chapel and in the plateau area, which was laid out in a rectangular block. This planting had a monumental character. Trees were arranged symmetrically on either side of the road, "their tall straight trunks rhythmically marking the solemn progress of a funeral *cortège*, like a guard of honour standing at attention." Even in areas where the roads were curved and winding, trees were planted on the margins rather than arranged in the middle of islets, artfully concealing and then revealing individual monuments, as in Mount Royal. In Notre-Dame-des-Neiges the monuments are more immediately visible as an ensemble. The effect is more like a well-treed urban streetscape than an English country estate.

Since its land had been cleared for farming in the 18th century, planting trees in Notre-Dame-des-Neiges was a priority. In the decade following 1855, more than 3,500 trees were purchased – elms, red and silver maples and other common trees. That number represents almost 70 per cent of the trees in the landscaped part of the cemetery today. There was never any ambition to create an arboretum of rare and exotic trees – 90 per cent of the trees comprise only eight species. Whereas 500 species have been counted in Mount Royal, the total in Notre-Dame-des-Neiges is only 59. The prevailing homogeneity of the treed landscape expresses order and calm, rather than emphasizing

FACING PAGE: *Notre-Dame-des-Neiges Cemetery, Montreal, Quebec*
The chapel is glimpsed in the distance.

*Notre-Dame-des-Neiges Cemetery,
Montreal, Quebec*
A row of family mausoleums.

strikingly individual specimens or surprising effects. The art of the Classical French garden landscape, as transmitted to New France by the Sulpician order in the gardens of their seminaries, very clearly modified the American Rural Cemetery ideal in Notre-Dame-des-Neiges.

As a Catholic cemetery, it was designed to include large public celebrations that combined religious, national and political purposes. In October 1855, three years after Ludger Duvernay (*Patriote*, editor of *La Minerve*, and co-founder of the Saint-Jean-Baptiste Society) had died and been buried in the old burial ground, his remains were transferred to the new cemetery of Notre-Dame-des-Neiges in an impressive ceremony that attracted more than 10,000 people. After the death in 1894 of Honoré Mercier (a co-founder of the

Parti National and the first nationalist premier of Quebec), it became the custom for crowds of pilgrims to come annually to honour and exalt his memory. Some 25,000 people gathered to meditate at Mercier's graveside in 1898. The fortieth anniversary of his death was commemorated by a mass at Le Gesù and a pilgrimage to his grave. His death date on October 30 linked the celebration of national memory with the annual celebration of Catholic doctrine relating to the communion of saints. The Feast of All Saints on November 1 was the occasion of grand processions and services, in some years attracting more than 50,000 people. On that day, visiting and tending graves was a communal and public occasion, supplementing if not replacing the relatively private observances of individual anniversaries

questionable claim that the French-Canadian race has two distinctive traits – Catholicism and nationalism.

Mount Royal Cemetery had no mandate to celebrate the minority status of the mostly anglophone Montrealers buried there, but made every effort to avert controversial memorials. The violent death in 1877 of Thomas Hackett, a member of the militantly Protestant Orange Order, resulted in fundraising among Orange Lodges ouside Montreal for the erection of a very large monument. The cemetery trustees permitted it to be placed, not in plain view, but near the entrance, where any breach of public order might be more easily stopped. Its unveiling in 1881 revealed much taking (and giving) of offence, however, and the shocked trustees insisted on the removal of one line of the monument's inscription. A blank space replaced the words "by an Irish Roman Catholic mob." Even so, a visitor today cannot but read in the remaining inscription an ancient grudge:

> *In Memory of*
> *Brother*
> *Thos. Lett Hackett, LOA*
> *Who was Barbarously Murdered*
> [blank space]
> *On Victoria Square*
> *When Quietly Returning from*
> *Divine Service*
> *12 July 1877*
> *This Monument was Erected by*
> *Orangemen and Protestants of*
> *The Dominion, as a Tribute to his Memory*
> *And to Mark Their Detestation of His Murderers*

The date of "12 July," when the Orange Lodge celebrated the victory of the Battle of the Boyne in Ireland in 1690, hints at the not-so-quiet nature of the lodge members' return from divine service. The monument does not so much honour Hackett's memory as glorify mutual detestation. It opposes letting a barbarous quarrel die. Montreal Orangemen

throughout the year.

Between 1858 and 1866, the Institut Canadien erected the Monument to the Patriotes of 1837–38, a massive grey stone obelisk prominently located on a small hill. Its purpose was to define an emerging French-Canadian identity, based on the liberal principles of the Patriote party, and honouring heroes of the political struggles. On the sides of the massive pedestal base, plaques list the names of the victims of the battles of Saint-Denis, Saint-Charles and Saint-Eustache, of those executed in Montreal, and of political exiles. But from the outset this monument has been a contested site of memory. The liberal ideology of the Institut was denounced in 1858 by the Bishop of Montreal. The monument's setting on consecrated ground resulted in the

apparently did not parade annually to the monument, however, but let it stand as a permanent gesture of their defiance.

Crowd scenes not wanted by either cemetery were occasioned by the affair of Joseph Guibord, a Catholic who died while under ban of the sacraments of the Church. Guibord was a member of the Institut Canadien, which had long been engaged in a quarrel with the Bishop of Montreal about prohibited books in its library. His remains were refused burial in the consecrated ground of Notre-Dame-des-Neiges and had to be interred in Mount Royal, while his widow pursued legal action. After six years of controversy, the court decided in favour of her appeal, but a riotous mob prevented the first attempt at reburial.

At the conclusion of the Guibord affair in 1875, the Bishop of Montreal, Mgr Bourget, took the high road in advising his parishioners:

Have an ever greater and greater religious respect for your cemetery, and enter into it only with fear and trembling. Do not turn it into a place of promenade and recreation, but make a pilgrimage there as often as you can. In travelling through it, consider it as the parish and the city of the dead.

The Bishop's pastoral letter emphasizes the difference between his view of a cemetery as an extension of the Catholic parish, and Mount Royal Cemetery's plan for welcoming a diversity of religious beliefs. One promoted group pilgrimages – even individual visitors were instructed to

Notre-Dame-des-Neiges Cemetery, Montreal, Quebec
The "Last Kiss" – also seen elsewhere, as in the Cimitero Monumentale, Milan – is a complex symbol, combining Sweet Death with the Kiss of Life, or Resurrection.

think of themselves as belonging to a greater parish – while the other encouraged private meditation. Many family mausoleums in Notre-Dame-des-Neiges are arranged in rows like streetscapes of houses in a city of the dead (like Père Lachaise in Paris), in striking contrast to the more isolated setting of, for example, the Molson family mausoleums in Mount Royal.

Both cemeteries contain an abundance of monuments of great artistic quality. In Notre-Dame-des-Neiges the Louis Archambault monument, sculpted by Alfred Laliberté, is exceptionally fine. The bronze portrait bust on a tall stone pedestal has a bronze relief banner bearing a fleur-de-lys lying across its base. A carpenter and building contractor, Archambault had in 1876 founded a mutual benefit association, the French Canadian Artisans' Society of Montreal,

to provide illness and death insurance coverage for Catholic French Canadians who were not Freemasons and did not belong to any other benevolent society forbidden by the Church. Several thousand members attended his funeral and raised funds to erect a monument in honour of "this worker's accomplishment," so distinctly "fraternal, national, religious and democratic" in character.

A broad range of figures from traditional religious iconography is to be found in the Catholic cemetery – the Madonna and Child, the Holy Family, the crucified and triumphant Christ, saints and angels. Works by European stonecutters tend to predominate in Canadian cemeteries, but in Notre-Dame-des-Neiges religious devotion is often combined with national purpose. Commissions for monuments have played a significant role in supporting the

BOTH IMAGES: *Notre-Dame-des-Neiges Cemetery, Montreal, Quebec*

careers of several outstanding Quebec sculptors.

Louis-Philippe Hébert is remembered as "the first Canadian sculptor of commemorative statues." One of his masterpieces is the Valois family monument, commissioned by Philomène Valois-Lussier to honour the memory of her mother, brother and husband, who died in 1893 and 1894. In October 1894 Hébert returned to Montreal from Paris, where he had spent six years studying the techniques of bronze casting and the art of modelling, and winning many honours in the Paris Salon. He had also completed many sculptures for public display in Quebec. His contract with his client specified that the statue would be nine feet tall, that the design model would be approved by Mme Lussier, that it would be cast in bronze in one of the best foundries in Paris, and that the price would be $3,500, to be paid in two installments.

Hébert's majestic Angel of Glory, positioned on an immense pedestal designed by Émile Brunet, triumphantly displays Hébert's talents and the modelling techniques he had acquired during his European years. The angel stands, holding in one hand a long cross and in the other hand, on the verge of being dropped, a floral crown. The symbolic pose follows a standard convention, but the Valois angel is remarkable for its grace of facial expression and delicacy of gesture, the suspended animation of its partly deployed wings, and (in the words of the poet Louis Fréchette) "Et puis, l'admirable draperie!" Fréchette's own bronze portrait bust in antique drapery, set on a plain granite column of modest size, made in 1909 by Alexandre Carli, proves that the excellence of monuments in Notre-Dame-des-Neiges does not depend on grandeur.

Another masterpiece by Louis-Philippe Hébert is the monument for Charles-Théodore Viau, a successful and respected manufacturer of biscuits. The Viau business remained in the family for a century after his death in 1898, and Viau is still said to be "a name virtually synonymous with biscuits in Canada." The magnificent stone structure of his monument, with its Neoclassical Roman sarcophagus, perhaps reflects Viau's interest in enlightened urban planning. His model town development of Viauville required "purchasers of lots to put up stone-façaded houses of no more than two storeys, set back from the sidewalk." Viau also paid a substantial sum for the church and parish of Saint-Clément to be established in Viauville. In tribute to his Catholic faith, the bronze mourning figure at his tomb holds up a cross toward his bronze relief portrait, and the ivy twining around the cross seemingly reaches out to form a living and evergreen frame for his portrait medallion. The relief effigy is not at all pretentious, but as accurate as a photographic portrait. Hs eyebrows, ears, mustache, chinline and receding hairline show the man as he was when he died at age 55. In fact, Hébert based his reproduction of these traits on an actual photograph of Viau.

The kneeling figure at the Viau monument is a *pleureuse* (weeper), an allegorical representation of grief. Many very fine examples of this European tradition are to be found in Notre-Dame-des-Neiges.

A mourner statue on the monument for Charles F. Pratt, who died in 1876, is a well-draped figure quite composed and restrained in her grief, standing on a sarcophagus and leaning slightly on the support of an antique urn. Carved in marble, she is thought to have been imported from Europe. Later mourners are more abandoned in their grief, with a tendency to collapse under the weight of their emotions. One bronze *pleureuse,* carved and cast in Italy, has apparently exhausted her tears and fallen into a torpor that anticipates the "MORS PAX AETERNA" ("death is eternal peace") engraved on the tomb of the brothers Oscar and Marius Dufresne (who died in 1936 and 1945).

Notre-Dame-des-Neiges also has many beautiful examples of another Italian sculptural tradition, the Mourning Angel. Some of these express a quiet melancholy as they contemplate a palm frond, the portent of eventual victory over death, while others are quite overcome with grief.

FACING PAGE: *Notre-Dame-des-Neiges Cemetery, Montreal, Quebec* Viau family monument, sculpted by Louis-Philippe Hébert.

C. THEODORE VIAU
1879 – 1938
EPOUX DE

CHARLES T. VIAU
1843 – 1898
EPOUX DE

THEOPHILE VIAU
1883 – 1939
EPOUX DE

Notre-Dame and Beechwood Cemeteries, Ottawa

Mount Royal and Notre-Dame-des-Neiges, separate but interconnected on their mountain site, set the highest of standards for cemeteries in Canada. In some ways their examples influenced the development of two Ottawa cemeteries some 20 years later, after a smallpox epidemic led to the closing of cemeteries in Sandy Hill, within the city limits. Beechwood Cemetery, established in 1873, is almost as large as Mount Royal Cemetery (160 acres compared to 165). However, Notre-Dame-des-Neiges is much larger than Ottawa's Notre-Dame (280 acres compared to 35).

Notre-Dame, established in 1872, was designed by Georges Bouillon, who was ordained two years later and became parish priest of Notre-Dame Cathedral. In the 1870s and 1880s he designed a number of church buildings in the Ottawa diocese. (His beautiful chapel of the Convent of Our Lady of the Sacred Heart in Ottawa is now installed in the National Gallery of Canada.) Although Bouillon was familiar with the American Rural Cemetery style, his plan for Notre-Dame has symmetrically arranged curvilinear roads, but in the newer areas the road layout follows straight right-angled or oblique lines. The topography is relatively flat, and the trees are planted in *allées*, as in Notre-Dame-des-Neiges. The cemetery is now overlooked by a 20th century high-rise urban development. It provides, not a pastoral retreat from the world, but a reminder that the fact of death cannot be ignored. In the midst of life we are in death. Notre-Dame was originally larger than it is now, and its northern boundary coincided with part of Beechwood's southern boundary, as with Montreal's adjoining cemeteries. The sale of 20 acres for urban development severed that picturesque connection.

Although Beechwood's western and northeast boundaries are fenced and open to streetscapes, an uncultivated forest forms a buffer along the west, northwest and north boundaries. Its Rural Cemetery plan was designed by architect Robert Surtees, who was City Engineer from 1876 to 1897. His other landscape projects included work for the Improvement Commission of Ottawa (the predecessor of the National Capital Commission) and pathways in the Experimental Farm. The Beechwood Cemetery Company also commissioned the construction of Beechwood Avenue from the St. Patrick Street Bridge at the Rideau River, to make a convenient and attractive road link from the centre of the capital to the main gate of the cemetery.

The Beechwood plan was laid out by Alpine Grant, a landscape gardener who had been one of the founders of Cataraqui Cemetery (Kingston) and was its first superintendent from 1850 to 1864. Grant was employed by Lord Monck, the first Governor General resident in Rideau Hall (not far from Beechwood Cemetery), to put the principles of picturesque landscape design into practice – first in the layout of Spencer Wood in Sillery (the neighbour of Mount Hermon Cemetery) and then as head gardener of Rideau Hall, from 1864 to 1868. Lord Monck had Grant construct a new entrance drive and plant numerous trees to create changing vistas along the approach to Rideau Hall. Grant put this experience to good use in Beechwood in laying out the road from the original entrance (now overgrown by trees). Although not as elevated as the land of Mount Royal Cemetery, Beechwood Cemetery is sited on some of the highest land in Ottawa. Views of central Ottawa are glimpsed through the trees, and some monuments, like that of Tommy Douglas, are positioned to frame a vista of Parliament Hill.

FACING PAGE: *Notre Dame Cemetery, Ottawa, Ontario*

FACING PAGE, FAR RIGHT: *Notre Dame Cemetery, Ottawa, Ontario*
The Laurier monument, sculpted by Alfred Laliberté.

The monument for Prime Minister Sir Wilfrid Laurier displays the excellence of artistic and technical skills developed in Canadian art foundries after the Great War. In its combination of architectural stone with full-size bronze figures, and its relief bronze wreath of maple leaves propped on the stone steps, it is reminiscent of war memorials. The eight figures sculpted by Alfred Laliberté stand around a tall pedestal bearing a stone sarcophagus. Their forms blend modernism and naturalism, and their gestures and postures illustrate a neoclassical grace. Neither pallbearers nor caryatids – female figures serving in classical architecture as ornamental supports, in place of columns – they are mourners, serving as representatives of national sentiment. Despite political differences, "the entire country was in mourning" at Laurier's death. Following a magnificent state funeral on February 22, 1919, more than 100,000 people escorted his coffin to Notre-Dame Cemetery.

Cataraqui Cemetery, Kingston

The influx of United Empire Loyalists from the American colonies, following the Revolution, was the beginning of the growth of Kingston as a British colony. In 1792, when Kingston had only 50 houses, St. George's Church was built next to the Lower Burying Ground, which had been in use since at least 1783. The funds for the church and the stipend for its first resident rector (the Reverend John Stuart, an American Loyalist and energetic missionary, clergyman and pioneer schoolmaster) were supplied by the Anglicans, but Scottish Presbyterians were also buried in its churchyard. In 1825, however, a fracas broke out when Archdeacon George Okill Stuart (Reverend Stuart's son) announced, just before a Presbyterian burial was about to take place, that Presbyterians were no longer welcome. In that year the Upper Grave Yard, formerly for military burials, was fenced off into three sections – English, Presbyterian and Roman Catholic. The Catholics also had an older churchyard next to St. Joseph's Church.

All of these old burying places were far too small for the rapidly growing population. By 1830 Kingston had 3,587 residents. Toronto then had only 2,800. From 1841 to 1844 Kingston was the capital of the United Province of Canada. In the summer of 1847 it was devastated by the typhus epidemic, in which 1,400 immigrants died shortly after disembarking at Kingston. Three years later, 66 prominent professional and business men and one woman purchased shares in a non-profit company incorporated to establish a non-denominational cemetery, to be located about three miles northwest of Kingston near the village then called Waterloo. Archdeacon Stuart was a shareholder, but in the end he obtained special permission to be buried (in 1862) in the Stuart Family Lair in the churchyard of St. George's. The Stuart Lair is an unroofed stone enclosure; its form and

name are rare in Canada. A "lair," meaning a place where one lies down to sleep (often used for animals, especially beasts of prey), also has a specifically Scottish meaning as a graveyard plot, "the resting place of a corpse." For the members of this particular Stuart clan, the family and church association had more distinction than the setting of a new cemetery. Other shareholders did not look back, but welcomed the new vision of the picturesque Rural Cemetery.

The landscape plan was designed by F. J. M. Cornell, whose father, Silas, had in 1838 designed Mount Hope Cemetery in Rochester, which was much influenced by Mount Auburn Cemetery near Boston. Notwithstanding intermittent political disagreements in the early 19th century (the Fenian Raids and the *Fugitive Slave Act*, among others), in many practical ways Canadians emulated American examples. Kingston and Rochester were linked by steamboat lines and numerous mercantile ties. Kingston newspapers in 1839, for example, advertised that the Rochester firm of Robbins & Hicks could supply marble tombs and gravestones through the authorized contractor, D. Prentiss of Kingston.

The elevated 70 acre property, known in 1850 as the "Grove" because it was "crowned by a grove of beautiful pine trees," had extensive views of the surrounding countryside, even including "a pretty glimpse of the bay." A large plan, printed in 1853 for circulation to prospective shareholders, shows the characteristic winding roads and curved paths of a Rural Cemetery layout. The picturesque landscape is introduced by the entrance lodge, with its board-and-batten wood siding, steeply pitched roof and gables decorated with pendant bargeboards. It is an appealing example of the Carpenter Gothic style promoted by Andrew Jackson Downing. In his influential books, *Cottage*

The "Rural Gothic" Gate Lodge.

Residences (1842) and *The Architecture of Country Houses* (1850),
which included patterns and plans for houses that were
meant to stand a little apart from ordinary vernacular style,
Downing set out to reform American taste. His "Gate-
Lodge in the English style" illustrates what he called "Rural
Gothic" picturesqueness: "that beautiful modified form of
Gothic architecture which we adopt from the English people; and which certainly expresses ... a union of domestic
feeling and artistic knowledge." Downing's well-chosen
words show how his Rural Gothic gate-lodge fits with the
desired aesthetic and domestic feeling of the Rural
Cemetery. Since "it is evident that all irregular cottages are
more costly" than ones with a square or rectangular plan,
this design "will not be chosen by any one with whom economy of first cost is a primary consideration," according to
Downing. "We offer it, however, either as an ornamental
cottage for some small family who desire a snug residence
for part of a year, or as a pretty gate-lodge for the entrance
to a gentleman's place." The entrance lodges in Cataraqui
Cemetery and Mount Hermon Cemetery in Sillery share
this American-influenced "Rural Gothic" picturesqueness.

The Anglican Christ Church mortuary chapel, built in
1870 on the one-acre "Church Lot" shown on the original
Plan, is a stone structure in a Gothic Revival style more
directly derived from English examples. The view of Christ
Church from the cemetery evokes an idealized picture of an
English country churchyard. But for the most part, Cataraqui
was designed in an American style, and its ongoing
improvements were based on American experience.

Alpine Grant's successor as superintendent was David
Nicol, who in 1884 made a tour "through the Eastern
States," visiting 10 Rural Cemeteries to gather information
that would support his recommendations to his board of
directors. His handwritten reports in the Cataraqui minute-
books make fascinating reading. At the Forest Hills
Cemetery in Boston, Nicol reported:

I was fortunate in finding the Supt Mr. Oliver Molton in his office. He is
a most genial old Yankee, who has occupied the same position for 27 years,

Large ornamental urn with an allegorical scene of Morning.

In every place Nicol noted policies of discouraging and removing railings, hedges and copings around grave plots. In Springfield Cemetery, for example, "it seems that in a few years the whole place will be entirely cleared of the offensive obstacles." The grounds of Mount Hope in Rochester:

are beautifully undulating and of a very diversified character, presenting much interesting natural beauty – which is however sadly marred by a very large number of unsightly railings. But here also they are by general consent being gradually removed and doubtless this cemetery will in the course of time become very attractive.

It is something of a shock to realize that the handsome wrought-iron chains and fences still surrounding a number of grave plots in Cataraqui are surviving relics of the superintendent's campaign against them. Like sections that were "laid out in geometrical figures, the stiffness of which does not accord with the modern style of landscape architecture," these "old-fashioned railings" were deplored as outmoded. Besides, they interfered with maintenance. Nicol had concerns about the uneven quality of groundskeeping in Cataraqui. Some plots were maintained by his work crew, some were privately tended, and others were neglected. The grounds of Cedar Hill Cemetery in Hartford, Connecticut, in contrast, were "laid out in the most approved modern manner" and were "highly improved:"

The most important particular is that no lots can be neglected because all the grounds on which improvements have been made are regularly mowed as often as needed, which during the early part of the season is about every ten days. It is considered that one man with horse and lawn mower can accomplish more than ten men with scythes and sickles, besides making it look much better.

A notable American-style improvement is the large number of cast iron and zinc ("white bronze") statuary, vases and fountains, ordered from the illustrated catalogues of the manufacturer J. L. Mott, New York, or the Canadian supplier John R. Peel of London, Ontario. The marvellous acanthus fountain – with its swan on a pedestal supported by pelicans plucking their breasts, in a basin bordered by a large circle of frogs and turtles – was assembled from a selection of component parts. Similar fountains can be found throughout North America, including Mountain Cemetery in Yarmouth, Nova Scotia.

Cataraqui's collection includes a large ornamental urn on a pedestal, about eight feet tall, for which was paid the sum of $228, including import duty. On one side a maternal angel with swirling draperies gathers two limp infants to her bosom. Their eyes are closed and mouths turned down in sorrow. On the other side, two angels mount heavenwards. The infant, sprouting his own smaller set of wings, partly supports himself on the maternal shoulder, while raising a flaming torch in his other hand. The scenes, copied from the famous reliefs of Night and Morning by the Danish sculptor Bertel Thorvaldsen, gain another level of allegorical meaning in this context.

Nicol selected large feminine mythological statues to grace specimen plantings of "groups of ornamental shrubs ... and some trees of highly coloured foliage, such as purple Beech." In his view, "the ground near the fountain, which the large pines now occupy and render ugly, is a very prominent spot in which ornamentation of this kind would appear to best advantage. A statue of Hebe pouring water form a pitcher into a cup would be an admirable ornament for the centre of a group of flowering shrubs, just where the pines now stand."

Mott's mail order Hebe – who was also chosen to ornament Temperance Fountains in a great many American cities – is no longer in Cataraqui. The figure who now stands near the grave of Sir John A. Macdonald has been identified from Mott's catalogue as "Rebecca." Her little urn suggests that she is metaphorically a source of water, although not an official Temperance Movement figure. In 1850 Macdonald, then an ambitious young lawyer and Tory representative of Kingston in the Legislative Assembly of Canada, was one of the cemetery company's first shareholders. In the Macdonald family plot (surrounded still by a handsome wrought-iron fence), his grave, marked by a simple cross with the inscription "AT REST," is one of Cataraqui Cemetery's most visited sites.

Every year on June 6, the anniversary of his death in 1891 has been commemorated by a public service of wreath-laying and remembrance. A lament – an air played by Scottish highland clans on occasions of death or calamity – is played on the bagpipes by the Fort Henry Guard piper. The speeches on this occasion are regularly interrupted by the sound of train whistles, as service continues on the nearby national railway line, which Macdonald was so instrumental in setting up, and trains still stop for passengers at the Kingston station a short distance from the cemetery.

Passenger trains are perhaps apt analogues for this cemetery, which provides ample accommodation for all classes. It is the resting place not only of Canada's founding prime minister, but also the bootlegger William Allen, who was well known in Kingston as "Dollar Bill," and many less famous former residents of the city. It is said that no one is a "true Kingstonian" until three generations of the family are buried in Cataraqui. Long-established Kingstonians may well have more than 100 family connections buried here. Queen's University, founded in 1841, the earliest degree-granting liberal arts college established in the United Province of Canada, purchased four lots which include plots for the families of eminent professors and principals of the university, such as the Reverend George Munro Grant, Robert Charles Wallace, William Archibald Mackintosh and John James Deutsch. Another lot purchased by Queen's includes the anonymous remains of those who donated their bodies to the School of Medicine. Medical students attend their burial services in gratitude for their contribution to the advancement of learning.

Cast-iron figure of *Rebecca* by the J.L. Mott Iron Works.

The Cataraqui Cemetery Company began with an ambition to develop "one of the most picturesque and beautiful cemeteries in the Dominion," and has succeeded admirably. Its appeal depends not so much on the distinction of its monuments as on their landscape setting. Relatively few of the earliest gravestones have survived, as most have been eroded by weather, removed or replaced. As superintendent David Nicol reported to the board, "About twenty-five good monuments have been erected during the year [1886/87] and a number of old slab headstones have been

taken away, and altogether the cemetery is really improved in appearance." His own burial place is part of a family plot that has a plain grey stone inscribed only "Daniel Nicol / died / Nov. 14, 1866 / aged 66 years," probably erected for his father, with whom David apprenticed at Hedderwick nurseries at Montrose, Scotland. His own marker is one of several small footstones, and reads only "David Nicol / 1829-1894." On the next plot is a small footstone for his son, who succeeded him as cemetery superintendent, inscribed merely "George Nicol / 1858-1923." It is almost as if the Nicols had in mind Sir Christopher's Wren's famous epitaph in St. Paul's Cathedral, London: "Lector, si monumentum requiris, circumspice" (Reader, if you seek a monument, look around you). The Nicols were modest, but also justifiably proud to let their work speak for them. Their burial place, not far from the rock quarry, on high ground that slopes down into a ravine, has a lovely view of the varied terrain.

The picturesque landscape today no longer owes anything to extensive views of the surrounding countryside, still less to "a pretty glimpse of the bay." Its beauties are inside its boundaries, and result primarily from the preservation of its various heights and ravines. The stream beds are mostly quite dry now, but contain drifts of wild buttercups, forget-me-nots and ferns. Many little arched footbridges cross them, and the ravine banks are filled with masses of day lilies. The very tall mature trees may be admired from several angles. Even the remaining groves of pines, which Nicol rather disliked and thought "monotonous," make a highly sympathetic setting for the uniform graves, "THE BIVOUAC / OF OUR / ARMY AND NAVY / DEAD" in the military plot, attracting the visitors' gaze from many viewpoints. Finally, Cataraqui's sense of uncrowded spaciousness gives it a serenity apparently natural, but not easily achieved.

Cataraqui's monuments are often unassuming and seldom proclaim their full stories. The reticent marker for Thomas MacLeod, who died December 16, 1960, merely states that he was a "SURVIVOR OF / ANTARCTIC EXPEDITIONS / R.F. SCOTT 1910 / E. SHACKLETON 1914 / E. SHACKLETON 1920." The monument for Sarah Ann Fraser, with its fine statue of a pensive woman with folded hands, reveals only that she was the "wife of Francis Fraser, Merchant Montreal" and "daughter of E.H. Hardy Esq. of Kingston," born in 1833, and "died whilst on a visit to her parents 8 July 1863." A handsome swagged urn monument, its baroque curves richly embellished with moss, bears a copper label engraved only with the word "WILSON."

A grey granite pedestal is crowned with a wreath of vigorously carved thistle flowers on which perches a finely detailed cast bronze bird, its eyes closed somewhat enigmatically. The monument commemorates William McIntosh, who died in 1858 aged 80 years, and Unie Chisholm, who died in 1861 aged 75. Below is engraved a phrase in Gaelic – "Cha till Sin tuílle" ("Return shall we never!"), a refrain from Sir Walter Scott's "Mackrimmon's Lament," likely in nostalgic reference to the song that Scott described as "but too well known from its being the strain with which the emigrants from the West Highlands and Isles usually [took] leave of their native shore." The verses that follow are attributed only to "D. Mc I." The poet seems to be Donald M'Intosh, the author of only one known published poem, called "Glimpses of Highland Superstition," and perhaps the son of Unie and William. His bleak lament combines the Scots' traditional sorrow over leaving their native shore behind with an unsentimental farewell to earthly life, untempered by any hope of future awakening.

> No more the mountain heath in Spring
> For us shall blossom fair
> No more the lark for us shall sing
> When soaring high in air
> Past are our hopes and fears on Earth
> Our pleasures and our pain
> The wail of Woe the laugh of Mirth
> Will wake us not again

FACING PAGE: Veterans' monuments on a cold, bright day.

The Necropolis and Mount Pleasant Cemetery, Toronto

A brief history of the earliest burying places of Toronto, during the 70 years since "Governor Simcoe began to build Castle Frank," was published by the *Globe* in November 1868. At that time, the military cemetery in Victoria Square (where Simcoe's 15-month-old daughter was then buried) was still used "exclusively for soldiers, their wives and children." The *Globe* noted that private burying grounds on estates like those of the Baldwin and Powell families, "in the neighbourhood of the Queen's Park" were no longer "retired rural spots, far from the hum of the busy city." By 1868, "houses [had] encompassed them round, and they no longer enjoy[ed] those amenities, their founders fondly imagined would ever belong to them." The earliest churchyards were inactive. Land granted to the Presbyterians 50 years earlier, between Duchess (now Richmond) and Britain streets, affected by the "Disruption" of the Church of Scotland in 1843, had become "a romantic little nook."

About a dozen moss-grown stones are scattered over it; a solitary cow crops the grass which covers the still visible mounds, and altogether it has more the appearance of an old country church-yard than anything in the city ... What may be the ultimate doom of this little landmark in our history we cannot tell. Probably in a few years, it will be built over, and the old Presbyterian burying ground will be amongst the things that were.

Other early burial places had filled up and closed. In 1844 the churchyard of the Anglican Cathedral of St. James had been replaced by St. James' Cemetery overlooking the ravine of the Don River, and in 1855 the Catholic ground around St. Paul's Church had been replaced by "the beautiful Cemetery of St. Michael's" on Yonge Street, south of Deer Park.

Following a petition in 1851 from the inhabitants of the rapidly growing village of Yorkville, the Potter's Field – the common burying ground opened in 1826 on six acres of farmland at the corner of Yonge Street and the Concession Road (known today as Bloor Street) – had also closed. It was replaced by a 15 acre site overlooking the Don Valley, to the south of St. James' Cemetery. According to the *Globe* report, "The land was in a miserable state at the time of the purchase, being filled with stumps and overgrown with rank grass." The purchasers were "three merchants of the city" who cleared the land, "obtained a charter from Government declaring it a common burying ground free to all, and at last sold it to the Trustees of the Potter's Field" (later named the Toronto General Burying Grounds Trust). The *Globe* was careful to indicate that the trust was a non-profit corporation.

Some time ago a cry was raised touching this Trust. Mercenary motives were imputed to the members of the Trust, and some people spoke as if they could pocket the profits, but this is, we are informed, an impossibility. The Trust is incorporated by an Act of Parliament, which contains clauses stringent enough to prevent any individual from touching a single farthing of the funds.

The trustees called the new cemetery the Necropolis. The name was linked to the revival of interest in classical antiquity, based on the archaeological investigation and partial restoration of ancient sites. Among the finest and most famous of these rediscovered sites were pagan tombs, and Neoclassical forms and concepts became associated with the 19th century movement to provide non-sectarian burial places. Many cemeteries established outside large cities of the living were named Necropolis, the ancient Greek word

meaning "city of the dead," an implicit signal that they would accommodate those with no local affiliation to an established church. The name of the earlier Potter's Field had more bluntly labelled those buried there as strangers – indigents, or visitors who had died far from home, not members of a local church. Its name, although charitable in intent, was somewhat tainted by its Biblical source. When the repentant traitor and disciple Judas Iscariot returned his ill-gotten 30 pieces of silver, the chief priests "took counsel, and bought with them the potter's field, to bury strangers in" (Matthew 27: 7). The Necropolis was a more cosmopolitan name. It suggested a less exclusive worldview, one somewhat more welcoming than the mere defining of "us" *versus* "them," the strangers.

Its beginnings included the reburial of the remains moved from Potter's Field. It is thought that between 1826 and 1850 more than 6,000 had been buried in those six acres near Yorkville. A large granite boulder in the Necropolis bears a bronze plaque commemorating "THE RESTING PLACE OF PIONEERS":

THE REMAINS OF 984 PERSONS WERE REMOVED TO THIS LOCATION AND SOME 364 OTHERS WERE REMOVED TO MOUNT PLEASANT CEMETERY BETWEEN THE YEARS 1851 AND 1881. THE INDIVIDUAL MONUMENTS WERE ALSO MOVED, BUT BEING MADE OF SOFT STONE, MOST OF THEM BECAME ILLEGIBLE FROM EROSION AND HAVE BEEN LAID FLAT ON THE PLOTS. REQUIESCAT IN PACE

In its 1868 article, the *Globe* commented: "It would be superfluous for us to enter upon a description of the beauties" of the Necropolis. "Its position, the picturesqueness of the scenery around, the taste displayed by Mr. Hayder in beautifying and ornamenting the grounds are known to everybody." The Necropolis and the nearby St. James' Cemetery, both overlooking the ravine of the Don River, were influenced by the picturesque aesthetic of the Rural Cemetery Movement. The landscape layout of St. James' was designed by John Howard, who first consulted a borrowed copy of a guidebook to Mount Auburn Cemetery. Howard was an English-born architect, surveyor, civil engineer and artist who had immigrated to Toronto in 1832. (In 1873 he deeded his Regency villa, Colborne Lodge, in its 165 acre estate, now High Park, to the city.) His landscape plan left, as the setting for a small mortuary chapel, the crest of a gently rising knoll, which has been called one of the finest building sites in Toronto.

From the street and the entrance to the cemetery there are striking views of the Chapel of St. James-the-Less, which was completed in 1861. It was designed by Frederic Cumberland and William Storm, English-born architects who had supervised the construction of St. James' Cathedral, following the destruction of the first cathedral in the 1849 fire that devastated Toronto's business district. The design of St. James-the-Less derives from the historic tradition of the English rural parish church. The beauty of its form rests on the fine details of its simple composition, its proportions and the excellence of its construction and materials – slate, wood and grey sandstone masonry – which lead some to see it as an early type of the Arts and Crafts Style. It has been described with lyrical precision by William Kilbourne and William Dendy:

With its monumentally heavy bell tower and its broach spire [an octagonal spire atop a square tower], it forms a pyramidal composition ... The tower is gracefully tall, to the tip of its needle-like spire, and yet its base is finished with a rough random-coursed masonry and a hugely spread buttress at the outer corner that makes it appear massive enough to be a modelled outcrop of living rock ... In St. James the Less, Cumberland & Storm eliminated all but the most expressive forms and effects, superbly manipulating light and shadow and a variety of materials.

The chapel has "a serene monumentality that is perfectly attuned to the picturesque cemetery and its emotional associations" and is "one of the few religious buildings in

Canada with the power to express not only the nineteenth century's fearful respect for death, but also its confidence in the pattern of life and in the afterlife beyond death."

Ten years after the completion of St. James-the-Less, the Necropolis trustees commissioned Toronto-born architect Henry Langley to design its mortuary chapel, superintendent's lodge, and entrance gates. Working with a smaller budget than Cumberland and Storm, Langley designed structures influenced by the American "Rural Gothic" style. Instead of the characteristic board-and-batten seen in Andrew Jackson Downing's pattern book, the lodge is clad with Toronto "buff" brick. Its most striking decorative features are the gable bargeboards with jigsaw-cut perforations. The entrance takes the form of free-standing gable bargeboards – a large one in the middle for carriages and small ones on either side for pedestrians. The chapel lacks bargeboards or other "Carpenter Gothic" details, but its spire is decorated with crockets and topped with an ornamental metal finial like those seen on Gothic Revival monuments.

During his long career, Henry Langley had a number of partnerships and trained numbers of younger architects. His churches of several denominations "left his stamp on the skyline of a great many Ontario towns." He worked on a number of projects for William McMaster, who was a trustee of the Toronto General Burying Grounds and a very wealthy Baptist. Langley had been born of Baptist parents, but in census records he most often identified his religious affiliation as Plymouth Brethren. He is buried in the Necropolis, where anyone, of any denomination (or even none), was welcome to purchase a plot.

The non-exclusiveness of the Necropolis is evident in several memorials. On April 12, 1838, despite appeals for clemency, Samuel Lount and Peter Matthews were hanged for their part in the 1837 Rebellion. Their bodies were taken down from the gallows and buried together in Potter's Field until 1859, when friends had their remains disinterred and removed to the Necropolis. Lount and Matthews are commemorated by a granite monument in the form of a broken pillar, erected in 1893, with a bronze plaque later installed at its base:

"PATRIOTS OF 1837"
THIS MEMORIAL IS TO HONOUR THE MEMORY
OF PETER MATTHEWS AND SAMUEL LOUNT
WHO, WITHOUT PRAISE OR GLORY, DIED FOR
POLITICAL FREEDOM AND A SYSTEM OF
RESPONSIBLE GOVERNMENT.

Also in the Necropolis is the family vault, set in the ground and covered with a heavy flat slab, of Charles Durand, a lawyer and author convicted of complicity with the Rebellion and also sentenced to be hanged, who spent years as a fugitive exile in the United States. Buried here too is William Lyon Mackenzie, the leader of the Rebellion.

One of the trustees of the Toronto General Burying Grounds was Robert Walker, Esquire, the proprietor of Robert Walker & Sons, retailer of quality goods to middle-class and wealthy clientele. His family monument in the Necropolis was erected before his own death and before the opening of Mount Pleasant Cemetery. The Walker monument is crowned by a Gothic Revival spire decorated by crockets. One side of the pedestal bears a plaque commemorating three of his sons who died as infants:

IN MEMORY OF
THE INFANT SONS OF
ROBERT & MARY WALKER
THOMAS FOSTER
DIED MAY 9.1842
AGED 24 DAYS
CYRUS
DIED OCT.14.1847
AGED 17 WEEKS
GEORGE FOSTER
DIED NOV.17.1854
AGED 2 DAYS

At its base are four splendid recumbent lions, looking as if they might have been carved from life.

The models for the lions were not found in the zoo in Riverdale Park, immediately to the south of the Necropolis, however, since the Riverdale Zoo did not open until 1894. (It closed 80 years later.) Purchased from the Scadding Estate in 1856, the park was originally 162 acres on both sides of the Don River. Citizen protests prevented the Necropolis from expanding into the park, and by 1872 the Toronto General Burying Grounds trustees realized that the cemetery's capacity would soon be challenged by the city's growing population. One year later, they purchased a 200 acre farm on the east side of Yonge Street in the Township of York, just north of the village of Deer Park (and north of the beautiful St. Michael's Cemetery, on the west side of Yonge Street). Its rural location and its name, Mount Pleasant Cemetery, were signals that it would emulate the Rural Cemetery pattern of Mount Auburn. Its location just beyond the northernmost stop of the streetcar line made it accessible to visitors and perhaps a popular destination, like Mount Auburn, for weekend strolls.

The site, combining plateau farmland and ravines with two creeks crossing through it to the Don River, had scenic potential, but the "wretched appearance" of the land, which was referred to as a "thistle farm," did not escape notice. It would require effort and artistry to transform it into a landscape. The landscape architect appointed by the trust was Heinrich Engelhardt, who was Prussian-born, had trained as a civil engineer in Berlin, and had emigrated to the United States in 1851. His experience as a landscape gardener in several American cities was said to include cemeteries in Virginia and North Carolina and assisting with Frederick Law Olmsted's New York Central Park. Engelhardt emigrated to Ontario in 1870 (in time to be recorded in the 1871 Census, which showed that nearly 10 per cent of the province's population had German roots). In the years following Confederation, many new provincial institutions required the construction of large buildings complemented by extensive grounds. As a qualified landscape gardener,

FACING PAGE: *The Necropolis, Toronto, Ontario*
Celtic Cross monument for William Lyon Mackenzie.

Engelhardt found rather scant competition in Ontario. He was soon occupied in drawing up plans for the provincial Institution for the Deaf and Dumb in Belleville, the Institution for the Blind in Brantford and the Ontario Agricultural College (now part of the University of Guelph), as well as for municipal parks and cemeteries in Brantford and Port Hope, and perhaps Picton.

In Belleville, the founding of a new cemetery had been mooted over many years since at least 1856, when the *Hastings Chronicle* had reported: "It is intended to model the projected Cemetery after that of Kingston, which is one of the most convenient and tasetefully laid out in the Province." In April 1872, a letter to the editor from a certain "H" was published in the Belleville *Weekly Intelligencer*:

Other towns are moving in the matter of public improvements. Picton will have a Cemetery; Port Hope is to have a beautiful Park, as well as a Cemetery; other towns of less pretentions than ours contemplate improvements of this kind, and shall Belleville be behind?

It has been strange to see, that a community like Belleville, can endure the sight of their neglected church-yard, and never agree upon the cemetery question ...

There is nothing more creditable to the people than the proper care and adornment of the resting places of the dead.

I hope you will keep the importance of this subject before your numerous readers, and that you will soon awaken our people from the strange lethargy they have fallen into about the Cemetery.

The town soon had its Belleville Cemetery on the shore of the Bay of Quinte, beautifully landscaped by Engelhardt. (The editor and publisher of the *Weekly Intelligencer* went on to become, briefly, prime minister. In 1917 Sir MacKenzie Bowell was buried, with due honours, in Belleville Cemetery.)

In 1872 Engelhardt published *The Beauties of Nature Combined with Art*, Canada's first book on landscape gardening. It included a chapter on "Graveyards and Cemeteries":

In some localities, the pent-up graveyard has given way to spacious cemeteries, many of which are admirably arranged and cared for. Such cemeteries are indeed an ornament to the locality where they are situated. Well may that city or town be proud, that can boast such a "city of the dead." Strangers visit such places with interest, while relatives and friends are led to higher and nobler aspirations, as they meditate amidst such places of solemn and yet graceful attractions.

It is most earnestly to be desired that every city, town, and village may have, at no distant day, one cemetery where all, of whatever creed or denomination, may rest side by side.

The chapter went on to advise that: "The site for a cemetery should be well chosen, at some distance from the turmoil and bustle of active life ... yet should be always easy of access. If the site chosen possesses natural advantages, such as hills and dales, groves and creeks, so much the better, but the improvements should agree and conform to the natural features of the place."

Engelhardt's book combined practical topics, such as drainage, with the contemplation of spiritual improvements: "It is the object of the art of landscape gardening not merely to please the eye, but to improve the taste, and to excite the various affections and passions of the mind to a love of the beautiful." The trustees of the Toronto General Burying Grounds, impressed both by Engelhardt's philosophy and his rough sketches for the new Mount Pleasant Cemetery, hired him to plan the landscape layout.

Engelhardt prepared an overall site plan and a detailed design for the western portion, which fronted on Yonge Street, the city's main north-south thoroughfare. He created an intricate system of curvilinear paths and roadways, which were carried over the water features by "neat rustic bridges." A creek was transformed into a series of small ponds or "lakelets," some with islets in the centre, connected by a series of cascades. Two white swans were imported from Germany to complete the picturesque effect. When the cemetery opened in November 1876, with Engelhardt as the newly appointed superintendent of the grounds, local newspapers reported favourably on the transformations of the landscape. The *Evening News* was confident that "when the plans of the company are brought to a termination Mount Pleasant will be one of the handsomest burying grounds in America." The *Mail* predicted: "In a few years the young trees which are now mere naked poles ... will be covered with foliage." The planting program begun by Engelhardt, and supported by the trustees for more than 125 years, has resulted in what many see as the finest arboretum in Canada. Hundreds of varieties of both native and introduced specimens may be identified with the help of small labels or a tree guide, complete with an alphabetical index and a map.

But all was not entirely peaceful at Mount Pleasant. In 1880 it was reported that dogs had eaten the swans. Differences of opinion arose between the trustees and the superintendent, who disliked certain monuments, which he said gave the cemetery "the appearance of a marble yard." Perhaps the trustees might have read with more care the chapter on "Monuments" in *The Beauties of Nature Combined with Art*.

If a monument be erected in a proper place, so as to afford a fine view, and in a chaste style, being at the same time surrounded with corresponding trees, shrubs, and flowers, it will charmingly ennoble the place.

If a monument be erected in memory of some departed friend, wife or husband, the most proper place would be some shaded grove or an island, or near a grotto, with a single weeping willow or cypress by its side: thus the whole place will assume the character of solemn resignation and internal peace ...

Any monument should be of a chaste and tasteful structure, and harmonious in all its proportions: its intrinsic meaning should be clearly delineated ... if this is not accomplished, the work will be a failure.

Engelhardt's chapter on "Statuary" observes that "statues have a tendency to excite cheerful impressions and emotions." Not every statue will do, however. "Grace in execution, faultlessness in form, and expression in character, and a proper relation to the surroundings, are indispensable requisites to them. Some," he continues, "have recommended that statues might be erected in small spots or plots of level ground; this, however, is objectionable, if the surrounding circumstances of the locality do not harmonize with such a design." The raising of the objection implies some fault in the form of the statue, but the greater problem is the perceived lack of harmony with its setting. Like Frank Lloyd Wright, who famously tried to control the furnishing of his clients' houses, the landscape architect was troubled when his vision was compromised by "objectionable" additions.

Even more prescriptive are the comments in the chapter on "Inscriptions."

Sepulchral monuments should bear in their inscription, the name, the date of birth and death of the deceased; it is against good taste to add to this the name of him who erected the memorial. But all other inscriptions are superfluous, provided the monument in itself is perfect in all its parts, and fully able to make the desired impression on the mind of the silent visitor.

In short, "inscriptions ought to be plain, short and expressive, *multum in parvo*." As the years passed, the compromises necessary to accommodating the various prevailing tastes of the cemetery's customers failed to moderate Engelhardt's strong opinions about chaste, appropriate and tasteful monuments. In 1888 the disharmonious relations between him and the trustees ended with his being fired. Until he died in 1897 of consumption at the age of 66, Engelhardt lived alone in a downtown rooming house. He left no will, nor any family outside Germany, and his grave in Mount Pleasant remained unmarked until 1991.

In 1915 the city expropriated a right-of-way for the construction of Mount Pleasant Road, which bisected the cemetery. In the 1930s the lakelets were filled in because they were expensive to maintain, and in the 1950s the excavation for the Yonge Street subway supplied soil for infilling and grading to provide more burial places. Despite these alterations, the western portion of Mount Pleasant Cemetery continues to benefit from the imprint of

Engelhardt's original design. Its nobler and more graceful monuments harmonize with their surroundings and, in fact, illustrate "the beauties of nature combined with art." Many later monuments bear plain and short inscriptions that would have pleased him. Perhaps the spirit of the place encouraged an expressive restraint.

As an outdoor gallery of museum of art and architecture, the cemetery is a subject for "ROMwalks," conducted tours sponsored by the Royal Ontario Museum. Participants meet their guides at the Yonge Street Gate, which is itself a notable landmark. Built of brick with limestone trim, the gate has broad, flattened Tudor arches and narrow turrets capped with small cupolas. With the original office, it forms a kind of gatehouse, screening the restful landscape within from the busy sidewalk and streetscape.

The social structures of the world outside find some parallels within the gates of most cemeteries. That does not mean that there is a proportional representation of the outside world. In Mount Pleasant there is no military section, for instance, as in Beechwood Cemetery (Ottawa),

Brookside Cemetery (Winnipeg), and Cataraqui Cemetery (Kingston). (The trustees opened the next Toronto Burying Ground, Prospect Cemetery, in 1890.) Mount Pleasant has only two monuments for volunteers of Toronto's 10th Royal Grenadiers, and the 48th Highlanders' plot and Memorial. But the Salvation Army has five plots for some 750 members. Fraternal organizations, founded as benevolent societies, are represented in the older section of the cemetery by grand monuments to mark their burial plots – the Masonic Order (1893), the St. Andrew's Society (1891) and the Independent Order of Oddfellows (1897). The I.O.O.F. memorial stands 27 feet high, not far from Yonge Street. It was cut from Indiana limestone and New Brunswick granite in a Yonge Street studio, and incorporates about 20 symbols having esoteric meaning for I.O.O.F. members.

In his book *Toronto: No Mean City*, Eric Arthur observed that "each phase of architecture in the nineteenth century finds an echo in the lettering and design in our older cemeteries." Perhaps the best examples are to be found not only in St. James' Cemetery and the Necropolis, as Arthur suggested, but also in Mount Pleasant. The most obvious "echo" is the Massey family mausoleum (completed in 1891), designed by E.J. Lennox, the architect of Toronto's third City Hall (built 1889–99). Both structures are made of massive blocks of red sandstone pierced by small arcades of round-arched windows and are inspired by the work of Boston architect Henry Hobson Richardson.

The Romanesque Revival design of the tomb is based on the form of a small church with a central tower, much compressed and made asymmetrical by a circular false stair-tower with a conical roof above a window arcade ... The apse is lit by a row of small windows set into the curve of the east wall and filled with stained glass depicting leaves and flowers; the overall effect is that of the nave and chancel of a small church. Most of the light, washing the interior in a mysterious radiance, comes, however, from windows set out of sight high in the tower. To crown the central tower Lennox designed a stepped pyramid roof on which he intended originally to place a very simple urn.

RIGHT: *Mount Pleasant Cemetery, Toronto, Ontario*
Detail of the Independent Order of Odd Fellows (I.O.O.F.) monument.

FACING PAGE: *Mount Pleasant Cemetery, Toronto, Ontario*

PAGE 148: *Mount Pleasant Cemetery, Toronto, Ontario*
Yonge Street entrance gates.

PAGE 149: *Mount Pleasant Cemetery, Toronto, Ontario*
Massey family mausoleum.

Hart Massey had purchased the premium triangular plot in the early 1880s, but did not begin to plan a mausoleum until the untimely deaths in 1884 of his eldest son, Charles, and in 1890 of his youngest son, Fred Victor. In place of the simple urn intended by Lennox, Massey subsitituted a large marble statue of the figure of Hope with her anchor of promise for "a peaceful haven after the Voyage of Life." No doubt, Engelhardt would have seen the sculpture as discordant in its surroundings, atop a monument otherwise "perfect in all its parts."

The Richardsonian Romanesque style in Toronto is evident in many buildings of substance and power. The Ontario Legislative Assembly Building, the George Gooderham House (which became the York Club in 1909), and grand houses on St. George and Jarvis streets are predominant in their settings and are built to last through the ages. It has often been noted that cemeteries founded in the high Victorian era took care to provide opportunities to make clearly defined distinctions between families of influence and those of moderate means. Private mausoleums certainly reflected the superior housing the affluent enjoyed during their lifetimes. A family mausoleum was built to impress its viewers and to make a statement about a family's status. Visitors to Mount Pleasant Cemetery may find themselves recalling the well-known couplet by poet B.K. Sandwell: "Toronto has no social classes / Only the Masseys and the masses."

In his recent guidebook to Mount Pleasant Cemetery, Mike Filey comments: "Without question the Massey mausoleum, which was erected at a cost of $25,000 and has 'lodgings' for twenty-three, is the most striking looking structure in the cemetery." It is in fact, in the opinion of many, the finest architectural work in the cemetery. But the reference to "lodgings" begs another observation. The Massey mausoleum has a meaning that is entirely unrelated to luxury housing. There are no creature comforts here. Another kind of message may be drawn from the silent "mysterious radiance" washing from high, unseen windows. Lennox's association with the Massey family in Toronto had begun in 1883 with his commission to build the Massey Manufacturing Company's head office on King Street West and Charles Massey's residence on Jarvis Street. But Charles had died before the house was completed, and it was acquired by his brother Chester (who raised two sons there – the actor Raymond Massey and Canada's first native-born Governor General, Vincent Massey). In addition to the impressive mausoleum, the Massey family also built three remarkable memorials to their dead, which serve all classes of the living – the Fred Victor Mission, the University of Toronto's Hart House, and Massey Hall on Shuter Street.

Mount Pleasant also has superb mausoleums built in classical temple style. The Eaton family in 1907 commissioned one modelled on the Maison Carrée, a Roman temple from the first or second century, in Nîmes, France. The stately portico with classically proportioned columns and capitals, entablature and triangular pediment establishes an undeniable dignity and seriousness or *gravitas*. The two sentinel bronze lions are recumbent, but more alert than the stone lions on the Walker memorial in the Necropolis. They were cast by the John Williams Bronze Foundry in New York, and their sculptor was also an American. The 1910 copyright is to Eli Harvey, a Paris-trained Quaker born in Ogden, Ohio. A foremost creator of realistic wildlife sculptures, Harvey had observed closely the Abyssinian lions in the menagerie of the *Jardin des plantes* in Paris. Not all components of the Eaton mausoleum are imported, however. Like the Massey mausoleum and others in Mount Pleasant, this one has a grate in the door that permits a visitor to look into the interior and see a stained-glass window, a radiant spot of light penetrating the gloom. The Eaton glass was created by the firm of Robert McCausland, founded in Toronto in 1850. The McCausland firm, the earliest continuing stained glass studio in North America, is still in business, and the McCauslands are the source of 75 per cent of all the existing stained glass windows in Canada. The glazed panels in Mount Pleasant mausoleums are visual echoes of those in many Toronto churches and homes.

Not far from the private Eaton, Cox (1905), Gage (1924) and other family mausoleums is the communal Mount Pleasant Mausoleum, Crematorium and Chapel (1917–20), designed by the noted architectural firm Darling and Pearson, which also designed the oldest parts of many important buildings in Toronto, including the Royal Ontario Museum, the Flavelle mansion (now the Faculty of Law building at the University of Toronto), Convocation Hall, the Toronto General Hospital and the Canadian Bank of Commerce headquarters.

Several outstanding monuments in Mount Pleasant reflect the most advanced artistic tastes of their time in Toronto. Three of them, all made by the Toronto sculptor Emanuel Otto Hahn, illustrate a range of artistic preferences. The first is dedicated to the Salvation Army personnel who lost their lives in the SS *Empress of Ireland* disaster. The ocean liner was struck by a Norwegian coal boat in the St. Lawrence River and sank in less than 15 minutes. Among those who drowned (187 crew and 840 passengers) were 167 Salvationists en route to the Army's World Congress in London, England. On the base of the stone, the epitaph is set in simple elegant bronze lettering:

IN.SACRED.MEMORY.OF.167
OFFICERS.&.SOLDIERS.OF.THE.SALVATION.ARMY
PROMOTED.TO.GLORY.FROM
THE.EMPRESS.OF.IRELAND
AT.DAYBREAK.FRIDAY.MAY.29.1914
COMMISSIONER.&.MRS.D.M.REES
COLONEL.&.MRS.S.C.MAIDMENT

...

MAJOR.&.MRS.H.FINDLAY..MAJOR.MRS.A.SIMCO
STAFF.CAPTAIN.&.MRS.A.MORRIS..STAFF.CAPTAIN.F.H
AYES
"GOD.IS.OUR.REFUGE.&.STRENGTH.A.PRESENT.HELP.
IN.TROUBLE".PSALM.46.1.

LEFT: *Mount Pleasant Cemetery, Toronto, Ontario*
Eaton family mausoleum.

FACING PAGE: *Mount Pleasant Cemetery, Toronto, Ontario*
The grave of Dougall King.

The sculpture combines realism with allegorical meaning. Hahn captured in stone the rough energy of a breaking wave. A single sea-bird hovers above, its wings spread wide. From an indefinite, almost formless background, a large cross emerges in shallow relief, projecting just enough at its top to support a crown of glory resting on a wreath of victory. The reverse side of the monument bears the standard Salvation Army crest, the circle of the sun surrounding the motto "BLOOD AND FIRE" and in the centre, a heraldic superposing of crossed swords, the letter S and the cross. Hahn's design adapted the crown of glory above the crest, a symbol familiar to the Salvationists. Similarly, his adaptation of the cross develops from the epitaph's oblique reference to Good Friday. The monument delicately balances the celebration of the Salvation Army's organization and faith with a recognition that their purpose is to offer support to others, and to help them in trouble of any kind.

Hahn's monument for Sir Byron Edmund Walker (1924) takes a more traditional form. It is a large flat stele carved in very shallow, almost two-dimensional, bas relief. In the middle is a representation of a smaller stele, filled with the slightly raised lettering of the epitaph – just the names, birth dates and death dates, followed by a quotation:

'ONLY THE ACTIONS
OF THE JUST
SMELL SWEET AND
BLOSSOM IN THE
DUST'

The quotation's source was a dirge in *The Contention of Ajax and Ulysses for the Armour of Achilles* (1658) by James Shirley. Its mediated reference to ancient history fits well with the character of the two angels standing in profile on each side. Each, with static pose, blank facial expression, folded wings, tidy hair and identical robes and sandals, mirrors the other image. The antique form of their robes and sandals is slightly modified by a reference to 1920s modern style, but the overall effect is decorous rather than art deco.

Edmund Walker (1848–1924) rose from unremarkable origins in the backwoods near Caledonia, south of Hamilton, to become a "Canadian Medici." Beginning in an exchange office at the age of 12, with a Grade 6 education, at a time when the American currency situation was complicated by the secession of 11 states from the Union, Walker went on to work in the recently formed Canadian Bank of Commerce and rose through the ranks to a position of national and international reputation. Like the Florentine bankers, the Medici, Walker was a patron of the arts and sciences. He was a significant benefactor of the University of Toronto and made essential contributions toward establishing the Royal Ontario Museum and the Art Museum of Toronto (now the Art Gallery of Ontario). His monument in Mount Pleasant is modest, quite the antithesis of Michelangelo's dynamic and radically new design for the Medici tomb. During his lifetime, Walker was embroiled in a number of controversies about contemporary art. Although he had helped to secure generous public funding for the National Gallery of Canada, its acquisition policy while he was chairman of the board drew criticism. Walker had definite likes and dislikes, and he was very accustomed to exerting influence. In controversies in the year or two before his death, the gallery was accused of showing favouritism to Canadian painters whose work was "labored, dull, and unimaginative." The National Gallery was called a "national reproach."

Hahn's work on the Walker stele is neither laboured nor dull, but his imagination appears under a certain constraint when compared to his monument for Lionel Cutten, who died in 1938. The two mourning figures sitting on a long high-backed bench, in their combination of realism with an enigmatic symbolism, bear comparison with the sculptures of Michelangelo. Their modernity reveals the German-born Hahn's European training and his awareness of nude or lightly draped figural traditions in European cemeteries. The exposed breasts of the women would perhaps have hardly been tolerated in another public space in "Toronto the Good," but they were, and are, accepted and even appreciated in the context of Mount Pleasant's landscape of mourning.

ARTHUR·FORBES·CUTTEN
BELOVED·HUSBAND·OF
AUDREY·BRUCE·PEARSON
AND CAROLYN BEAVER WISHART
AUDREY·BRUCE·PEARSON
BELOVED·WIFE·OF
ARTHUR·FORBES·CUTTEN
DIED·MARCH·8·1982

ANNIE·ROWENA
BELOVED·WIFE·OF
LIONEL·FORBES·CUTTEN
DIED·OCTOBER·16·1932

LIONEL·FORBES·CUTTEN
BELOVED·HUSBAND·OF
ANNIE·ROWENA
DIED·AUGUST·21·1938

CAROLYN·BEAVER·WISHART
BELOVED·WIFE·OF
ARTHUR·FORBES·CUTTEN

HELEN·GERTRUDE
BELOVED·WIFE·OF
WILLIAM·LUTZ·MONCUR
DIED·JANUARY·6·1933

CUTTEN

IN·SACRED·MEMORY·OF·167
OFFICERS·&·SOLDIERS·OF·THE·SALVATION·ARMY
PROMOTED·TO·GLORY·FROM·THE·"EMPRESS·OF·IRELAND"
AT·DAYBREAK·FRIDAY·MAY·29·1914
COMMISSIONER·&·MRS·D·M·REES
COLONEL·&·MRS·S·C·MAIDMENT
BRIGADIER·W·S·POTTER·BRIGADIER·H·WALKER
BRIGADIER·&·MRS·HUNTER·MAJOR·&·MRS·D·L·CREIGHTON
MRS·H·FINDLAY·MAJOR·MRS·A·SIMCO

CAPTAIN·P·ILES
CAPTAIN·FLORES
CAPTAIN·J·MYERS
CAPTAIN·&·MRS·J·DODD
CAPTAIN·G·WHITMORE
CAPTAIN·M·McGRATH
CAPTAIN·C·BROOME
LIEUTENANT·S·ROLAND
CORPS·CADET·A·REES
CORPS·CADET·A·REES

ABOVE: *Mount Pleasant Cemetery,
Toronto, Ontario*
Cutten family monument, sculpted
by Emanuel Otto Hahn.

LEFT: *Mount Pleasant Cemetery, Toronto,
Ontario*
Detail of the SS *Empress of Ireland*
monument.

Hamilton Cemetery

❧ Hamilton Cemetery is the oldest municipally owned and operated cemetery in Canada. In 1848 the city acquired a tract of land on the northwest outskirts of town, next to Christ's Church Anglican Cemetery, which had opened in the previous year. The non-denominational Burlington Heights Cemetery opened in May 1850. By the end of the century, both Christ's Church and the Anglican Church of the Ascension, which had opened its cemetery in 1851, were troubled by financial and maintenance problems. The three cemeteries were unified in 1900 under the management of the city and renamed Hamilton Cemetery.

The city's original land purchase may have been prompted by the death in March 1848 of William Case, a physician who had immigrated in 1805 from New Hampshire to the "Head of the Lake." For many years, he was one of only two medical practitioners in the large Gore District, which included Burlington, Ancaster and Grimsby. Dr. Case had provided medical services to the British troops garrisoned on Burlington Heights in 1812, and also to the wounded and ailing among the American invaders. When the British regimental surgeon was recalled, Dr. Case's new house was converted for two years into a military hospital. He and his family were respected and his 11 children included the area's most able physician in the next generation. But he had made it known that he was an agnostic, and the Anglican Church refused to bury his remains. Space for his burial was provided by the Hamilton family in their private burial ground.

In the 1950s road construction caused the graves in the old family burial ground to be removed to the Hamilton Cemetery. A plaque erected by the Hamilton Medical Society on Case's sarcophagus monument in 1927 ends with the words, "This grave also marks the first burying ground in Hamilton." That is to say, the plaque commemorates the pioneer burying ground of Hamilton's founding family, now itself buried beneath the heavily travelled Jolley Cut, which

RIGHT: Bruce family Celtic Cross.

FACING PAGE: Tuckett family mausoleum.

links the older part of the city to the "mountain" heights to the south.

The Burlington Heights site is picturesque, with a view overlooking the shallow waters of Cootes Paradise, the great "V" of the Niagara Escarpment rising behind it as a backdrop. It is located on York Boulevard, Hamilton's most scenic entrance. William Hodgins, the City Engineer between 1853 and 1856, is known to have designed the limestone Gothic Revival gate lodge, and may have laid out the typically Rural Cemetery plan, with curvilinear roads shaping irregular islets. From 1856, the Assistant City Engineer was the architect Robert Surtees, who moved in the 1860s to Ottawa, where he designed Beechwood Cemetery.

Burlington Heights is filled with historic sites, many now invisible to most eyes and marked only by memorial plaques. It is part of the Iroquois Bar, a giant glacial sandbar deposited during the last ice age along the shoreline of Lake Iroquois. Separating Cootes Paradise from Hamilton Harbour (formerly Burlington Bay), the Bar was a meeting and burial place for aboriginal peoples long before European settlement. Richard Beasely, the first settled European they traded with, had his home there. A plaque has been erected on the site of his now-vanished cabin, where he entertained Lieutenant-Governor John Graves Simcoe and his wife on their second visit in 1796. Burlington Heights had been so named by Simcoe on his first visit three years earlier, in nostalgic memory of one of his favourite places back home, in its Yorkshire spelling Bridlington.

The place of the garrison's encampment on the heights has almost disappeared from sight. When immigrant ships arrived in Hamilton Harbour filled with cholera-stricken passengers, the citizens of Hamilton at first refused to let passengers disembark, but they were persuaded by George Hamilton to let the cholera victims use the abandoned military barracks as a hospital and temporary shelter. No records were kept of their burial places. The return of cholera in 1854 resulted in the burial of 391 victims in unmarked graves, and the Spanish influenza outbreak from October 1918 to January 1919 necessitated the mass burial

of 264 men, women and children. A rock bearing a plaque was placed in 1926 to mark "the resting place / of these unknown / soldiers immigrants / and citizens."

Hamilton Cemetery is also the place where the monument known as "the lost war memorial" was found in the 1960s, after its location had been forgotten for several decades. In 1898 it was erected by public subscription "to the memory of the non-commissioned officers and privates of the British Army who died between 1862 and 1868." The granite needle was never really lost, but the lettering of its inscriptions had become difficult to decipher.

The defensive earthworks erected by the garrison troops in 1812 are still a prominently visible feature of the cemetery, since they provided the setting for a row of mausoleums. Most prominent is the Greek temple mausoleum built for William Eli Sanford (1838–1899), surmounted by a nine-foot-tall sculpture of Hope wearing classical robes. Her right hand of grace is raised heavenward, and her left rests on the anchor of faith. The anchor image is sometimes seen as ironic, since Sanford's sudden death came by drowning at his summer home on Lake Rosseau, when his boat capsized after his anchor got wedged in the rocks. Sanford was a staunch Methodist, however, and the choice of the Hope sculpture follows the example set most eminently by the Methodist Masseys in their family mausoleum at Mount Pleasant Cemetery.

Like the Masseys, Sanford had supported many philanthropic causes. He was particularly concerned for the welfare of orphan children, since he had himself been orphaned at the age of six. From a 21st century perspective, there is irony to be found in Sanford's seeing himself as a benefactor, not an exploiter, when he provided employment for some of the orphan children in his warehouses and factories. His philanthropy was supported by his immense wealth, which he had acquired by his timely move into the manufacture of ready-made clothing in 1861. By 1871 his company had "sales of $350,000 and an inside work-force of 455. The next largest of the city's 35 tailors or clothing manufacturers had sales of only $40,000 and employed a mere 15 workers. Indeed, the business was the fourth largest employer in Ontario ... By comparison, Toronto's biggest clothing establishment produced $110,000 worth of goods and employed 124 workers."

W.E. Sanford also speculated in real estate, becoming one of the largest landowners in Manitoba after undertaking to drain the Big Grass marsh and Westbourne bog. In Hamilton, he twice renovated his house, which he named "Wesanford." The second renovation took two years, cost about $250,000, and resulted in a stately 56-room mansion with lavish furnishings, a pinnacled tower, a colonnaded portico and a circular drive. His mausoleum, built at a cost of $100,000, was not cheap either, but was perhaps a more lasting investment. Wesanford mansion was demolished in 1938.

George Elias Tuckett (1835–1900) died a few months after Sanford, and his mausoleum is also set into the 1812 ramparts. Tuckett's reputation as a tobacco manufacturer, a patron of saloons, a director of the Hamilton Jockey Club, and thereby an abettor of gambling, was quite different from that of the Methodist Sanford. Tuckett's mausoleum is not like Sanford's, a classical temple set on the heights, but an architectural expression of the force needed to withstand the rampart's mass and support the weighty layered roof. The heavy squared cross is less like a Christian motif than an ornament holding down the roof, like the lid of a canister.

Between the Tuckett and Sanford tombs is the relatively unassuming mausoleum for Thomas C. Watkins (1818–1903), the retailer who founded The Right House department store. He was the first in Hamilton to build a modern high-rise building for his store, to hire female sales-clerks and to establish a charge account system and a local delivery service. He was also a Methodist and member of the Sons of Temperance. The low wrought-iron gate hangs open, seeming to encourage visitors rather than keeping them out.

The small-scale perfection of the Land Family Vault, in the form of a miniature Gothic chapel, is even more appealing. It was built in 1853 and may be the oldest mausoleum in

Canada. Robert Land was one of the earliest Loyalist settlers in the Hamilton area. Sentenced to death as a British spy by a military court in New York in 1779, Land was released for trial in a civil court, but skipped bail and managed to escape the country, settling at the Head of the Lake five years later. In 1791 his wife and six of their seven children, who had been evacuated to New Brunswick, determined to resettle in the Niagara area. They journeyed by way of their old homestead in Pennsylvania, by then owned by the oldest son, a supporter of the American cause, who failed to persuade them to join him. Instead, a surprise awaited them in Upper Canada, where the family was reunited after 12 years of believing that they had been separated by death. The patriarch was buried in the family burying ground in 1818. His son Robert, Colonel Land, had a long military career in various local militia, from 1804 until his retirement in 1847 at the age of 75. Soon after the opening of the Burlington Heights Cemetery, he had the Land Family Vault built. His father's remains were re-interred so that the family might never be parted again.

It has been claimed that Hamilton is one of the most Scottish of Canadian cities, and monuments to the influence of the Scottish diaspora in the 19th century are seen throughout Hamilton Cemetery. As in Mount Pleasant, the burial plot of the St. Andrew's benevolent society is marked by a large saltire, or X-cross. St. Andrew, the patron saint of Scotland, is said to have been martyred on such a cross, having begged his executioners not to use the standard pattern, as he was unworthy to be crucified in the same manner as his Saviour.

Many of the most beautiful Celtic Crosses in Canada are monuments for people of Scottish descent, and a large number of them stand in Hamilton Cemetery. The Celtic Cross incorporates the ancient pre-Christian symbol of the solar cross, a circle surrounding a cross with arms of equal length. Ireland's conversion to Christianity by St. Patrick in the fifth century was followed by the gradual evolution, through the next 400 years, of what became known as the Irish High Cross. A later renewal of interest in Irish culture and native antiquities grew into a literary and artistic movement known as the Celtic Revival. Casts of two historic High Crosses were exhibited with great success at the 1853 Dublin Industrial Exhibition, and in 1857 Henry O'Neill published his *Illustrations of the Most Interesting of the Sculptured Crosses of Ancient Ireland*. Versions of the High Cross quickly became fashionable cemetery monuments in Victorian Dublin and the rest of the country. One of the most famous in England is the monument of John Ruskin, a pioneer of the international Arts and Crafts movement. Carved with elaborate bosses and interlaced strapwork, the revival crosses are fine examples of the British Arts and Crafts aesthetic.

The base of the Bruce family cross in Hamilton Cemetery bears the clan motto "FUIMUS" ("We have been," that is, our ancestors were kings of Scotland). The front face of the stone is filled with panels of intricately knotted interlace, punctuated with bosses. On one panel, the laces become vines sprouting stylized trefoil leaves. William Bruce (1833–1927), born in the Shetland Islands, Scotland, was a teacher and astronomer who "practised an ornate style of engrossing; his penned and illuminated addresses became internationally renowned and were sent to Queen Victoria, the Prince of Wales, and Kaiser Wilhelm, among others." He was also a founder of the Hamilton Art Gallery, donating 32 paintings by his late son, William Blair Bruce, who had trained in Paris, to form the nucleus of the Gallery's collection.

William Hendrie (1831–1906), who was born in Glasgow and immigrated to Hamilton in 1855, made his fortune by improving the freight delivery system connected with the great railway expansion. At the peak of his cartage business, he owned 300 draft horses and had extensive interests in livestock breeding. (The monument to his most famous racehorse, Martimas, is still an attraction at the Royal Botanical Gardens, although whether the horse is actually buried there is a matter of debate. The rich purse from the 1898 Futurity Stakes was donated by Hendrie, who was opposed to racetrack betting, to build the Martimas Wing at the Hamilton General Hospital.) The Hendrie

cross has a grand simplicity. Its plain surfaces bear only a crest with the motto "FIDELITER" ("faithfully") and a central boss, intricately carved with an innovative mix of motifs – a rugged rope border, a wreath of thistles and a dynamic wheel in the centre.

The Lucas cross, embellished on all four sides by intertwined luxuriant foliage, with a splendidly vigilant winged lion, commemorates Richard Alan Lucas, who had established a successful wholesale grocery business, importing goods from the world and exporting fruit from the Niagara peninsula. He died on March 15, 1917, just a fortnight after

LEFT: The Colonel Land family mausoleum.

FACING PAGE: Sanford family mausoleum.

RIGHT: Detail of the Malloch family Celtic Cross.

FAR RIGHT: Detail of the Hendrie family Celtic Cross.

his son, Major Frederick Travers Lucas, was killed in action near Vimy. Not far away stands the Kellogg cross, studded with at least 24 bosses, four rampant lions and a few dozen serpents-with-ears, interlaced as in an illuminated Celtic manuscript.

In contrast to the ebullience of these crosses is the modernist stone sculpture of a Celtic bard, chanting an ode while plucking his lyre. The inscription – "IN LOVING MEMORY OF MY HUSBAND / JOHN SLOAN / GORDON A.R.C.A. [Associate of the Royal Canadian Academy of Art] / 1868 . 1940 . ARTIST . POET . RACONTEUR / AFTER LIFE'S FITFUL FEVER / HE SLEEPS WELL" – seems to have been carved by his widow, HORTENSE CROMPTON / MATTICE GORDON

A.R.C.A. / 1886 . 1961 . ARTIST . TEACHER . FRIEND." Both John and Hortense Gordon were well-known painters and teachers. They lived the artistic bohemian life full of avant-garde work, summers in Europe, and a great circle of friends. John Gordon was noted for his wit and mercurial temperament. His epitaph makes a rather surprising allusion to the "Scottish play." Shakespeare's Macbeth is speaking to Lady Macbeth about the man he murdered, and now envies: "Better be with the dead, / Whom we, to gain our peace, have sent to peace ... / Duncan is in his grave; / After life's fitful fever he sleeps well" (*Macbeth*, 3: 2). The phrase is probably best understood out of its original context, as a literary fragment shored with a trenchant wit against John Gordon's ruin.

Ross Bay Cemetery, Victoria

In 1850 the Hudson's Bay Company acquired land east of Fort Nisqually from the Songhees Nation (then called the Chilcowitch). The bay in the Strait of Juan de Fuca was named after Isabella Mainville Ross, the widow of Charles Ross, the company's chief trader, who died of a sudden illness in 1844, not long after arriving to supervise construction of the fort. In 1853 she purchased 156 acres of waterfront land and had a farmhouse built for herself and the four youngest of their nine children. The farm income was not sufficient to provide for her large family, however, and as the years passed, Isabella Ross had to sell parcels of the property. She died in 1885 and was buried within sight of her former house. Her cemetery plot was but a tiny portion of the land that had once been in her possession.

The cemetery trustees purchased 12 acres in 1872. Landscaping began in October, and plots were offered for sale the following March. The original landscape plan, by local architect Edward Mallandaine, had winding carriage-ways designed to take advantage of the site's contours and to feature vistas across the Strait of Juan de Fuca to the snow-capped Olympic Mountains in the distance. The road from the entrance gates led to a semi-circular carriage-way as a focal point. By the 1980s this focus seemed redundant, and the area was divided into plots, where the new grave markers illustrate changes in design from those of the previous century. In the older parts of the cemetery, many plots are surrounded by curbstones, low railings or cast-iron fences, and several are paved with stone or concrete. In 1893 and 1906 the city of Victoria bought land for the cemetery's expansion, but its present size of 27.5 acres is still smaller than most Rural Cemeteries. The greatest change over the last century is the growth of mature trees. The original trees were stunted and sparse; an archival photograph from 1885 shows a few small trees dominated by monuments. Now the full-grown trees have created verdant settings sheltering, or in some cases competing with, the monuments. The city's Parks Department planted most of the trees in the 1930s and 1940s. Cuttings from them have been a resource for city landscaping, so that the cemetery is not only a sylvan retreat in itself, but has contributed to the general greening of Victoria's boulevards.

The trustees had intended the cemetery to be open to all burials without religious restrictions, but the Church of England and the Roman Catholic Church forced them to reserve segregated portions for their denominations. Presbyterians, Wesleyan Methodists and the Reformed Episcopal Church then also took reserved sections, leaving only 10 per cent of the entire site available for the general public. A public outcry led to an investigation, resulting in the first three churches paying the purchase price of their reserved lands in 1879. The other sections were made available to all, under the administration of the city's Cemetery Board.

Victoria's role as a port city on the Pacific coast brought a certain number of isolated strangers, who were buried in its Potter's Field section – the destitute and friendless and nameless. But it also attracted a rich diversity of communities. The southwest corner of Ross Bay Cemetery, which at one time extended all the way to the beach, was set aside for "Heathens," the name then applied to non-Christians. It was the burial place for aboriginals who had not converted to Christianity, Japanese Buddhists, and Chinese, before the Harling Point Chinese Cemetery was established in 1903. The Sikh community practised cremation, at one time on open pyres in Ross Bay Cemetery. The ashes were not interred, but scattered on the flowing water.

Examples of Ross Bay's stone scupture gallery:

TOP LEFT: An imported monument for Sir Joseph Trutch.

TOP RIGHT: A stone by George Kirsop in memory of his wife.

BOTTOM RIGHT: Gilardi's monument for Leila Engelhardt.

BOTTOM LEFT: Unsigned monument for Willie Hickey.

FACING PAGE: A small chair for David Campbell, "A little Hero."

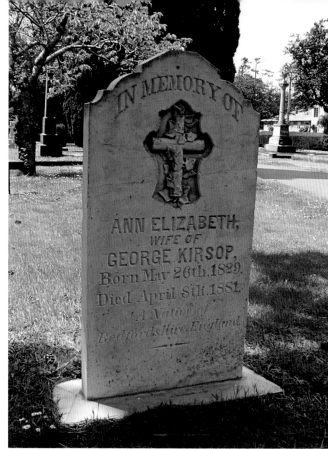

162

Awareness Society in 2002. Its silhouette acknowledges a traditional form without replicating it. Neither is the epitaph a traditional one; it is a deliberately contemporary expression of historical memory.

In Memory of Nancy & Peter Lester,
who came to Victoria in 1858 in
search of equal rights.
Nancy Davis Lester
Born in Haddensfield,
New Jersey in 1810
Died in Victoria, BC in 1892.

In June 1858 she wrote this letter
from San Francisco to a friend:
"The excitement relative to the Fraser
River gold mines prevails here to a
considerable extent. Many coloured
persons have left for that region and
many more are making preparations to go.
Indeed it seems a Providential provision
for us who are so oppressed."

She was survived by her husband
Peter Lester
Born in South Carolina
about 1814
Date and place of death unknown
He was a leader of the anti-slavery
movement in Philadelphia and San
Francisco in the 1840s and 1850s.
In Victoria he was a bootmaker,
tinsmith, painter and merchant for
many years.

The cemetery's segregation policy was based on religion, not race. Some 600 African-Americans who came from California in 1858 and 1859 during the Fraser River gold rush were buried according to their church affiliation. The Church of England section includes the grave of Rebecca Gibbs, a laundress who lived for many years in the gold rush boom town of Barkerville. Her grave was unmarked until 1998. The present marker includes her poem "The Old Red Shirt," which was originally published in the *Cariboo Sentinel*. The grave marker for Nancy Davis Lester was erected by the Old Cemeteries Society and the BC Black History

Ross Bay Cemetery's relatively small size and late date detract not at all from its qualities as an exemplary Victorian-era cemetery. It is especially rich in beautifully

ABOVE: A tree transformed into a living monument by marks of remembrance etched into its trunk.

FACING PAGE: Figure of Hope on George Kirsop's monument for Annie Deans.

carved and well-preserved monuments in a variety of late 19th and early 20th century styles. Good stone was available from British Columbian quarries. Sandstone from Haddington Island was frequently used until about 1885, and grey granite was obtained from Nelson Island, Texada Island and Granite Island. Imported materials were also in demand. Red granite was brought from New Brunswick, Sweden and Scotland, blue and grey marble from Vermont, and white marble from Vermont, Scotland, Sweden and Italy. Complete monuments were sometimes imported. Some fine examples of White Bronze works were transported by rail from St. Thomas, Ontario.

An imported stone monument commemorates Sir Joseph Trutch, British Columbia's first Lieutenant-Governor after Confederation, who is buried in Somerset, England, and the family of his brother-in-law, Peter O'Reilly, who came from England in 1859 and held many appointments in the colonial administration. The white marble cross draped with a floral wreath, from which petals fall unto its base, was made by Sanders of Euston Road, London.

Most monuments, though, were made locally. The Old Cemeteries Society has collected much information about Victoria's many stonecutters and sculptors whose works are displayed in the cemetery. Excellent opportunities to work in this rapidly evolving city attracted many stoneworkers. The construction of the Provincial Parliament Buildings, the Empress Hotel and Craigdarroch Castle evoked a civic pride, which is also expressed even in small individual monuments in this outdoor sculpture garden. George Rudge, for instance, the son of a marble dealer in New Brunswick, moved from San Francisco and Seattle to Victoria in 1875, and a number of his sons also became stonecutters. Thomas Bradbury, born in Lancashire, England, moved to Victoria in 1887, where he combined monument making with importing granite from Scotland, being an agent for the Vancouver Granite Quarries, and directing the construction of the Parliament Buildings.

M. Gilardi, a native of Lombardy, Italy, began working as a marble cutter in Victoria before 1890. The white marble monument for Leila Engelhardt, who died in 1884 at age 9, is a broken column, signifying her truncated lifespan. The column is draped with a fringed veil and covered with flowers cut in their bloom. The detailed carving demonstrates Gilardi's gifted marble cutting. Another child's monument for Willie Hickey, who died in 1889, has similar motifs, but was unsigned by its maker.

George Kirsop, one of the most prolific and skilled monument makers in Victoria, came in 1875 from his native Newcastle-upon-Tyne, England. Kirsop must have carved the beautifully understated white marble tablet in memory of his wife, who died in 1881. A simple cross, covered with delicate ivy leaves, is embedded in a deep recess whose curved outline relates subtly to the curves outlining the top of the stone. The carving skill is that of a virtuoso who loves a challenge. The design is somewhat reticent, since ivy may have many meanings. In this context, it suggests evergreen life attached to a Christian faith in the promise of the Cross. Her inscription, after 125 years, still looks as if it were cut quite recently. The tablet for Kirsop himself, next to his wife's, has the same design, but although he died 16 years later, his stone is more weathered and worn than hers. It would appear that he chose the better quality of marble for her monument.

The tablet for Eden White (1846–1884) "A Native of / Marsh Balden, near Oxford, / England," also shows Kirsop's skill in carving reliefs in a deeply recessed setting and his interest in original motifs – in this instance, the angel's profile and collar-like wings. The upper border of the tablet is also unique. The monument for the Wood family in the Church of England section includes Kirsop's white marble sculpture of a downcast mourner with her right hand holding a floral wreath and resting on a classical urn.

Kirsop's monument for Annie Deans (1832–1890) is grander. A white marble sculpture of a figure personifying Hope stands on a high pedestal, with inverted flaming torches carved in relief on each corner. Wearing a draped chiton in classical style and a single star as a crown, she points heavenward with her right hand while her left holds a scroll and rests on an anchor. All these attributes signal her meaning, that life is not extinguished beyond the veil of death. The anchor of hope in God's promise is an image of "strong consolation" drawn from Paul's epistle to the Hebrews: "Which hope we have as an anchor of the soul, both sure and steadfast, and which entereth into that within the veil" (Hebrews 6: 18, 19). The scroll is the book of life, in the form of the ancient roll or volume, and the star is the promised crown of glory. The sculpture is an allegorical representation of Presbyterian hope in salvation.

Charles Moss (1821–1877) worked as a moulder at the Albion Iron Works, where the cast-iron fence around his grave was made. The elaborate moulds used in its manufacture – draped lamps on the corner posts, oak leaves and acorns, and stringed harps – illustrate the skills of his trade. The truncated sandstone obelisk, carved by George Kirsop, bears symbols of Charles Moss's affiliation with the Independent Order of Odd Fellows. The three-linked chain is an emblem of the I.O.O.F., originally formed in 18th century England as a working-men's social and benevolent association. The hand holding a heart is a symbol admonishing I.O.O.F. members not merely to earn wages, but to put their heart into their work.

Two well-known monuments represent small things left behind by the dead. A bronze fire helmet, resting on a concrete pillow inscribed "Fred," commemorates Fred Medley, a fireman who was killed on duty in 1925. A marble baby's chair holds sculpted booties and socks, with the inscription, "A little Hero." David Campbell died in 1913, only 17 months old.

Even in this outdoor sculpture gallery, many monuments use only words to convey messages to those left behind. The most unusual is that erected by John Dean (1850–1943), who as a candidate for political office had been unsuccessful in winning over the electorate. His plain grey stone is treated almost like advertising space bought for the expression of his views, in capital letters. The stone was erected in 1936, while he was still alive, and it is said that he used to travel by streetcar to place bouquets on his own grave-plot. It was exceptionally strong-minded of Mr. Dean to have inserted a later line into his inscription, above a caret. He was still capable of afterthoughts, but not of removing a superfluous apostrophe:

ARTFUL POLITICIANS ARE ITS BANE
IT IS A ROTTEN WORLD, ˄ *IT'S SAVING*
GRACE IS THE ARTLESSNESS OF THE YOUNG
AND THE WONDERS OF THE SKY.

John Dean also donated land for a public park, named in his memory, at the top of Mount Newton, a place for contemplating the wonders of the sky.

OLD CANADIAN
CEMETERIES

A VISUAL TOUR

PREVIOUS PAGE: *Seeley's Bay area, north of Kingston, Ontario*
Fog-bound cemetery in late winter along Highway 15.

RIGHT: *Notre-Dame-des-Neiges Cemetery, Montreal, Quebec*

BOTTOM LEFT: *Mount Pleasant Cemetery, Toronto, Ontario*

BOTTOM RIGHT: *York Cemetery, Toronto, Ontario*

TOP LEFT: *York Cemetery, Toronto, Ontario*

TOP RIGHT: *Wallbridge Cemetery, Belleville, Ontario*

BELOW: *Highway 2, near Welcome, Ontario*

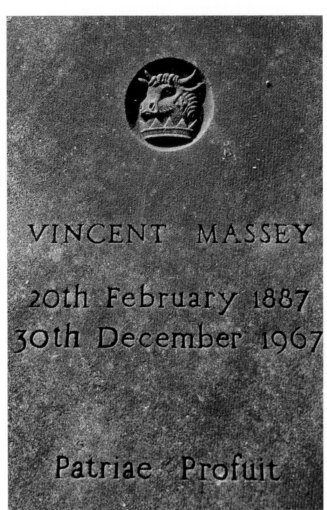

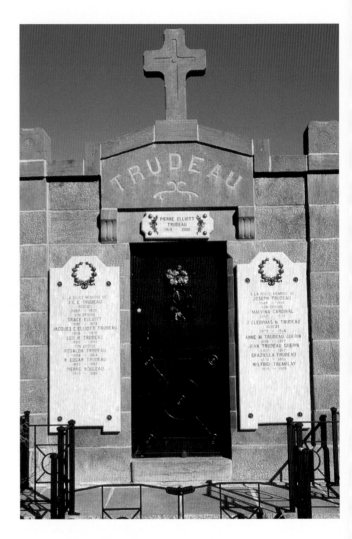

St James' Cemetery, Toronto, Ontario
Monument for Paul Kane.

St. Mark's Cemetery, Port Hope, Ontario
First Canadian-born Governor-General of Canada.

St. Rémi de Napierville, Quebec
Prime Minister Pierre Trudeau's family vault.

FACING PAGE: *Alert Bay, Northwest Territories*
On the shore of the Arctic Ocean, crosses erected
for a crew killed on a supply run.

NEXT PAGE: *Heritage Cemetery, Cobourg, Ontario*

Cemetery at Chantry, Leeds County, Ontario

Notre-Dame-des-Neiges Cemetery, Montreal, Quebec

Heritage Cemetery, Cobourg, Ontario

St. Michael's Ukrainian Orthodox Cemetery, Gardenton, Manitoba

St. Andrew's on the Red, near Selkirk, Manitoba

Mount Pleasant Cemetery, Toronto, Ontario

York Cemetery, Toronto, Ontario
Monument for Tim and Lori Horton.

The Old Burying Ground, Fredericton, New Brunswick

Sacred
To the Memory of
MARMADUKE HARE BRADSHAW
Son of
FRANCIS BRADSHAW of this Place
Surgeon and SARAH his Wife
who by falling into a Pot of boiling Water
was to dreadfully scalded but he survived
the accident but a few Hours.
He died on the 6TH Day of May 1800
Aged 5 Years 6 Months and 18 Days.

Placentia, Newfoundland

Mount Pleasant Cemetery, Toronto, Ontario

Marble Island, Hudson Bay
Whaler's grave.

ABOVE: *Notre-Dame-des-Neiges Cemetery, Montreal, Quebec*
Monument for Robert Bourassa.

RIGHT: *Hirsch Community Cemetery, near Estevan, Saskatchewan*

NEXT PAGE: *Cataraqui Cemetery, Kingston, Ontario*

UNKNOWN

GR... MEL REBMANN
ER... JULY 27, 2001
IF TEARS COULD BUILD A STAIRWAY
AND MEMORIES A LANE, I'D WALK
RIGHT UP TO HEAVEN DARLING AND
BRING YOU HOME AGAIN
MUM & DAD

ABOVE: *Mount Pleasant Cemetery, Toronto, Ontario*

RIGHT: *Fairview Lawn Cemetery, Halifax, Nova Scotia*

FAR RIGHT: *Mount Pleasant Cemetery, Toronto, Ontario*

FACING PAGE: *Trent Valley Cemetery, Hastings, Ontario*

ERECTED
TO THE MEMORY
OF AN
UNKNOWN CHILD
WHOSE REMAINS
WERE RECOVERED
AFTER THE
DISASTER TO
THE "TITANIC"
APRIL 15TH 1912

Newtown, Bonavista North, Newfoundland

Saint-Jean-Port-Joli, Quebec.

St. Ann's First Nation Parish, near Duncan, British Columbia

LEFT: *Groesbeek Canadian War Cemetery, Nijmegen, Holland*

BELOW: *Notre Dame Cemetery, Ottawa, Ontario*

ABOVE: *Botanical Cremation Gardens, Beechwood Cemetery, Ottawa, Ontario*

BELOW: *Little Plume Cemetery, near Swift Current, Saskatchewan*

FACING PAGE: *Mount Royal Cemetery, Montreal, Quebec*

ABOVE: *Church of England Cemetery, St. John's, Newfoundland*
FACING PAGE: *Holy Sepulchre Cemetery, Hamilton, Ontario*

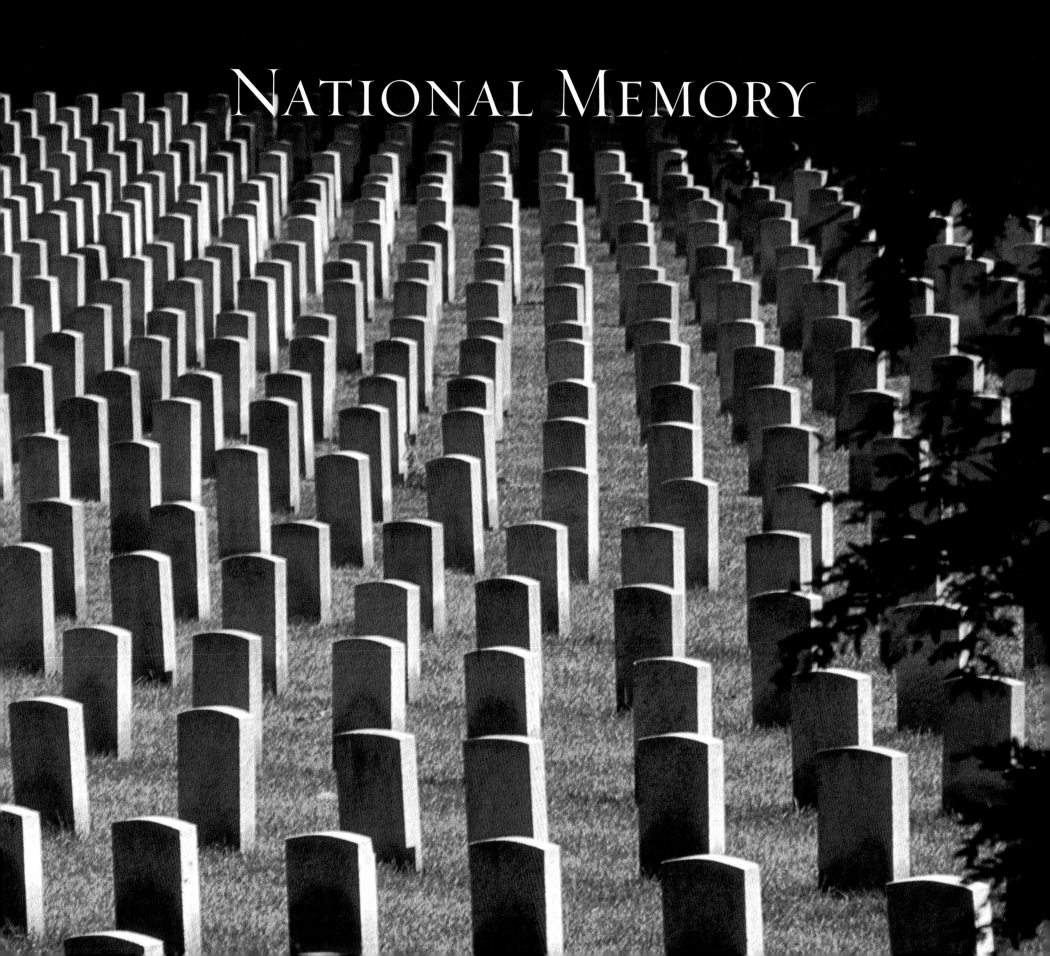

National Memory

NATIONAL MEMORY

Lest we forget

❧ "Show me the manner in which a nation cares for its dead, and I will measure with mathematical exactness the tender mercies of its people, their respect for the laws of the land and their loyalty to high ideals." The quotation from William Gladstone, four times prime minister of Britain between 1868 and 1894, is especially pertinent to war memorials. For better and worse, nations have historically defined their boundaries by wars, and a nation's essential character may be measured by its commemoration of its war dead. National memory is most explicit in burial grounds and cenotaphs honouring those who died in battle.

In the United States, a nation established by armed revolution and tested by a civil war in which more than 600,000 died, Abraham Lincoln's Gettysburg Address has been part of American national memory ever since the president was requested to make "a few appropriate remarks" at the consecration on November 19, 1863, of the Gettysburg Cemetery for the Union war dead:

Fourscore and seven years ago our fathers brought forth, upon this continent, a new nation, conceived in liberty, and dedicated to the proposition that all men are created equal.

Now we are engaged in a great civil war, testing whether that nation, or any nation so conceived, and so dedicated, can long endure. We are met on a great battle-field of that war. We have come to dedicate a portion of it, as a final resting place for those who died here, that the nation might live. This we may, in all propriety do. But, in a larger sense, we cannot dedicate — we cannot consecrate — we cannot hallow, this ground — The brave men, living and dead, who struggled here, have hallowed it, far above our poor power to add or detract. The world will little note, nor long remember what we say here; while it can never forget what they did here.

The appropriateness of Lincoln's celebrated remarks lies not only in his memorably succinct phrasing, but also in his focus on the future. Remembrance of these dead and the resolution that they shall not have died in vain are requisite for the generation of new life. "It is rather for us, the living [to] be dedicated to the great task remaining

FACING PAGE: *Tomb of the Unknown Soldier, Ottawa, Ontario*

PAGE 188–189: *Woodland Cemetery, Hamilton, Ontario*
Veterans' area.

before us ... that we here highly resolve that these dead shall not have died in vain; that the nation shall have a new birth of freedom, and that government of the people by the people for the people, shall not perish from the earth." War memorials not only celebrate the sacrifice made by the dead, and honour them for their devotion and dedication, but also remind the living of our obligation to carry on the struggle for a better life.

The war dead are not the only ones requiring a memorial. The disasters of war affect survivors as well, particularly those who have to cope with death on a catastrophic scale. They have also struggled bravely and their dedication ought not to be forgotten. Calamities of disease and other civilian disasters also require places in national memory.

Seven Years' War

❧ The small Hôpital-Géneral cemetery, dating from 1710 and still in use, is the final resting place of more than 1,000 French, British, Canadian and Aboriginal men who died during the Seven Years' War (1756–63).

In June 1755, just a few days after Quebec's Hôtel-Dieu was incapacitated by a fire, 400 sick soldiers and sailors disembarked in the first arrival of regular French troops, and the Hôpital-Général was transformed into a military hospital. The arrival of Montcalm's troops in the following year brought another 600 sick men from their trans-Atlantic voyage directly to the hospital wards. The ravages of fever ended only in March 1759, just three months before the arrival of the English forces. Their bombardment of Quebec brought a large number of civilians, seeking refuge beyond the range of English cannon-fire. The English fired approximately 40,000 cannonballs into Quebec during the siege, reducing much of the town to ruins.

The battles of Montmorency, the Plains of Abraham and Sainte-Foy followed in quick succession. According to the custom of the time, those who died on the battlefields were buried in common graves. The wounded were carried to the hospital, where the nuns impartially cared for French, British, Canadian or Aboriginal men. Those who died in hospital, regardless of which side they had fought for, were buried in common graves in the hospital's cemetery – Catholics in consecrated ground and Protestants on the other side of the surrounding wall. The nuns not only coped with providing care under extreme duress but also prepared a *relation*, or missionary report, to their order in France, a vividly written record of the disasters of this war:

Another pen than mine would be needed to paint the horrors that we had to see and hear during the twenty-four hours that the transfer of the wounded continued, the cries of the dying and the suffering of the affected ... After having set up more than five hundred beds ... there still remained as many again to find a place for. Our barns and stables were filled with these poor unfortunates. We had sixty-two officers in our infirmaries, thirty-three of whom died. One could see nothing but severed arms and legs.

The nuns also preserved a register, in which were inscribed the names, rank and company name and sometimes the place of residence, of more than 1,000 military men buried in the cemetery between 1755 and 1760. It was this register that made possible the modern memorial which incorporates the names of those men – like the Vimy Memorial, with its catalogue of names of Canadian soldiers who died in France on the battlefields of the First World War. It is also reminiscent of American Civil War cemeteries, where men who fought on opposing sides share a common fate and burial place.

In 1760 the Hôpital-Général returned to caring for aged and infirm civilians, and its cemetery served the parish of Notre-Dame-des-Anges. The unmarked military graves began to fade from memory. The end of the 20th century brought a renewed recognition of the national significance of this small burial place. The Seven Years' War Memorial, with its inscriptions of the names of the buried soldiers, was inaugurated in 2001. Following a solemn cortège from

Hôpital-Général Cemetery, Quebec City, Quebec
The double nature of this national site of memory is recognized by Pascale Archambault's sculpture *Traversée sans retour* (Crossing with no return). Two incomplete figures of men grapple aggressively across a wide crevice in a slab of stone, both oblivious to the lifeboat below.

the Chapel of the Ursulines in the old city, the remains of Lieutenant General Montcalm, who had been mortally wounded on the Plains of Abraham, were transferred to a new mausoleum in the cemetery where so many of his soldiers were buried.

The leader of the English forces, General James Wolfe, mortally wounded on the same battlefield, was buried at his family's parish church, St. Alfege's, in Greenwich, near London. According to a legend repeated in years past, before fighting his last battle Wolfe recited lines from Thomas Gray's "Elegy Written in a Country Church-Yard" and added, "Gentlemen, I would sooner have written that poem than take Quebec." Wolfe's own copy of Gray's *Elegy*, bearing his handwritten notes, is perhaps a more authentic

record. Next to these words from Gray's finale, "The Epitaph" – "Here rests his head upon the lap of Earth / A Youth to Fortune and to Fame unknown" – Wolfe added this marginal comment: "Yet were he on this score less happy?" Although Wolfe has occasionally been characterized as melancholic, his admiration for Gray's poem reflects an 18th century concept of happiness. Was the life of this unknown youth necessarily "less happy" than the life of a famous hero? To some moderns that concept may seem austere, but it was then worthy of great popular esteem. General Wolfe's comment even seems to anticipate a 20th century view of history – that the lives of unknown footsoldiers are as worthy of celebration as those of famous generals.

War of 1812

❧ On October 13, 1812, Major General Sir Isaac Brock, commander of the British forces in Upper Canada, was killed by an American sharpshooter while his troops repelled the invading force. The battle of Queenston Heights greatly influenced the determination of the Crown and the general population to defend British North America. Brock's death was instrumental in marshalling public opinion against the Americans, with whom Canadians had many connections, both familial and commercial. In 1824 his remains were reburied at the foot of a stone monument erected by the government of the Province of Upper Canada, with support from public subscription. Brock's Monument, as it was always called, was 40 meters tall and designed to be seen by the vanquished Americans on the other side of the Niagara River. Upper Canadians had a respect verging on adoration for the man they deemed responsible for their national survival. Their patriotic pride was much offended on Good Friday in 1840, when the original monument was destroyed by a massive blast of gunpowder, allegedly set off by an American who sympathized with the 1838 Upper Canada Rebellion.

A new monument, dedicated in 1853, was designed by architect William Thomas. It is an even loftier and more impressive column, 56 meters high, surmounted by a statue of Brock. Winding stairs inside the column were restored, allowing visitors to enjoy a prospect of the heights sucessfully defended by Brock's troops.

The design of the second Brock's Monument was obviously influenced by the design of Nelson's Column, the centrepiece of Trafalgar Square in London. Admiral Nelson, one of the British Empire's best-loved heroes, lost his life in 1805 at the Battle of Trafalgar. Like Brock, Nelson was killed by a sharpshooter while his men were defeating the enemy. The Nelson monument is a granite column 56 meters high, which supports a statue of the hero. Nelson's column is an enlarged copy by William Railton of the columns of the Roman

temple of *Mars Ultor*, the god of war as the avenger. Acanthus leaves cast from British cannons decorate the top, and at the base are bronze relief panels depicting Nelson's four great victories, cast from armaments captured from the French. William Thomas, who immigrated to Toronto from England in 1843, undoubtedly knew Nelson's Column well and used it as his model. In the scale of military greatness, General Brock was not quite the equal of Admiral Nelson, nor is his monument quite as superb. But the two columns are comparable both in scale and in the inspiration of Neoclassical design. Both demonstrated how popular hero-worship could be encouraged and celebrated for nationalist purposes.

The Military Burying Ground, which forms part of Victoria Memorial Square, is the oldest existing European burial place in Toronto. It was opened in 1794 in the Military Reserve land in "a clearing in the brushwood" some distance from Fort York, as the place of interment for men of the garrison, their wives and children. It contains an estimated 500 graves (although the *Globe* in May 1900 referred to "more than 800 graves"). One of the earliest was for Lieutenant-Governor Simcoe's 15-month-old daughter, Katherine, who died while the family was living in their portable canvas house near the Queen's Rangers camp. When the York garrison was defeated and briefly occupied in 1813, the American invaders buried the dead of both sides in rather hasty fashion along the lakeshore. Through the rest of the War of 1812, York was a hospital station for men wounded in battle, and John Strachan, then the garrison chaplain, noted that he was conducting up to eight burial services each day.

The ground was closed to further burials in 1863, and its maintenance almost immediately became a concern. From the time that the original forest surrounding it had been cleared, the burying ground had been protected only by a picket fence. In the 1830s, lots for private residential villas were auctioned off from part of the Military Reserve. The development plan shows the broad avenue of Wellington Place linking Clarence Square, named after the previous

FACING PAGE: *Brock's Monument, Queenston Heights, Ontario*
An aerial view of Brock's Monument, towering above the Queenston Heights battlefield.

PAGE 196: *Victoria Memorial Square, Toronto, Ontario*
Walter Allward's *Old Soldier.*

PAGE 197: *Old Burying Ground, Halifax, Nova Scotia*
Welsford-Parker Monument.

king, William IV (formerly Duke of Clarence), to Victoria Square, named after the heir to the throne. But by the end of Queen Victoria's long reign, industrial redevelopment had overtaken the area.

In the 1880s the Government of Canada, which owned Victoria Square, cancelled a 21 year lease when the lessee failed to maintain the fence surrounding the Garrison Cemetery. Its neglected condition and incidents of vandalism had become a matter of public concern. The *Globe* reported that a farmer had been observed driving away with headstones in his wagon. The city appointed a Military Burial Ground Commission, which made a survey of the 344 grave mounds that were still visible then, and had the square improved for use as a public park. But in 1895 the clandestine removal of more headstones, including that of Simcoe's daughter ("in place a couple of months back"), was reported. The Army and Navy Veterans' Association persuaded City Council to change the name of the park to Victoria Memorial Square and began a long campaign to raise funds to honour the dead of the War of 1812: "It should be a sacred duty of the citizens to put up some memorial stone at this historic spot."

In January 1907 the monument was finally completed. Seventy veterans and many citizens, led by the mayor, gathered in Victoria Memorial Square to unveil the "Old Soldier" by the sculptor Walter Allward. His earlier commissions in Toronto, for the figure of Peace for the Northwest Rebellion Monument at Queen's Park and the South African War Memorial on University Avenue, had showed his preference for combining allegorical meaning with individual portraiture. His last and greatest project, the monumental Vimy Memorial for Canadians lost or killed in the First World War, would reveal the same strong interest. The Toronto architect Frank Darling, a member of the committee judging the design competition for this monument, was also on the international panel that selected Allward for the Vimy Memorial project. No doubt the Vimy panel members were influenced by the very favourable reception of "The Old Soldier." The half-length

figure was praised for depicting not only "the indomitable courage of a fine British type" but also "the horror of war … through the poignant pathos of the aged and broken veteran."

The sculpture's power was evoked again in 1919, when maimed veterans of the First World War were frequently seen on the streets of many other Canadian communities:

To see the Old Soldier one must make an excursion into a slum of Toronto, a shabby little park or base-ball ground called Portland Square … here indeed is a little neglected shrine of art. For the half figure of a soldier, with his empty coat sleeve and his eager, wonderful old face is absolutely haunting … In this bit of comparatively early work, Mr. Allward gets right away from so-called "portrait study," or a Victorian symbolism which would depict by the conventional figure of a veteran in uniform the idea of patriotism, to something vital and real.

Characteristically, Allward's concept went beyond the narrowly defined terms of his commission. He did not portray a soldier killed in action, one of those who "shall not grow old, as we who are left grow old: / Age shall not weary them, nor the years condemn." Allward's "Old Soldier" has grown old and weary, with just one arm. He represents those veterans whose life after battle has demanded long years of courage, another aspect of the disasters of war.

In the 21st century this formerly shabby little square is a community park. It was described by Jane Jacobs as a potential "urban jewel, rescued from a wasteland of neglect and forgetfulness." The rehabilitation project includes the identification of grave locations by means of remote sensing using a resistivity meter. Just 18 of the original grave markers survive. In a misguided rehabilitation some years ago, the stones were taken from their original locations, positioned horizontally and set in concrete, and have as a result suffered damage from accelerated erosion. They have been removed for conservation, cleaning and storage, until they can appropriately be re-installed. The improved amenities enhancing community use of this park will provide a setting for the continuing interpretation of this richly historical place.

Crimean War

❧ The imposing Welsford-Parker Monument in the Old Burying Ground, Halifax, commemorates Major Augustus Welsford and Captain William Parker, two Nova Scotians serving in the British Army during during the Crimean War (1853–56), who died at the siege of Sebastopol. It is a rare early example of a war memorial erected by public subscription to commemorate individuals who died in foreign combat. Residents of Halifax had closely followed news of the war, not only through personal letters and military dispatches, but in reports sent from the field by William Russell (the world's first war correspondent) and published in *The Times* of London. They could also read Welsford's obituary in the *Illustrated London News*: "The major was a general favourite, and his loss is sincerely deplored in his native place. For three years ending in 1852 his regiment was stationed in Halifax, and he endeared himself to a very numerous circle of friends."

The end of the year-long siege in September 1855 was celebrated in Halifax by an estimated 10,000 to 12,000 people who enjoyed the night-time bonfires and illuminations, as the *Morning Journal* reported:

A triumphal arch ... produced a fine effect. Transparencies graced the front of the Court House and New Market, such as the flags of England, Turkey and France crossed, and above them the words "VICTORY" and "GLORY TO ALLIES" "SEBASTOPOL HAS FALLEN." H.M. Ship Boscamen was beautifully illuminated and decorated. Dartmouth looked well from this side.

The monument design by George Lang, a Scottish-born stone mason was a classical triumphal arch surmounted by a lion, symbol of English military strength. The lion was carved from a single 14-ton block of sandstone from New Brunswick. The result was a splendid "physical manifestation of the mood of [the] community at one particular moment," expressing the spirit of Halifax in the 1850s.

Northwest Rebellion

❧ The Northwest Rebellion ended with the Battle of Batoche in May 1885. On the battlefield were 27 dead from both sides. The cemetery at the battlefield has been recognized since 1923 as a National Historic Site. The mass grave of Métis who died in the battle is marked by nine wooden crosses, enclosed within a modest picket fence. Gabriel Dumont, who commanded the Métis forces, was buried there when he died in 1906. A memorial in Ottawa commemorates two members of the "Sharpshooters Company" of the Governor General's Foot Guards. Their regiment had originally been formed in Quebec City in 1861 as a volunteer company of civil servants. When the civil service moved to Ottawa in 1865, the corps came with it. The Prince of Wales (later King Edward VII) became their Honorary Colonel, and they adopted the plumes of the Prince of Wales as their badge. The corps was called out on active service because of the Fenian threat in 1866, and in 1884 four of its members volunteered for the Nile Expedition to relieve General Gordon at Khartoum, but it did not come under fire until the Battle of Cut Knife Hill. The two men commemorated in Ottawa were the regiment's first fatalities.

Designed by British sculptor Percy Wood, the monument displays relief portraits of Private William B. Osgoode and Private John Rogers, and a bronze statue of a guardsman wearing his plumed headgear, resting on arms reversed. It was installed in 1888 at a downtown site now occupied by the Chateau Laurier hotel. Its later relocation to Nepean Point, farther from the Parliament Buildings, may reflect a shift of opinion about the rights and wrongs of the conflict in which the lives of these two men were sacrificed.

Mount Pleasant Cemetery in Toronto has two monuments connected with the Northwest Rebellion. The Fitch family monument is an architecturally elaborate miniature granite temple structure, sheltering a bronze bust effigy of Lieutenant William Charles Fitch of the Royal Grenadiers, "killed in action at Batoche, N' W' T'." The pedestal is decorated with the bronzed scabbard of his sword and a bronze medallion, which bears an enigmatic heraldic device – the Latin motto "SPES JUVAT" ("Hope delights") and a fierce lamb's head with a sword. Two other members of Toronto's Tenth Battalion of the Royal Grenadiers, Private Thomas Moor and Private Isaac Thomas Hughes, are commemorated in a 14-foot-high monument, unveiled in 1887 in the presence of 400 members of the regiment. The stele presents an elaborate architectural structure for a relief carving of insignia, military regalia, and weapons and armour from classical antiquity.

First World War

❧ In 1917 Canada, as part of the British Empire, became a member of the Imperial War Graves Commission. In no previous war had individual graves been provided for ordinary soldiers who died on the fields of battle. The commission was established to administer orderly burial, to establish permanent cemeteries and to determine how to memorialize the dead and missing. Its work was guided by several fundamental principles: that no privately erected memorials would be permitted on the battlefields; that each of the dead should be commemorated individually by name either on a headstone over the grave or by an inscription on a memorial if the burial was unknown; that headstones and memorials should be permanent; that headstones should be uniform; and that there should be no distinction made on account of military or civil rank, race or creed. The remains of those who died in battle were buried in rows with almost identical headstones. The graves of the wounded who died in Canada were marked by headstones of the same design. These are "the crosses row on row" that mark the military burial sections in Canadian cemeteries.

Where climate permitted, the commission's cemeteries in Europe were "laid out to the standard of an English coun-

ABOVE: *Mount Pleasant Cemetery,*
Toronto, Ontario
Fitch family monument.

RIGHT: *Mount Pleasant Cemetery,*
Toronto, Ontario

try garden in harmony with the character of their surroundings," following the precepts of the celebrated English horticulturist Gertrude Jekyll. To create a sentimental association between the gardens of home and the foreign field where the soldiers lay, the cemeteries were planted with species native to the member countries wherever possible. Thus maples were planted near Canadian graves. But these European graveyards were not enough for Canadians, most of whom could not hope to visit them. War memorials in Canada were needed.

The Peace Tower, built between 1919 and 1927 in front of the Parliament Buildings in Ottawa, is a free-standing campanile with a carillon, a feature meant to recall the bell towers whose sounds were heard across the fields of France and Flanders. The idea of preserving remnants of battlefields finds expression in the Memorial Chamber, where the walls are lined with stone from France and Belgium, and the floor is paved with stone from grounds where Canadians died. The Book of Remembrance on display honours the memory of 619,636 Canadians who served abroad during the First World War.

The remains of the 66,655 who lost their lives while serving overseas were not repatriated for burial. Of those, 19,660 were posted "missing, presumed dead" and have no known graves. In Canada, as in England and France, men whose deaths could not be confirmed by personal identification haunted the collective imagination. In 1920 a French unknown soldier was buried beneath the Arc de Triomphe in Paris and a British "Unknown Warrior" in Westminster Abbey in London. Eighty years later, the Tomb of the Unknown Soldier was installed as a complement to the National War Memorial in Ottawa.

FAR LEFT: *The Great War Memorial,*
Thunder Bay, Ontario

LEFT: *The Great War Memorial,*
Burlington, Ontario
Sculpted by R.V. Lewis and
Florence Wyle.

Throughout the 1920s, funds were raised in thousands of Canadian communities to build memorials to those local men – often remembered as "boys" – who did not return home from the Great War. A few practical buildings were constructed, but almost all memorials were dedicated, permanent cenotaphs. Some took the form of Scottish stone cairns, some were architectural limestone or granite structures, and some were sculptures representing Canadian soldiers in bronze or marble. After decades of exposure to the open air, many now require expensive restoration.

The Cenotaph in Hamilton, Ontario, unveiled in 1923 by Governor General Viscount Byng of Vimy, was originally funded by more than $5,000 raised by Hamilton branches of the Canadian Club. In 1953 alterations costing $2,000 were sponsored by the United Council of Veterans. By 2004 urgent repairs costing $120,000 were needed, and there was "no money for such work in the city budget."

The Hamilton Cenotaph, flanked by columns supporting sculptures of helmets and other equipment used by Canadian troops, is a replica (like others throughout the British Empire) of the Cenotaph in Westminster, London. The eminent architect Sir Edwin Lutyens was given 14 days by the British prime minister, Lloyd George, to design and produce a temporary wood and plaster structure for the peace celebrations on July 19, 1919. It met with such immediate popular acclaim that it was rebuilt in Portland Stone for Remembrance Day in 1920. The massive monolith, a high pedestal supporting a garlanded casket, has a deceptively simple silhouette, but its lines are subtly complicated by artful mathematical calculations. Its surfaces, which appear to be flat, are actually imperceptibly curved, exhibiting entasis, a refinement of Greek architecture seen (for example) in the Parthenon.

Lutyens' drawings show that he meant the vertical sides to taper so that their imagined extensions would meet at a point 1,000 feet in the air. The horizontal lines of the steps at the base made a part of large circles with a radial centre point 900 feet below the ground. "The Secret of the Cenotaph" is that the Cenotaph is not only what you see. It is invisibly buried deep in the earth and also linked with an unseen point in the high heavens. Its visible outline can also be read as the grip of a sword, with its base the hand guard, and its blade sheathed in the earth. A patriotic reference may have been intended to the Arthurian legend, the Matter of Britain, where the hilt of Excalibur is found in a stone in a graveyard, waiting for the "Rightwise King Born of all England" to grasp it. But more generally, and more in the spirit of the Peace Conference of 1919, the Cenotaph-sword was a symbol of the ancient prophecy (not yet fulfilled) that "nation shall not lift up sword against nation, neither shall they learn war any more" (Isaiah 2: 4).

Montreal sculptor G.W. (George) Hill was commissioned to make memorials in Montreal, Westmount, Sherbrooke, Lachute and Magog in Quebec, Pictou in Nova Scotia, Morrisburg in Ontario, and many other places, including Charlottetown and Harbord Collegiate Institute in Toronto. The costs for restoring the Charlottetown memorial in 2001 were comparable to the original payment to Hill. By 2003 the memorial commissioned by Harbord Collegiate staff and students had fallen into disrepair. The bronze soldier's rifle had lost its bayonet, and the memorial needed protection from skateboarders. It seemed at first that no one would take responsibility for financing the memorial's restoration: "In Ottawa, the Canadian heritage department says it isn't into war monuments, while Veterans Affairs is focused on the large installations at Dieppe, Vimy and 11 other battlefields in Europe. It has no funds to maintain hundreds of small monuments of varying allure across Canada." The Toronto District School Board was "deficit-ridden," and the mandate of the Harbord Foundation was solely to provide student bursaries: "The heritage of academic excellence and ethnic tolerance pioneered at Harbord Collegiate is the most important tradition of all ... 'The bursaries are for the living, the students of today ... If we have to choose, then the students are more sacred than the monument.'" The Harbord Club alumni organization, along with Harbord's current staff and students, raised donations and provided an estimated $200,000 to restore the bronze fig-

FACING PAGE: *Harbord Collegiate Institute, Toronto, Ontario* "Our Soldier" War Memorial, sculpted by George W. Hill.

ure and its granite pedestal and to build a new protective wall bearing the names of Harbord Collegiate's Second World War dead. At its rededication on November 11, 2005, the sculpture was named "Our Soldier." The community of students, staff and alumni had taken proud ownership of him.

The undetermined responsibility for maintaining and restoring this particular sculpture, and the dismissive tone of the slighting reference to "hundreds of small monuments of varying allure across Canada," ought to be set in appropriate artistic and community contexts. Many of Canada's most talented sculptors received these commissions. The proliferation of monuments sponsored by schools and other local institutions was prompted by a widespread need to commemorate neighbours and colleagues lost in the war. The chosen designs tended to be representational rather than allegorical, reflecting the belief that soldiers should be honoured as individuals. It is perhaps ironic that the names of so many of their sculptors have been almost forgotten.

In April 1922, the "Burlington and Nelson Citizens' Memorial In Honor of the Men of Burlington and Nelson Township who served in the Great War 1914–1919" was unveiled by "His Excellency General The Right Honorable LORD BYNG, of Vimy, G.C.B., G.C.M.G., M.V.O., Governor General of Canada, and Commander-in-chief." Clearly, Lord Byng unveiled one local war memorial after another. It was the first and, so far, the last visit to the town by a Governor General of Canada, and it was also the first and, so far, the best public sculpture unveiled in the city. The typescript records of the Burlington Memorial subscription committee indicate that its cost was $6,150. From the remaining balance, $100 was given to the Veterans Association and the Veterans Women's Auxiliary, and $40 was retained for the maintenance of the monument. Its restoration in 2000 (paid for by the city and the province's millennium fund) cost $30,000.

The committee also recorded the terms of their commission. On the side of the granite pedestal were inscribed "the names of all the boys who were killed, or died in harness overseas, from the Town of Burlington and the township of

P.L.McGAVIN R.F.C. + 2nd Lt D.H.McGIBBON R.A.F.

Gnr A.McINTOSH 9th Bde C.F.A. + Lt G.K.MACKENDRIC

IE R.A.F. + Lt G.L.B.MACKENZIE 3rd Bn + Capt W.

McLAUGHLIN 2nd Bn + Lt H.J.MACLAURIN 16th Bn

+ Lt D.G.MACLEAN R.F.C. + Lt G.D.McLEAN Tank

LENNAN R.N. + Capt D.D.MACLEOD 49th Bn + Cpl

K.MACPHERSON 42nd Bn + Gnr S.M.MACPHERSO

HELL K.Shrops L.I. + 2nd Lt J.R.MAGUIRE W.York R. + Lt H

MALLOUGH C.A.M.C. + Lt M.E.MALONE 15th Bn + 2nd

TIN 58th Bn + Pte I.B.MARTY 75th Bn + Pte W.A.MARWO

R.A.F. + Lt G.J.MEC

von H.MICH

C

C

C.A.M.C. + Maj

NEWCOMBE

Lt

NICHOLSON

VARSITY

DENT

BODY

Nelson," and on the back "the names of the principal battles, which the Canadians took an active part in." The sculpture itself required more consideration:

The Committee set to work to study designs of a monumental nature. From the first, the Committee was impressed with the figure of the Victory Statue, used in Toronto for the Victory Loan Campaign; this brought them into communication with Mr. R.V. Lewis, the sculptor of that statue, but he was not in favour of using that model for a permanent memorial; ... his idea being that the statue ... should be as near as possible a representation of a soldier just returning to the trenches, with that determined look on his face, which was characteristic of all our men.

... The statue, as we have said, is entirely of bronze and depicts an infantry soldier standing at ease in a great-coat; the bottom is torn off, as was usual, fully equipped for the trenches: under his steel helmet, he wears a wool Balaclava helmet, knitted by the women of Canada, his face is calm, but shows that determination, which enabled them to carry on through all difficulties and dangers.

Funding and erecting monuments continued during the great Depression of the 1930s. One outstanding example is the Belgian War Memorial erected on the Boulevard Provencher in Saint Boniface near Le Club Belge, the social club of the Belgian immigrant community. The project of honouring their fallen countrymen was greeted with enthusiasm, and funds were raised and the monument erected within a year. It commemorates the suffering that followed Germany's 1914 invasion of Belgium. The sculptor was Hubert Garnier, whose family had immigrated from France to Saint Boniface in 1913. Garnier had studied art in Winnipeg, Chicago and Vancouver and apprenticed with sculptors in Paris, New York and Chicago. The monument to the Belgian dead of the First World War has two figures sculpted in stone on a base of large irregular stones. The standing figure contemplates his fallen comrade.

In neighbouring Winnipeg, a cenotaph competition resulted in public controversy when the sculptor of the winning design was discovered to be Emanuel Hahn, who had been born in 1881 at Reutlingen, Würtemburg, Germany, and had, at the age of seven, emigrated with his family to Toronto. He was not granted the commission. A second competition was held, requiring all applicants to state that they were Canadian-born. The winner was Elizabeth Wyn Wood, born near Orillia, but unfortunately she had recently married her teacher, a native of Germany – Hahn, in fact – and her Winnipeg project also did not get commissioned. Cenotaphs in Petrolia and Alvinston, Ontario, as well as numerous other monuments, were designed and completed by Hahn, and his work is familiar to all who handle Canadian coins. The Caribou quarter and the Bluenose schooner dime are his designs.

The unveiling of the last large memorial, that commissioned by the residents of Welland and Crowland, Ontario, was scheduled for the Labour Day holiday, September 4, 1939. Louis Temporale completed the stone cutting, which was based on a full-size clay model sculpted by Elizabeth Wyn Wood. Her design departs from the usual representation of a single soldier to include an additional heroic figure, a woman. Both figures symbolize "Service and Sacrifice," not only of those who fought in foreign lands, but also of those who supported the war effort at home. On September 3, England again declared war on Germany. The Great War had not ended all war. Speakers at the unveiling the following day had to refer to the commemoration of "the War Dead of the last Great War" at the opening of "what may prove to be a conflict of longer duration and a harder and more bitter struggle." With inscriptions added later for the dead of the Second World War and the Korean War, this and all the earlier memorials now serve as community gathering places for annual observances on Remembrance Day.

FACING PAGE: *Hart House, University of Toronto, Ontario*
World War I Memorial.

National War Memorials

Monuments sprang up in communities across Canada, but there was also popular pressure to erect national memorials for annual ceremonial observances of remembrance. The signing of the Peace Treaty in Paris, 1919, was celebrated by a victory parade that included a march past a "great catafalque" temporarily erected beside the Arc de Triomphe. In London, the British celebration featured Lutyens' Cenotaph, which was also meant to be a temporary structure. "Cenotaph" is derived from the Greek words *kenos* and *taphos* meaning "empty tomb." This type of memorial originated in the importance attached by Greeks in the classical era to the proper burial of their dead. If recovery of the corpse was not possible, either because of defeat in war or because death took place at sea, the ancient Greeks built a cenotaph. A *sema* (a piece of stone or a stone figure) substituted for the missing body an external sign of the invisible dead, who was kept alive in memory by the inscription on the stone. This concept gripped the imagination of many in Britain, and the victory parade in London was barely over before the question of making the temporary cenotaph a permanent structure in Whitehall began to attract attention and support. It was transformed into a permanent memorial by the "sentiment of millions." Canada has two national cenotaphs, one in Vimy and one in Ottawa.

Vimy, France, was the site of Canada's first national cenotaph. In 1922 the French nation granted the people of Canada the use for all time of the land for the park and memorial. Designed by Walter Allward, the Vimy Memorial stands on Hill 145, overlooking the Canadian battlefield at one of the points of the fiercest fighting in 1917. Inscribed on its ramparts are the names of 11,285 Canadian soldiers who were posted "missing, presumed dead" in France. The same number of Canadian trees and shrubs are planted in the large surrounding park (which preserves the contours of part of the battle-devastated field). When the memorial was unveiled in 1936, King Edward VIII said it was "a memorial to no man, but a memorial for a nation." Its base bears the inscription, in English and French: *"To the valour of their countrymen in the Great War / and in memory of their sixty thousand dead this monument is raised by the people of Canada."*

The memorial's ramparts and towering pylons were constructed of very durable limestone from an ancient quarry in Yugoslavia. The same material was used for the 20 allegorical figures, twice as large as life, which were carved on site over a period of 10 years by stonecutters working from plaster casts made from Allward's original life-size clay sculptures. Allward said that his idea for the memorial was inspired by a dream:

When things were at their blackest in France, I went to sleep one night after dwelling on all the muck and misery over there ... I dreamed I was in a great battlefield. I saw our men going in by the thousands and being mowed down by the sickles of death ... Suffering beyond endurance at the sight, I turned my eyes and found myself looking down on an avenue of poplars. Suddenly through the avenue I saw thousands marching to the aid of our armies. They were the dead. They rose in masses, filed silently by and entered the fight to aid the living. So vivid was this impression, that when I awoke it stayed with me for months. Without the dead we were helpless. So I have tried to show this in this monument to Canada's fallen, what we owed them and we will forever owe them.

Allward also described the meaning and form of his allegorical design:

At the base of the strong impregnable walls of defence are the Defenders, one group showing the Breaking of the Sword, the other the Sympathy of the Canadians for the Helpless. Above these are the mouths of guns covered with olive and laurels. On the wall stands an heroic figure of Canada brooding over the graves of her valiant dead; below is suggested a grave with a helmet, laurels, etc. Behind her stand two pylons symbolizing the two forces — Canadian and French — while between, at the base of these, is the Spirit of Sacrifice, who, giving all, throws the torch to his Comrades. Looking up they see the figures of Peace, Justice, Truth and Knowledge, etc., for which they fought, chanting the Hymn of Peace. Around these figures are the shields of Britain, Canada and France. On the outside of the pylons is the Cross.

In this context, the cross on the Vimy Memorial may be compared to the Cross of Sacrifice designed for the Imperial War Graves Commission by the architect Sir Reginald Blomfield, who declared that he had "taken immense pains" to create a symbol that would be free of the "cusps and crockets" associated with the Gothic church style favoured by "antiquaries": "What I wanted to do in designing this Cross was to make it as abstract and impersonal as I could, to free it from any association with any particular style and above all, to keep clear of any of the sentimentalities of Gothic. This was a man's war far too horrible for any fripperies, and I hoped to get within range of the infinite in this symbol of the ideals of those who had gone out to die." Like Allward, Blomfield had aimed at creating a symbol that excluded no form of belief.

The recent restoration and rehabilitation of the Vimy Memorial may help prove the truth of Winston Churchill's prediction:

We know the mutability of human arrangements, but even if our language, our institutions, and our Empire all have faded from the memory of man, these great stones will still preserve the memory of a common purpose pursued by a great nation in the remote past and will undoubtedly excite the wonder and the reverence of future ages.

The National War Memorial is situated in a position of power, on Confederation Square near Parliament Hill in Ottawa. Its form, a high narrow granite arch, expresses a complex combination of two symbolic traditions. The classical triumphal arch, through which victorious armies paraded, was built to celebrate the successes of war. The most famous example was the Arch of Titus in Rome, built after the imperial conquest of Judea in the Jewish Wars (66 –70 AD). Its sculpted reliefs illustrate the triumphal parade of Roman soldiers carrying the spoils of war, sacred objects looted from the destruction of the Temple in Jerusalem.

The terms of the competition for the design of the Canadian War Memorial stipulated that no attempt should be made to glorify war. The international competition made it implicit that there would be no celebration of especially Canadian military prowess, and it was understood that

Ottawa was no imperial capital. The design by Vernon March of England successfully transformed the tradition of the triumphal arch. Unlike the arches of Paris and Rome, the elevated arch in Ottawa is not meant for parades of military forces. Only the larger-than-life sculptures can pass through it. The 22 allegorical figures atop the memorial arch are not celebrating victory, but anticipating demands to be made on them in the struggle they are going forward to meet. They represent the "Great Response of Canada," or more particularly the volunteer response of hundreds of thousands of individual Canadians who answered the call to serve during the war. The memorial's location alters the traditional perspective in another way: viewers are not expected to join in or follow behind the army. Rather, the figures of historic self-sacrifice are moving on a higher plane – not expecting a welcoming return home, but rather a higher destiny.

Much simplified from the elaborate classical tradition, this modernist arch is unadorned by sculpted reliefs celebrating victory and fame. Originally the monument bore the sole inscription "1914–1918." It was rededicated in 1982, when the bronze numerals "1939–1945" and "1950–1953" were added to commemorate Canada's war dead in later wars.

In May 2000 the remains of an unknown Canadian soldier who died near Vimy Ridge were repatriated from France and buried in front of the Memorial in the Tomb of the Unknown Soldier designed by Canadian sculptor Mary-Ann Liu. A granite sarcophagus has a cast-bronze cover, a sculpture representing key elements of the stone carving on the altar of the Vimy Memorial – a medieval sword, a helmet of the type worn in the First World War, branches of maple leaves and laurel leaves, which symbolize both victory and death. Far from commemorating a war to end all war, this memorial includes on one corner piece a poppy, which is said to represent "those who may fall in future conflicts."

The headstone from the Unknown Soldier's grave at Vimy was also relocated to Ottawa. It is the only artifact in the Memorial Hall in the new War Museum. The single window in the Memorial Hall is located so that on Remembrance Day at 11:00 a.m. a shaft of sunlight falls precisely on the headstone.

The Irish Memorial

Grosse-Île, despite its name, is a not-very-large island only three miles long and a mile wide, lying mid-channel in the St. Lawrence River, 30 miles east of Quebec City. From 1832 until 1937 the island served as a quarantine station for the Port of Quebec, then the main port of arrival for European immigrants to Canada. Now it is a National Historic Site commemorating the importance of immigration to Canada during the period from the early 19th century to the First World War. The tragic deaths on Grosse-Île of more than 6,000 Irish immigrants, particularly during the typhus epidemic of 1847, are commemorated by the Irish Memorial.

The quarantine station was established in the context of a great increase in immigration from the British Isles, particularly Ireland and Scotland, after the end of the Napoleonic Wars in 1815. From around 1830, an average of 30,000 immigrants – approximately two-thirds of them from Ireland – began to arrive annually in Quebec. This unprecedented influx took place at the time when the second cholera pandemic had begun raging in Britain in 1831. The numbers of immigrants arriving on Canadian shores began to increase almost twofold, and the risks of an epidemic heightened with the arrival of every overcrowded and insanitary ship. As a means of containing this dreaded disease and preventing its spread into Canada, the colonial authorities set up a quarantine station on Grosse-Île. But by 1832 there was insufficent space on the island to deal with the numbers of sick passengers, which were increasing at an alarming and uncontrollable rate. By mid-June ships were bypassing the island, and more than 25,000 people landed directly in Quebec City. By summer's end 51,422 immigrants had entered, and almost 3,300 deaths were reported in the city and on Grosse Île. The number of sick immigrants dwindled in the following year. The station had to deal with another cholera outbreak in 1834, but then remained relatively quiet until 1847, when a far greater tragedy began to unfold.

The tragic events of that year stemmed from the Great Irish Famine (1845 to 1849). During those years of hunger the population of Ireland declined by more than two million. One half of them died from starvation, disease or malnutrition, while the other half emigrated. (The population of Ireland is even today smaller than in 1841.) An unprecedented number of Irish people sought refuge in Canada. In the 1847 shipping season, more than 100,000 immigrants sailed for Quebec; in previous years, the average number had been 25,000 to 30,000. Most were Irish. Already weakened by malnutrition and starvation, they had been crowded aboard sailboats that were unfit for transporting human cargo. Although ships normally took an average of 45 days to make the crossing, 26 of those that set sail in 1847 took over 60 days. The passengers reached their destination in a deplorable state, many already infected with typhus, a disease that soon reached epidemic proportions.

At Grosse Île, the situation was precarious. Although the quarantine station had been enlarged, it was barely equipped to meet the demand, and its staff were overworked. There was a medical staff of three, headed by Dr. George Douglas. The first ship to arrive, 10 days after preparations were completed, was the *Syria,* discharging 231 passengers, of whom 84 needed admission with typhus fever. Only two weeks after the opening, Dr. Douglas had 850 patients in his hospital and a further 500 on board ships awaiting admission. Week by terrible week more arrived. Several ships had to lie at anchor and await inspectors and medical personnel. Usually quarantines averaged six days, but that year several vessels had to stay for over 20 days. Records from 1847 show that 398 ships were inspected at Grosse Île and 441 in Quebec. Seventy-seven carried more than 400 passengers each. Seventy-three ships were from Liverpool, the main port of departure, and 24 were from Bremen, Germany. The rest were all from Ireland – 50 from Limerick, 33 from Cork, 29 from Glasgow, 27 from Dublin, 26 from Sligo, and 21 from Belfast.

An objective historical account notes that during the first decades of the quarantine station's history, the Canadian government had no control over British emigration, which

BELOW: *Grosse-Île, Quebec*
Gravesite plot of Irish immigrants
who died of typhus.

FACING PAGE: *Grosse-Île, Quebec*

was managed by colonial authorities, and that "the operation of the station was characterized by haste, improvisation, and trial and error, without any real understanding of the causes, spread and treatment of infectious diseases." The terrible experience of thousands of Irish immigrants undoubtedly taught "a number of essential lessons" in medical treatment and efficiency, and one historian has concluded that "in the final analysis [their] death and suffering were not in vain." That conclusion would not have satisfied the Ancient Order of Hibernians, who in 1909 erected the Irish Memorial, a 50-foot high Celtic Cross cut from Irish stone, with inscriptions in English, French and Gaelic. The English reads:

To the sacred memory of thousands of Irish who, in order to preserve their faith, suffered famine and exile, and, victims of typhus, ended their sorrowful pilgrimage here, comforted and strengthened by the Canadian Priests. Those who sow in tears reap in joy.

The French inscription is comparable, but the Gaelic blessing has a more bitter political edge:

Children of the Gael died in their thousands on this island having fled from the laws of the foreign tyrants and an artificial famine in the years 1847-48. God's loyal blessing upon them. Let this monument be a token to their name and honour from the Gaels of America. God Save Ireland.

The Irish cemetery was laid out in 1832 on a plateau between two crags located southwest of Cholera Bay. It holds over 6,000 of Grosse Île's 7,553 individual burial plots. Individual burials were performed until 1847, when long trenches were dug to serve as mass graves. Grosse Île has become a point of pilgrimage.

The numbers of Irish buried at Grosse Île are overwhelming, but so also are the proportions of Irish survivors who started new lives in this new world. Between 1829 and 1851, 60 per cent of all immigrants who came through the port of Quebec were Irish. In the 85 year period from 1829 to 1914 a total of 661,000 Irish immigrants arrived through the port. Thousands died at sea in the cholera and typhus epidemics, in addition to those who reached this island, only to die so close to their intended new home. Many of the survivors had to make new lives for themselves without the children or spouses who had accompanied them when they left Ireland a few weeks earlier. The poignancy of this cemetery lies not merely in the scale of the Irish catastrophe, but in its bitter-sweet intermingling of hope and woe.

MARY	MURPHY	JAMES	NUGENT	ELLEN	PURCELL	BRIDGET	RIGNEY
MARY	MURPHY	JOHN	NUGENT	HUGH	PURCELL	JOHN	RIGNEY
MARY	MURPHY	ELIZA	NUGENT	B.	PURCELL	THADEUS	RIGNEY
MICHAEL	MURPHY	JAMES	O'BRIEN	EDWARD	QUANE	BRIDGET	RIORDAN
MICHAEL	MURPHY	JOHN	O'BRIEN	JOSEPH	QUIGLEY	DANIEL	RIORDAN
PATRICK	MURPHY	JOSEPH	O'BRIEN	MARY	QUIGLEY	JOHN	RIORDAN
PATRICK	MURPHY	MARGARET	O'BRIEN	MICHAEL	QUIGLEY	MARGARET	RIORDAN
PATRICK	MURPHY	MARY	O'BRIEN	THOMAS	QUIGLEY	JANE	RITCHIE
ROSE	MURPHY	MICHAEL	O'BRIEN	THOMAS	QUIGLEY	THOMAS	RITCHIE
SUSAN	MURPHY	PATRICK	O'BRIEN	WILLIAM	QUIGLEY	ANDREW	RIVLACH
SUSAN	MURPHY	TIMOTHY	O'BRIEN	MARTIN	QUIGLEY	JAMES	ROACH
SYBIL	MURPHY	DOMINICK	O'BRIEN	JOHANNA	QUILLIGAN	MARTHA	ROACH
THOMAS	MURPHY	HELEN	O'CONNELL	MARY	QUILTEY	ELIZA	ROBB
THOMAS	MURPHY	HUGH	O'DONNELL	ANN	QUINES	MARGARET	ROBERT
THOMAS	MURPHY	SYDNEY	O'DONNELL	ELLEN	QUINLAN	ALEX	ROBINS
THOMAS	MURPHY	MICHAEL	O'DONNELL	MARGARET	QUINLAN	GEORGE	ROBINS
THOMAS	MURPHY	JAMES	O'DONOGHUE	MARY	QUINLAN	JAMES	ROBINS
TIMOTHY	MURPHY	ANN	O'DOWD	CATHERINE	QUINLAN	JANE	ROBINS
ANN	MURPHY	BARNET	O'HARA	CATHERINE	QUINN	JOHN	ROBINS
ANN	MURRAY	MICHAEL	O'HARA	CHARLES	QUINN	JOHN	ROBINS
ANTHONY	MURRAY	NELLY	O'HARA	EDWARD	QUINN	MARY	ROBIN
CATHERINE	MURRAY	THOMAS	O'HARA	GEORGE	QUINN	MARY	ROBIN
CHARLES	MURRAY	SARAH	O'HARE	JAMES	QUINN	THOMAS	ROBIN
DANIEL	MURRAY	MARGARET	O'HART	JAMES	QUINN	WILLIAM	ROBIN
DENIS	MURRAY	ROSE	O'HART	JAMES	QUINN	ALLISON	ROCH
ELIZA	MURRAY	CATHERINE	O'HOY	MARY	QUINN	JOHN	ROCH
ELLEN	MURRAY	MARY	O'LEARY	MARY	QUINN	JAMES	ROCK
GEORGE	MURRAY	THOMAS	O'LEARY	MARY	QUINN	JOHN	RODD
JOHN	MURRAY	BRIDGET	O'MALLEY	MARY	QUINN	JOHN	RODD
	MURRAY	JOHN	O'MALLEY	ROBERT	QUINN	FRANCIS	RODG
LUKE	MURRAY	CATHERINE	O'NEILL	ROGER	QUINN	MARY	RODG
	MURRAY	JOHN	O'NEILL	THOMAS	QUINN	ELLEN	ROG
	MURRAY	MARY	O'NEILL	TIMOTHY	QUINN	MARY	ROG
	MURRAY	MARY	O'NEILL	WILLIAM	QUINN	MATTHEW	ROG
MARY	MURRAY	MARY	O'NEILL	ANN	QUINTON	MICHAEL	ROG
	MURRAY	STEPHEN	O'NEILL	MARGARET	QUIRKE	PATRICK	ROG
MICHAEL	MURRAY	WILLIAM	O'NEILL	MARY	QUIRKE	ELIZABETH	ROB
MICHAEL	MURRAY	EDWARD	O'REILLY	MARY R.		MARGARET	RON
PATRICK	MURRAY	PATRICK	O'REILLY			MARY	RON
THOMAS	MURRAY	ELLEN	O'SHAUGHNESSY	MARY	RAFFERTY	MARY A.	RON
ELLEN	MURTAGH	THOMAS	O'SHAUGHNESSY	JAMES	RAHILLY	MAURICE	RON
ELLEN	MURTAGH	DOMINIC	OATES	ELIZA	RAY	BRIDGET	ROO
GARET	MURTAGH	DONALD	OATES	GEORGE	RAY	MARY	ROO
ANN	MYLAN	JACOB	ONIOV	HENRY	REABURN	MARY	ROO
		ALEXANDER	ORR	HENRY	REABURN	PATRICK	ROO
				MARY	REABURN	ALEXANDER	ROS
				ANN	REDDY	CATHERINE	ROS

The Inuit Memorial

Tuberculosis, once known as "consumption," has had an enormous impact on history. Until quite recently the disease was the leading cause of death in Europe and America, killing and incapacitating millions of people, many in their youth. Millions more – the survivors – were orphaned, widowed, ruined and devastated by the breaking-up of their families. Until the discovery of the antibiotic streptomycin in the 1940s, the only treatments were surgical collapse (or removal) of the tubercular lung and a regime requiring quarantine, total bed rest, good food, fresh air and time in vast amounts. From the 1890s sanatoriums were built by philanthropists to provide a place for working people for whom rest and good nutrition at home and travel to private institutions were impossible. In Canada, sanatoriums were developed with the aim of treating every case of tuberculosis. By 1953, 19,000 beds were occupied. Treatment lasted a year and a half on average, but patient stays of three years were common, and some spent 10 to 15 years in "sans."

The Inuit were very susceptible to the virus. In the 1950s more than one-third of them were infected, and uncontrolled epidemics devastated northern communities. During outbreaks of the highly communicable disease, the Canadian government sent medical teams equipped to make chest x-rays throughout the north. Those found to be infected were immediately quarantined and sent to hospitals in the south for treatment. In the early years the death rate was high. The disease was often far advanced before it was detected by the x-ray test, and effective drug treatments were not available. Inuit patients suffered from the loss of their families and community, and at first received little support to help them fight their illness. The experience of a patient in the Mountain San in Hamilton exemplifies their initial bewilderment and dislocation. Knowing no English, he was treated by a Chinese doctor, whom he took to be a fellow Inuk:

But the doctor did not speak Inuktitut to him — simply came in each day, smiling, even laughing, and said a few unintelligible words in English. The patient struggled to work out why a fellow Inuk would behave in this manner. The only explanation he could come up with was that there must be some sinister intent — that he was going to die, and that is why he had been brought there.

He later recovered and returned home to tell this story, but a number of his fellow Inuit patients died far from home between 1956 and 1963 and were buried in paupers' graves in Woodland Cemetery. In some instances their families were never informed. Years later, surviving family members who travelled thousands of miles to say prayers over their graves were troubled to find their burial places unmarked. Inuksuit — figures made of unworked stones — have been erected as memorials in Mastuijatch Cemetery within Quebec's Mount Hermon Cemetery. The memorial in Hamilton commemorates the Inuit patients who died while in the sanitorium, and also pays tribute to the carvings they made there.

Since prehistoric times the Inuit have made carvings from stone and bone for ritual use. For them, sculpting was not the specialty of artists, but part of their traditional practice of many useful skills. All tubercular patients were encouraged to take up arts and crafts such as needlework, knitting, drawing and leatherwork, to exercise muscle tissue and alleviate boredom. Patients could work on carvings while confined to bed, although they had to wear masks to protect their lungs from the fine soapstone dust. For some, this aspect of their tuberculosis treatment changed their lives.

Kenojuak Ashevak, now generally regarded as Canada's foremost Inuit artist, was sent to Parc Savard Hospital in Quebec City, where she stayed from early 1953 to the summer of 1955, narrowly escaping death several times. Her craft work there caught the eye of James Houston, who with his wife, Alma, promoted Eskimo art through the Canadian Handicrafts Guild. The Houstons developed a market for these artworks, which were sold through the Hudson's Bay Company and Eskimo Cooperatives. By 1962 Kenojuak's

drawings, reproduced as prints, had gained so much recognition that her art was featured in a National Film Board production. The money she earned from the film enabled her husband, Jonniebo, to purchase his own canoe, achieving independence as a hunter. Kenojuak's life was changed, but increasing fame and financial success did not separate her from traditional Inuit culture. She did not think of herself exclusively as an artist, but continued to travel with her husband every summer to their old campsites to hunt and fish.

In February 1958, *Maclean's* magazine featured sculptures made by Inuit patients at the Mountain San in Hamilton. They made 200 carvings a month, which found a ready market in the San gift shop, retailing for more than $50,000 a year. The sanatorium ordered regular shipments of soapstone from a Quebec quarry and took 30 per cent commission on the sales. In 1995 Inuit sculptures that had been kept on display in the lobby of the San became models for a white granite monument erected in Woodland Cemetery. At its crest is a large Ookpik, the Inuktitut name for the Snowy Owl that hunts by day over its range in the Arctic tundra. Scenes cut in relief depict Inuit catching seals through the ice in the traditional way, hunting for their livelihood.

The scenes show a persistent longing to return from the foreign ways of "whitemen's land" to traditional Inuit life. This longing is poignantly illustrated by the experience of David Mikeyook. In October 1952, he escaped from the San, wearing only pyjamas, light summer pants and a dressing gown, and taking with him only a jackknife and razor blades. Concealing himself in the small wilderness on the escarpment near the hospital, he survived for two months by his hunting skills, snaring rabbits and other small game. He was found dead, but it is unlikely that he simply wished to die. Rather, he wished to take up again his life and livelihood.

The English spellings of Inuit names vary — Mikeyook or Mikiuk. Those commemorated by the Inuit memorial in Woodlands Cemetery have their names engraved in both English and Inuktitut characters.

Maritime Disasters

In 1912 the world was stunned by the sinking of the "unsinkable" liner *Titanic* on her maiden voyage. Of the 1,500 passengers who perished in the disaster, 1,175 would have the sea as their final resting place. The White Star Line immediately chartered four Canadian vessels, including three based in Halifax, to take on the grim task of recovering the victims' remains. Of the bodies recovered, 119 were buried at sea; about 60 were unidentified at the time and 49 remain unidentified. Of the 209 recovered for burial on land, 44 victims remain unidentified. One hundred and fifty were buried in Halifax: 121 in the non-denominational Fairview Lawn Cemetery, 19 in the Mount Olivet Catholic Cemetery and 10 in the Baron de Hirsch Jewish Cemetery. The graves are marked by rows of stark, simple, black granite headstones, all inscribed with the same date: April 15, 1912. There are no special memorial headstones or other tributes. Many graves do not display names, just numbers signifying the order in which they were retrieved from the North Atlantic. In Fairview Lawn Cemetery the graves are laid out in curved lines to resemble the hull of a ship. The lines on the right are broken to represent the side of the *Titanic* that struck the iceberg. The graves face, coincidentally, the same direction as the wreck at the bottom of the Atlantic. During the summer, an average of 10 busloads of visitors each day visit the Fairview Lawn Cemetery.

Much less impressive is the burial place of most victims of the catastrophic Halifax explosion of 1917, which occurred in the narrows of the harbour between Dartmouth and Halifax. The collision between the *Mont Blanc*, a French munitions ship laden with high explosives, and the *Imo*, a Belgian relief ship, caused the largest explosion in history, prior to the atomic bombs over Hiroshima and Nagasaki. The Halifax blast was followed by a tsunami that swept the waterfront. More than two miles of the city was destroyed, 6,000 people were left homeless, 10,000 were injured and over 2,000 people died.

In the epilogue to her recent book on the explosion, Laura M. MacDonald mentions the official memorial in Needham Park, where an annual memorial service is held on the morning of December 6, but also draws attention to the "modest patch of land on Bayers Road across from the rock outcropping that signifies the entrance to the South Shore," where the unidentified dead are buried: "To enter the graveyard, visitors must park in the driveway to an apartment building and enter through the side gate. A modest monument sits in the middle of the field, but, unlike other memorials, there are no names to represent those buried there. Particularly now, when names have become the simple, defining element of so many memorials, the modesty and anonymity leaves visitors with a terrible sense of injustice."

The circumstances of the terrible calamity perhaps colour MacDonald's sense of injustice. Many residents of the north end of Halifax lived very modest lives. Their names were not as widely recognized as, say, the first-class passengers on the *Titanic*. Whole families were wiped out, leaving no one to remember. Frantic survivors searched through the hospitals and returned to their neighbourhood time after time, in hopes of finding clues to the whereabouts of a missing spouse or child. MacDonald's book draws on a collection of hundreds of interviews with survivors, and brings individuals to life by retelling many unforgettable stories. Billy Duggan, who had been working on Minesweeper *P.V. VII*, walked through the city to his home. Finding it and his aunt's and uncle's homes destroyed, he felt sure that his wife and children were dead. But he found them at the Camp Hill hospital, exhausted, stunned or weak from blood loss, but all alive – Lottie, Irene, Bessie, Helena, Lydia and Kenneth. A soldier had freed Irene, who was hanging from a splintered beam, and Bessie and Helena had rescued their mother and the others from the rubble. "Then he asked to see baby Gordon, just three weeks old. It must have been an awful moment, the longest pause he ever heard. Lottie told him that they had forgotten the baby."

FACING PAGE: *Fairview Lawn Cemetery, Halifax, Nova Scotia*
Memorials to those lost in the sinking of the *Titanic*.

The memorial for Swissair Flight III is exemplary in its restraint and respect for the privacy of the dead – a monument that does not record the names of the dead need not leave a sense of inadequate or uncaring memory. A slab of granite cut in two is very simply engraved on the polished sides facing south toward St. Margaret's Bay, where the airplane crashed with an impact so strong that the tremor was felt for miles. The inscriptions, in English and French, are simple acknowledgments of fact. The memorial for the dead makes no distinction of religious affiliation:

IN MEMORY OF
THE 229 MEN, WOMEN AND CHILDREN
ABOARD SWISSAIR FLIGHT III
WHO PERISHED OFF THESE SHORES
SEPTEMBER 2, 1998

THEY HAVE BEEN JOINED TO THE
SEA AND THE SKY

MAY THEY REST IN PEACE

The restrained form of the final prayer avoids any specifically Roman Catholic association with RIP, or *Requiescat in Pace*. None on board the plane survived, but the inscription on the other half of the stone acknowledges that their survivors include not only those who had known them in their lifetimes, but also those who shared in the distress of the disaster's aftermath:

IN GRATEFUL RECOGNITION OF
ALL THOSE WHO WORKED TIRELESSLY
TO PROVIDE ASSISTANCE IN THE RECOVERY
OPERATIONS AND COMFORT TO THE FAMILIES
AND THEIR FRIENDS DURING A TIME OF DISTRESS

The memorial is very close to Peggy's Cove, where one can see what is said to be the most picturesque and most photographed lighthouse in the world. Its picture-postcard quality as a lighthouse is not diminished by the fact that its original usefulness has been lost. The Swissair Flight III memorial is also much visited and photographed. But it proves quite impossible to capture an adequate image of this site. No postcards or memorabilia are sold. The inscribed stones serve to focus the visitor's view toward the place of impact, but again one cannot avoid trying to take in visually all the great expanse of sea and sky. The rugged natural landscape of rock scraped clean by the ice age, but still tenaciously gripped by the roots of persistent plants, seems to offer the larger background history of the polished and inscribed memorial stone. The memorial's designers have added to this site just enough meaning to create a wordless poetry of intimations that can neither be translated nor lost in translation.

The Luminous Veil

❦ The Prince Edward Viaduct spans the Don Valley, the largest of Toronto's ravines, connecting Bloor Street on the west with Danforth Avenue on the east. Designed by architect Edmund Burke and engineer Thomas Taylor to accommodate pedestrians and vehicles as well as a lower-level deck for a future subway line (not constructed until a half-century later), it has been designated a National Historic Civil Engineering Site. It is an outstanding work of art and engineering, exemplifying beauty of form and function, and representing "a moment in the city's history when public infrastructure was considered an artefact of aesthetic and cultural significance." The viaduct, completed in 1919, is a landmark structure. It towers above the Don River and Don Valley Parkway and offers dramatic views, especially from viewing places along the balustrade and the handrail on both north and south sides of the pedestrian way.

Its construction was celebrated in Michael Ondaatje's novel *In the Skin of a Lion* (1987) as one of the defining moments in the physical and cultural development of the city. Ondaatje also represented a darker aspect of the bridge through the character of the daredevil Nicholas Temelcoff: "His work is so exceptional and time-saving he earns one dollar an hour while the other bridge workers receive forty cents. There is no jealousy towards him. No one dreams of doing half the things he does. For night work he is paid $1.25, swinging up into the rafters of a trestle holding a flare, free-falling like a dead star."

It is Temelcoff who rescues the nun who is blown off the bridge while it is still under construction: "She disappeared into the night by the third abutment, into the long depth of air which held nothing, only sometimes a rivet or a dropped hammer during the day." Ondaatje's novel is itself a structure held together by tension like that of "the three hinges of the crescent-shaped steel arches [that] knit the bridge together." The title and epigraph of the novel are drawn from the ancient epic *Gilgamesh*, where the hero Gilgamesh,

grieving for his dead friend, goes in search of Utnapishtim, who has been given everlasting life: "The joyful will stoop with sorrow, and when you have gone to the earth I will let my hair grow long for your sake, I will wander through the wilderness in the skin of a lion." Ondaatje's celebration of life includes its balance of grief.

Over the course of its history, the beautiful Prince Edward Viaduct became a "suicide magnet," second in North America only to San Francisco's Golden Gate Bridge, and earned among the mental health community in Toronto the title, the "Bridge of Death." Its notorious allure still attracts people in distress, but since 2003 suicidal intentions have been thwarted by the Luminous Veil. The barrier saves some lives; those who feel an impulse to jump are forced to pause and reflect, and may take the opportunity to seek help. On both sides and at both ends of the bridge are public telephones with prominent signs for the Help Line number of a Distress Centre.

The design of the veil by Dereck Revington in collaboration with Yolles Engineering Solutions, while respecting the integrity of the historic viaduct, takes a distinctly contemporary form. An oscillating double layer of cables and thousands of slender stainless steel rods are held in tension by a "V" truss suspended by a series of galvanized steel bowstring masts. The cruciform masts may be seen as crosses memorializing those whose lives ended at the viaduct; but "the shimmering, tremulous quality" of light reflected from the veil of bright steel cables also has the power to evoke thoughts about "the ephemeral and tenuous nature of the divide between life and death." In traditional grave marker symbolism, the veil represents what is hidden to us on this side of the great divide. The Luminous Veil is designed not to hide the views of the Don Valley, and its interpretation goes beyond the traditional context to include the contrasting theme of connection. The individual rods are very slender and derive their strength from being held in tension and supported. The lightweight but strong network may be seen as an emblem that (like the viaduct itself) celebrates the overcoming of divided or contrary forces.

READING MONUMENTS

READING MONUMENTS

The Meanings of Stones

The original definition in English of "monument" – "a sepulchre, place of sepulture" – became obsolete as it evolved into new meanings – "a written document, record," and later "a structure of stone or other lasting material erected in memory of the dead, either over a grave or in some part of a sacred edifice." This evolution of meaning reflects a history of the multiple purposes of grave monuments. They preserve the living memory of the dead and protect the remains from deliberate or accidental disturbance.

They also defend the living from being inadvertently exposed to the dead. In Jewish and other traditions, contact with the contents of a grave is said to cause ritual impurity or uncleanness. It was the custom to whitewash tombs so that they might be recognized at a distance, and defilement avoided. Reference to this practice has become part of the English language, through the familiar Biblical account of the scribes and pharisees being reproved as hypocrites: "Woe unto you, scribes and Pharisees, hypocrites! for ye are like unto whited sepulchres, which indeed appear beautiful outward, but are within full of dead men's bones, and of all uncleanness" (Matthew 23: 27). "Whited sepulchre" has become a recognized metaphor for hypocrisy. Another narrative of this reproach, less well known, refers explicitly to the danger of pollution represented by *unwhited* sepulchres: "Woe unto you, scribes and Pharisees, hypocrites! for ye are as graves which appear not, and the men that walk over them are not aware of them" (Luke 11: 44).

Cemetery monuments balance their several purposes in various ways. The protection of the graves, so that no one will walk over them, is a priority for some. Protective grave covers include flat stones called ledgers or recumbent slabs, which resemble the monumental paving that covered graves beneath floors inside pre-Reformation churches. Later on, slabs were sometimes raised on four or six short pedestals, forming table stones.

Both slabs and table stones tend to be very large, heavy stones with room for lengthy epitaphs. The names and dates of all the members of large families may be listed, or tombs of military officers may be filled with detailed accounts of their honours and achievements. To decipher these large horizontal texts, the reader is compelled to bow over the tomb. Chest tombs, also called altar tombs, are even more massive, with spaces for

FACING PAGE: *Mount Pleasant Cemetery, Toronto, Ontario*

PAGE 218–219: *Church of England Cemetery, St. John's, Newfoundland*

carvings and inscriptions on the side and end panels as well as on the top.

Coped stones, which have narrow raised central panels with sloping sides, are variants of the recumbent slab. Some are ridged and gabled like roofs, the ridges taking the shape of a cross. St. Mark's churchyard in Niagara-on-the-Lake has several coped stones with crosses. One slab has a recumbent Celtic Cross carved in shallow relief. On one of its side margins, inscribed in an elegant open Gothic script, is a brief identification: "Thos. Halliday Watt. Surgeon &c. Died Dec. 16. 1880." Others have higher profiles with steeply raked planes.

Since they cover single graves, these stones do not aggrandize the human scale. Sometimes a child-size recumbent slab lies by the side of a parent's slab. In the Toronto Necropolis, mother-and-daughter monuments take the shape of partly unrolled scrolls, their ends filled with simple floral emblems. The raised lettering on the small scroll tells a short tale:

OUR BIRDIE GEORGEINA / PHILLIPS / HORSMAN. / DIED Feb. 21. 1871, / AE. 17 MO'S. 4 D'YS.

On the larger stone the raised lettering reads:

MY BELOVED WIFE / HANNAH HORSMAN, / DIED AT UXBRIDGE ONT. / NOV.12, 1876, AGED 30 Y'RS 7 MO'S. / GONE BUT NOT FORGOTTEN.

Later, in smaller inscribed lettering, a postscript was added:

ALSO / ALBERT ABRAHAM. / INFANT SON OF THE ABOVE. / DIED 27 SEPT. 1877, / AGED 10 MO'S 21 DAYS.

Albert's mother lived just a few days after his birth.

Headstones, or tablets, were derived from monumental wall tablets inside churches. Tablets from the 18th and early 19th century have varied silhouettes – simple rectangles or complex shapes with pronounced shoulders and intricate angular projections. "Domed" tablets with rounded or Gothic pointed-arched tympanums may have had symbolic reference to archways marking a passage to immortal life. Many graves marked by headstones originally had smaller footstones, but few of these remain. A trend toward wider, lower and more uniform headstones followed the First World War, and later the smaller plaque, made of granite or bronze and inlaid rather inconspicuously in the turf, was favoured. Such plaques, representing merely a signature and years of birth and death, offer minimal identification and a message occluded from all but graphologists.

Many monuments from the late 19th and early 20th century are more imposing. Pedestal tombs stand alone or support various kinds of sculpture, such as urns, crosses, columns, obelisks or statuary. Composite architectural monuments also took elaborate forms. A typical example is the Meakins family monument in Hamilton Cemetery. with four pink granite columns supporting an entablature that in turn supports a large obelisk. Meakins & Sons were furniture makers who moved from Montreal in 1850 and become the first cabinetmakers in Hamilton to use machinery in their business. By 1881 the firm was so successful that a new larger factory was built. Charles William Meakins was himself a designer and carver who handcrafted furniture for his church and made the patterns for the fountain erected in Gore Park to celebrate the official opening of the municipal waterworks. His monument is an architectural fantasy exemplifying and celebrating the potential of machine manufacturing. It is dated 1881 and its maker is prominently identified as E. Martin & Son.

Monuments mark places of personal memory – most immediately, the memory of those we knew in life. Someone dear to us has gone before us into the grave. Such graveside experiences are sombre, marked by intense feelings of loss. To be present at an interment is a shock to our feelings. Our connection to another person's life, felt to be an integral part of our own, has been severed. Though we yet live, we feel that part of our shared lives, indeed part of our being, is also buried with the dead. The grave marker supports the very personal task of surviving and bearing this loss. Visiting the burial site, caring for it, and bringing flowers and other tokens of remembrance are part of the experience of bereavement. Mourning is shaped and expressed by the performance of these rituals, in which personal grief is set within the larger context of a common cultural tradition.

Choosing or commissioning a monument is a significant task for the bereaved. Its design speaks about an individual life, but its design vocabulary is informed by traditions common to its time and place. In older graveyards, gravestone motifs have a local character determined by the skills of the artisans and the beliefs of the community. Although the visual patterns show countless variations in detail, they are fundamentally repetitive. Such conformity confirms the undeniable fact that we are all travelling to the same end and is oddly reassuring. This recognition of common mortality may come into conflict, however, with the wish to celebrate the value of one particular, irreplaceable life. The tensions produced by these contraries result in occasional innovative surprises in gravestone design.

Ultimately, grave monuments are neither personal nor familial, but more general reminders of the past. They are the essential markers of the long historical memory of our generations and our cultures. Through them we honour our predecessors, who in their lifetimes made our country ready for us who follow them. Burial grounds are records of our debts as a people and a nation.

This may be a sign unto you, that when your children ask their fathers in time to come, saying, What mean ye by these stones? Then ye shall answer them ... and these stones shall be for a memorial unto the children of Israel for ever. (Joshua 4: 6–7)

For anyone interested in cultural traditions and their transmission and evolution, the stones in historical graveyards are full of significance. Layers of complex public and private meaning, never to be fully explicated, are to be found in their words and images. Their inscriptions include a vast range of quotations and allusions, especially to religious or philosophical texts. Even when the individuals commemorated may be unknown to us, there are sermons in these stones, lessons in life addressed to all passers-by.

Their symbolic images may be read as part of an elaborate and extensive code. Gravestone emblems raise perennially fascinating questions for which there are no easy answers. The equivalents provided by some brief guides — *Anchor* means "hope," *Bell* means "mourning," *Column* means "noble life," and so on — have limited usefulness and are unsatisfactory. They reduce a complex symbol to a simple rebus, like puzzles given to children who are just learning to read and need pictographs to help them guess the meanings of the big words.

Visual imagery is more than a substitute for literacy. When most people in medieval Europe were illiterate, the great stained glass windows in their cathedrals presented very complex stories that could be interpreted over and over again. Their pictures were not simply "worth a thousand words." Over years and centuries, words change in ever-renewing contexts, and every retelling enriches a story's meaning. Even today, in an age of general literacy, our imaginations are still deeply engaged by a living oral tradition, the retelling of old stories. Our strongest links with a great wealth of traditional meanings are symbolic images. Although they may be found in many places, the happy hunting grounds for them are burial places.

The Necropolis, Toronto, Ontario
Recumbent slabs for Hannah Horsman and her daughter.

Mausoleums

Victorian cemeteries took care to provide opportunities to make clearly defined distinctions between families of influence and those of moderate means, and they reserved spaces for private mausoleums, designed to provide extra security and to make impressive statements about family status.

The original Mausoleum at Halicarnassos – built in the mid-fourth century BC in memory of King Mausolos and celebrated as one of the Seven Wonders of the ancient world – became the prototype for magnificent monumental tombs. The tomb of Mausolus has been in ruins for centuries, but the generic name continued to have resonance. In the 18th century it was not unusual for great estate owners to build a family mausoleum in their park. The Dedlocks' tomb in Charles Dickens' *Bleak House* had real-life parallels throughout England, most notably the superb Castle Howard Mausoleum in Yorkshire.

Mausoleums reflect the superior housing the affluent enjoyed during some part of their lifetime. They are anomalous buildings, however, since they do not change through time. Funerary architecture, precisely because it is never renovated for new uses or adapted to accommodate new styles, has been said to be the purest and most complete statement of architecture, the most practical of the arts.

The nobleman's mausoleum in the park ... is magnificent in its finality, alone in the landscape, undisturbed by daily use by the mere living. An appropriate mausoleum should appear to be an edifice for the housing of the dead ... to provide a suitable setting for the dead to lie, and the balanced, serene plans of so many mausolea mirror the repose of the dead body lying still for eternity.

*St. Mark's Anglican Church Cemetery,
Niagara-on-the-Lake, Ontario*
Carnathan-Baur mausoleum.

In Canada, most of the largest and finest family mausoleums are found in major cities, where manufacturers and merchants acquired large fortunes. In St. James' Cemetery, a mausoleum was built for James Austin, who was born in Ireland in 1813, emigrated to Toronto and apprenticed at the age of 16 to the printer William Lyon Mackenzie. When he died in 1897, he was president of the Dominion Bank and the Consumers' Gas Company. In 1866 he outbid other wealthy competitors to purchase Spadina, the house built by William Baldwin on the escarpment overlooking the city. Austin demolished the Baldwin home and built a grander Spadina, in which four generations of his family lived until it was donated to the city in 1982, to be preserved as a museum of high-Victorian style. His subdivision and sale of building-lots on Spadina's extensive grounds "probably realized about $200,000, a healthy profit on his original invest-

ment of $14,000 for the entire property" 23 years earlier. His investment in St. James' Cemetery was equally far-sighted. The Austin mausoleum is still in use by family members. Faithful servants, also considered part of the family, were buried within the fenced area around it.

The Carnathan-Baur mausoleum in St. Mark's Cemetery, Niagara-on-the-Lake, is a modern adaptation of a classical form. Tuscan columns frame exquisitely made bronze doors. In front stands a strikingly elegant urn/planter sculpted in Art Deco style. Dorothy Carnathan married Charles Baur, a son of an eminently successful family in Terre Haute, Indiana, but after his death she returned to her birthplace and built this monument for him and her parents. Mausoleums often bear no inscription except the family surname, but this one has two poetic inscriptions that mingle religious sentiments with more secular feelings. "Until the day break and the shadows flee away" comes from the Song of Solomon 2: 17. Another verse is from Cardinal Newman's hymn "Lead, Kindy Light": "And with the morn those angel faces smile / Which I have loved long since, and lost awhile." The lily of the valley sculpted in the urn's garland also may refer to the Song of Solomon, 2: 1: "I am the rose of Sharon, and the lily of the valleys."

Most recent mausoleums are large structures for public use, but private mausoleums are still being built today. In the Woodland Cemetery, Hamilton, the owners of a company manufacturing mattresses that promise enjoyment of "the Ultimate in quality sleep ... night after night ... for the rest of your life" have erected a granite mausoleum, with a landscape setting including a copper-domed Serenity Gazebo. Engraved on the pediment over the door is the message:

ASK YOURSELF WHAT YOU WOULD LIKE TO BE DOING IF TIME AND MONEY WERE NO OBJECT / THAT IS EXACTLY WHAT YOU SHOULD BE DOING NOW.

Woodland Cemetery, Hamilton, Ontario
Patterson mausoleum.

Skulls

A gravestone needs no special emblem to make it a reminder of death, or *memento mori*. A popular 20th century reference book, *Brewer's Dictionary of Phrase and Fable*, glosses the Latin phrase as "an emblem of mortality, such as a skull; something to put us in mind of the shortness and uncertainty of life." An 18th century definition would have been more candid and explicit. The *memento mori* is not so much an emblem of "uncertainty" as a reminder of the one absolute certainty that all life however long or short – ends in death.

No one visiting a cemetery can fail to note this obvious conclusion. Perhaps for that very reason, most gravestones carry a message to the living that goes beyond the reminder that they must die. In Canada, most *mementi mori* are to be found in Nova Scotian cemeteries, which contain our greatest wealth of 18th century stones. But even there, the skull is represented on only a few gravestones. Sometimes the reminder of mortality and the warning that death ends our opportunity to amend our lives are spelled out in the epitaph:

> O Mortal woman Behold thy Fate
> How short the time how swift the Date
> But when shall i Return from this
> To Rectify what's done Amiss.

On other stones we find the pictorial emblem of the skull, or death head. It is often combined with crossed thighbones, an oblique reference to the ancient custom of removing bare bones from their original burial place after a number of years, and stacking them in ossuaries, or bone-houses. Most of these skull-and-crossbones images are schematic. Although their sculptors may appear to have had primitive technical skills in the tradition of folk art, their visual impact is powerful.

A frequent accessory to the skull-and-bones imagery is the hourglass, emblem of the fact that our time is finite. The metaphorical sands measuring the hours of our lives will surely run out. Labels may explicitly spelling out the message

Old Burying Ground, Halifax, Nova Scotia
Skull and crossbones on a stone for Nathanael Peirse, "who departed this Life Jany. 26. 1755. AEt. 70."

"HOMO / MEMENTO / MORI" – "remember, man, you must die."

The *memento mori* seldom stands alone, without a more hopeful message. The skull-and-bones emblem in the setting of a consecrated Christian cemetery is very different from the meaning of superficially similar emblems on a bottle of poison, or a pirate flag. As sailors in the 18th and 19th centuries knew very well, the Jolly Roger was simply a death threat, a warning that victorious pirates made no pledge to take prisoners for ransom. For the faithful Christian, in contrast, death could win no final victory, for the grave's apparent prisoners had already been redeemed.

The winged skulls on the gravestones of Puritan Planters in Nova Scotia are explicit emblems of victory over death, as are the later Soul Effigies. Sometimes the latter are referred to as cherubs or even *putti*. The Hebrew *cherubim*, however, were powerful winged creatures – the prophet Ezekiel had a vision of them, each with four faces and four wings, wheeling in the middle of the air. These cherubs became confused with classically derived *putti* – "little men" – in Renaissance art, where they were no longer mighty spiritual beings, but pudgy babies with wings. (The ubiquitously reproduced *cherubini* by Raphael are examples.) The winged infants displayed on many gravestones by the mid 19th century were no longer strenuous Soul Effigies, but perhaps only sentimental images.

Freemasonry Symbols

❧ Of the hundreds of fraternal organizations indicated by acronyms or symbols on Canadian gravestones, none is more prominent than the Ancient Brotherhood of Free and Accepted Masons. The earliest Masonic lodges in British North America were held under field warrants in military regiments. There was a regimental lodge in Annapolis Royal from 1738 and in Halifax from 1752. The powerful Masonic presence in the Halifax Old Burying Ground illustrates the social and political prominence of the Freemasons in the newly founded colonial capital. Lodges of the Scottish Rite were chartered from 1819 to 1867 in Quebec City, Montreal, and 16 other towns in present-day Nova Scotia, Prince Edward Island and Newfoundland. The Protestant Irish and Scottish men who were Freemasons in the new colonies had strong reasons to remember connections with their earlier homes on the other side of the Atlantic.

Old Burying Ground, Halifax, Nova Scotia
Masonic motifs combined with a reminder, "HOMO MEMENTO MORI."

Freemasonry has been described as a system of morality veiled in allegory and illustrated by symbols. Although the meaning of some Masonic symbols may be esoteric, others derive from common traditions and are intelligible even to uninitiated. The Masonic tools of square and compasses represent rectitude and measured control, the virtues required for the building of individual moral character as well as for the sound construction of sacred and secular public buildings. Other tools of the ancient craft of masonry also symbolize the life-shaping power of the upright code of conduct valued by freemasonry – the plumb line, the maul and chisels.

More elaborate Masonic gravestones may include representations of Euclidean geometry, stars with five and six points, the triple tau (representing an acronym for the Temple of Jerusalem) and other allegorical references to ritual practices of the order. The disembodied All-Seeing Eye expresses the belief that no action, however secret or hidden, is invisible to the Supreme Being or Deity. Rays of energy stream out from the eye in all directions, dispersing enlightenment.

Masonic representations of the sun and moon usually have facial features marked by serious, even stern, expressions. Like other Masonic emblems, these not only mark an individual's association in the brotherhood, but also codify the meaning of fraternal traditions. Both rise and set in predictable cycles of absence and return – the sun rules by day, the moon by night. For millennia, long before the solar source of energy in our particular universe began to be understood in any scientific sense, the sun was worshipped as a universal symbol of power. Sunrise, bringing light out of darkness, is an obvious emblem for seeing truth and finding knowledge and understanding. The moon reflects the sun, whose radiance, despite its apparent diurnal interruption, is unending. The sun always lights one half of our world, even when it seems to us to have set.

The lunar cycle is similarly deceptive. As the moon wanes and then waxes, it always reflects a full disc of solar light, but to our limited view only once each month. The Masonic moon is always shown as a crescent, growing from its apparent death to full strength. The omnipresence of these two lights made them essential symbols in the Hermetic tradition, which has been linked with the origins of Freemasonry.

Two columns, or pillars, symbolize part of the Temple of King Solomon in Jerusalem and refer to the legend of the sudden death of the Temple's master builder. The somewhat mysterious depiction of Death taking the Temple builder in a surprise attack from behind is occasionally seen on Masonic gravestones. The rites of initiation into the frater-

nity incorporate both this legend and the ancient Egyptian myth of the death, burial and resurrection of Osiris. An allegory of a journey, trials and rebirth into the brotherhood is central to Masonic texts and practices, which require recognizing and facing the necessity of death.

The very strong connection between Freemasonry and the cemetery reform movement in the 18th century was no mere coincidence. Rural Cemeteries and monuments in Egyptian and Neoclassical styles were influenced by Freemasonry, especially by way of Napoleonic France.

BELOW LEFT: *Mount Pleasant Cemetery, Toronto, Ontario*
Detail of the Masonic monument.

BELOW RIGHT: *Old Burying Ground, Halifax, Nova Scotia*
Freemasonry symbols.

Obelisks

✤ For centuries, Europeans reinvented Egyptian architectural motifs – pyramids, obelisks, pylons, lotus columns and inscriptions – to make design statements that had special appeal for connoisseurs of ancient history. The 19th century rediscovery of Egyptian style gave it a wider impact, not only reaching a popular audience, but also involving a revived awareness of a long-dead culture, or cult. It began with Napoleon's invasion of Egypt in 1798, a military disaster, but one that occasioned the publication of a magnificent pictorial encyclopedia, *Description de l'Égypte*. Its images were immediately and widely disseminated. Publishers of family Bibles were not slow to see the commercial advantage of adding historical authenticity to pictorial representations of Joseph and his brothers in Egypt, or the events of the Exodus. The depiction of Aaron stretching out his hand to call up a plague of frogs no longer showed a medieval European town in the background, but the Nile with suitable architectural details. One of the few permitted Sabbath entertainments in many households was the perusal of the illustrated Bible, a treasured family possession. As a result, the forms of Egyptian columns and obelisks became accepted as an authorized vision of scriptural texts.

The French discovery of the Rosetta Stone permitted the deciphering of Egypt's ancient hieroglyphics. The Egyptian Book of the Dead, whose meaning had been lost for 1,400 years, was intelligible once again. Not that many actually read the ancient papyrus, of course, but translations were published. It was enough to know that the tombs of the Egyptian necropolis were built in the expectation of resurrection, judgement and triumph over death, and that the ancient Egyptians viewed death as the beginning of an extended afterlife for the soul, which after thousands of years would be reunited with the body. Egyptian dwellings for the living, built of clay and supported by bundles of papyrus stalks, were but temporary lodgings. In contrast, the abodes of embalmed bodies awaiting the return of their souls were built of stone and were meant to be solid and secure for the ages. The longevity, if not absolute permanence, of ancient Egyptian monuments influenced a growing wish to erect more lasting monuments in 19th century cemeteries.

The obelisks erected by the pharaohs were immense. The one now standing in Rome (after previously standing for more than 1,700 years in Egypt) is more than 30 meters tall and weighs 230 tons. Roman emperors, undeterred by transportation difficulties, regarded obelisks as portable souvenirs from their conquered Egyptian colony. The result of the fall of the Roman Empire was, in time, the fall of the looted obelisks in neglected gardens and circuses. But a few hundred years later, they were unearthed and erected again and, along with other ancient ruins, revered for their antiquity.

After the opening of the Suez Canal in 1869, a pair of obelisks in Alexandria was offered for relocation to London and New York City. For the next decade or more, the engineering challenges presented by their transport and erection caught the fascinated attention of newspaper journalists and their readers. The one being towed to London on the cylindrical barge *Cleopatra* was nearly lost at sea in a sudden gale, and it took 112 days to haul the other through the streets of New York, from the West 96th Street pier to Central Park. In both new locations the bases contained time capsules — lead boxes filled with newspapers, coins, a dictionary, the Bible and other markers of contemporary civilization.

True obelisks are monolithic. They are shaped as a tall square, tapering shaft, like a petrified ray. At the top is a 60-degree-angle pyramidion, which in Egypt was usually sheathed with a bright metal to reflect the rays of the sun like a beacon or heliograph. Their original service to the powerful solar deity in Heliopolis was long dimmed before they arrived in smoky northern cities. A 20th century engineer and historian has given one obelisk a voice:

In the middle of Central Park in New York stands a tall stone on a quiet, wooded knoll. It has stood here for 70 [now 125] years and in that time has witnessed the neighbouring streets swell in activity from suburban quiet into the busiest thorofares of all time. It has watched great buildings grow from the ground and it has been dwarfed by their eminence and bulk. It can, in all truth, say: "I have witnessed this great change in only one-fiftieth of my existence, for in my youth in Egypt I have had Moses look on my face, and Joseph has paused within my shadow. I have seen a great city, as great as yours, burn and disappear and I have stood near the sea for 2000 years to witness another great city blossom and die. Be not proud, for I shall exist when all this brick and steel about me has crumbled into dust!

The obelisks in Canadian cemeteries are often much taller than neighbouring stones. Although they would clearly be dwarfed by the Egyptian originals, they reflect something of the authority and stability of those ancient inscribed stones, whose creative power was meant to perforate clouds and disperse negative forces that threatened to obscure the sun. Polished granite obelisks, when seen from the correct angle, are also heliographs, mirroring the sun's rays from their pyramidal points.

LEFT: *Mount Pleasant Cemetery, Toronto, Ontario*
Heliograph point of a tall obelisk.

FACING PAGE: *St. Andrew's Presbyterian Church Cemetery, Beaverton, Ontario*

Neoclassical Monuments

❧ Neoclassicism involves adopting motifs from the cultures of ancient Greece and Rome, and making them new. The Neoclassical style in funerary art and architecture represents a selection from a broad range of Greek and Roman traditions. Broadly speaking, the renewal of the classical inheritance continued (with interruptions) virtually from the time when the original models were nearly new themselves. The monuments of ancient Greece and Rome illustrate their builders' powerful inventiveness in renewing traditional forms. Innovations in style, from the tombs of Mycenae to late Hellenistic and Græco-Roman times, reflect one-and-a-half millennia of changing beliefs about the celebration of life and death.

Stele are usually elaborate and elegant. Their prototype is the Roman stele, an upright slab – like the headstone, but larger – decorated with relief carvings. Sir Edmund Walker commissioned an exceptionally fine one in Hamilton Cemetery to commemorate his father, mother and unmarried sister. The basic data are simply declared on the reverse, in handsomely shaped metal letters set into the stone. On the front, the stone base, shallow pilasters and simple pediment make an understated architectural frame for the bas-relief, a nearly two-dimensional picture, in cast bronze. Walker, a "Canadian Medici" and patron of contemporary Canadian artists, commissioned this monumental sculpture from Walter Allward, who had recently completed his work on the Vimy National Memorial. The figure of a mourner, holding broken flowers in one hand, is hooded and wrapped in a garment that appears to be a shroud. Her eyes are closed

Hamilton Cemetery, Hamilton, Ontario
Detail of the Walker stele by sculptor Walter Allward.

as if anticipating her own death. At the top of the panel is the raised inscription "HE GIVETH HIS BELOVED SLEEP." The lettering is, again, beautiful, but it is quite inconspicuous, like the lettering at the base: "W S ALLWARD SCVLPTOR." Walker's own monument in Mount Pleasant Cemetery is also a stele.

The sarcophagus was also part of the Neoclassical revival. The classical casket was so called from the Greek words meaning "flesh-eating." The limestone coffin consumed the corpse, hastening its decay. The most famous Neoclassic burial, or rather reburial, in modern times is Napoleon's Tomb in his crypt in the Église du Dôme, Hôtel des Invalides, Paris. The Emperor's majestic sarcophagus consists of six coffins, each container inside another – oak on the exterior, ebony, lead, another lead, mahogany, tin-plate. The purpose of these multiple encasements seems to have been to prevent – rather than encourage – the consuming of Napoleon's body, which according to legend is uncorrupted.

The tomb of Camillien Houde (1889–1958) in Notre-Dame-des-Neiges Cemetery is a stone sarcophagus made in Italy which is said to be a replica of Napoleon's tomb. Houde was first elected to the Legislative Assembly of Quebec in 1923 and was defeated and re-elected many times at the federal and provincial polls, in addition to being mayor of Montreal in almost every year between 1928 and 1940, and from 1944 to 1954. These vicissitudes of political fortune were interrupted by Houde's exile from 1940 to 1944 in an Ontario internment camp, following his outspoken opposition to conscription during the Second World War. Perhaps Houde saw certain parallels between his career and that of the little corporal.

The Neoclassical sarcophagus is a type of monument, rather than an actual casket. Like the Neoclassical urn, it is not a container, but a symbolic form. Many notable monuments in the 20th century illustrate an evolution of the sarcophagus into modern shapes in which Ionic capitals, scrolls and bands of egg-and-dart enrichments express the classical language of architecture in new voices. The Holton monument, among others in Hamilton Cemetery, is a modern

rendition of the Roman sarcophagus of Cornelius Lucius Scipio Barbatus (third century BC, now in the Vatican museum), which became the model for a great many memorials in cemeteries on both sides of the Atlantic. The Clifford Sifton tomb (1929) in Mount Pleasant Cemetery has rows of classical acroteria, but is a modern complex of Doric fluted columns supporting an understated, implicit reference to the sarcophagus tradition.

The Latin *urna* is a vase whose form is a rounded or ovoid body on a circular base. The noun is derived from the verb *urere*, "to burn," perhaps because urns were originally made of earthenware. Among the ancient Romans and Greeks, the urn was in common use for holding and carrying various contents, including water, vote ballots, or lottery tickets. Its special use as a cinerary urn, to preserve the ashes of the dead, gave to its classical form an enduring symbolic signifi-

Mount Pleasant Cemetery, Toronto, Ontario
The Sifton monument, with Neoclassical details.

BELOW LEFT: *Union Cemetery, Oshawa, Ontario*
Grave of R.S. McLaughlin, co-founder of General Motors Company.

BELOW RIGHT: *Ross Bay Cemetery, Victoria, British Columbia*
Williams family monument, a draped urn supported by four attached columns.

cance, even in places where cremation was not generally practised. In fact, the urn was displayed on a great many monuments in cemeteries where the practice of cremation would have been shunned. In these contexts it had an entirely representative value. Whether it was an almost two-dimensional relief incised on a flat tablet stone, or a solid sculpture, it was not meant to be taken for a real urn – a useful vessel with a hollow interior that might be filled with ashes. These urns would never be opened to reveal their contents. They are not so much imaginary urns as objects that represent what cannot be known or imagined. They stand for a concealment of the

evidence of the material changes to the body after death and also suggest the barrier of ignorance about changes to the life of the spirit after death.

Many sculpted urns on funerary monuments are draped with sculpted veils, further emblems of what is hidden to mortal experience and comprehension. Their size is also significant. Urns are small containers to encapsulate what in life was a much larger body – "Alasse, how small an Urne contains a King!" It is said that the Roman Emperor Severus, who died on a campaign in Britain, sent for his urn shortly before his death and addressed it with the words, "Little Urn, thou shalt contain what the whole World could not before."

The Walmsley monument in Mount Pleasant Cemetery is an elegant composition of Neoclassical motifs in stone and bronze, enriched but dignified. The columns, entablature and pediment make an architectural frame for the bronze epitaph panel, which is enriched with a Greek key border and small lion heads. All form an elaborate background for a massive stone urn with bronze fittings – handles, a swagged veil, and panels of stylized wave patterns. At the top of the urn burns a stone flame.

Many urn monuments are crowned with finials of flame. The flaming urn became a very well-known emblem as the gilded copper emblem at the top of the monument for the Great Fire of London. Commonly known as "The Monument," the colossal stone column designed by Robert Hooke and Christopher Wren became the archetype of the genre, and its name has come to mean a structure "intended to commemorate a notable person, action, or event." Its design influenced the Nelson Column in London and Brock's Monument at Queenston Heights, as well as thousands of cemetery monuments of lesser measure but imposing in their own context. The flaming urn was Hooke's design. It won out over Wren's proposal, a sculpture of the mythical phoenix arising from its own ashes, which was rejected because perching a great bird with wings outspread atop a column 61 meters high would have presented practical difficulties related to wind resistance.

Hooke's urn conveyed the same symbolic meaning – the

Fire of Restoration rising from the ashes, which were all that remained of four-fifths of London City in 1666. Hooke was a man well learned in the New Science and had conducted advanced experimental research in the chemistry of combustion. His intention was not to depict a cremation process in a cinerary urn. Rather, his flaming urn, and others in burial places around the world, figures a meaning as full of mystery as the fabled phoenix. The flame of a new life rises from a substance that has burnt out, in which there is literally nothing left to burn.

The Monument inspired many grand columnar monuments. In Ross Bay Cemetery, the grave of John Boyd, a dealer in groceries and liquors who died in 1890, is marked by a pedestal with a finely proportioned and detailed Corinthian column supporting a wreathed urn. In Cataraqui Cemetery, the Gildersleeve plot on the crest of a small hill has two prominent monuments. A very tall Ionic column, supporting an urn with handles, commemorates Henry Gildersleeve. The third generation of a family of shipbuilders in Connecticut, he immigrated to Upper Canada in 1816 and became "the father of steam navigation on the Bay of Quinte and the upper St. Lawrence," as well as a banker, magistrate and successful Kingston citizen. After his death in 1851, his son Overton, at the age of 26, took over the flourishing shipping and shipbuilding business. To overcome competition from railways and other boatlines, Overton Gildersleeve sped up journey times and cut his passenger rates. "Usually he offered passage between Kingston and Belleville, including stateroom and berth, for 5s., but during one season he provided the same service for 15d." His death at only 34 years of age caused the family to erect a broken column, signifying that his life had been cut short.

The Neoclassical urn and the lamp sometimes appear almost interchangeably on gravestones. The lamp bears some similarity to a flaming urn, since in ancient times it too was made of clay, but it had a handle and a nozzle for the wick of twisted flax, and contained olive oil or naphtha for fuel. The lamp has a religious significance connected with many well-known passages in Jewish and Christian scrip-

ABOVE: *Mount Pleasant Cemetery, Toronto, Ontario*
Walmsley family monument.

LEFT: *Cataraqui Cemetery, Kingston, Ontario*
Two columnar monuments for the Gildersleeve family.

Old Burying Ground, Halifax, Nova Scotia
Urn motif.

ture. The word sometimes translated as "a candle" is not a tallow rod with a wick, but an earthernware oil lamp. The psalmist sings, "For thou wilt light my candle: the Lord my God will enlighten my darkness" (Psalm 18: 28). However, "there shall be no reward to the evil man; the candle of the wicked shall be put out" (Proverbs 24: 20). "The spirit of man is the candle of the Lord" (Proverbs 20: 27) is a text central to the Jewish tradition of *Yahrzeit* (the anniversary of a death), when a lamp or candle is kept burning.

In the Christian New Testament, the image of the spirit of man as the candle of the Lord is given an expanded interpretation.

Ye are the light of the world ... Neither do men light a candle, and put it under a bushel, but on a candlestick; and it giveth light unto all that are in the house. Let your men so shine before men, that they may see your good works, and glorify your Father which is in heaven. (Matthew 5: 14–16)

In Biblical times, household lamps were kept alight continually, and during the Exodus the children of Israel were commanded to bring for the tabernacle "pure olive oil beaten for the light, to cause the lamp to burn always" (Exodus 27: 20). This was the Biblical type for memorials such as the everlasting flame on Parliament Hill in Ottawa. For Christians, a chapter that gives an account of the last judgement, determining who shall gain entrance to the kingdom of heaven, begins with a parable of ten virgins – five wise, who "took oil in their vessels with their lamps," and five foolish, "who took their lamps, and took no oil with them" (Matthew 25: 1–13). Thus the lamp symbol summarizes a multiplicity of scriptural references very familiar to observant Jews and Christians. More generally, however, the undying flame and the earthenware lamp are symbols of the spirit within the body, which is made of earth and must return to it.

The inverted torch is also a Neoclassical funerary symbol. Sometimes the flame is extinguished, signifying the end of life, and sometimes it continues to burn upside down (contrary to physical possibility), signifying a transformation of the spirit. An outdoor version of the more domestic lamp, the torch is meant to be held high, carried, and passed from hand to hand. Its association with endurance and with victory makes it appropriate in war memorials: "Take up our quarrel with the foe: / To you from failing hands we throw / The torch; be yours to hold it high."

The Willow

The Weeping Willow is often seen in combination with Neoclassical urns and obelisks. The Willow has a form suggesting that its branches are bowed in grief, and since it grows beside streams, may suggest rivers of tears flowing in sympathy. It has no special religious meaning, although the exile from Israel of the Jews during the Babylonian Captivity inspired a psalm (and in turn a memorable Reggae song) with the willow-and-stream motif:

By the rivers of Babylon, there we sat down, yea we wept, when we remembered Zion. We hanged our harps upon the willows in the midst thereof. For there they that carried us away captive required of us a song ... How shall we sing the Lord's song in a strange land? If I forget thee, O Jerusalem, let my right hand forget her cunning. (Psalm 137: 1–5)

The willow represents a very ancient belief that the natural world is affected by strong human feelings and shares our sorrows. When our emotions are of sufficient intensity, they will find expression outside ourselves and will even animate the natural world. Not all sorrow is for bereavement. Lost love has been memorably expressed through the images of weeping willows on gravestones.

Whether as sculpted reliefs or simple incised outlines, willows are beautifully represented in a great variety of artistic styles.

Old Burying Ground, Halifax, Nova Scotia
Urn and willow motif on a monument "SACRED / To the Memory of / Capt. James Fullerton," who died in 1838.

BOTTOM LEFT: *Old Burying Ground, Halifax, Nova Scotia*
Urn and willow motif in the tympanum of a monument for Thomas Lawlor, his wife Susanah and their son Thomas, "who departed this Life" in 1772, 1782 and 1778.

BOTTOM RIGHT: *Town Point Cemetery, Chebogue, Nova Scotia*

Jewish Symbols

❦ The teachings of the Christian New Testament have their roots in the Hebrew scriptures known to Christians as the Old Testament. In the Hellenistic world, both Christians and Jews decorated their catacombs and places of worship with figures representing Biblical scenes, heroes and animal figures, as well as more abstract motifs. Both Jews and Christians have varied widely in their interpretation of the second of the Ten Commandments: "Thou shalt not make unto thee any graven image, or any likeness of any thing that is in heaven above, or that is in the earth beneath, or that is in the water under the earth." The more liberal interpretation of this prohibition depends on the following verse: "Thou shalt not bow down to them, nor serve them" (Exodus 20: 4, 5). In general, Jews have followed a stricter interpretation than most Christians, respecting the fuller explication:

Take ye therefore good heed unto yourselves: for ye saw no manner of similitude on the day that the Lord spake unto you in Horeb out of the midst of the fire: Lest ye corrupt yourselves, and make you a graven image, the similitude of any figure, the likeness of male or female, The likeness of any beast that is on the earth, the likeness of any winged fowl that flieth in the air, The likeness of any thing that creepeth on the ground, the likeness of any fish that is in the waters beneath the earth. (Deuteronomy 4: 15–18)

Roselawn Cemetery, Toronto, Ontario

Instead, Jewish symbolism includes a few particular images connected with religious observances and – since the 18th century – the six-pointed star (the hexagram), said to be the device on the Shield of David (the *Magen David*).

Jewish grave markers tend to be simple and understated. Plain low headstones, or recumbent slabs that cover and protect the grave, predominate. The plots of many 19th century graves may also be defined by masonry borders or retaining walls, often surmounted by low iron or masonry fences. In parts of the Baron de Hirsch Affiliated Cemeteries in Montreal, grave plots are covered with uniform simple low floral carpets of densely planted red and white begonias – a delicate form of protection.

Part or all of the inscriptions on Jewish gravestones may be in Hebrew, which is read from right to left. The date of death may be written according to the Hebrew calendar, which begins 3,760 years before the date accepted as the beginning of the Christian or Common Era. Often a date in the current millennium, after the year 5000, will omit the letter for 5. For example, the year 5680 will be written as 680. Then the civil, or Gregorian, calendar year may be simply calculated by adding 1,240 – keeping in mind that the Hebrew year begins with Rosh Hashana, in the month of September according to the Gregorian calendar.

During the *Shivah* (seven-day) period of mourning and on the *Yahrzeit* or anniversary of death, a lamp or candle is kept burning. The emblem of a small oil lamp, often seen engraved on Jewish gravestones, shares with the similar Christian emblem a reference to the text of Proverbs 20: 27: the spirit, or soul, of a man is the candle, or lamp, of the Lord. The Hebrew proverb has various English translations and is open to more than one interpretation. The lamp may be the word of the Lord, providing spiritual enlightenment for travellers through life, according to the psalmist: "a lamp unto my feet, and a light unto my path" (Psalm 119: 105). It may also represent a spiritual spark of the *Shekinah*, the omnipresent divine immanence. The *Shekinah* itself manifests the Talmudic saying that death is the moment when two worlds, the living and the eternal, "kiss" one another.

A passage in the Talmud says that in the world to come the saints will bask in the radiant light of the *Shekinah*. In this world, the radiance of the *Shekinah* shines through the fingertips of the Kohen as he performs the priestly blessing, according to Numbers 6: 22–27:

Baron de Hirsch Affiliated Cemeteries, Montreal, Quebec

And the Lord spake unto Moses, saying, Speak unto Aaron and unto his sons, saying, On this wise ye shall bless the children of Israel, saying unto them,
The Lord bless thee, and keep thee:
The Lord make his face shine upon thee, and be gracious unto thee:
The Lord lift up his countenance upon thee, and give thee peace. And they shall put my name upon the children of Israel; and I will bless them.

Only the descendants of the tribe of Aaron are eligible for priesthood. For the priestly benediction, the hands are raised (Leviticus: 9: 22), with the middle finger and ring finger parted. It is said that the ability to perform this gesture naturally is a trait inherited only by the Kohen families. The gesture of blessing is an emblem depicted on gravestones of these descendants; often their family name (Cohen, Cohn, Caine and other spelling variations) also indicates their pedigree.

Star Trek fans know that Leonard Nimoy, the actor who played Spock, based his Vulcan Salute on the priestly blessing, which he recalled seeing as a child when taken by his grandfather to the synagogue. Spock's blessing was the mundane "Live long and prosper." *Star Trek* actors apparently had to manipulate their fingers off-screen before raising their hands into the camera frame.

The Levite washes the hands of the *Kohen* before he delivers the blessing, and thus the emblem of the ewer or pitcher and bowl is found on gravestones of members of the tribe of Levi. A candelabrum is an emblem for the mother of a family, whose weekly task of kindling the candles on Friday evening summoned a spiritual light to mark the beginning of the Sabbath day of rest. An open book is often chosen as an emblem for one who has studied the Torah and observed its precepts. Another symbol found on Jewish monuments is the lion of the tribe of Judah, the house of King David.

ALL IMAGES: *Roselawn Cemetery, Toronto, Ontario*

פ"נ האשה החשובה

מרת ליבע טאמארע

ב"ר אשר אנטשיל הלוי

נפטרה ד' חשוון תר"פו

ת נ צ ב ה"

Effigies

Effigies are lifelike portraits of the dead. In Roman Egypt, the facial features of the dead were depicted in an encaustic medium on wooden panels, which were placed over the face of the mummified corpse. Vivid effects were created using pigmented beeswax, especially living gleams of light in the eyes. These portraits were clearly related to ancient Egyptian beliefs about the afterlife. The impulse to preserve visual memories of individuals on monuments persists in the modern tendency to reproduce an image in an enamelled photograph or (more recently) to etch it by laser on polished granite.

Photographs are said to have a posthumous existence, according to critical theorists who have focused on the invention of photography as a great epoch in the history of the world. By freezing a subject at a moment in time, the camera immediately registers that moment as in the past and thereby defers it to some future time, when the living persons will, invariably, be dead. Although all portraits stimulate the persistence of visual memory, photographs haunt us with a particular aura of lost time. They celebrate the contingency of our lost memories.

Effigies now usually refer to lifelike sculptures that preserve visual memories of lost lives with a peculiar intensity. The living likeness is there, but is fixed and transformed. The portrait physically incorporates a translation from life into stillness, a changeless realm. The strong magic of effigies is central to the transformation in the final scene of *The Winter's Tale*, where Shakespeare's audience is unaware that Hermione is not dead, as we thought, but alive. She stands like a statue, while the "widower" Leontes marvels "To see the life as lively mock'd as ever / Still sleep mock'd death" (5, 3). The fulfilment of his wish that his wife could return to life has an extraordinary impact, even for those who already know the complete tale, because Shakespeare so brilliantly dramatizes the contradictions central to all effigies.

The "Marble Lady of Chebogue" in Yarmouth, Nova Scotia, may have been intended as an effigy. The Dr. Webster who arrived in Yarmouth in 1791 was the first of six generations of physicians that continued for 170 years. The second Dr. Webster studied medicine in Edinburgh and brought home a Scottish bride whom he met there. When she died 30 years later, he commissioned a local sculptor, S.F. Raymond, to carve a full-sized figure from a block of white Indian marble. This exotic material – the same stone used for the dome of the Taj Mahal – was transported to Yarmouth harbour by sea. The sculptor was asked to portray a lass reaping grain with her sickle, in remembrance of the Websters' meeting in the Scottish Highlands (and perhaps in reference to William Wordsworth's "Solitary Reaper"). In fact, she is shown in repose on a sheaf of grain. It is said that Raymond's model was a ceramic match holder representing a woman standing by a wheat sheaf, and that the match holder is still in the possession of the Webster family. The marble lady appears to be resting quite comfortably on the ground, with no thought of a grim reaper. Alas, her enigmatic appeal has not defended her from vandals, who have broken off parts of her feet.

Mount Royal Cemetery, Montreal, Quebec Bronze effigy of Master Fred Ulley, Boy Soprano (1884–1899), sculpted by George W. Hill, with the inscription: "We cannot lodge in granite or in bronze souls more vast than earth and sea and sky."

Victorian Gothic Revival

❦ Historicism was the characteristic trait of Victorian architects, who made a conscious attempt to adapt older styles for use in the modern era. The fashion for Gothic Revival style carried an overwhelming message of spiritual sincerity and holiness. Those who were active in the revitalization of the Anglican and the Catholic faiths in Victorian England were involved in controversies about church architecture. They wanted to recreate the spiritual energy of the 13th century, which they saw expressed in Gothic churches built then. In 1836, A.W.N. Pugin published his immediately famous *Contrasts*, which has been described as a "witty and impassioned plea in words and pictures for a return from the ugly, materialist world of his day to the noble, beautiful, and eminently Christian Middle Ages." Following Pugin, a great many newly built Gothic Revival churches soon made the pointed-arch window a common symbol of church architecture. The designs of many 19th century monuments reflected those recent architectural trends.

The best-known Gothic memorials in England were the Eleanor Crosses, which marked the 12 resting spots for the bier of Edward I's Queen, Eleanor of Castile, during her funeral journey in 1290 from Lincoln to Charing Cross in London. Those who saw the slender spires of decorated Gothic pillars and arches then were inspired to pray for the soul of the Queen. In fact, her soul's well-being was not so utterly dependent on the charity of strangers. An immense amount of wealth was invested to ensure that religious observances and prayers would be continued, and even that she would have "ii [two] wexe tapers brennynge upon her tumbe both daye and nyghte, which so hath continued syne the day of her buryinge to this present daye."

When the Prince Consort of Queen Victoria died in 1861, nine architects were commissioned to prepare competing designs for the Albert Memorial in Kensington Gardens. The winner was a highly elaborate Gothic Revival shrine inspired by the Eleanor Crosses. These renowned examples of royal

Beechwood Cemetery, Ottawa, Ontario
Monument with Victorian Gothic revival elements.

piety led many Canadians, especially those with ties to England, to erect Gothic Revival spires, richly embellished with carved crockets, finials, trefoils, quatrefoils and other foliate decorations. Unlike the royal memorials, however, their niches and canopies did not usually enshrine effigies.

In Hamilton Cemetery, the monument above the Brown family vault more closely resembles one of the Eleanor Crosses, of which only three remain, at Waltham, Hardingstone and Geddington. The stone on the Brown monument is quite worn, almost as if it were six centuries old rather than dating from the mid 19th century.

The Cross

❧ The cross most often seen in Canadian cemeteries has the Latin "†" shape, with the horizontal arm centred on the upper half of the upright shaft. The three ends of the cross may be floriated, with projections symbolizing leaves or petals of a living tree. These symbolize the cross as the tree of life – the tree that takes away the curse of death that followed Adam and Eve's original transgression with the tree in the Garden of Eden. Crosses in grave markers may also be adorned with a floral wreath or a palm branch, both symbols of victory.

The cross, in various forms, is a very ancient symbol. Its use as a Christian symbol began in the mid-fifth century. A Greek cross, with four arms of equal length, is found on a sarcophagus from that period now in the Vatican Museum. The legend of the finding of the original "True Cross" in Jerusalem by Helena, the aged mother of Emperor Constantine, was dated a century earlier, in the year 326. Like the veneration of its fragmentary relics, the earliest symbolic representations of the cross were associated with the conversion to Christianity of the emperor who turned the Roman Empire from persecuting to supporting the Church. In his *Life of Constantine* (*circa* 340), Eusebius wrote that a vision of a Cross of Light prompted the emperor's conversion, and that he thenceforth commanded that images of the cross be carried at the head of all his armies as a sign of salvation, a safeguard against every adverse and hostile power. Finally, Constantine commissioned a statue of himself to be set up in Rome, holding a Cross of Victory. The "monumental inscription" engraved on the cross declared, "By virtue of this salutary sign ... I have preserved and liberated your city from the yoke of tyranny." No longer perceived as a subversive force hostile to the Roman Empire, Christianity was now seen as its safeguard. And no longer was the cross an embarrassing symbol of a felon's death – as St. Paul had observed – a "stumblingblock," a "weakness," and even a "foolishness" to non-believers (I Corinthians 1:

23, 25). It was transformed into a paradoxical symbol of triumph over death. The cross replaced the earlier symbol of Christian belief, the fish, and in the seventh century the Crucifixion itself began to be visually represented.

During the English Reformation, Protestants repudiated the imagery of the Crucifixion. Even the ancient rood crosses in their churches were destroyed by iconoclasts. The cross itself began to be identified as a Catholic symbol, and today most crosses on gravestones are in Roman Catholic cemeteries. The angels or archangels attendant at the Cross are also frequently represented. Beside the numerous wrought-iron crosses in German Catholic churchyards, several stone monuments bear this image. In the St. Boniface churchyard in Maryhill, Ontario, one wrought-iron grave marker is crafted with two angels at the sides of a leafy cross that contains a small cast-iron crucifix.

ABOVE: *Notre-Dame-des-Neiges Cemetery, Montreal, Quebec*

LEFT: *Cemetery, near Creignish, Cape Breton, Nova Scotia*

FACING PAGE: *Notre Dame Cemetery, Ottawa, Ontario*

St. Mary's Roman Catholic Cemetery,
Kingston, Ontario
Angel of the Resurrection, sculpted
by Giulio Monteverde of Genoa,
Italy.

Angel Statuary

Saints and holy persons, frequently portrayed in Roman Catholic churches, also figure as sculptures in cemeteries. Angel statuary, however, is found in both Roman Catholic and Protestant or non-denominational cemeteries. According to one guide cataloguing graveyard symbols, the Angel may mean many things – "rebirth, resurrection, protection, judgement, wisdom, mercy or Divine love." Those who commissioned angelic images in centuries past did so in the context of a great wealth of legends about angels. They were familiar with dozens of stories, in the Bible and elsewhere, where angels played various roles. In the 20th century other meaningful stories were added, including a reference made by Mohandas Gandhi in a well-known quotation: "It is foolish to think that by fleeing, one can trick the dread god of death. Let us treat him as a beneficent angel rather than a dread god. We must face and welcome him whenever he comes."

Gandhi's perception of death as a "beneficent angel," or kind messenger, has much in common with the Jewish tradition of two angels of death, Gabriel, the messenger of mildest death, as well as the feared Sammaël. Many more angels in Jewish, Muslim and Christian traditions have individual names and special functions. Indeed, there is such a multitude of the heavenly host that trying to identify just one meaning for any specific stone angel appears to be itself an almost meaningless task. Many strands of meaning are usually braided together.

In the 19th century, Kingston was a major port of arrival for immigrants intending to settle in Upper Canada or Canada West. Most of them were Irish, and hundreds of them were deathly ill when their barges entered the harbour. Despite the quarantine station at Grosse-Île, Kingston suffered a cholera plague in 1832. During the summer, 97 of the 255 afflicted immigrants died. The great typhus epidemic of 1847 killed more than 1,400 in a town that then had just over 6,000 residents. The dying immigrants were hastily unloaded from their barges. Their remains were loaded onto death carts and given hurried burials in trenches in a field near the General Hospital, sprinkled with quicklime, and covered with a large mound of earth. For the inhabitants of Kingston, it was a "scene of unspeakable woe." Almost 60 years later, at the unveiling of a commemorative statue near the hospital, the Archbishop said that "God alone and the recording angel" could bear to keep account of "the excruciating pain of body and sorrow of soul, of the tears and agonizing groans of the famine-stricken, fever-hunted children of Ireland that expired here." His reference was to an Angel of the Last Judgement in the Book of Revelation: "And I beheld, and heard an angel flying through the midst of heaven, saying with a loud voice, Woe, woe, woe, to the inhabiters of the earth by reason of the other voices of the trumpet of the three angels, which are yet to sound!" (Revelation 8: 13).

The Kingston monument, which has been relocated from the original mass grave site to a corner of St. Mary's Roman Catholic Cemetery, represents an Angel of the Resurrection holding up a small open book in one hand and in the other the inverted trumpet hanging down, pending the sounding of the last trumpet. The figure represents the seventh angel in the Book of Revelation, "who had in his hand a little book open": "And I went unto the angel, and said unto him, Give me the little book. And he said unto me, Take it and eat it up; and it shall make thy belly bitter" (Revelation 10: 2, 9). It is often observed that Victorians were more realistic about death than people in later times, who have been more sheltered from the experience of seeing others die. But scenes of mass mortality such as the typhus epidemic would have been very bitter to swallow and must have far too closely resembled the apocalypse. Seeing them provoked an understandable reaction in the Victorian viewers – a wish to forget such horrors, to leave them unrecalled as things of the past and to focus on progress toward a better future. In Kingston the site of the typhus burial mound contained no memorial for 60 years.

The statue was carved in white marble by Giulio Monteverde of Genoa, Italy. Monteverde was one of a school of sculptors active in Italy whose works were internationally renowned. The Christ figure mounted above the chapel in the Recoleta, the oldest and most aristocratic cemetery of Buenos Aires, was created by him, as was the much-photographed seductive angel for the tomb of Francesco Oneto (1882) in the Staglieno Cemetery in Genoa. The Staglieno was famed as a gallery of monuments that enchanted countless American visitors. Mark Twain described it in his best-selling book *Innocents Abroad* (1869), and commented that the Staglieno would continue to be remembered "after we shall have forgotten the palaces." Twain's celebration of the new sculptures, to the disadvantage of "blemished" ancient classics, was very influential in the New World:

On either side ... are monuments, tombs, and sculptured figures that are exquisitely wrought and are full of grace and beauty. They are new and snowy; every outline is perfect, every feature guiltless of mutilation, flaw, or blemish; and therefore, to us these far-reaching ranks of bewitching forms are a hundred fold more lovely than the damaged and dingy statuary they have saved from the wreck of ancient art and set up in the galleries of Paris for the worship of the world.

The Monteverde Angel was a snowy-white figure of grace and beauty, with no flaw or blemish, and it still retains an apparent newness. He does not evoke the terror of the "mighty angel [who] cried with a loud voice, as when a lion roareth: and when he had cried, seven thunders uttered their voices." He is utterly quiet, and it is difficult to imagine his having the "power over waters to turn them into blood, and to smite the earth with plagues [until] their dead bodies shall lie in the street of the great city" (Revelation 10: 3; 11: 6, 8). The people of Kingston, who had seen such things in their own streets, had no appetite for a reminder of that vision. Only the arrival in 1881 of Bishop Cleary, who had studied in Rome and knew Monteverde's angel in the cemetery of San Lorenzo fuori le Mura, prompted the erection of a memorial for Irish Catholic victims of the typhus epidemic.

One of the best-known cemetery memorials in Canada is fictional – Margaret Laurence's *The Stone Angel* (1964). Hagar Shipley never knew her mother, who died giving birth to her – an all-too-common fact of life in Canadian prairie towns in the 1870s. Although Hagar at ninety is "rampant with

RIGHT: *Mount Hope Roman Catholic Cemetery, Toronto, Ontario*
Mourning angel with symbols of death and resurrection – Cross, palm frond and Easter lilies.

RIGHT: *Mount Hope Roman Catholic Cemetery, Toronto, Ontario*
Mourning angel with symbols of death and resurrection – Cross, palm frond and Easter lilies.

FAR RIGHT: *Notre-Dame-des-Neiges Cemetery, Montreal, Quebec*

FACING PAGE: *Wallbridge Cemetery, Belleville, Ontario*
Angel monument for Susanna Moodie.

memory," she doubts that her mother's memorial still survives: "I wonder if she stands there yet, in memory of her." Hagar is sardonic, even cynical, about her father's proud purchase – "my mother's angel that my father bought in pride to mark her bones:"

... my father often told me she had been brought from Italy at a terrible expense and was pure white marble. I think now she must have been carved in that distant sun by stone masons who were the cynical descendants of Bernini, gouging out her like by the score, gauging with admirable accuracy the needs of fledgling pharaohs in an uncouth land.

Her wings in winter were pitted by the snow and in summer by the blown grit. She was not the only angel in the Manawaka cemetery, but she was the first, the largest, and certainly the costliest.

White marble was available from North American quarries such as those in Vermont and Nova Scotia, but white Italian marble was famous, not only for its purity (certain chemical constituents of other marble cause it to darken with time) but also for its artistic pedigree. Since Roman times, the supply of white marble in Italy's Carrara Mountains has provided the nearly perfect medium for great masters – Michelangelo, Bernini, Canova and Thorvaldsen – as well as for countless anonymous stonecutters. The purity, the historical artistic tradition, and even the costliness of Italian marble statuary, made it very desirable. Visitors to Victorian cemeteries will notice, like Hagar, that stone angels were modelled from standard patterns. Nonetheless, the traditional stonecutter's handcraft trade was not an ignoble or fraudulent one, and Hagar's description of the production of her mother's stone angel is perhaps too dismissive. The stonecutters in Italy (and elsewhere) were the artistic descendants of Bernini's studio assistants, not Bernini himself. Even in Classical times, stonecutters did the mechanical work of enlarging and reproducing a sculpture from a smaller clay model, or from the original bronze, using a precisely accurate gauging system of points.

Hagar also complains about the angel's pure whiteness:

"Whoever carved her had left her eyeballs blank." She might have preferred the ancient practice of painting sculptures. The Alexander Sarcophagus, for instance, sculpted by Praxiteles and painted by Nicias, displayed a colour scheme of tan hair, light yellow skin, purple toga and magenta mantle. In some marble sculptures the stone skin was left *au naturel*, but in almost all cases the eyes, eyebrows, eyelids and eyelashes were coloured. The ancients may have shared Hagar's prejudice against a stone figure "unendowed with even a pretence of sight." But after two thousand years, even the mild Mediterranean climate has slowly worn away the paint, altering our perception of what Greek sculpture looked like. Sculptors from Bernini to Thorvaldsen made no pretense of lifelike colour. Their aim was to create an impression of life from blank material.

The Canadian climate, as Hagar points out, is harsher. More destructive than blowing snow and blown grit is acid rain, fuelled by the internal combustion automotive engine. Sulfurous compounds absorbed in water molecules eat away exposed calcite limestone surfaces, causing irreversible permanent damage.

Hope Statuary

Among Protestants who wanted to erect a nine-foot statue on their family gravesites but may have regarded angels as perhaps too Roman Catholic, Hope was the allegorical figure of choice. She is robed like an angel, but has no wings and has a large anchor, in reference to St. Paul's image of "the hope set before us" in the face of death: "Which hope we have as an anchor of the soul, both sure and stedfast, and which entereth into that within the veil" (Hebrews 6: 18, 19). For Methodists like the Massey family, the Anchor of Hope was especially associated with hymns written by Charles Wesley ("Thou art the anchor of my hope / ... Surely thy death shall raise me up, / For thou hast died that I may live"). Even better known was the popular hymn "We Have an Anchor," written in 1882 by Priscilla Jane Owens:

When our eyes behold through the gathering night The City of Gold, our harbour bright, We shall anchor fast by the heavenly shore With the storms all past for ever more.

The anchor emblem alone, without a figure, is sometimes represented in relief on tablet monuments as a symbol of hope, and occasionally a real anchor is transplanted for use as a memorial. In Ross Bay Cemetery, a family with a long connection to the Danish navy and who had lived for years in the Danish Virgin Islands placed an authentic Danish naval anchor on their family plot in 1990. On the eastern seacoast, anchors were combined with a large rock outcropping to form a memorial in the Old Burial Ground in Liverpool, Nova Scotia. The plaque, which includes a conventional image of the anchor of hope, reads:

GOD'S MERCY
OUR HOPE In memory of the crew of the
BEAM TRAWLER JUTLAND
foundered at sea March 11 1920
These crossed anchors recovered
from fishing banks on Jutland's
previous trip are placed as a
symbol of our HOPE that their
souls are resting in eternal peace.

FAR LEFT: *Liverpool Common Burying Ground, Liverpool, Nova Scotia*
Crossed anchors as a symbol of hope in memory of the crew of the Beam Trawler *Jutland*, foundered at sea in 1920.

LEFT: *Notre-Dame Cemetery, Ottawa, Ontario*
Figure of Hope.

A LA DOUCE MEMOIRE DE
FRANCOIS ANTOINE MULLER
DECEDE LE 27 NOVEMBRE 1914
A L'AGE DE 66 ANS & 10 MOIS

Mourners

Traditionally, mourners were female. They occasionally represent an individual "magnificent widow" but are more often symbolic evocations of romantic grief. Their stage presence derives from theatrical tradition. The tragic chorus in classical drama voiced the emotional content of the catastrophe, while the actors were caught up in the events. The chorus of woe mediates between actors and audience, heightening the intensity of grief, so that we can experience the catharsis of pity and fear. *Pleureuses* may be muted and restrained, but generally express an intensity of feeling that is utterly different from the stuffy Victorian tradition of hiring an undertaker's "mute" (like Oliver Twist) to carry a weakly symbolic clean handkerchief.

TOP AND BOTTOM LEFT: *Notre-Dame-des-Neiges Cemetery, Montreal, Quebec*

BOTTOM RIGHT: *Notre-Dame-des-Neiges Cemetery, Montreal, Quebec* Mourner figure with a floral tribute.

FACING PAGE: *St. Boniface Cathedral Cemetery, Manitoba*

Rustic Monuments

"Rural life" and "rustic life" share their essential root meaning – life in the country as opposed to the town. But over time, "rustic" gradually acquired extra layers of meaning – primitive, unrefined and rough. Then, as the circumstances of life became ever more smooth, refined and sophisticated, people began to view plain and simple or "rustic" things in a more positive light. Even during the reign of Elizabeth I, a writer could declare that "the whole life rustike is hurtless, simple, and most of all framed to the true order of Nature." People learned to admire examples of "rude," or country, workmanship, especially those constructed of stones in their natural undressed state, or tree branches left rough-hewn and still clad in their bark.

By the mid-Victorian era, this admiration for natural rusticity culminated in artificial simulations, so that garden benches apparently built from undressed logs might actually be made of cast iron. Rustic cemetery monuments in Canada and the United States generally date from the quarter-century beginning in the early 1880s. They are carved from limestone. The craftsmen may have been local, or the sculptures may have been shipped by rail from centres of production in American Limestone Belt areas in Illinois or Indiana. Smaller monuments were ordered from catalogues or copied from design books. But there are also elaborate and finely crafted examples made by carvers who may be identified by their characteristic styles.

Some monuments, sculpted in the form of a cairn of stones, are small imitations of large-scale precedents – Megalithic structures built as multi-chambered shelters for the dead during the New Stone Age and Bronze Age. Individual cairns were made more recently as special memorials of events, or to commemorate a person of special distinction. "Cairn" is a word with Celtic history. The Highland Scots referred to an old custom in a Gaelic expression, (in translation) "I will add a stone to your cairn." Rustic monuments, however, are not heaps of stones, or even pyramids of rough stones cemented together, but are sculpted from single blocks of limestone. In place of the cairn's metal plaque, they often have a sculpted stone label or scroll on which the epitaph is inscribed.

Rustic tree stones may be quite lifelike. They have often fooled the eye of casual visitors, who at first assumed they were looking at a real tree trunk whose branches had been lopped off. Their sculptors sometimes added details of continuing life, such as oak leaves with acorns, ferns, ivy twining up the bark, birds, or even squirrels perching on the abbreviated stubs of branches. These representations of life and death follow "the true order of Nature," and their meaningfulness derives from our experience of the natural world. In what may be the oldest book of the Bible, Job raises the question: "If a man die, shall he live again?" He observes a great contrast between the life of a tree and human life:

For there is hope of a tree, if it be cut down, that it will sprout again, and that the tender branch thereof will not cease.

Though the root thereof wax old in the earth, and the stock thereof die in the ground; Yet through the scent of water it will bud, and bring forth boughs like a plant.

But man dieth, and wasteth away: yea, man giveth up the ghost, and where is he?

As the waters fail from the sea, and the flood decayeth and drieth up: So man lieth down and riseth not: till the heavens be no more, they shall not awake, nor be raised from their sleep. (Job 14, 14, 7–12)

As Job's friend candidly points out to him, this is "unprofitable talk" and offers no religious consolation (Job 15, 3).

Severed stone trees as emblems of an abbreviated earthly life that nevertheless remains rooted and bound to eternal life are sometimes found in Jewish cemeteries. They are carved less naturalistically than the rustic style of the Gentiles. Most rustic cairns and tree stones owe little to religious traditions, offering instead an impression of natural-

FACING PAGE, LEFT: *St. Mark's Anglican Church Cemetery, Niagara-on-the-Lake, Ontario*
Rustic tree stump cross with the words, in twig lettering, "GONE HOME."

FACING PAGE, RIGHT: *Cataraqui Cemetery, Kingston, Ontario*

ism. Some, however, are composites — representations of crosses made of untrimmed tree branches are sometimes mounted on representations of stone cairns.

Lambs

Visitors to 19th century burial grounds cannot help noticing the high incidence of mortality among infants and young children. Family gravesites often record year after year the loss of newborn babies or toddlers, or commemorate the deaths of several young children in a single epidemic. The suffering of these children, and the grief of their surviving parents and siblings, is frequently expressed in memorials in the form of a resting lamb — meek, gentle, innocent and weak. Lamb memorials were so much in demand that they were manufactured *en masse* and illustrated in mail-order catalogues. Their poignancy is not diminished by their frequency. Indeed, when manufactured lambs that were originally all the same are now compared, they will be seen to have acquired individual identities from exposure to the elements over the years.

The lamb symbol has two aspects. It incorporates a stark recognition of the impossibility, then, of saving many children from premature death and provides a consolation for the survivors. The first aspect is a transformation of the archaic rites of offering an innocent victim — "as of a lamb without blemish and without spot" (I Peter 1: 19) — as a burnt sacrifice. The practice is recalled in the ancient story of the patriarch Abraham being commanded by his God to sacrifice his son, Isaac. The death of a child, no matter how common, appears unnatural, against parental feeling, an involuntary sacrifice. The Christian tradition transforms the ancient image by identifying the Son of God as "the Lamb of God, which taketh away the sin of the world" (John 1: 29). The Anglican service for the burial of a child reminded parents that God "spared not his own Son, but delivered him up for us all."

A more consoling interpretation of the lamb symbol is found in the same service, in the well-known words of Psalm 23: "The Lord is my Shepherd … Yea, though I walk through the valley of the shadow of death, I will fear no evil; for thou art with me; thy rod and thy staff they comfort me." This image of comfort is brought into focus by a quotation from Isaiah 40:11: "He shall feed his flock like a shepherd; he shall gather the lambs with his arm, and carry them in his bosom." The figure of the recumbent lamb is thus not only a victim, but also one who, in the words of the burial prayer, has been taken into the safe-keeping of eternal love.

Union Cemetery, Calgary, Alberta

Lambs in Hamilton Cemetery. The monument on the lower right is cast in zinc, or "White Bronze."

Doves

Bearing an olive branch, the dove symbolizes peace. It is also a sign of promise of salvation from the forces of destruction. In the ancient story of the great "flood of waters ... upon the earth," Noah's ark is built "to keep some seed alive": "And God remembered Noah, and every living thing ... and the waters asswaged ... And the dove came in to him in the evening; and lo, in her mouth was an olive leaf pluckt off: so Noah knew that the waters were abated from off the earth" (Genesis 7: 3 and 8: 1, 11).

The record of the baptism of Christ in the Gospel of St. John adds a Christian layer of meaning to Noah's dove, as it becomes the visible form of the Holy Spirit in the Christian Trinity of Father, Son and Holy Ghost: "And John bare record, saying, I saw the Spirit descending from heaven like a dove, and it abode upon him ... but he that sent me to baptize with water ... said unto me, Upon whom thou shalt see the Spirit descending ... the same is he which baptizeth with the Holy Ghost. And I saw, and bare record that this is the Son of God" (John 1: 32–34). The gravestone motif of the dove descending from heaven is therefore a symbol of faith in Christian baptism as the salvation of spiritual life from death.

A red sandstone grave marker in Ross Bay Cemetery for a dentist who died at the age of 26 in 1874 – Thomas Mills Bowden, "Native of Bowmanville, C.W. [Canada West, now Ontario]" – bears the inscription "Asleep in Jesus." The dove descends in a recessed trefoil, another symbol of the

RIGHT: *Notre-Dame Cemetery, Ottawa, Ontario*
Modernist sculptural interpretation of a dove.

FAR RIGHT: *Ross Bay Cemetery, Victoria, British Columbia*
Dove and flower motifs.

Trinity. The plucked branch carried in its mouth is elaborated in three acanthus leaves, which appear to be architectural supports for the Gothic arch crowning the tablet. In Woodhouse near Simcoe, Ontario, on the gravestone of William Howick's wife, Jemima, who died in 1855, the descending dove bears a branch that partly conceals a book on one side and a trumpet on the other, with an hourglass standing at the side to signal the brevity of mortal life. The book of life and trumpet are symbols of the Last Judgement of the quick and the dead, and their meaning is spelled out in the inscription:

> *We must all appear before the judgment*
> *seat of Christ, that every one may*
> *[repent?] the things done in the body accor-*
> *ding to that he hath done.*

> *Gardiner SC*

The "SC," an abbreviation for the Latin *sculpsit*, indicates that Samuel Gardiner was the maker of the stone. The doves on these stones appear to have been carved not from a standard pattern, but from real birds, though not necessarily from life. In pioneer times wild pigeons were hunted for food. Passenger pigeons were still numerous in North America in the 1850s and did not become extinct until the 1890s.

A monument from the 1870s is draped with a tasselled veil, drawn back to reveal that the dove lying on the sacrificial altar at the base of the stone is about to be received and taken above the clouds into heaven. A damaged stone in St. Andrew's churchyard, Niagara-on-the-Lake, commemorates Joseph [Gaston?], who died in 1854, aged 18 months. The verse suggests that the dove represents his spirit, which has flown away from earthly mortality:

> *Our lovely Infant Joseph rests,*
> *Beneath this sod of clay.*
> *His spirit slumbers with the blest,*
> *Untill the Judgement day.*

TOP: *St. Andrew's Presbyterian Church Cemetery, Niagara-on-the-Lake, Ontario* Dove with an olive branch on a broken gravestone for an infant.

MIDDLE: *Ross Bay Cemetery, Victoria, British Columbia* Dove with olive branch motif.

BOTTOM: *Old Woodhouse United Church Cemetery, Vittoria, Ontario* Dove with olive branch, Bible, hourglass and resurrection trumpet on the gravestone for Jemima Howick, who died in 1855.

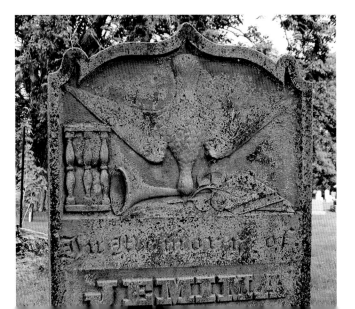

Hands

❦ Hands are universally recognized as a kind of metaphor technically known by the (much less universally recognized) term *synecdoche* – a part is used to signify the whole. "Hands" was a commonly used term for "workmen," and agreeing to "lend a hand" always means the involvement of much more than that one appendage. So hands on gravestones are useful *synecdoches*, evoking the presence of the whole person. Occasionally a sculpted hand whose proportions are not quite correct is seen on a gravestone, but models for hands are easily found, and many stonecutters mastered the art. They were happy to add a hand even when it was not strictly necessary for the symbolic meaning. In Economy, Nova Scotia, for instance, a bouquet of flowers, cut short in the bloom of life and already fading, is not set in a vase but is held in the hand, like an offering. It is a more personal gesture.

Throughout the 19th century, the handshake was a common everyday practice, often occurring in greetings, in leave-takings and in confirming business deals. Even today it may formalize (or take the place of) a written contract. The persistence of this ancient gesture may be traced in certain archaic forms of our language. For hundreds of years, the "handfast" or "hand-promise" meant one contract in partic-

ular – the betrothal of a couple was solemnized by their joining hands. The antiquity of this form of espousal is evident in Roman law, where *manus* referred to the power of a husband over his wife – hence the expression "to ask for a woman's *hand* in marriage." Various gravestones from ancient Greece show sculpted reliefs of husband and wife solemnly clasping hands in lasting commemoration of their vows.

The handclasp is frequently repeated, with individual variations of detail, on Victorian gravestones. The many representations of clasped hands, showing traces of a husband's formal shirt and button or cufflink and a wife's lacy sleeve, are modern abridgements of ancient designs, where the hands extended from the folds of togas. The emblem has many layers of meaning. The gesture marks a farewell to earthly things, but also implies the hope of a future reunion. In one oval vignette on the gravestone for Thomas Corris in Ross Bay Cemetery, both hands emerge from curling clouds, representing Heaven. As Corris (1783–1885) died at the age of 102, it is likely that in death he anticipated joining many friends who had predeceased him.

Two white marble stones in the Trinity Lutheran Cemetery in Fisherville, Ontario, were carved by the same stonecutter for men who died in 1882. They both show a handclasp between a woman and a man; her open sleeve on the left contrasts with his simple cuff, and his grasp shows more vigour than hers. The stone for Valentine Kiefer, aged 75, who had emigrated from Rhenish Prussia 40 years earlier with his wife and five children, bears the legend, "He's at rest." Since Kiefer's wife had died in 1863, the image is perhaps a sign of their hoped-for reunion in death, after 20 years of separation. On the tablet for John Race, only the word "Farewell" is added to the image. He was born Johannes Valentin Rees in Bad Bergzabern, Rheinbaiern. The spelling of his name changed to Rays and then Race after he arrived in 1851, accompanied by his wife, Elizabeth, their first son and a son born at sea – the survivor of twins. Her two brothers sponsored their journey. Census records from 1852 show that all three families lived in a single-storey log house with their aunt and uncle, who had settled in Rainham Township in

RIGHT: *Church of England Cemetery, St. John's, Newfoundland*

FACING PAGE, TOP: *Hillcrest Cemetery, Lunenburg, Nova Scotia*

FACING PAGE, RIGHT: *Lunenburg, Nova Scotia*

FACING PAGE, LEFT: *Mennonite Cemetery, near Pickering, Ontario*

1834. John's father, Johannes Rees Sr., came in 1861 and died a few months later, in the same year that John's youngest child died at the age of two. Such a life as John Race's might be summarized as a series of farewells. But, on the other hand, it might also be viewed as a series of helping hands and tokens of support. His family's journeys were made possible by friends who lent them money to pay the fare.

In the same cemetery in Fisherville are white marble tablets with relief carvings of an open Bible held in a hand with the thumb pointing to the text. All are inscribed in German in Gothic lettering and were carved at about the same time, in 1868–69, clearly by the same stonecutter. A similar group of stones in the cemetery of Economy shows the carver's preference for the index finger pointing up to the holy text. Sometimes the books have unlettered pages. Others have texts from the Bible, such as "I know that my Redeemer liveth" (Job 19: 25).

The emblem of the hand pointing heavenward may be seen as the same gesture, but minus the Bible. The viewer is not so much admonished to study scriptural text as to focus on the world to come and the promise of resurrection for the blessed who "die in the Lord." Several of the hands in Economy point to heaven as the eternal home. On the memorial for the young wife of John McLaughlin, a feminine hand, which looks almost like a delicate glove, points to a slender ribbon being drawn up out of sight and bearing the words "Gone home." On the gravestone for Edwin and Robert, the sons of Aghsah and Robert Morrison, a masculine hand points emphatically to the same words at the top of the stone.

More unusual are the three-dimensional cast-iron hands, supported by elaborate latticework, seen in various cemeteries in New Brunswick and Nova Scotia. These could be easily shipped ready-made from the foundry, and the appropriate name and date could be added later within the small frame, perhaps on stone or on a panel under glass. Many have lost their original nameplates. All of them, however, are marked with the maker's name and the registration date of his mould – "W.H. Faulkner R.D. 1884." As a result,

genealogical surveys of cemeteries in the two provinces have claimed to identify quite a few last resting places of a certain W.H. Faulkner, of whom nothing is known save the year of his death, 1884.

The broken chain, like the broken blossom, is an emblem of life cut short too soon. The memorial erected in St. Mark's Cemetery in Niagara-on-the-Lake by the parents of William McMillan, "who met with his death while in the employ of the O. & Miss. R.R. Co. at Lebanon, Mar. 11, 1867, AE 22 Yr's and 7m's," shows a hand coming down gently to grasp the fragmentary chain of life and draw it upward.

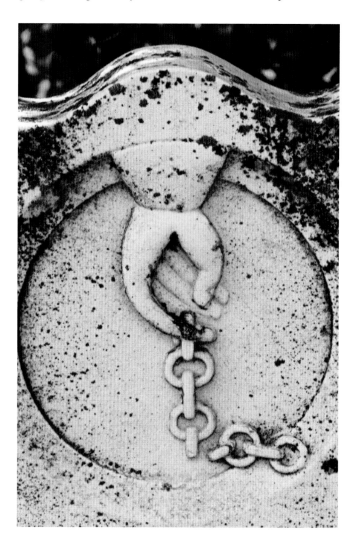

Flowers

Flowers are the most evocative, and in some ways the least explicable and most poignant, of gravestone images. Floral wreaths and arrangements are commonly offered, at funerals and gravesites, as emblems of the beauty and brevity of human life.

As for man, his days are as grass; as a flower of the field, so he flourisheth. For the wind passeth over it, and it is gone; and the place thereof shall know it no more. (Psalm 103: 15–16)

Our brief flourishing is a blossom whose natural purpose is only to fruit and seed the next generation. The broken blossoms marking graves of those who died too soon for that regeneration are, from a completely natural viewpoint, quite fruitless and lacking in meaning. But, as horticulturalists have known forever (or perhaps since the first garden in paradise), the reproductive function of flowers is by no means our only reason for celebrating their tremendous beauty.

RIGHT: *Malpeque, Prince Edward Island*

FAR RIGHT: *Boston Mills Cemetery, Boston Mills, Ontario*

Epitaphs

Reading epitaphs has a particularly fascinating appeal. Numerous books containing nothing but quotations from gravestone inscriptions have been published, but such collections are poor substitutes for the pleasures of discovering for oneself the epitaphs on monuments in old cemeteries. Reading the words hand-cut into the stone has a deeper and more direct appeal. It is not uncommon for an old tombstone to display half-a-dozen different styles of lettering, which are not easily replicated in modern fonts. And although a good photograph can represent the letters more faithfully, it does not capture the thrill of discovery – no enthusiastic bird-watcher would prefer to see a photograph, rather than find a rare bird in its natural habitat. A gravestone in its proper setting has an immediacy of impact, and its authenticity is evident – unlike some dubious epitaphs in anthologies. (Is there truly an epitaph somewhere for a tired housewife – "Don't mourn for me now, don't mourn for me never, I'm going to do nothing for ever and ever"?)

The worn lettering of ancient inscriptions may be difficult to decipher, but the challenge only adds to the enjoyment. Ultimately, the charm of old epitaphs derives from the knowledge that the letters were painstakingly cut long ago, and were meant to endure to a distant future. The text has been waiting for years, decades or centuries for you, dear reader, to come along. And now that the letters have caught your attention, you will receive a message sent to you from someone you never knew. Each one is unique – its publication is an edition of one copy. Even if its verse and sentiments may be inscribed on hundreds of similar stones, the message is very personal.

William Wordsworth, a poet much inspired by the capacity for memory and remembrance, began his "Essays upon Epitaphs" with a quotation from William Camden (1605), by way of John Weever's *Ancient Funerall Monuments Within the United Monarchie of Great Britaine* (1631). According to Camden, the invention of epitaphs "proceeded from the presage or fore-feeling of immortality, implanted in all men naturally." Wordsworth commented that "without the consciousness of a principle of immortality in the human soul, Man could never have had awakened in him the desire to live in the remembrance of his fellows":

Mere love, or the yearning of kind towards kind, could never have produced it. The dog or horse perishes in the field, or in the stall, by the side of his companions, and is incapable of anticipating the sorrow with which his surrounding associates shall bemoan his death, or pine for his loss; he cannot preconceive this regret, he can form no thought of it; and therefore cannot possibly have a desire to leave such regret or remembrance behind him.

The presage of immortality finds expression in a legion of epitaphs in which the dead speak to the reader from beyond the grave. Whether or not they make a claim for immortality or a personal resurrection, their words live on:

Death is a debt that's nature's due
Which I have paid and so must you.

————

As you are now, so once was I,
As I am now, so you will be,
Prepare for death, and follow me.

————

Oh cruel Death, I felt thy power,
You call'd in an unguarded hour.
My blooming friends, a warning take,
And with God your peace do make.

———

My flesh shall slumber in the ground,
Till the last trumpet's joyful sound,
Then burst the chains, with Sweet Surprise,
And in my Saviour's image rise.

————

Reader, pause, behold your fate,
Death will arrest you soon or late;
Your dearest interest is to have
Your bliss secur'd beyond the grave.

A modern version of these "sermons in stones" is found in Belleville Cemetery. The message to the unknown reader is about what "LIFE" is and isn't about. It is machine-engraved, entirely in upper-case letters, on granite. Above the text are laser-cut images of a young boy playing hockey and baseball. He died in 1998 in his thirteenth year.

LIFE. Life isn't about keeping score. It's not about how many people call you and it's not about who you've dated, are dating, or haven't dated at all. It isn't about who you've kissed, what sport you play, or which guy or girl likes you. It isn't about who is right, who is wrong, who succeeded and who failed. It's not about your shoes or your hair or the colour of your skin or where you live or go to school. In fact, it's not about money, clothes, or possessions you have: life isn't about having lots of friends or if you are alone and it's not about how accepted or unaccepted you are. Life just isn't about that.

But life is about who you love and who you hurt. It's about how you feel about yourself. It's about trust, happiness and compassion. It's about sticking up for what you believe in and replacing inner hate with love. Life is about avoiding jealousy, overcoming ignorance and building confidence. It's about what you say and what you mean. It's about seeing people for who they are and not what they have. Most of all, it's about choosing to use your life to touch someone else's in a way that could never have been achieved otherwise. These choices are what life's about.

Most epitaph texts have greater economy of expression. The Latin phrase used by Heinrich Engelhardt in his chapter on epitaphs – "*Multum in parvo*" ("Much in little") – seems apt, since Latin is the language renowned for aiming at the most powerful expression in the fewest possible words. Engelhardt, the designer of both Belleville and Mount Pleasant cemeteries, would have approved the brevity of the epitaph on the Flavelle tomb in Mount Pleasant.

TWO THINGS STAND LIKE STONE. KINDNESS
IN ANOTHER'S TROVBLE. COVRAGE IN YOVR OWN

The stoicism of the Flavelle inscription is enhanced by the use of the traditional Roman V for U in the inscription.

Sir Joseph Flavelle, who died in his eighty-second year in 1939, did not choose to economize on the epitaph for financial reasons. He left an estate of over six million dollars. A school drop-out at the age of 13, Flavelle went to work for a mediocre meat-packing operation, which he turned into "one of the most efficient and prosperous on the continent." He was chairman of the Imperial Munitions Board during the First World War, turning around an "ineffectual and inefficient" organization, and "did much to secure victory for the Allies." He worked on boards and commissions connected with the Royal Ontario Museum, the Toronto General Hospital and the University of Toronto, and "was almost single-handedly responsible for the establishment of the Ontario Research Foundation." Among his own troubles were the death of a seven-month-old daughter in 1888 when he was starting out in business, the death of his wife in 1932 (when he built the underground Flavelle vault, unique in Mount Pleasant), and the accusation that he had profiteered during the First World War by selling tainted bacon to the military (he was exonerated). His tomb bears another Latin motto related to his life's work: "PACE ET BELLO PARATVS" ("in peace and war prepared").

Occasionally an epitaph is addressed not to an unknown reader, but to the surviving family.

Farewell my wife and darling child
This world I bid adieu
Dear wife now my life is past
My love to you so long did last
Now for me no sorrow take
But love my child for my sake.

Other epitaphs express the lamenting voices of survivors.

So unaffected so compos'd a mind
So firm yet soft, so soft, yet so refin'd
Heav'n as its purest gold with torture tried
The saint sustain'd it, but the woman died.

———

Sleep well, sweet Babe, and take thy rest.
God called thee home, He thought it best.

———

Elizabeth wife of Capt. Savage
Royal Engineer
Who after a long and painful
illness which she bore with
the utmost Christian Fortitude
and Resignation, Departed this
Life on board the Lord Suffield
Transport, off Cape
Breton Octr. 6th
1828. Aged 28 Years.
Leaving a most Disconsolate
Husband and six young Children
To Lament the loss of one of the
Best and most Affectionate of
Wives and Fondest of Mothers.

Wordsworth notes the "benign influence" of reading such favourable epitaphs:

When a Stranger has walked round a Country Church-yard and glanced his eye over so many brief Chronicles, as the tomb-stones usually contain, of faithful Wives, tender Husbands, dutiful Children, and good Men of all classes; he will be tempted to exclaim ... 'Where are all the bad people buried?'

But he confesses that although he is not "so far lulled" as to believe he has found "the eye or central point of a rural Arcadia," he finds visiting the graveyard a refreshing break from the usual afflictions of life.

Lower Durham Cemetery, Lower Durham, New Brunswick
A homemade grave marker created by pouring concrete into a frame. The reversed lettering, created by sticks in the frame, was an unexpected result as the frame was constructed without understanding that a mirror image would be reproduced.

Rushes Cemetery near Crosshill, Wellesley Township, Ontario
The epitaph takes the form of a cryptogram. See p. 306 for the solution.

GONE HOME

BEAN

HENRIETTA   SUSANNA

S V W E T B S A 15 S T M O R E
E I R T E 2 Y D & H N S 10 H E
M I A D 17 & S H T N O A R M T
N A Y D H D . N E F S M Y E H E
E N S O W M . A B E O 2 D 26 T T
E V & E I R O M I F S G E E E
H R S 27 D I I E T W R 7 A O M
D A U H T A N M I S A 8 6 B . T
H T S E S M E R E T E L I E S .
Y E A I P H N I T A Y R I P M
E W N 8 6 5 A G E D 23 A P E L
E R N H S N W F W O I D T D H
I G A I 2 D I E H D E 27 H G O
T F R M O B T R N W N E V N A
F S O G D U A E O I H A E M Y

READER MEET US IN HEAVEN

It is such a happiness to have, in an unkind World, one Enclosure where the voice of detraction is not heard: where the traces of evil inclinations are unknown; where contentment prevails, and there is no jarring tone in the peaceful Concert of amity and gratitude.

Rarely does a hint of complaint intrude a "jarring tone" into an epitaph. In most cases, even the cause of death is not mentioned. In the Old Burying Ground in Halifax, the Glen gravestone with its unfamiliar words and spelling, delivers an oddly troubling message:

Janet Glen died 17th Decr 1826 aged 77
Wm Glen died of synanche trachealis
9th May 1827 Aged 7 1/2
Ar Glen died of synanche maligne
14th May 1827 Aged 4 1/2
STRANGER
Whether has desease or medical
omission cladmeast in their last
Claith

The "puzzle stone" in the Methodist Rushes Cemetery near Crosshill, Ontario, was erected by Samuel Bean to commemorate his first two wives, Henrietta and Susanna, who died in 1865 and 1867. (He married a third time, returned to the United States to live in New York and Iowa, and died at sea off the coast of Cuba in 1904.) When Henrietta died seven months after their marriage, he devised a funeral card as a puzzle square, 19 letters across and 19 down. When read in a spiral outward from the middle letter, it revealed the following message:

In memoriam Henriettah Furry Bean. Born in Penn married in Philadelphia to Samuel Bean MD and went with him to Canada leaving all her friends behind. Died in Linwood the 27th of Sep 1865 after an illness of 11 weeks aged 23 years 2 months and 17 days. She was a model wife 1 of 1000 much regretted by her sorrowing husband and all who knew her. Lived a godly life for 5 years and died happy in the Lord Peace be to her ashes. So mote it be.

The death of his second wife, who bore a daughter before dying in April 1867, prompted Dr. Bean to have a cryptic epitaph carved in stone. Above both wives' names is the emblem of a hand pointing heavenward, with the words "GONE HOME." At the base of the tablet is a direct message: "Reader! meet us in heaven." The overgrowth of lichen has been cleaned off the original stone, but the lettering is weathered after 150 years, and in 1982 Wellesley Township and the Wellesley Historical Society had a duplicate made in durable granite, with the letters picked out in black. To decode the inscription, the reader must start with the seventh letter in the seventh line, going counter-clockwise in a spiral – "IN MEMORIAM" – then zigzagging up and down for "HENRIETTA," then skipping up to zigzag again – "1ST WIFE OF S BEAN MD." The rest of the puzzle (for those too impatient to complete the task) – punctuated and converted into upper and lower case – follows:

... who died 27th Sep. 1865, aged 23 years, 2 months and 17 days, and Susanna his 2nd wife who died 27th April, 1867, aged 26 years, 10 months and 15 days. 2 better wives 1 man never had, they were gifts from God but are now in Heaven. May God help me to meet them there.

The textual cryptogram of the Bean epitaph is idiosyncratic indeed. It is strange that he should have felt a need to explicate the meaning of the common and very intelligible visual symbol – a hand pointing heavenward – with a verbal explication, "GONE HOME." In the 1860s, every graveyard visitor could easily have decoded that emblem.

The stones cut by the one-of-a-kind "J.W. Sculptor" are also filled with text. The elaborately lettered stone for James and David Hunter, in Windsor, Nova Scotia, ends with a verse that begins by hailing the Reader: "Lo!"

Lo! Here I ly with my dear Soul
All covered with cold clay
Hopeing with Joy to meet our Lord
At the ETERNAL DAY.

LASTING MEMORY

LASTING MEMORY

Recalling the Past

❧ "Lasting memory" is an oxymoron or contradiction in terms. Forgetting is, after all, an essential and even necessary part of the human condition. We forget so much in our own lives – how shall we not inevitably lose, piece by piece, memories of the lives of others? In the long perspective, memory is scarcely less evanescent than the experience of life itself.

And yet – our yearning for permanence is human too. What is more characteristic of our species than our capacity for recollecting the past and reshaping it for present and future use? Of much current interest to historians is the topic of how the reciprocal relationship between remembering and forgetting affects the perception of historical experience and the production of historical narrative. The relationship is examined by Paul Ricoeur in his recent *Memory, History, Forgetting*, which has been called "a landmark work in philosophy." Cemeteries and monuments may be seen as having a role at the ground level of this intriguing topic.

Memories attach themselves to material things and places. Cemeteries are places of memory in their origin and purpose, and particular monuments are dedicated to preserving future memory. If these places and things are not conserved, the memories associated with them become fragmentary and recede from the forefront of collective consciousness. It follows that the task of preserving these materials has great mnemonic value.

Most historical graveyard monuments were intended to be lasting, even everlasting. But, unless they are protected by conservation and restoration, their outdoor locations expose their materials to weathering and eventual decay. The landscape settings of these places are also vulnerable – not only to natural forces, but to the all-too-human urge to put land to new use.

Conserving the future of memory in Canada's historic cemeteries has depended, and will continue to depend, on community awareness, political will and economic resources. The manner in which a nation cares for its dead cannot be dissociated from its historical and continuing identity.

FACING PAGE: *Madill Church Cemetery, Huntsville, Ontario*

PAGE 268–269: *Notre-Dame-des-Neiges Cemetery, Montreal, Quebec*

Wooden Markers

A wooden cross simply made from two pieces of wood was a memorial easily made by pioneers with limited skills, time or resources. These crosses were sometimes treated with coats of whitewash, but in pioneer burial places they were often left to weather until their inscriptions faded and the forgotten sign itself fell into decay. Wooden grave markers can nevertheless last for a surprisingly long time in our Canadian climate.

For at least 100 years a wooden marker stood in the graveyard of the White Chapel, the earliest Methodist church in Prince Edward County, built in 1809 in Hallowell, near Picton, Ontario. When it was photographed in the early 1970s, no painted or carved inscription remained to identify the name or dates of the life it was meant to commemorate, but there were distinct traces of decorative carving. It is likely that the marker had originally been larger and symmetrical, with three small circular motifs or crockets on each side of the large central one. A wooden board in Ross Bay Cemetery, Victoria, marked the graves of some descendants of Isabella Ross, after whom the bay was named. The outline of the decorative crockets on each side of its tympanum is reminiscent of those remaining on the White Chapel marker. Its inscription shows a combination of raised and incised lettering. Having been exposed to the weather for a century or more, it was taken into storage and replaced with a stone marker.

A delicately crafted wooden tablet with elegantly cut raised lettering, a verse epitaph and decorative details including a draped Neoclassical flaming urn commemorates a young woman who died in Halifax in 1801, one year after the construction of St. George's Anglican Round Church. During the restoration of the "Little Dutch Church," the marker was discovered inside the church tower. Its fortuitous preservation proves that not all wooden grave markers were crudely or amateurishly made.

Rankin Inlet, Nunavut
Crosses marking children's graves.

SACRED
TO THE MEMORY
OF
Elizh. R— Wright —
daughter of Charles &
Elizabeth Wright —
who departed this
Life Septr: 23: 1801. Aged
16 Years & 11 Months

Mourn not for me my parents dear
I am not dead but Sleeping here
As I am now so must you be
Prepare for death & follow me

TOP: *St. Peter's, Selkirk, Manitoba*

FAR LEFT: *Hillcrest Cemetery, Lunenburg, Nova Scotia*
A wooden tablet has been left standing where it was found, carefully supported by brackets so that it may be preserved as long as possible in its original setting. Nothing is known of its date or the identity of the person whose grave it marked.

LEFT: *Little Dutch Church, Halifax, Nova Scotia*
Delicately carved wooden tablet for Elizabeth Wright, now stored inside.

Stones

Found stones without inscriptions were simple grave markers. The Pioneer Cemetery established in 1833 at West Mabou Harbour in Cape Breton has some graves marked by stones without names or dates. This place has a Gaelic Catholic ambiance. A tall wooden cross stands against the skyline of the Mabou Highlands, and the former site of the early church is marked by a traditional Scottish fieldstone cairn.

Fieldstones were also split to make a flat surface, which might be roughly engraved. The Pine Grove cemetery in Middleton, Nova Scotia, includes a marker for "M[ar]y Woodbery," who died in 1808, one "In Memory of Lydia Wife of J. Woodbery, d. Jul 24[?] 180[7?]" and one for "Ja[mes?] Woodbery," who died in 1817. Although the final "Y" is crowded off the baseline on the smaller stones, the letters are shaped with care. These monuments appear to have been homemade by those who remembered professional traditions from the years before their immigration.

At the other extreme from these modest fieldstones, perhaps found in and cleared from the pioneers' own fields, are the very large natural stones occasionally imported to mark graves in large cemeteries. There are handsome boulders in Mount Pleasant Cemetery, Toronto. One is a fitting monument for the eminent geologist Arthur P. Coleman (1852–1939). In addition to achieving academic honours at the University of Toronto, the Royal Society of Canada, the Geological Society of America, the Royal Canadian Institute and the Royal Geographical Society, Coleman was a pioneer explorer of the Canadian Rockies and the Selkirks. He made eight exploratory trips between 1884 and 1908, making his last Alpine Club of Canada expedition in his eighties. Glaciers were his primary geological interest – Mount Coleman, Coleman Lake and Coleman Glacier are named after him. Perhaps an expertise equal to Coleman's would be required to determine how many hundreds of millions of years the monumental boulder took to travel here

Pine Grove Cemetery, Middleton, Nova Scotia

from its place of formation. But even if it was at one period a glacially transported erratic, an amateur can see that no glacier deposited it exactly here. Much human effort and resources were needed.

Like other monumental stones, great and small, this large metamorphic stone might be seen, by someone seeking out symbolic significance, as a sample from the literal rock of ages undergoing changes through relatively short æons of secular time. Changes in other kinds of stone may be seen even in the much shorter spans of human lifetimes. Old cemeteries are excellent places to observe changes being effected in stone over a few decades, as weather and pollution take their unfortunate toll.

Sandstones were locally available in Canada – olive-grey Wallace sandstone in Nova Scotia, Sackville red sandstone in New Brunswick, and red-brown, grey and mottled Medina varieties in southern Ontario, especially from the Forks of the Credit or the Credit Valley. The development of railways also made sandstone from the United States readily accessible. Sandstones were popular building materials and were quite easily worked by gravestone cutters, who could create complex patterns of both deep and shallow relief in their lettering and pictorial emblems. Some have worn very well. Others were

TOP: *Mount Pleasant Cemetery, Toronto, Ontario*
Large piece of granite as a fitting monument for an eminent geologist.

FAR LEFT: *Mount Pleasant Cemetery, Toronto, Ontario*

LEFT: *Old French Cemetery, Lunenburg, Nova Scotia*
The Old French Cemetery in Lunenburg contains a small stone that is cleft by a cross and engraved "N. PAUL / 1754."

susceptible to water penetration – spalling or contour scaling, efflorescence, or "face bedding," the splitting off of layers along the bedding planes.

Slates, with their smooth fine-grained appearance and subtle colouring of grey, blue-grey, grey-green or black, were easily carved in shallow relief and incised lines. The tradition of slate headstones was brought to Canada by Planters from New England. Slate in Canada typically came from the Eastern Townships in Quebec or was imported from Vermont and other eastern states or colonies. Slates are very durable and resistant, but may sometimes delaminate, or split apart in layers.

"Marble" derives from the Greek word *marmaros*, meaning any hard stone, but in fact marbles are soft enough to be carved quite readily. The category of marble is defined by the American Standards for Testing Materials as a crystalline rock, of various compositions and textures, which "must be capable of taking a polish." Marble gravestones exposed to atmospheric pollution do not long retain a polish, however, as their surfaces decay and dissolve and more and more of the stone is converted into gypsum or erodes away. Marbles are metamorphic rocks, formed by

extreme heat and pressure from clay or lime marls, dolomite or limestone.

Limestones are sedimentary rocks, composed mostly of calcium carbonate in the form of calcite. There are many variations of colour – from Kingston brownish-blue to Ottawa brownish-grey to Queenston silver-grey to Quebec brown-grey and blue-grey, and many other varieties – all of which normally weather to a lighter shade of grey. Ordinary non-metamorphic limestone is more easily carved than marble, but it lacks some of marble's most valuable qualities – primarily the permanence and beautiful nearly-white colour that made it the stone of choice for sculptors of ancient Greece. Italian white marble is calcite limestone, a metamorphic rock that has many variations in chemical composition, colour, texture and susceptibility to weathering. The name "marble" is applied not only to calcite limestone but also to limestone that is mostly dolomite. Although less susceptible to acidic damage, dolomite contains magnesium and is therefore more susceptible to erosion. When left to weather, it will in time crumble like sandstone.

FACING PAGE, LEFT: *Notre-Dame-des-Neiges Cemetery, Montreal, Quebec*

FACING PAGE, RIGHT: *Old Burying Ground, Halifax, Nova Scotia*
Sandstone monument with deeply cut lettering and high relief carvings of an urn and soul effigies within an egg-and-dart border.

LEFT: *Loyalist Cemetery, Digby, Nova Scotia*
Finely engraved shallow relief of a soul effigy on a slate stone in memory of "Mr THOMAS HOLDSWORTH / who died at sea Sept. 9. 1798."

Bronze

Exegi monumentum aere perennius
regalique situ pyramidum altius
quod non imber edax, non Aquilo impotens
possit diruere aut innumerabilis
annorum series et fuga temporum.
Non omnis moriar multaque pars mei
vitabit Libitinam.

Horace, *Odes* III, xxx

Bronze memorials have been held in esteem ever since classical times, and the eminence of bronze as a sculptural medium has never been diminished. Horace boasted that he had erected for himself "a monument more lasting than bronze" (and also higher than the pyramids), a monument that neither rain, nor wind, nor the passage of numberless years, nor the flight of time itself, could corrode and wear away. And it is true that his poetry has outlasted many of the statuary memorials of his fellow citizens of Imperial Rome. His ode claims that his "greater part" will avoid Libitina, the Roman goddess of the dead, in whose temple was sold everything needed for funerals, including monuments. His confidence – "I shall not die completely" – was certainly not misplaced. For anyone less poetically gifted than Horace, however, bronze is the best material for capturing a lifelike portrait, even if it will not last quite forever.

Bronze – an alloy of copper and tin – will resist corrosion, if well maintained. A great open-air collection of bronze sculptures is dispersed across Canada, in the form of memorials erected after the First World War. Conservation treatments in recent years have restored the original vitality of their facial expressions.

Cast Iron

New furnace technology in the 18th century made it less costly to produce cast iron, an alloy with a high carbon content that makes it more resistant to corrosion than either wrought iron or steel. Durable, strong, relatively light and easily transported, suitable for mass production systems and with the potential for moulding in almost any shape, the metal soon played a pre-eminent role in industrial and urban development. Cast iron made possible the huge growth of railroad transportation, water systems and street lighting and machinery-filled factories. It also prompted bold new advances in architectural technology, including the fabrication of cast-iron storefronts.

The production of grave markers was a spin-off from this enormously successful industry. It is more common, however, to find cast-iron fencing, fountains or garden furniture in a cemetery than grave markers. Skeptics may have been influenced by the teaching about spiritual housekeeping in the Sermon on the Mount:

Lay not up for yourselves treasures upon earth, where moth and rust doth corrupt, and where thieves break through and steal ... But lay up for yourselves treasures in heaven, where neither moth nor rust doth corrupt, and where thieves do not break through nor steal: For where your treasure is, there will your heart be also. (Matthew 7: 19–21)

Oxidation, or rusting, occurs rapidly when cast iron is exposed to moisture and air. Once a rust film forms, its porous surface acts as a reservoir for liquids, causing further corrosion. If not arrested, this process will continue until the iron is entirely consumed, leaving nothing but rust.

St. Mary's Cemetery, New Brunswick

Zinc or "White Bronze"

In many groupings of grave markers dating from the late 1880s and early 1890s, one or two will be found that are completely impervious to the organic growths that blight neighbouring stones – black spots, lichens and mosses. Unlike marble stones nearby, which may be quite worn from exposure to rain, snow, fog and atmospheric pollution, the details of the inscriptions and designs on these few markers are as crisp as when they were new. Their characteristic bluish-grey colour indentifies them as "white bronze." They are actually made of zinc.

All of these monuments originated with the Monumental Bronze Company in Bridgeport, Connecticut. In 1879 the founders of this company perfected new methods of making zinc "more than 99% pure," fusing the cast parts with hot zinc (rather than soldering the joints with an alloy), sandblasting the fused casts, and then applying a secret patented surface treatment to speed the process whereby zinc, when exposed to air, develops a protective coating of zinc carbonate. More than 100 years later, the results of these technological advances prove the enduring truth of advertisements for this product:

White Bronze solves one of the great questions of the day, being pronounced by scientists as practically indestructable. It does not corrode or change its color; moss will not grow on it, and as it does not absorb moisture, it is not affected by frost.

The promotion of white bronze was as innovative as its manufacture, for sales of these markers depended on agents selling from catalogues. These were illustrated with a comprehensive array of pictorial motifs, verses and quotations, from which the purchaser could select items to be fused to the basic form, often in the shape of an obelisk. The company declared that each marker was "made to order" and that the selection offered in the catalogue was superior to what was available in show rooms where local stonecutters dis-played partially pre-carved memorials. Company artists would even produce custom-made sculptures or bas-reliefs from portraits or photographs. These individual effigies were an expensive option, however. The menu of designs in the catalogue provided great choice and greater economy.

Production costs of casting the parts and assembling the monuments were low. Since the larger monuments, such as obelisks, were hollow, and zinc is much lighter than stone (heavier than iron, but not as heavy as lead), transportation costs were also modest. Subsidiary plants were set up, including one in St. Thomas, Ontario, which was the source for white bronze monuments throughout Canada. Prime Minister John A. Macdonald's National Policy of protective tariffs against American imports had been adopted in 1879. St. Thomas, now calling itself the "Railway City" or the "Railway Capital of Canada," had 26 rail lines pass through town, including in 1872 the line that took a shortcut through Canada from New York to Chicago. Among its immense tonnage of railway freight were the white bronze monument components that arrived from Bridgeport. The finished monuments are to be seen from Nova Scotia to Victoria, and in all the communities in between that had access to a train depot in the 1880s. Many of them are clearly marked on the base: "White Bronze Co. St. Thomas, Ont."

In 1914 the American government took over the Monumental Bronze Company, and its production was converted to munitions for the Great War. But the demand for these monuments had already declined rapidly from the turn of the century. As their novelty value wore off, their imitation of stone became less and less convincing. Even the marketing of zinc under the name of white bronze began to prompt unfavourable comparisons with real bronze, an alloy of tin and copper which, as it aged, formed a beautiful and much-prized patina. White bronze, in contrast, continued to look oddly new.

Sculptures cast in real bronze were made by famous artists, or at least by original craftsmen who worked within a centuries-old tradition. The anonymous artists of the Monumental Bronze Company, on the other hand, made wax models for the casting of various motifs – flowers, crowns, hand-clasps – but had nothing to do with the assembly of these parts on the "made-to-order" monument. Finally, the wide selection offered in the catalogues did not result in the variety or individuality that might have been expected. A few bestselling styles, seen again and again, are identical across the continent. In comparison, a motif carved over and over in stone markers, even by the same sculptor, will have individual variations, enhanced by differing patterns of weathering and wear.

White bronze memorials have been as durable as was predicted in 1885 in *Scientific American* magazine. Zinc corrosion has occurred only in severely polluted industrial environments. The largest sculptures, such as those erected by American towns to commemorate the Civil War, have been affected by a very slow creep of the metal, but in Canadian graveyards the only visible damage is the theft of bolted panels, which were designed to be removable for the subsequent addition of names and dates.

FAR LEFT: *Trinity United Church Cemetery, Shelburne, Nova Scotia* "White Bronze" monument for three "beloved children of Abbie & Gideon W. Harlow," who died in 1886. "Little Freddie" is commemorated on the reverse side of the small tablet.

LEFT: *Ross Bay Cemetery, Victoria, British Columbia* "White bronze" obelisk from 1886, embellished with fringed and tasselled drapery and figured patterns.

Granites

❧ By the 1880s, residents in North America had had time to observe that its rigorous climate and the effects of the first decades of acidic air pollution were eroding epitaphs and decorative carvings on what were meant to be enduring stone memorials. "White bronze" was marketed as a man-made product more lasting than stone, but what was first seen as a technological improvement on what had been fashioned by nature soon began to look merely synthetic, a simulation of the real thing. That modern technology was soon replaced by a promotion campaign for an ancient material. The Barre Granite Association began to market Vermont granite as "the Rock of Ages," a trade name registered in 1914. According to the association, Barre Gray granite "is nearly as hard as sapphire. It can be exposed to weather forever without crumbling or staining." It will preserve memory "for all time."

Granites are rocks of igneous (or sometimes metamorphic) origin that tend to be hard, heavy, durable and acid-resistant. Experimental commercial processes of polishing granite had begun in the 1830s, and the display of a piece of machine-polished and incised granite at the 1851 Great Exhibition in London spurred further development of the industrial process. The use of polished granite radically changed the design of monuments. The earlier form, a tablet with relief or incised engraving on the front face, was replaced by three-dimensional obelisks, columns, pedestals and monuments based on architectural forms. Large globe monuments, for instance, were much more effective in polished granite than in other kinds of stone. The side of the sphere reflecting the sunlight contrasts more obviously with the penumbra of the other half. This celebration of light is also enhanced when an obelisk is made from polished granite. Softer stone or zinc may reproduce the shape of the obelisk, but not its symbolic role as a heliograph, or reflector of sunlight.

Granite is also a very effective material for representing metamorphic change. Smooth polished surfaces, recording particular names and dates, can be shown as emerging in part from rough pieces of rock. More than uniformly finished stones, these monuments evoke a sense of the ancient formation of rock. Their almost subliminal references to past millennia supply a context closer to that of stoicism than to a concept of Eternity – despite the message of the "Rock of Ages" hymn. Machine-cut granite is also capable of creating various depictions of the metamorphosis of the stone tomb into foliage. Stylized acanthus leaves seem to grow from the smooth stone surfaces of monuments in a kind of metamorphosis. These beautiful forms have great decorative value, but they also very subtly suggest the æons-long process of transformation of elements from rock to life-forms, and vice versa – "Dust to dust," seen in a geological time frame.

Granite is suitable for pedestal tombs and columns, arches and diverse other architectural elements. In older cemeteries new granite *tempietti*, small temple shelters that will remain bright and shiny, are sometimes erected to protect fragile older sculptures, that are weather-worn and damaged by pollution or vandalism.

TOP LEFT: *St. Mark's Anglican Church Cemetery, Niagara-on-the-Lake, Ontario*
Polished granite globe monument reflecting solar illumination.

BOTTOM LEFT: *St James' Cemetery, Toronto, Ontario*
Unusual curled cartouche, bearing an inscription, apparently carved from the stone beneath.

LEFT: *Mount Pleasant Cemetery, Toronto, Ontario*
A new granite pavilion shelters a damaged monument.

Conserving the Future of Memory

Conserving the Future of Memory

It is accepted that cultural properties in art galleries and museums require the services of professional conservators. Historic cemeteries are outdoor museums whose treasured contents are obviously even more exposed and in need of professional care. They are at risk, even including risks associated with conservation projects. Cleaning, repairing and restoring old monuments require expertise and should be attempted only by those trained in techniques and materials under the supervision of professional conservators training to work with old cemetery monuments. Irreversible damage has too often been the result of good intentions. Common kitchen cleansers are never suitable for use on historic stones, and even the gentlest effective treatment – washing with small quantities of clean water – should not be attempted if there is any risk of temperatures falling to the freezing point before the stone has dried out. The removal of lichens is another risky project. The growths will return in a short time, since tombstones provide their ideal environments, and most types are harmless to stone, other than forming soil which will promote the growth of mosses. It is advisable only to control their accumulation by gently brushing off loose material, and removing mosses and other small plants by hand. Recarving inscriptions that have become almost illegible, or painting the lettering, is a most unfortunate practice. Enthusiasts should even abstain from making rubbings (following the example of brass rubbings from monuments in old churches in England), which eventually cause damage to the stones

The historical integrity of the site is all too often damaged in the name of cleaning it up, or maintaining it more easily. Its authentic natural heritage may be unknowingly uprooted, even as well-meaning gardeners plant assorted "wild flowers." Removing monuments from their original settings to re-arrange them in a setting of concrete is a practice that has been deplored for decades, but still occurs. Countless numbers of tablet headstones have been laid flat on the ground so that lawnmowers are ridden over them, and they slowly sink below the sod. The only good aspect of this practice is that the stone is often better preserved than it would be if exposed to air pollution. The unfortunate aspect is that once the stone is gone from sight, the spot is generally believed to have been always an unmarked pauper's grave, or even never a burial place at all.

All cemeteries are vulnerable to malicious, as well as careless, damage. Racism, and calendar dates such as Halloween or full moons have prompted nights of destruction and dishonour. Making it against the law for any visitors to be in burial grounds after sunset

FACING PAGE: *Cape Freels, Bonavista North, Newfoundland*

PAGE 284–285: *Lunenburg, Nova Scotia*

would make it easier for police to monitor and prevent these shocking scenes. Less well publicized, but very alarming because so difficult to control, is the theft of some of Canada's most beautiful and valuable sculptures from Notre-Dame-des-Neiges and other cemeteries. Such things often turn up in antique stores or on the black market, even on eBay. It is strange that their purchasers do not feel uncomfortable about putting these grave monuments, beautiful as they are, in their gardens. (Perhaps their comfort has been conditioned by seeing so many funerary objects taken from other cultures in museum collections.) Even more distressing is the possibility that stolen bronzes may be melted down and used for scrap metal – the apparent fate of certain huge sculptures by Henry Moore and Lyn Chadwick, and even war memorials, recently taken from outdoor sites in the United Kingdom.

The final threat to historic burial places is their closure and transformation into redevelopment sites. Visitors to the necropolis in Toronto are usually surprised to learn that the trendy shops and hotels of Yorkville were built on a cemetery that was closed and cleared between 1851 and 1881, and tend to assume that such closures no longer happen. They are misinformed. The pressure for development sites is even more acute now than in the 19th century. Burial grounds, like the rest of our built heritage, cannot rely on sentiment for their survival. Many of the oldest pioneer sites are near routes that have become busy highways, and stand in the way of engineering improvements and expansion.

The survival of Canada's historical cemeteries thus far is in large part due to their friends – groups of volunteers who have worked with passion and dedication to preserve them for the future. From Mahone Bay in Nova Scotia to Pittsburg Township in Ontario and the Old Cemeteries Society of Victoria, these long efforts have found satisfying rewards. Their work is not complete, however. Their greatest achievement has been an ongoing work-in-progress and their success have been accomplished in sustaining partnerships with municipal provincial and federal departments and institutions.

One example is the Old Burying Ground Foundation in Halifax, and the preservation of what is now widely appreciated as an outdoor museum and major tourist attraction. St. Paul's Anglican Church was responsible for providing burial services and keeping records, but did not own the Old Burying Ground and derived no income from it until 1777, when it passed a resolution that "all strangers" (those who were not members of St. Paul's) would be charged the sum of ten shillings for the burial of "their deceased relation or acquaintance." Although the land was granted to the Church in 1793, a Deed from 1801 explicitly stated that Protestant Dissenters "still have and forever hereafter shall have good right and claim to bury their dead in the said ground commonly called the Old Burying Ground." This non-denominational claim to the right to preserve the ground thwarted three attempts – in 1844, in the early twentieth century, and again in the early 1980s – by St Paul's to sell redevelopment rights after the cemetery closed. The Old Burying Ground experienced several periods of neglect and was badly vandalized during the notorious V.E. Day celebrations at the end of the Second World War. The Welsford-Parker Monument (installed at its entrance in 1860) is credited with granting it "a second lease on life," when Victorian improvements gave it a more park-like appearance and connection with its urban setting. The latest restoration was initially prompted by the visit of Pope John Paul II to Halifax in 1984. Local conservationists formed the Old Burying Ground Foundation, a volunteer organization, to achieve adequate financial support for the ongoing project of maintaining, restoring, photographing, cataloguing and interpreting the site. Their application to the Historical Sites and Monuments Board of Canada resulted in this becoming in 1991 the first cemetery to be designated a National Historic Site. Seven more cemeteries were designated National Historic Sites between 1992 and 2000. Others form part of Parks Canada sites, and since 1999 the Government of Canada has implemented a program designed to protect and honour the grave sites of Canadian prime ministers.

In comparison, the United States established its National Register of Historic Places in 1966, and more than 928 cemeteries and burial grounds have been identified and documented as being of historical importance to the nation. The National Trust for Historic Preservation, an American trust whose mandate is to be "a source of training and education, information, financial assistance, and networking opportunties for preservation leaders," has published one of the most comprehensive guides for friends of old cemeteries, *Preservation of Historic Burial Grounds*.

When English Heritage, the British government's statutory advisor on the historic environment of England, published its first *Register of Parks and Gardens of special historic interest in England* between 1983 and 1988, only 14 cemeteries of national importance were included. As the general appreciation of designed historic landscapes increased in the 1990s, it became clear that many more cemeteries deserved a place on the register. Another 80 were added in 2001 and 2002, and criteria were developed for assessing sites in the near future for a National Register of Cemeteries. *Paradise Preserved*, a joint publication of English Nature and English Heritage and available on their websites, is a comprehensive introduction to the assessment, evaluation, conservation and management of historic cemeteries.

Circumstances in Canada differ in some ways from those in the United States and Britain, but it is encouraging to know that a National Register of Canadian Cemeteries, or Provincial Registers of Historic Cemeteries, would not have to invent the wheel. We have much to learn from other nations about recognizing the historical and natural value of cemeteries. Like "Doors Open," which originated in France as "La Journée Portes Ouvertes" in 1984 and spread to Scotland in 1990, we can adapt that foreign experience here. Doors Open Ontario, launched by the Ontario Heritage Trust in 2002, had 1.5 million visits to hundreds of heritage properties across the province in the first four years of the program. Almost every town that participated in Doors Open included one or more historic burial places. And the Ontario Heritage Trust has honoured many of these burial places with its commemorative plaques. This gives grounds for hope for the conservation of memory in Ontario.

A Tale of Two Pioneer Burying Grounds

❧ Across the country, the future of pioneer burying grounds has always been in doubt. Some have survived cycles of neglect and degradation, concern and restoration. Sad tales of lost burial places may be weighed in the balance with success stories of those that have been saved. The Tansley Burying Ground (in use from 1815 to 1905) in Burlington, Ontario, has vanished completely from sight, and almost as completely from community memory. In the 1970s it had not been forgotten, but it was nevertheless closed and disposed of. In contrast, the exemplary history of the Old Protestant Burying Ground (in use from 1784 to 1873) in Charlottetown, Prince Edward Island, offers encouragement and a number of pertinent lessons to anyone engaged in similar struggles. Almost every circumstance and challenge to its survival is typical of Canada's earliest burial grounds.

Dundas Street has one of the longest histories in Canada. Proposed in the 1790s by Lieutenant-Governor John Graves Simcoe, the "Governor's Road" soon became "the spinal cord which supported the settlement of southern Ontario." As Highway No 5, it is on its way to becoming one of the most-travelled roads in the province. In 1815 the last will of Henry Magee deeded an acre of land from his farm on Dundas Street, west of Twelve Mile Creek, "for the benefit of the Inhabitants of the said Township of Nelson for a Burying Ground, Church and School House and for no other purpose." With its mills, stagecoach change point, inns, post office and farms, Crooks' Mills (later St. Ann's, and finally known as Tansley) was very prosperous. For a time in that pre-industrial era, it may have been a bigger business centre than nearby Hamilton. But Tansley dwindled into a small hamlet with only a few old houses and was eventually amalgamated into the town of Burlington.

By the mid-1970s, Magee's community burying ground had somehow become a site for burying a natural gas line and telephone cables. It had lost its fence, and the construction of a new bridge over the Creek had taken away a good portion from its unfenced ground. The Burlington Historical Society voiced its concern to the city, which produced the information that "most" of the remaining tombstones were broken, and that "this Cemetery was used primarily for the burial of paupers." Where all the supposed paupers had come from was not at all clear. It was merely assumed that Tansley had always been a poor place to live. Furthermore, "unfortunately, this Cemetery has now become poorly situated in that the Halliday Homes factory lies to the north and west and the Gas station lies to the east of it." The Historical Society, which only a few years earlier had been successful in marking another pioneer burial ground with a memorial cairn, asked permission to erect a memorial plaque on the Tansley site. In response, the society received a letter of regret from the owner of the neighbouring factory. While his company "would have no objection to a discreet sign being placed on the cemetery property," he said, its own property was for sale, "and it is conceivable that a new owner might object to such a sign." Despite the distress of many, the Tansley cemetery was closed in 1978 and cleared under the *Ontario Cemeteries Act*. The remains from six or eight graves were relocated to another cemetery. A local newspaper reported that 400 burials had occurred there, but there were no early records. It was clear that the title for the graveyard property had never been transferred to another owner, but the burial ground had no board or representative. The operator of the gas station recalled: "There were 35 to 40 tombstones in there at one time ... They just seemed to vanish." Other Tansley residents said that horses had been allowed to graze there, and after that "for years and years the cemetery was a jungle."

Since even a discreet sign might have been objectionable to purchasers of the neighbouring property, the place of the former Tansley Burying Ground has never been marked. Today almost no one has even heard of Tansley. The history of its burial ground is recalled with some degree of apprehension by those responsible for maintaining other pioneer graveyards. Many pioneer churches on Dundas Street are still active, and their churchyards are faithfully maintained by resourceful descendants, but they are all too close to 21st century traffic. How will the Anglican and Methodist pioneers, who set their churches and burial grounds on opposite sides of the Governor's Road, be accommodated in time to come? It is more than possible that our historical memory will be further diminished.

In the contrasting case of the Charlottetown Old Protestant Burying Ground, land was deeded to the Anglican church in 1826 "for the purpose of being used as a place of Burial for the parish of Charlotte aforesaid and for no other use trust intent or purpose whatsoever." Even before its closure, its deferred maintenance was found objectionable. In 1857 the *Guardian* noticed that efforts were being made to improve its appearance: "The outside fences have been repaired and straightened and the ground cleared of underbrush. Many of the head stones and railings are in deplorable state, and others are tumbling down." Thirty years later, the *Patriot* reported that work had begun "to repair the fences ... and otherwise improve the appearance of the place," but the ground was still "the eye-sore it [had] been during the last few years."

Perhaps in no respect have the people of Charlottetown fallen to a greater extent behind their neighbours in the other Provinces, and particularly in the United States, than in the matter of ornamenting their cemeteries. We do not believe in wasteful lavishness in building expensive monuments to the departed, but certainly all such places, whether new or old, should be kept neat and free from rubbish of every kind. A hint in regard to the state of many of the plots in the Old Burying Ground ought to be sufficient.

Funds were repeatedly supplied by various benefactors, and repairs and improvement were repeatedly carried out. Nevertheless, from time to time the local newspapers found it necessary to offer stronger hints. In 1915 the *Daily Examiner* regretfully noted: "Nothing whatever has been done towards improvements of the old Cemetery on Malpeque Road, in which the Protestants of olden times are sleeping."

The fence around it is still dilapidated, and the place is still open to stray cattle, pigs, and poultry. The rubbish of last year's growth still lies about the graves of "loved ones gone." Who, among all the heirs to the results of their labours, will lead a movement to change the disgraceful condition of what ought to be regarded as a "sacred spot."

In the following year, the *Guardian* eloquently heralded the most recent project of conservation and restoration:

If there is a spot in or around the city that we have a right to respect and to preserve sacredly, it is this spot, where the City's fathers and mothers lie buried. And yet no spot sacred or otherwise has been so sadly and so persistently neglected. A walk through this neglected ruin today; a look at its broken memorial stones, – old fashioned and unpretentious it is true ... a look at its unkempt paths, and its unrecognizable graves cannot but compel the conclusion that if we have not dishonoured the graves of our fathers, we have most shamefully neglected them ...

The City should take pride in the preservation instead of letting it become an eyesore and reproach. We owe more than this to those who sleep in the old cemetery, we owe more to ourselves than to let these historic stones be trampled and broken.

We trust that citizens generally, but particularly those whose kindred lie buried there, will cooperate with those who are making efforts to redeem this once hallowed spot from defamation.

Perhaps the *Guardian*'s recognition in 1916 of what was owed to the dead by the living reflected, in part, the strong sense of remembrance that was characteristic of the period of the Great War.

By the mid 20th century, in contrast, what predominated was a sense of an urgent need to build for the future – tacitly, for a temporary short-term future. In 1956, and again in 1962, the mayor asked the Burying Ground committee to consider turning it into a park – removing all monuments and grading and levelling the grounds "with flower beds and trees and benches for our Senior Citizens to sit upon and enjoy the lovely outdoors in the twilight of their own lives."

Perhaps the City could erect 1 large fitting Memorial in the Centre, giving the history and any other data of interest. Seems such a waste as years go by ... I am addressing a similar letter to Bishop MacEachren re the old Catholic Cemetery:

It is striking that only the elderly – or "Senior Citizens" – are linked to the context of a Memorial, as if "history" could be of interest only to living memory and must naturally die out "as years go by." The Old Protestant Burying Ground committee declined both proposals. The old Catholic Cemetery was less fortunate; very few stones remain there. (In 2003 Hurricane Juan uncovered a number of old Catholic gravestones that had apparently been dumped as fill along the Victoria Park breakwater.)

The 1947 the *Guardian* had published a survey made by Miss Elsie Cambridge, a summer visitor from Woodstock, Vermont, along with a critical commentary.

Undoubtedly, this cemetery has known the twin evils of vandalism and neglect. Chiefly to be deplored are the following: badly leaning monument shafts, a considerable number of once wantonly smashed slabs which have been "repaired" in a quite unseemly manner – in such a manner, often to amount to further desecration; several fine sarcophagi are lying in heaps; and here and there are such debris as the utterly useless remains of old iron fences and broken stone posts which once guarded family plots ...

As already mentioned, one of the present objectionable features is the all too apparent evidence of careless repair work. Stones that could have been neatly repaired at little expense, have been rudely daubed with cement and stuck together in such an untidy and unlovely manner.

In 1978 the *Guardian* celebrated the most recent restoration project, deplored the historic cemetery's having become a favourite drinking spot for "rubbies" and reminded its readers of a better American example (as the *Patriot* had done more than 70 years earlier): "Charlottetown could have its own little Mt Auburn."

Anyone who has visited Mt Auburn Cemetery in downtown Boston knows that a beautiful cemetery can be maintained in the heart of a city or town

of any size. Mt Auburn with its sculpted tombstones and crypts, ancient trees, vast lawns and wondrous array of flowering shrubs contributes something important and moving to all who pass by.

By the end of the 20th century, the Old Protestant Burying Ground had again fallen on hard times:

Over half the remaining stones had fallen over, or were leaning badly; only two sarcophagi remained upright; and bushes had grown up all over the grounds. All sorts of debris and garbage and empty bottles had accumulated. The fences were either completely gone, or in very bad repair. The area had once again become a place for drunks and loiterers to congregate. On occasion a person was known to have slept in an open-ended sarcophag[us] that was still standing ... irregularities were occurring both day and night in the Burying Ground.

A Millennium Grant gave timely support to the committee's work, and an editorial in the *Guardian*, "Cemetery Project A Worthy Cause," praised the result:

For years we criticized its neglected state and encouraged anyone who would listen to help the cause of those who have been trying to spruce it up.

For years the old graveyard ... was an eyesore because of its unkempt and derelict state. It was also a target of vandalism ... The project has been a worthy one. Our cemeteries are sacred places. They mark the final resting place of those who've gone before us. All of us walk this earth for a limited time. The passing of time should not diminish the significance of what we do or undermine the contributions we make to our families, our community, our society. The restoration of the Old Protestant Burial Ground gives due honour to those who lie there.

The Old Protestant Burying Ground in Charlottetown faced the same challenges to its future as numerous other Canadian historical graveyards. What made it a survivor? Certainly it was fortunate in having a committee that could resist the city's offers of flower beds and trees and benches in exchange for removing its graves and gravestones. Many burial grounds had no living voice to speak on their behalf when the owners of neighbouring properties declared them objectionable. It was fortunate, too, in the distinctly high quality of the city's journalism. The *Guardian* especially well expressed its readers' underlying consciousness of the historical graveyard's value to Charlottetown.

Finally, its committee sought historical evidence to supplement the evidence of the remaining gravestones. Committee members gathered data from an inventory made in 1917 of the 799 gravestones then remaining, from Elsie Cambridge's survey of 596 stones in 1947, and from George Wright's catalogue in 2000, when just 450 stones could be identified. In addition, they searched out information in sextons' ledgers, St. Paul's Anglican Church records, and sources in the Prince Edward Island Public Archives and Records Office. As a result, they were able to compile a Master Burial List of approximately 3,250 names; it continues to be updated as more information is discovered. Although only 556 graves have (so far) been located, those buried in more than 2,500 unknown graves still have their names – and even in some instances their life-stories – recorded.

Thus, as Charlottetown celebrated its 150th anniversary in 2005, the city's support for the preservation and restoration of "this tarnished treasure" found its reward not only in a public amenity – "a place of quiet beauty alongside a busy avenue" – but also in a living history of those upon whose lives the city and the province were founded. The enrichment of meaning in our present-day lives is vitally dependent on a community of memory. In contrast to the American suburb once memorably dismissed by a former resident – "there is no *there* there" – contemporary Charlottetown has come to recognize that the "*here*" emphasized in the inscriptions of so many gravestones is a real place. This truth was eloquently expressed by the poet Judy Gaudet in the Old Protestant Burying Ground's fundraising brochure:

Imagine a city underground. It is the Charlotte Town that used to be. Here are many prominent people ...

Here's bandleader Galbraith's wife Susan. Here are auctioneers, wheelwrights, soldiers and blacksmiths. Theophilus DesBrisay, the first Anglican Rector, who served for 47 years, is here with his wife, children and grandchildren. Here are the joiners, carriage builders, tinsmiths, teachers and poets. John LePage's wife and children are here. Printers, tax collectors, tavern keepers, turners, doctors, and architects are here. Here are butchers, bankers, stationers, millers, masons, saddlers and harness makers. You might think work could go ahead as usual in the city under the ground. Life and Death. ...

John Ross, the publisher, lost his young son in the same year the Charlotte Town fire took his business ... Eliza Taylor, wife of Neil Graham, the ship's carpenter, died in childbirth. His second wife died that way too.

Many women did. Many children died, But we all have our time. And it may be that they are not in this city under the ground at all, "but amidst the stars and near the throne" as one stone claims for a lost Knight child. But should we not pay some honour to the place where they were last seen? Surely if we forget them, and their lives, their contributions and their humanity, the city above ground will be the poorer.

More
Stories in
Old Stones

From 1914 to 1920, Wallace Stegner lived part of his boyhood in the area of the Cypress Hills, on the border of Saskatchewan and Alberta. A driving tour through the Hills, now part of an interprovincial park, includes the grounds of the Cypress Hills Massacre of 1873 and Fort Walsh, the headquarters of the North West Mounted Police from 1878 to 1882, and also the little cemetery up the hill from the fort. In his memoir *Wolf Willow*, Stegner observes that the history of the Plains frontier was there "in a capsule, condensed into the life-span of a reasonably long-lived man."

From grizzlies, buffalo, and Indians still only half possessed of the horse and gun, the historical parabola to Dust Bowl and near-depopulation covered only about sixty years.

But as a child and "until a quarter-century after [he] left the place," he "never knew a scrap of that history."

In the world's old places, even the New World's old places, not only books reinforce and illuminate a child's perceptions. The past becomes a thing made palpable by monuments, buildings, historical sites, museums, attics, old trunks, relics of a hundred kinds; and in the legends of grandfathers and great-grandfathers; and in the incised marble and granite and weathered wood of graveyards.

Stegner calls the story of his return "Capital of an Unremembered Past" and comments: "The very richness of that past as I discover it now makes me irritable to have been cheated of it then." He learns that "the Cypress Hills discovered they had a history when the Old Timers' Association of Maple Creek planted some historical markers in 1942":

In the old post cemetery, where the police graves were identifiable but the civilian ones a scramble of unmarked mounds, they erected crosses, and where they knew, they placed the appropriate names: Clark, Dumont, LaBarge, Quesnelle, McKay, Chief Little Bird — white, métis, Scotch halfbreed, Indian. ... The foundations of Farwell's [trading] post were still faintly discernible after nearly seventy years, but the battlefield they could locate only through the memory of an old métis who as a boy of eighteen, in 1880, had kicked up human bones while herding the police beef herd on that ground.

"Once discovered, history is not likely to be lost," Stegner concludes. That would be comforting, if true. The historical parabola of near-depopulation, however, casts some doubt on his conclusion. Old grave-yards and cemeteries are places full of historic cultural and natural treasures. But, like other treasure hoards, they need guardians. In the absence of preservation measures, without effective protection and conservation, their historic natural and cultural treasures of old cemeteries will be lost forever.

In time, all the works of humankind must be so lost. Even the most ancient stone monuments will not last forever. Their inscriptions may be deciphered for only a few thousand years at most. It is their premature ruin that is regrettable and even culpable. The re-use of old burial grounds for present profit is objectionable to many people, and prompts a bitter-ness comparable (in some ways) to Hamlet's quip – "Thrift, thrift, Horatio, the funeral baked meats / Did coldly furnish forth the marriage tables." The redevelopment of historic burial grounds raises questions about our transmission of history. Will future generations thank us for paving over, or building over, the graves of their predecessors? Or will they mourn the irreversible loss of historical monuments?

Hans Christian Andersen explored an aspect of this question in "The Old Grave-Stone" (1852). The stone, with its almost worn-out inscription and hourglass emblem, lies in the courtyard of a house, near the kitchen door. Children play on it, and kitchen maids lay copper saucepans on it to dry. The master of the house recalls that his father bought it

from the graveyard of the old church of the convent which was pulled down, and ... the monuments and the grave-stones sold ... Most of them were cut in two and used for paving stones, but that one stone was pre-served whole, and laid in the courtyard.

An old man, who looks "old enough to be the grandfather of all present in the room," is struck by his childhood mem-ory of "the very worthy old couple" whose gravestone this was. He remembers overhearing the distressed widower speaking of his wife:

"I was, as I have said, a boy, and only stood by and listened to what the oth-ers said, but it filled me with a strange emotion to listen to the old man, and

to watch how the colour rose in his cheeks as he spoke of the days of their courtship, of how beautiful she was ... And then he talked of his wedding-day; and his eyes brightened, and he seemed to be carried back ... to that joy-ful day of hope, long passed away. And yet there she was, lying in the next room, dead – an old woman, and he was an old man, speaking of the days of hope, long passed away. Ah well, so it is; then I was but a child, and now I am old, as old as Preben Schwane then was. Time passes away, and all things change ..."

The old man recalls Preben's old house, which was con-sidered, by the road inspectors, "too old and rotten to be left standing":

"Afterwards, when the same fate befell the convent church, and the grave-yard was destroyed, the grave-stone of Preben and Martha, like everything else, was sold to whoever would buy it ... The paved street now passes over the resting place of Old Preben and his wife; no one thinks of them any more now."

And the old man who had spoke of all this shook his head mournfully, and said, "Forgotten! Ah, yes, everything will be forgotten!"

All this has been heard by the youngest child in the room, who stands on a chair to look out into the yard, "where the moon was pouring a flood of light on the old gravestone – the stone that had always appeared to him so dull and flat, but which lay there now like a great leaf out of a book of history."

The young boy, a *persona* of the storyteller Andersen, determines that, through him, "the obliterated inscription on the old, weather-beaten gravestone [shall] go forth to future generations in clear, golden characters." His story has a hopeful ending: "The beautiful and the good are never for-gotten, they live always in story or song."

But it might be pointed out that "the beautiful and the good" are not the whole story. Cemeteries are not just places of golden legends. In truth, nothing human is alien to them. It is desirable to preserve, as much as we can, their authen-tic comprehensiveness for future generations. We have no right to sacrifice, selectively, the memory of those who pre-deceased us.

NOTE FROM THE PHOTOGRAPHER

Dealing with the emotional subject of cemeteries, the photographer must convey their meaning and significance without trivializing the individuals buried there. The essence of every cemetery begins with those who reside there. Every stone has a story, and it is quite humbling to think of each stone representing the life of another person.

In the attempt to capture the essence of a burial ground, the photographer needs to include as much variety as possible. Without sufficient variety, cemeteries have a tendency to look the same. The remarkable thing about a land as enormous as Canada is that it naturally provides enough variety that distinctions between burial grounds become apparent. A cemetery in Newfoundland will look different from a burial ground in Saskatchewan, simply because of where they are situated. Distinctions are also found in the materials used in different regions; you'll find Sackville red sandstone in New Brunswick and brownish-blue limestone in Kingston, Ontario. The materials often used in earlier times were driven by local availability. This variety of material, along with varying regional styles of workmanship, often tied to heritage, creates a sense of regional style that is reflected in *Old Canadian Cemeteries*.

The most important elements, especially for this subject matter, are light and weather. Cemeteries are somber places; they are places of reverence while also being places of hope. The early morning light and the glow of the setting sun, given their connotations with life and death, can produce more meaning here than almost anywhere else. Weather conditions, too, add a different meaning to an image: the mystique of fog over a cemetery, or of fog and snow together, reads much differently than fresh snow on a crisp winter morning. It is with these conditions that the photographer can capture the regional styles and geographical distinctions, while creating something that is interesting and unique. As such, the photographer can approach the subject matter, not solely as the photography of cemeteries, but instead as the photography of the Canadian landscape.

John du Toit

Canton Cemetery, Canton, Ontario
One of my favorite cemeteries is this small burying place in Canton, Ontario. The double row of cedars provides a beautiful contrast with the autumn foliage. Dr. Currelly, the principal founder of the Royal Ontario Museum in Toronto, established the cemetery. As well, Canton cemetery is the resting place of Sgt. Edward Edwin Dodds, one of 29 Canadian soldiers to receive the United States Congressional Medal of Honor. Of the 29 soldiers, Dodds is the only one to be buried in Canada.

LITERARY PERMISSIONS

NOTES TO THE TEXT

These notes are provided as a tool for those who wish to learn more about the subjects covered in this book. The notes are presented chronologically by subject heading, with corresponding page numbers in the text. Cited texts are listed as SOURCES, other information is listed as NOTES.

Discovering Historic Canadian Graveyards 12-15

SOURCES
Eudora Welty, Country Churchyards, 8, 10.

NOTES
"The Russ' Creek Cemetery is a priceless jewel of Ontario's natural and cultural heritage," May 10, 2006, correspondence to the Mayor and Council, Township of Alnwick-Haldimand, from Linda Pim, Ontario Nature Conservation Policy Analyst.

H.A. Engelhardt, the landscape designer of two Rural Cemeteries in Ontario – Belleville Cemetery and Mount Pleasant Cemetery, Toronto – published a book with the title *The Beauties of Nature Combined with Art* in 1872.

Stories in Old Stones 16-17

SOURCES
Alice Munro, *The View from Castle Rock*, 30, 40, 50, 84–86.

A New World 21-23

SOURCES
Michael Francis Howley, "The Old Basque Tombstones at Placentia," 83, 86, 90.

Robert McGhee, *The Last Imaginary Place*, 169–170.

Mounds and Cairns 23-25

NOTES
"Cairnpapple" means a pile of loose stones. Prehistoric cairns are the source of the more recent Scottish practice of building memorial cairns of smaller size. The tradition was brought to Canada by settlers from the Orkney Islands and other parts of Scotland. See Marion Heath, *Stories from Stones*.

First Nations and Christian Missions 26-28

SOURCES
The translation of Malaspina's report is quoted from Edward L. Keithahn, *Monuments in Cedar*, 40.

A.Y. Jackson, *A Painter's Country*, 89–90.

David A. Nock, "Edward Francis Wilson" (1844–1915), DCBO.

Scott Trevithick, "Evangelical and Aboriginal Religion in the Shingwauk Indian Residential School: The Case for Deeper Scholarly Engagement with Religious Discourse, Ritual and Meaning," 11, 12, 16, 17, 19.

Wilson's correspondence is quoted in Trevithick, 17. The passage from John Grant, *Moon of Wintertime: Missionaries and the Indians of Canada in Encounter since 1534* (Toronto: University of Toronto Press, 1984), 245, is quoted in Trevithick, 12.

Christian Burial and Cemetery Reform 29-32

SOURCES
The Register of Parks and Gardens: Cemeteries, English Heritage website: english-heritage.org.uk

James Stevens Curl, *Death and Architecture*, 135–167, 244–264.

Charles Dickens, "The City of the Absent," in *The Uncommercial Traveller*, 233–240.

Charles Dickens, *Bleak House*, chapters 18, "Lady Dedlock," 66, "Down in Lincolnshire," and 67, "The Close of Esther's Narrative."

Rudyard Kipling, *The City of Dreadful Night*, chapter 8.

NOTES
The 20th century brought an ironic reversal to the concept of care "in perpetuity" in Victorian England's private cemeteries. Some of the most successful joint-stock companies failed to provide funds for continued maintenance after all their grave plots were sold. Great cemeteries were left to a slow decline of decayed gentility, and forms produced by creative human energy were taken over as habitats for natural flora and fauna. In recent years, volunteer not-for-profit organizations have been incorporated for the purpose of supporting the restoration and preservation of great monuments, tombs and landscapes in neglected cemeteries.

Kipling's title, *The City of Dreadful Night*, referring to Calcutta as a whole, was borrowed from James Thomson's 1882 poem of the same name, inspired by London. By the time of Kipling's visit, the old part of South Park Street Cemetery had become weathered and forlorn, "a scene of utter desolation," with "rust-eaten railings" and defaced mounds of masonry.

In Paris a Napoleonic decree banned burial within or immediately outside churches. In 1784 subterranean quarries had been consecrated as catacombs by the Archbishop of Paris. By an Order of Council, the medieval graveyards and the Cimetière des Innocents were cleared and their contents stored in the enormous new ossuary.

Loudon (1783–1843) was buried in Kensal Green. See "John Claudius Loudon and the Garden Cemetery Movement," in Curl, *Death and Architecture*, 244–264. Strang, like Loudon, was a Scot. His *Necropolis Glasguensis: With Osbervations* [sic] *of Ancient and Modern Tombs and Sepulture* (1831) is quoted by Curl, 244.

Mount Auburn Cemetery 35

NOTES

Jacob Bigelow's *History of the Cemetery of Mount Auburn* (1860) is quoted on the National Park Service website for Mount Auburn. Dr. Bigelow, a Boston physician and Harvard professor, was the first to propose the founding of the cemetery. Website: nps.gov/nr/twhp/wwwlps/lessons/84mountauburn

Cemetery Reform in Canada 36-38

SOURCES

Thomas Chandler Haliburton, *The Clockmaker*, 70.

———. "Yarmouth Mountain Cemetery Since 1860," Walking Tour Brochure and records in the Yarmouth County Museum & Archives.

James Stevens Curl, *The Victorian Celebration of Death*, 188–189.

Cremation 38-40

SOURCES

James Stevens Curl, *The Victorian Celebration of Death*, 188–189.

NOTES

Loudon, in *The Gardeners' Magazine* (1843), quoted in Curl, *Death and Architecture*, 263–264. "Pile" may have been a misprint for the less familiar word "pyre."

Certain lines of Service's poem, published in *Songs of a Sourdough* (1907), were related to controversies of the day. "I'm asking that you won't refuse my last request ... So I want you to swear that, foul or fair,

you'll cremate my last remains." On the Dawson Trail, the promise to fulfill McGee's last request is hampered only by a lack of fuel until the finding of the derelict ship on the marge of Lake Lebarge: "Then 'Here,' said I, with a sudden cry, 'is my cre-ma-tor-eum.'" But the poet makes the most of the narrator's wrestling "with grisly fear" and "dread" – "Then I made a hike, for I didn't like to hear him sizzle so" as "the greasy smoke in an inky cloak went streaking down the sky."

Green Burial 40-41

SOURCES

Robin Marantz Henig, "Fat Factors," *The New York Times Magazine*, August 13, 2006. Henig quotes Jeffrey I. Gordon, M.D., Director, Center for Genome Sciences, Washington University, St. Louis.

William Wordsworth, "Essays upon Epitaphs," 337–338, and "The Brothers," 402– 414.

Historic Burying Grounds 45-48

SOURCES

Bruce A. Parker (in collaboration), "Richard Hatt" (1769–1819) and David Gagan, "George Taylor Denison of Rusholme" (1816–1873), *DCBO*.

Robert L. Fraser, "Richard Hatt" in *The Dictionary of Hamilton Biography*, I, 96–100.

George T. Denison and John H. Martin, *A Chronicle of St. John's Cemetery on the Humber*, 4, 6, 22.

Lois Corey and Melanie Blum, eds. *A Grave Matter: Cemeteries of Ancaster*.

NOTES

The letter from the Reverend James Jones, in the Anglican Church Archives, Montreal, is quoted in Brian Young, *Respectable Burial: Montreal's Mount Royal Cemetery*, 5.

Catherine Parr Traill is often quoted in discussions of Canada's pioneer cemeteries. According to Carol

Martin, *In Memory of Chelsea's Historic Cemeteries*, 83, the diary entry was made on 29 August 1832, as the Traills stopped in Cobourg, Ontario.

Acadian Church Yards 49-51

SOURCES

John Winslow, *Les Acadiens dans la région de Grand Pré en 1755 selon la liste du lt-col. John Winslow / Lt. Col. John Winslow's List of the Acadians in the Grand-Pré Area in 1755.*

Sally Ross, "Acadian Cemeteries in Nova Scotia: A Survey."

Mather B. DesBrisay, *The History of the County of Lunenburg.*

Anselme Boudreau, edited by Father Anselme Chiasson, *Chéticamp: mémoires*, 91, 111.

Père Anselme Chiasson, *Chéticamp: histoire et traditions acadiennes*, 163.

J.-Alphonse Deveau, "Pierre Le Blanc" (c. 1720–1799), *DCBO*.

NOTES

In 2003 Sally Ross and Deborah Trask studied 61 Acadian cemeteries in 42 parishes. I am indebted to them for generously sharing their knowledge. For the "invisible heritage" of Acadian cemeteries, see Ross, 19. She concludes that wooden crosses were the customary gravemarkers for Acadians before the Deportation, quoting from the missionary Father Pierre Maillard's report in 1745 that New England soldiers attacking a Mi'kmaq settlement had destroyed their burying place, "and all the crosses, planted on their graves, broke into a thousand pieces" (Ross, 2).

DesBrisay, p. 79, quotes the "long mysterious exodus of death" from Henry Wadsworth Longfellow's poem "The Jewish Cemetery at Newport" and "Where every severed wreath is bound" from a poem by Felicia Hemans, "Burial of an Emigrant's Child in the Forest."

Foreign Protestants 52-56

SOURCES

St. George's Church and Community website: collections.ic.gc.ca/churchandcommunity

Andrew W. Cranmer, *The Little Dutch Church Burial Ground: A Survey of the Grave Stones in their Present State.*

Deborah Trask, *Hier Ruhet in Gott: Here Rests in God: Germanic Gravestones in Lunenburg County.*

NOTES

The duke's German title was Braunschweig-Lüneburg. Lunenburg County in Virginia, founded in 1746, was also named in honour of the Hanoverian kings. Both British colonies anglicized the name by adding an 'n.'

Ruhe suggests a more lasting peace than *Friede*, the word used for more political, and temporary, peacetime in this world. However, one of the German words for graveyard is *Friedhof*.

The translation of the record in the Heyson family Bible has been adapted from that published by DesBrisay, 389, and quoted by Trask. The last words of the Zwicker inscription are illegible. The translation offered for "*40 her nach [...]*" is "and 40 afterwards [left to mourn her]." My alternative version extends the emphasis of the epitaph: that Zwicker and all her descendants have died, or will die, *im Herrn*, "in the Lord." This is meant to be a record of life, both mortal and everlasting, not of mourning. The Hebrew word translated as "rose" or "Rose of Sharon" in the English version, and as "lily" in the Lutheran translation, is now thought to refer to the autumn crocus.

Congregationalist Planters 57-59

SOURCES

Allan I. Ludwig, *Graven Images: New England Stonecarving and its Symbols, 1650–1815*, xxv.

Deborah Trask, *Life How Short, Eternity How Long: Gravestone Carving and Carvers in Nova Scotia,* 13.

The New Light and Soul Effigies 60-63

SOURCES

J. M. Bumsted, "Henry Alline" (1748–1784) and B. C. Cuthbertson, "John Payzant" (1749–1834), DCBO.

James Doyle Davison, *What Mean these Stones?: The Restoration of the Old Horton–Wolfville Burying-ground.*

Deborah Trask, "J.W., Folk Carver of Hants County, Nova Scotia."

Deborah Trask, *Life How Short, Eternity How Long,* 18–23, 71–80.

NOTES

Gaspereau Press in Kentville, Nova Scotia, has undertaken a project of designing a new typeface for digital composition by 2010, the 250th anniversary of the arrival of the New England Planters. The "Horton Revival" type will be based on letterforms used by the Horton Carvers. Website: gaspereau.com.

United Empire Loyalists 64-66

SOURCES

The United Empire Loyalists' Association of Canada (UELAC) website: uelac.org

Protestant Burying Ground, Quebec City 67-68

SOURCES

In collaboration, "Alexander Munn" (1766–1812), DCBO.

Anglican Churchyards 69-73

SOURCES

Alfreda (Bingle) Jeffries, *From Generation to Generation:*

A History of St. Andrew's Anglican Church, Grimsby, Ontario, 1794–1994, 9–10, 14, 105–106.

David Ouellette, "James Crooks" (1778–1860), DCBO.

Janet Carnochan, *Graves and Inscriptions in the Niagara Peninsula,* available online: sandycline.com/history

Fred Habermehl and Donald L. Combe, *Stones, Saints & Sinners: Walking Tours of Niagara-on-the-Lake's Large Historic Cemeteries.*

NOTES

A maker of fences in the 19th century advertised a new kind of fence as being "bull-strong, horse-high, and pig-tight," according to Ian Frazier, "Hogs Wild," *The New Yorker* (December 12, 2005), 71.

The McCausland firm is still in business in Toronto, after 150 years.

Elgin Cathedral, the "Lantern of the North" in Scotland, has a great many table stones. Both Crooks transcriptions are from Carnochan; the stone of Mary Butler, the widow of William Crooks Junior, has since broken. The seizure of the *Lord Nelson* had been declared illegal by a U.S. court in 1817. The schooner, which was promptly armed and put into action for the Americans forces under the new name of the *Scourge*, sank in a sudden squall on Lake Ontario. The famous wreck still lies at the bottom of the lake.

The Morrison and Wilson inscriptions were recorded by Janet Carnochan, whose work has preserved information about inscriptions and graves that have since been lost.

Methodist Burying Grounds 74-76

SOURCES

Victor Shepherd, "The Methodist Tradition in Canada," available online: victorshepherd.on.ca/Other%20Writings/the_methodist_tradition_in_canada.htm

NOTES
William Fawcett's story is the basis for a novel by his great-grandson Robert James: *Reader Be Thou Also Ready*. Fredericton: Broken Jaw Press, 2000.

I am indebted to Richview/Willow Grove Pioneer Cemetery Restoration Project Coordinator Randall Reid for information about the history of the Richview cemetery.

Quaker Cemeteries 77-79

SOURCES
Anon. The Children of Peace Cemetery, 90.

David L. Newlands, *The Orthodox Friends Burying Ground, Yonge Street, Newmarket, Ontario*.

NOTES
The Mason-Dixon Chat Forum website shares the following information: "James Lundy, of Company 'C,' 179th New York Infantry, died September 10, 1864, of disease contracted in the trenches before Petersburg. His body was brought home to the village of Sharon (Ontario), and there laid to rest."

African-American Cemeteries 80-81

SOURCES
William Faulkner, "Pantaloon in Black" (1940), reprinted in *Go Down, Moses* (1942), 135–159.

John Michael Vlach, "Graveyard Decoration," *The Afro-American Tradition in Decorative Arts*.

Owen Thomas, "Anderson Ruffin Abbott" (1837–1913), DCBO.

New Germany 82

SOURCES
Nancy-Lou Patterson, "The Iron Cross and the Tree of Life: German-Alsatian Gravemarkers in Waterloo Region and Bruce County Roman Catholic Cemeteries."

NOTES
The "Weilers of Maryhill" plaque was erected in the churchyard in the summer of 2000 on the occasion of a reunion of "500 descendants of all these Weilers." In the United States, the iron crosses in more than 70 German-Russian burial places in the plains, especially in central North Dakota, have been much studied and declared National Historic Sites.

Ghost Town Graveyards 83

SOURCES
Johnnie Bachusky and Susan Foster website: ghost-townpix.com/alberta/mtn.htm

Karen Buckley, "Mountain Park Cemetery, Alberta, Canada."

New Iceland 84-85

SOURCES
Nova Scotia Icelanders website: nova-scotia-icelanders.ednet.ns.ca

Betty Jane Wylie, *Letters to Icelanders: Exploring the Northern Soul*, vi–vii.

Gudbrandur Erlendsson, translated by Anna S. Bjornson, *Markland: Remembrance of the Years 1875–1881*.

Ukrainian Cemeteries 86-89

SOURCES
Frances Swyripa, "Ancestors, the Land, and Ethno-religious Identity on the Canadian Prairies: Comparing the Mennonite and Ukrainian Legacies."

NOTES
Although the timing of the *Provody* festival connects liturgically with saving the souls of the dead from Purgatory, still, families thoroughly enjoyed these celebrations. Swyripa mentions an archival photograph showing the men drinking beer and playing cards.

Ukrainians' long experience in cultivating wheat arrived in Canada before the Ukrainians them-

selves. A spring wheat strain from Galicia has been called the "first Ukrainian immigrant to Canada." In 1842 David Fife, who farmed near Peterborough, Ontario, obtained a sample in Glasgow from a Danzig ship unloading wheat from the Ukraine. He found that it matured 10 days earlier than other types of wheat, making it very suitable for the short Canadian growing season. The hardy Ukrainian wheat, named Red Fife because of its colour, transformed the Canadian economy and was influential in opening up the prairies for cultivation. By 1928 about 85 per cent of all spring wheat grown in Canada was Marquis, a hybrid of Red Fife.

Chinese Cemeteries 90-92

SOURCES
Edward Mills, "Chinese Cemetery, Harling Point, Oak Bay, British Columbia," Historic Sites and Monuments Board of Canada Agenda Paper 1995–18.

Japanese O-Bon 93-94

NOTES
The wartime memories of the Japanese Canadian residents of Chemainus, British Columbia, were recorded in a series of biographical vignettes in Catherine Lang's *O-Bon in Chimunesu: A Community Remembered*.

Jewish Cemeteries 95-97

SOURCES
David and Tamar de Sola Pool, *An Old Faith in the New World: Portrait of Shearith Israel, 1654–1954*.

Jacqueline Hucker, "Beth Israel Cemetery," Historic Sites and Monuments Board of Canada Agenda Paper 1992–98.

NOTES
The New York Shearith Israel congregation, whose first burial ground dated from 1656, kept close ties

with the Shearith Israel congregation in Montreal from its founding in 1768. Their 1829 congregation decision is quoted in de Sola Pool, *An Old Faith in the New World*, 309.

The Old Burying Ground, Halifax 102–109

SOURCES

Phyllis R. Blakeley, "Richard Bulkeley" (1717–1800), Judith Fingard, "Charles Inglis" (1734–1816), and Jane Hollingworth Nokes, "William Lawson" (1772–1848), *DCBO*.

Jacqueline Adell, "The Old Burying Ground, Halifax, Nova Scotia," Historic Sites and Monuments Board of Canada Agenda Paper 1991–95.

Deborah Trask, *Life How Short, Eternity How Long*, 28–31, 58–69.

NOTES

For Daniel Shatford, see the Canadian Heritage website: chin.gc.ca

In 1991 the Old Burying Ground, Halifax, became the first cemetery in Canada to be designated a National Historic Site.

The quotation on the Lawson stone from Job 1: 21 incorporates an allusion to the recent births of the children: "Naked came I out of my mother's womb, and naked shall I return thither: the Lord gave, and the Lord hath taken away; blessed be the name of the Lord." The transcription in Adell reads "loud mansions." My variant, "allotted" or destined mansions, fits the sense of the poem, with an added hint that the children's rooms in heaven were not quite ready for their early arrival. The reference to the children as saints suggests a Puritan confidence that they are among the elect; their lot is to be chosen for salvation.

Mount Hermon and St. Patrick's Cemeteries, Sillery, Quebec 110–113

SOURCES

Charles Bourget, "Chapels of Rest and Cemeteries: Significant development between the 17th and 20th centuries," Quebec Religious Heritage Foundation website: patrimoine-religieux.qc.ca/cimetiere/cimetieree.htm

Christina Cameron, "Charles Baillairgé" (1826–1906) and Fernand Ouellet, "Joseph Masson" (1791–1847) (re John Strang), *DCBO*.

Mount Royal and Notre-Dame-des-Neiges Cemeteries, Montreal 114–129

SOURCES

Robert Comeau, "Louis Archambault" (1814–1890), Yves Lacasse, "Louis-Philippe Hébert" (1850–1917), Stanley Brice Frost and Robert H. Michel, "Sir William Christopher Macdonald" (1831–1917), and Paul-André Linteau, "Charles-Théodore Viau" (1843–1898), *DCBO*.

Brian Young, with photographs by Geoffrey James, *Respectable Burial: Montreal's Mount Royal Cemetery*.

Nathalie Clerk, "Le cimetière Mont-Royal, Outremont et le cimetière Notre-Dame-des-Neiges, Montréal, Québec," Historic Sites and Monuments Board of Canada, Rapport 1998–38 and Rapport Supplémentaire 1998–38A.

Witold Rybczynski, *A Clearing in the Distance: Frederick Law Olmsted and America in the 19th Century*, 14.

Pierre-Richard Bisson, Mario Brodeur, and Daniel Drouin, *Cimetière Notre-Dame-des-Neiges*.

NOTES

Mount Royal Cemetery and Notre-Dame-des-Neiges Cemetery were the first Rural Cemeteries in Canada to achieve recognition as National Historic Sites.

Two Solitudes, the title of Hugh MacLennan's 1945 novel, comes from a well-known quotation from Rainer Maria Rilke: "Love consists in this, that two solitudes protect and touch and greet each other."

A report in *La Minerve*, 14 December 1852, described Notre-Dame-des-Neiges as "the Island of Montreal's most beautiful site in its elevation and terrain. It appears that the Board is ready to spare no effort to make it completely suited for its destined purpose, and to make of it a second Père Lachaise." Quoted in Clerk, 169. My translation.

Mount Royal Cemetery Annual Reports, 1874 and 1877, quoted in Young, 33, and Clerk, 164.

There were 43 European Burial places on Montreal Island prior to Mount Royal Cemetery. Some are listed here in more than one group. The data are displayed in Andrée Héroux's map and chronological graph in Bisson et al, 184–185.

Montreal Cemetery Company Annual Report, 1852, quoted in Clerk, 164–165, and Young, 25.

Mount Royal Cemetery Annual Report, 1865, quoted in Young, 30, 33.

Mount Royal Cemetery Annual Report, 1899, quoted in Young, 110–111, 119.

The metasequoia was planted as a memorial to Dr. Ernest Henry "Chinese" Wilson, the renowned botanist and plant-hunter. Brochures are provided in both English and French on "The Trees of Mount Royal Cemetery" and "Bird Watching in the Mount Royal Cemetery."

The interpretation of the *allées* of trees is from Bisson et al., 46. My translation.

Hackett's funeral was protected by 1,200 delegates from Toronto, Kingston, Ottawa and elsewhere; Young, 73–75.

Mgr Bourget's pastoral letter is quoted in Clerk, 173. My translation.

Notre-Dame and Beechwood Cemeteries, Ottawa 130-131

SOURCES

Réal Bélanger, "Sir Wilfrid Laurier" (1841–1919), *DCBO*.

Rhona Goodspeed, "Beechwood Cemetery, Ottawa, Ontario," Historic Sites and Monuments Board of Canada Agenda Paper 2000–46, and "Notre-Dame Cemetery, Ottawa / Vanier," Historic Sites and Monuments Board of Canada Agenda Paper 2000–47.

NOTES
The Beechwood Cemetery has published "Great Canadian Profiles" of more than 250 men and a few women, with historical notes and a guide to their burial locations.

Cataraqui Cemetery, Kingston 132-137

SOURCES
Linda Cyr, *Expressions in Stone: The Art of Cataraqui Cemetery.*

A. J. Downing, *The Architecture of Country Houses.*

Paul R. King, "Cataraqui Cemetery: A Condensed History."

Jennifer McKendry, *Weep Not for Me: An Illustrated History of Cataraqui Cemetery, Kingston, and Into the Silent Land: Historic Cemeteries and Graveyards in Ontario.*

NOTES
Descriptions of the "Grove" by J.H. Meacham in the *Illustrated Historical Atlas of Frontenac, Lennox & Addington Counties, Ontario* (1878) and C.W. Cooper in *Prize Essay. Frontenac, Lennox & Addington* (1856) are quoted in McKendry, *Weep Not for Me*, 8.

David Nicol's reports in the Cataraqui Cemetery Minute Books are held at Queen's University Archives, Kingston.

The Necropolis and Mount Pleasant Cemetery, Toronto 138-153

SOURCES
Edith G. Firth, "John George Howard" (1803–1890), Douglas Richardson and Angela K. Carr, "Henry Langley" (1836–1907), Ronald J. Stagg, "Samuel Lount" (1791–1838), Ronald J. Stagg, "Peter Matthews" (1789 or 1790–1838), in collaboration, "William McMaster" (1811–1887) and David Kimmel, "Sir Byron Edmund Walker" (1848–1924), *DCBO*.

Ontario Heritage Foundation, "Mount Pleasant Cemetery."

Eric Arthur, *Toronto: No Mean City.*

Nathalie Clerk, "Mount Pleasant Cemetery, Toronto, Ontario," Historic Sites and Monuments Board of Canada Agenda Paper 2000–03.

Sally Coutts, "Easeful Death in Toronto: A History of Mount Pleasant Cemetery."

Pleasance Crawford, transcription of "The Cemeteries," The *Globe* (Toronto), Nov. 21, 1868.

Pleasance Crawford, "H.A. Engelhardt (1830–1897): Landscape Designer."

Pleasance Crawford, "Engelhardt, Heinrich Adolph (1830–1897)."

William Dendy and William Kilbourn, *Toronto Observed: Its Architecture, Patrons, and History*, 81-83, 141-142.

H.A. Engelhardt, *The Beauties of Nature Combined with Art*, 8–9, 11, 124–126.

Mike Filey, *Mount Pleasant Cemetery: An Illustrated Guide.*

G.P. de T. Glazebrook, *Sir Edmund Walker*, 147.

NOTES
The letter in the Belleville *Weekly Intelligencer* is part of the Pleasance Crawford fonds in the City of Toronto Archives, Fonds 232, Series 773, File 48. Reports in the Toronto newspapers in the 1870s and 1880s are cited by Clerk, 10–12, from citations by Crawford in "H.A. Engelhardt (1830–1897): Landscape Designer," 171–172.

Mike Filey, "Hart Almerin Massey," *Mount Pleasant Cemetery: An Illustrated Guide*, 152–154.

Hamilton Cemetery 154-160

SOURCES
Peter Hanlon, "William Eli Sanford" (1838–1899), and David G. Burley, "George Elias Tuckett" (1835–1900), *DCBO*.

T. Melville Bailey, ed., *The Dictionary of Hamilton Biography*, vol. I, entries for William Bruce, William Case, Robert Land. Sr. and Thomas C. Watkins.

Elizabeth Manneke, *History in Hamilton Cemetery.*

John Terpstra, *Falling into Place.*

NOTES
A monument has been erected "To Honour / The Diligence Of The Late / GARY WINSTON HILL / In Disclosing The Burial Site / Of Hundreds of Dear Souls / (Young and Old) / Who Died From: / THE CHOLERA EPIDEMICS / 1832 to 1854." Gary Hill's untimely death interrupted his project of researching the history of the cemetery and raising public awareness about its value; his work is now being carried on by other volunteers.

Ross Bay Cemetery, Victoria 161-165

SOURCES
The Old Cemeteries Society of Victoria website: oldcem.bc.ca

John Adams, *Historic Guide to Ross Bay Cemetery, Victoria, B.C., Canada.*

NOTES
Charles Ross was buried in the first graveyard, which was closed in 1855. There is a memorial to him in Pioneer Square.

Lest We Forget 191-192

NOTES

Abraham Lincoln, Draft of the Gettysburg Address: Nicolay Copy, November 1863; Series 3, General Correspondence, 1837–1897. The Abraham Lincoln Papers at the Library of Congress, Manuscript Division (Washington, D.C.: American Memory Project, [2000–02]): http://memory.loc.gov/ammem/alhtml/alhome.html

Seven Years' War 192-193

SOURCES

Wellington Place Neighbourhood Association website: wellingtonplace.org

Jean-Claude Parent, "Le cimetière des Héros, Québec," Historic Sites and Monuments Board of Canada Rapport 1998–42.

NOTES

"Relation de ce qui s'est passé au Siège de Québec, et la prise du Canada; par une Religieuse de l'Hôpital Général de Québec [1765]," quoted by Parent. My translation.

Wolfe's copy of Gray's "Elegy," one of the treasures of the Thomas Fisher Rare Book Library at the University of Toronto, is illustrated and discussed in Charlotte Gray, The Museum Called Canada: 25 Rooms of Wonder, 292–297.

War of 1812 194-196

SOURCES

Michae J. Rudman, "The Old Garrison Burying Ground," Fort York Archives (1996): fortyork.ca.

NOTES

The City of Toronto has declared that, "at no time will human remains be disturbed" during the rehabilitation of the square.

Alexandrine Ramsay, The Globe, January 5, 1907, Illustrated Section, and Katherine Hale, The Canadian Magazine, January, 1919, 77–78, are quoted on the Wellington Place website.

The lines including "Age shall not weary them" are quoted from Laurence Binyon's poem "For the Fallen" (1914).

Crimean War 197

SOURCES

Susan Buggey, "George Lang" (c. 1821–1881), and Susan Buggey and Garry D. Shutlak, "David Stirling" (1822–1887), DCBO.

Sally Coutts, "Welsford-Parker Monument, Halifax, Nova Scotia." Historic Sites and Monuments Board of Canada Agenda Paper 1989–40.

First World War 198-205

SOURCES

"SOS for our cenotaph: War memorial needs $120,000 in repairs by VE Day anniversary," Hamilton Spectator, February 16, 2005.

Victoria Baker, Emanuel Hahn and Elizabeth Wyn Wood: Tradition and Innovation in Canadian Sculpture.

Andrew Crompton, "The Secret of the Cenotaph."

John Deverell, "Harbord WWI statue is losing the battle," Toronto Star, December 23, 2003.

Nora A. Reid, Local Architectural Conservation Advisory Committee Designation Report for the Welland-Crowland War Memorial, Chippewa Park, website: welland.library.on.ca

James Rusk, "Our Soldier is refreshed, rededicated: Dignitaries join Harbord students, grads at restored First World War memorial," Globe and Mail, November 12, 2005.

More than 5,100 memorials have been posted on the National Inventory of Canadian Military Memorials website: orces.gc.ca/hr/dhh/memorial/engraph/home_e.asp?cat=+2

"We Will Remember," War Monuments in Canada website: cdli.ca/monuments

NOTES

In 1960 the Imperial War Graves Commission's name was changed to the "Commonwealth War Graves Commission." See Veterans Agency website: veteransagency.mod.uk

Records for the Burlington War Memorial are in the Burlington Historical Society Archives.

For Florence Wyle, see the biography produced by Library and Archives Canada for the website "Celebrating Women's Achievements … Women Artists in Canada," created in 2002 and updated in 2005.

National War Memorials 207-208

SOURCES

Laura Brandon, "History as Monument: The Sculptures on the Vimy Memorial."

Hansard record of Churchill's speech in the British House of Commons, May 4, 1920, quoted on the Veterans Agency website: veteransagency.mod.uk

NOTES

The interview with Allward in 1921 is quoted in Brandon. The Vimy Memorial was designated a National Historic Site of Canada in 1997. The project of its restoration was under the direction of Canada's Department of Veterans Affairs in cooperation with the Commonwealth War Graves Commission. The Memorial was rededicated on April 9, 2007, the 90th anniversary of the battle of Vimy Ridge. Jane Urquhart's novel The Stone Carvers not only made many Canadians familiar with the name of Walter Allward, which had almost faded from national memory, but also enriched her readers' understanding of the Vimy Memorial's power to insist on "prodigious feats of memory from all who come to gaze at it," 378.

The Irish Memorial 209-211

SOURCES

André Charbonneau, "1847: A Tragic Year at Grosse Île" and André Sévigny, "Quarantine and Public Health: The Changing Role of Grosse Île, September 1995," Parks Canada website: www.pc.gc.ca/lhn-nhs/qc/grosseile/natcul/natcul1b_E.asp

In 1997 Parks Canada published *1847, Grosse Île: A Record of Daily Events*, by André Charbonneau and André Sévigny.

Mary Mullins website on her pilgrimage to Grosse Île: homepage.tinet.ie/~mcmullins/grosse-ile.htm

The Inuit Memorial 212-213

SOURCES

Pat Sandford Grygier, *A Long Way from Home: The Tuberculosis Epidemic among the Inuit*, 115–116.

Maritime Disasters 214-216

SOURCES

Laura M. MacDonald, *Curse of the Narrows: The Halifax Explosion 1917*, 282.

NOTES

As MacDonald notes, marked gravesites can be found in the Mount Olivet and St. John's cemeteries.

The Luminous Veil 217

SOURCES

Marco L. Polo, "The Luminous Veil: Transforming Memory and Meaning at Toronto's 'Bridge of Death,'" 23.

Michael Ondaatje, *In the Skin of a Lion*, 31, 34, 35.

Mausoleums 224-226

SOURCES

Christopher Armstrong, "James Austin" (1813–1897), *DCBO*.

James Stevens Curl, *Death and Architecture*, 4.

Obelisks 230-231

SOURCES

Bern Dibner, *Moving the Obelisks*, 7.

Neoclassical Monuments 232-236

NOTES

The Urn quotations and the Monument definition are cited from the Oxford English Dictionary. The Severus anecdote is recounted in various classical sources.

The Willow 236-237

NOTES

The Latin name of the weeping willow, *Salix babylonica*, refers to the scriptural text. However, current horticultural opinion is that the tree translated as "willow" was really the Euphrates Poplar, *Populus euphratica*, the most common tree along the Euphrates River. Our weeping willow is apparently native to China and never grew in Bible lands.

Jewish Symbols 238-241

NOTES

The Jewish year represents the number of years since creation, calculated by adding up the ages of people in the Bible back to the time of creation, in the seventh Hebrew month (September or October). For conversion to the Gregorian calendar year, subtract 3,761 or 3,760.

Effigies 242

SOURCES

William Shakespeare, *The Winter's Tale*, 5: 3.

Deborah Trask, *Life How Short, Eternity How Long*, 54, 56, 96.

NOTES

The Websters' son Isaac was a sea captain. The memorial indicates that he died in Yokohama, Japan, on board the *Iranian* (a 3,000-ton cargo ship).

Victorian Gothic Revival, 243

SOURCES

Edward Blore, *The Monumental Remains of Noble and Eminent Persons* (1826), quoted in Curl, *Death and Architecture*, 83.

The Cross 244-245

SOURCES

Eusebius, *History of the Church from Christ to Constantine*.

Angel Statuary 246-250

SOURCES

Jennifer McKendry, *Into the Silent Land*, 229.

NOTES

McKendry notes the archbishop's reference to an Angel of the Last Judgement.

Hands 260-261

SOURCES

Sandra Tennant and Dwight Wadel, Trinity (Holy Ghost) Evangelical Lutheran Church and Cemetery, Fisherville, Ontario: History, Tombstone Transcriptions and Founding Families.

Deborah Trask, *Life How Short, Eternity How Long*, 48–50.

Epitaphs 263-267

SOURCES

Waterloo Region Branch OGS website: water-looogs.ca/cemeterypics/RushesCemetery.html

William Wordsworth, "Essays upon Epitaphs," 323, 337–338.

Carole Hanks, *Early Ontario Gravestones*, 67, 94.

Zinc or "White Bronze" 280-281

SOURCES

Rotundo, Barbara. "Monumental Bronze: A Representative American Company," 263–291.

Deborah Trask, *Life How Short, Eternity How Long*, 51–52, 96.

NOTES

The advertisement for W.H. Coffin, White Bronze agent, in Cape Sable Advertiser, Barrington, Nova Scotia, Oct. 13, 1887, is quoted in Trask, 51.

Granites 282-283

SOURCES

Barre Granite Association website: barregranite.org/guild.html

Conserving the Future of Memory 287-289

SOURCES

The Old Cemeteries Society of Victoria website: oldcem.bc.ca

Jacqueline Adell, "The Old Burying Ground, Halifax, Nova Scotia," Historic Sites and Monuments Board of Canada Agenda Paper 1991–95.

Tamara Anson-Cartwright, *Landscapes of Memories: A Guide for Conserving Historic Cemeteries: Repairing Tombstones*.

Gordon D. Smithson, *Milton Cemetery: Pittsburgh Township*.

Lynette Strangstad, *Preservation of Historic Burial Grounds*.

English Heritage and English Nature. Paradise preserved: An introduction to the assessment, evaluation, conservation and management of historic cemeteries (2002).

A Tale of Two Pioneer Burying Grounds 290-293

SOURCES

Records in the Burlington Historical Society Archives, including John Quinsey, "Nelson Township Cemetery No. 10, Tansley Pioneer Cemetery," Halton-Peel Branch, OGS (1995).

Mary Byers and Margaret McBurney, *The Governor's Road: Early Buildings and Families from Mississauga to London*, 3.

George Wright, *Who Departed This Life: A History of the Old Protestant Burying Ground, Charlottetown, Prince Edward Island*, 13, 16–17, 19–21, 64, 67, 70–71, 73, 75–78.

NOTES

Gertrude Stein, having chosen to live in Paris, was recalling – reluctantly – Oakland, California, in her *Everybody's Autobiography* (1937).

More Stories in Old Stones 294-295

SOURCES

Wallace Stegner, *Wolf Willow: A History, a Story and a Memory of the Last Plains Frontier*, 127.

Hans Christian Andersen, "The Old Gravestone" (1852).

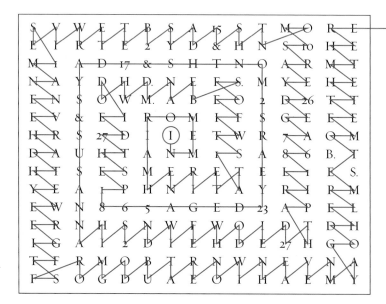

Solution to the Dr. Bean Stone
To decipher the stone, start at the 7th letter in the 7th line, "I," indicated here with a circle. Go down to the "N," then over to the "M," then up to the "E." Continue with the red line as it makes a counter-clockwise spiral and then begins to zigzag at the "H" of "HENRIETTA." Notice the exaggerated zig from the "A" of "HENRIETTA" to the "I" of "1ST." Continue to follow the red line through the code until it is solved and you finish at the "E" in the top right corner. Notice too the initials S. B. that are not part of the solution. Instead they serve as the signature for Dr. Samuel Bean, the creator of the code, and the survivor of two lost wives, Henrietta and Susanna.

Saints & Sinners: Walking Tours of Niagara-on-the-Lake's Large Historic Cemeteries. Niagara-on-the-Lake, Ontario: Niagara Historical Society, 1995.

Haliburton, Thomas Chandler. *The Clockmaker: Series One, Two and Three.* Edited by George L. Parker. Ottawa: Carleton University Press, 1995.

Hanks, Carole. *Early Ontario Gravestones.* Toronto: McGraw-Hill Ryerson, 1974.

Hardy, Sandra J. *Pennsylvania German and German-American Gravestone Language and Symbol Guide.* [no place] Sandra J. Hardy, 2003.

Heath, Marion. *Stories from Stones: Cairns of Ontario.* Ottawa: Borealis Press, 2003.

Henig, Robin Marantz. "Fat Factors," *The New York Times Magazine,* August 13, 2006.

Hershey, Mary Jane Lederach. *This Teaching I Present: Fraktur from the Skippack and Salford Mennonite Meetinghouse Schools, 1747–1836.* Studies in Anabaptist and Mennonite History no. 41. Intercourse, Pa: Good Books, 2003.

Howley, Michael Francis, Archbishop. "The Old Basque Tombstones at Placentia." In *Transcriptions of the Royal Society of Canada.* Ottawa: 1902, Section II: 79–92.

Hucker, Jacqueline. "Beth Israel Cemetery." Historic Sites and Monuments Board of Canada Agenda Paper 1992–8.

Hudson, Deborah. *Oakville's Black History.* Oakville, Ontario: Oakville Museum, 2000.

Jackman, Edward J. R. *A Quiet Gentle Surprise: A*

History of Saint Michael's Cemetery, Toronto, Ontario, Canada. Toronto: Catholic Cemetery Association, 1980.

Jackson, A.Y. *A Painter's Country: The Autobiography of A.Y. Jackson.* Toronto: Clarke, Irwin, 1958.

Jeffries, Alfreda (Bingle). *From Generation to Generation: A History of St. Andrew's Anglican Church, Grimsby, Ontario, 1794–1994.* Grimsby, Ontario: St. Andrew's Parish Church, 1994.

Kalman, Harold. *A History of Canadian Architecture.* 2 vols. Toronto: Oxford University Press, 1994.

Keithahn, Edward L. *Monuments in Cedar.* Rev. ed. Seattle: Superior, 1963.

Keister, Douglas. *Stories in Stone: A Field Guide to Cemetery Symbolism and Iconography.* Salt Lake City: Gibbs Smith, 2004.

King, Paul R. "Cataraqui Cemetery: A Condensed History," *Families* 19, no. 4 (1980): 343–356.

Kipling, Rudyard. *The City of Dreadful Night (1888).* Collected in *From Sea to Sea and Other Sketches: Letters of Travel.* New York: Charles Scribner's Sons, 1899.

Lang, Catherine. *O-Bon in Chimunesu: A Community Remembered.* Vancouver: Arsenal Pulp Press, 1997.

Linden, Blanche M.G. *Silent City on a Hill: Picturesque Landscapes of Memory and Boston's Mount Auburn Cemetery.* 2nd ed. Amherst: University of Massachusetts Press, 2007.

Ludwig, Allan I. *Graven Images: New England Stonecarving and its Symbols, 1650–1815.* 3rd ed. Hanover: Wesleyan University Press, University Press of New England, 1999.

MacDonald, Laura M. *Curse of the Narrows: The Halifax*

Explosion 1917. Toronto: HarperCollins, 2005.

Maclean, Hugh D., Rev. *A Rare Gift within its Gates: The Story of St. Mark's Anglican Church, Niagara-on-the-Lake, Ontario, Canada.* Niagara-on-the-Lake, Ontario: T&C Associates, 1980.

Manneke, Elizabeth. *History in Hamilton Cemetery.* Hamilton: Hamilton Municipal Cemeteries, 2000.

Martin, Carol. *In Memory of Chelsea's Historic Cemeteries.* Chelsea, Quebec: Castenchel Editions, 2005.

Matthews, Samantha. "At Home in the Necropolis." *The Mausolea & Monuments Trust Newsletter* (May, 2001).

McGhee, Robert. *The Last Imaginary Place: A Human History of the Arctic World.* Toronto: Key Porter Books, 2004.

McIlwraith, Thomas. "Graves and Monuments." In *Looking for Old Ontario,* Toronto: University of Toronto Press, 1997.

———, and Mark Hummer. "Grave and Nave: An Architecture of Cemeteries and Sanctuaries in Rural Ontario." *Ontario History* XCVII, no. 2: 138–159.

McKendry, Jennifer. *Weep Not for Me: An Illustrated History of Cataraqui Cemetery, Kingston.* 2nd ed. Kingston, Ontario: Jennifer McKendry, 2000.

———. *Into the Silent Land: Historic Cemeteries and Graveyards in Ontario.* Kingston, Ontario: Jennifer McKendry, 2003.

Medland, Harvey. *Tombstone Tales from Ontario Cemeteries.* Willowdale, Ontario: The Ontario Historical Society, 2000.

Miles, Joan, and Pleasance Crawford. *The Heritage and*

Natural Features of Prospect Cemetery: A Walking Guide, Toronto: Prospect Cemetery, 1988.

Millar, Nancy. *Once upon a Tomb: Stories from Canadian Graveyards.* Calgary: Fifth House, 1997.

Mills, Edward. "Chinese Cemetery, Harling Point, Oak Bay, British Columbia." Historic Sites and Monuments Board of Canada Agenda Paper 1995–18.

Milner, William Cochran. *History of Sackville, New Brunswick.* 1934. Reprint. Sackville: Tribune Press, 1970.

Moore, Christopher. *Grave Sites of Canadian Prime Ministers / Lieux de Sépulture des Premiers Ministres du Canada.* Ottawa: Parks Canada, 2000.

Munro, Alice. *The View from Castle Rock.* Toronto: McClelland & Stewart, 2006.

Newlands, David L. *The Orthodox Friends Burying Ground, Yonge Street, Newmarket, Ontario.* Newmarket, Ontario: Young Street Monthly Meeting, Religious Society of Friends (Quakers), 1983.

Nora, Pierre, ed. *Les lieux de mémoire.* Paris: Gallimard, 1997.

Ondaatje, Michael. *In the Skin of a Lion.* Toronto: Vintage Canada, 1996.

Parent, Jean-Claude. "Le cimetière des Héros, Québec." Historic Sites and Monuments Board of Canada Rapport 1998–42.

Patterson, Nancy-Lou. "The Iron Cross and the Tree of Life: German-Alsatian Gravemarkers in Waterloo Region and Bruce County Roman Catholic Cemeteries." *Ontario History* LXVIII, no 1: 1–16.

Polo, Marco L. "The Luminous Veil: Transforming

Memory and Meaning at Toronto's 'Bridge of Death.'" *Journal of the Society for the Study of Architecture in Canada (JSSAC / JSÉAC),* 29: no 3, no 4: 19–26.

Quinsey, John. "Nelson Township Cemetery No. 10, Tansley Pioneer Cemetery." Halton-Peel Branch, Ontario Genealogical Society. 1995.

Ricoeur, Paul. *Memory, History, Forgetting.* Translated by Kathleen Blarney and David Pellauer. Chicago: University of Chicago Press, 2004.

Robertson, J. Ross. "The Military Cemeteries." *Robertson's Landmarks of Toronto. Toronto:* J. Ross Robertson, 1894.

Robinson, David. *Saving Graces: Images of Women in European Cemeteries.* New York: W. W. Norton, 1995.

Robinson, William. *God's Acre Beautiful or The Cemeteries of the Future.* London: The Garden Office, 1880.

Ross, Sally. "Acadian Cemeteries in Nova Scotia: A Survey." *Markers* XXII (2005): 1–33.

Rotundo, Barbara. "Monumental Bronze: A Representative American Company." In *Cemeteries and Gravemarkers: Voices of American Culture.* ed. by Richard E. Meyer. Ann Arbor, Michigan: UMI Research Press, 1989.

Rybczynski, Witold. *A Clearing in the Distance: Frederick Law Olmsted and America in the 19th Century.* Toronto: HarperFlamingo Canada, 1999.

Schwartzman, Arnold. *Graven Images: Graphic Motifs of the Jewish Grave Stone.* New York: Harry N. Abrams, 1993.

Slaney, Catherine. *Family Secrets: Crossing the Colour Line.* Toronto: Natural Heritage Books, 2002.

Sloane, David Charles. *The Last Great Necessity:*

Cemeteries in American History. Baltimore: Johns Hopkins University Press, 1991.

Smith, Edwin, Olive Cook and Graham Hutton. *English Parish Churches.* London: Thames and Hudson, 1976.

Smithson, Gordon D. *Milton Cemetery: Pittsburgh Township.* Rev ed. Kingston, Ontario: Pittsburgh Historical Society, 1979.

Stegner, Wallace. *Wolf Willow: A History, a Story and a Memory of the Last Plains Frontier.* Toronto: Macmillan of Canada, 1955.

Stevens, Maynard G. *Where They Rest in Peace: A Guided Tour of Seven Historic Cemeteries in Kings County, Nova Scotia.* Kentville, Nova Scotia: Gaspereau Press, 2001.

Strangstad, Lynette. *Preservation of Historic Burial Grounds.* Washington: National Trust for Historic Preservation, 2003.

Swyripa, Frances. "Ancestors, the Land, and Ethno-religious Identity on the Canadian Prairies: Comparing the Mennonite and Ukrainian Legacies," *Journal of Mennonite Studies* (2003).

Tennant, Sandra and Dwight Wadel. *Trinity (Holy Ghost) Evangelical Lutheran Church and Cemetery, Fisherville, Ontario: History, Tombstone Transcriptions and Founding Families.* Fisherville, Ontario: Trinity Lutheran Church, 2004.

Terpstra, John. *Falling into Place.* Kentville, Nova Scotia: Gaspereau Press, 2002.

Trask, Deborah. *Life How Short, Eternity How Long: Gravestone Carving and Carvers in Nova Scotia.* Halifax: The Nova Scotia Museum, 1978.

———. "J.W., Folk Carver of Hants County, Nova Scotia." In *Puritan Gravestone Art II*, The Dublin Seminar for New England Folklife: Annual Proceedings 1978. Boston: Boston University, 1978.

———. *Hier Ruhet in Gott: Here Rests in God: Germanic Gravestones in Lunenburg County*. Mahone Bay N.S.: Mahone Bay Museum, c. 2003. (Revised from a paper first published in Margaret Conrad, ed., *Making Adjustments: Change and Continuity in Planter Nova Scotia, 1759–1800*. Fredericton: Acadiensis Press, 1991. 140–152.)

Trevithick, Scott. "Evangelical and Aboriginal Religion in the Shingwauk Indian Residential School: The Case for Deeper Scholarly Engagement with Religious Discourse, Ritual and Meaning." Paper delivered at the Decolonizing History Colloquium, Toronto: University of Toronto at Mississauga, November 11, 2005.

Urquhart, Jane. *The Stone Carvers*. Toronto: McClelland & Stewart, 2001.

Vlach, John Michael. "Graveyard Decoration," *The Afro-American Tradition in Decorative Arts*, Cleveland: The Cleveland Museum of Art, 1978: 139–147.

Welty, Eudora. *Country Churchyards*. Jackson: University Press of Mississippi, 2000.

Williams, Pamela. *Death Divine: Photographs of Cemetery Sculpture from Paris, Milan, Rome*. Don Mills, Ontario: P. Williams, 1995.

———. *Last Kiss: More Photographs of Cemetery Sculpture from Genoa, Vienna, Milan*. Don Mills, Ontario: P. Williams, 1999.

———. *In the Midst of Angels: Photographs of Sculpture from the Cemeteries of Europe and Beyond*. Don Mills, Ontario: P. Williams, 2005.

Willsher, Betty. *Understanding Scottish Graveyards*. 3rd ed. Edinburgh: Council for Scottish Archaeology and National Museums of Scotland, 2005.

Winslow, John. *Les Acadiens dans la région de Grand Pré en 1755 selon la liste du lt-col. John Winslow / Lt. Col. John Winslow's List of the Acadians in the Grand-Pré Area in 1755*. Grand-Pré: Société Promotion Grand-Pré, 2002.

Wood, Eric S. *Historical Britain*. London: The Harvill Press, 1995.

Wordsworth, William. "The Brothers" (1800), *William Wordsworth: The Poems*, 2 vols, edited by John O. Hayden. New Haven: Yale University Press, 1981. I, 402–414.

———. "Essays upon Epitaphs" (1809, 1810), *William Wordsworth: Selected Prose*, edited by John O. Hayden. Harmondsworth: Penguin Books, 1988.

Worpole, Ken. *Last Landscapes: The Architecture of the Cemetery in the West*. London: Reaktion Books, 2003.

Wright, George. *Who Departed This Life: A History of the Old Protestant Burying Ground, Charlottetown, Prince Edward Island*. Charlottetown: Acorn Press, 2005.

Wylie, Betty Jane. *Letters to Icelanders: Exploring the Northern Soul*. Toronto: Macmillan Canada, 1999.

Young, Brian. *Respectable Burial: Montreal's Mount Royal Cemetery*. Montreal-Kingston: McGill-Queen's University Press, 2003.

INDEX